# Risk Assessment and Treatment

# Risk Assessment and Treatment

Edited by

Michael W. Elliott, CPCU, ARM, AIAF, MBA

2nd Edition • 2nd Printing

**The Institutes**
720 Providence Road, Suite 100
Malvern, Pennsylvania 19355-3433

# Foreword

The Institutes are the trusted leader in delivering proven knowledge solutions that drive powerful business results for the risk management and property-casualty insurance industry. For more than 100 years, The Institutes have been meeting the industry's changing professional development needs with customer-driven products and services.

In conjunction with industry experts and members of the academic community, our Knowledge Resources Department develops our course and program content, including Institutes study materials. Practical and technical knowledge gained from Institutes courses enhances qualifications, improves performance, and contributes to professional growth—all of which drive results.

The Institutes' proven knowledge helps individuals and organizations achieve powerful results with a variety of flexible, customer-focused options:

**Recognized Credentials**—The Institutes offer an unmatched range of widely recognized and industry-respected specialty credentials. The Institutes' Chartered Property Casualty Underwriter (CPCU®) professional designation is designed to provide a broad understanding of the property-casualty insurance industry. Depending on professional needs, CPCU students may select either a commercial insurance focus or a personal risk management and insurance focus and may choose from a variety of electives.

In addition, The Institutes offer certificate or designation programs in a variety of disciplines, including these:

- Claims
- Commercial underwriting
- Fidelity and surety bonding
- General insurance
- Insurance accounting and finance
- Insurance information technology
- Insurance production and agency management
- Insurance regulation and compliance
- Management
- Marine insurance
- Personal insurance
- Premium auditing
- Quality insurance services
- Reinsurance
- Risk management
- Surplus lines

**Ethics**—Ethical behavior is crucial to preserving not only the trust on which insurance transactions are based, but also the public's trust in our industry as a whole. All Institutes designations now have an ethics requirement, which is delivered online and free of charge. The ethics requirement content is designed specifically for insurance practitioners and uses insurance-based case studies to outline an ethical framework. More information is available in the Programs section of our website, TheInstitutes.org.

**Flexible Online Learning**—The Institutes have an unmatched variety of technical insurance content covering topics from accounting to underwriting, which we now deliver through hundreds of online courses. These cost-effective self-study courses are a convenient way to fill gaps in technical knowledge in a matter of hours without ever leaving the office.

**Continuing Education**—A majority of The Institutes' courses are filed for CE credit in most states. We also deliver quality, affordable, online CE courses quickly and conveniently through CEU. Visit CEU.com to learn more. CEU is powered by The Institutes.

**College Credits**—Most Institutes courses carry college credit recommendations from the American Council on Education. A variety of courses also qualify for credits toward certain associate, bachelor's, and master's degrees at several prestigious colleges and universities. More information is available in the Student Services section of our website, TheInstitutes.org.

**Custom Applications**—The Institutes collaborate with corporate customers to use our trusted course content and flexible delivery options in developing customized solutions that help them achieve their unique organizational goals.

**Insightful Analysis**—Our Insurance Research Council (IRC) division conducts public policy research on important contemporary issues in property-casualty insurance and risk management. Visit www.Insurance-Research.org to learn more or purchase its most recent studies.

The Institutes look forward to serving the risk management and property-casualty insurance industry for another 100 years. We welcome comments from our students and course leaders; your feedback helps us continue to improve the quality of our study materials.

Peter L. Miller, CPCU
President and CEO
The Institutes

# Preface

*Risk Assessment and Treatment* is the assigned textbook for the ARM 55 course in The Institutes' Associate in Risk Management (ARM) designation program. This text provides learners with a broad understanding of the assessment and treatment techniques for the major categories of risk faced by all organizations, with an emphasis on hazard (insurable risk).

The first part of the course takes a holistic approach by explaining risk assessment techniques, such as root cause analysis, that can be applied to all of an organization's risks (hazard, operational, financial, and strategic). It also details risk treatment alternatives, including risk transfer, and the benefits of accepting risk when pursuing an opportunity.

The remainder of the course discusses ways to assess and treat various types of risks. These include emerging risks and those traditionally addressed by risk management. Examples of emerging risks include cyber risk, social media risk, climate change risk, reputation risk, regulatory risk, and supply chain risk; those traditionally addressed by risk management include legal risk, property risk, personnel risk, environmental risk, and motor fleet risk. The last assignment explores the role of smart products and data analytics in risk assessment and control.

The Institutes are grateful to the insurance professionals who contributed to this text, including the individual members of the Risk and Insurance Management Society (RIMS) and the Public Risk Management Association (PRIMA), who gave us feedback on the relative importance of various topics covered in the course. In addition, Tom Worischeck, CSP, ARM, provided important updates to the fleet risk assignment.

We are also grateful to the individuals who helped develop previous forms of the content, including manuscript reviewers and various advisory committee members. In particular, The Institutes would like to thank James Kallman, PhD, ARM, CRM, for his valuable insight.

For more information about The Institutes' programs, please call our Customer Success Department at (800) 644-2101, email us at CustomerSuccess@TheInstitutes.org, or visit our website at TheInstitutes.org.

Michael W. Elliott

# Contributors

The Institutes acknowledge with deep appreciation the contributions made to the content of this text by the following persons:

Susan Crowe, CPCU, MBA, AIC, ARe, ARM, API

Beth Illian, CPCU, AINS, AIS

Laura J. Partsch, JD

# Contents

# Segment A

# Segment A

**Assignment 1**
Introduction to Risk Assessment and Treatment

**Assignment 2**
Root Cause Analysis

**Assignment 3**
Business Continuity Management

**Assignment 4**
Physical Property Risk

# Introduction to Risk Assessment and Treatment

## Educational Objectives

**After learning the content of this assignment, you should be able to:**

▷ Describe the nature of risk assessment and the risk assessment process.

▷ Describe the major risk identification and analysis techniques.

▷ Describe the risk treatment process and risk treatment techniques.

▷ Describe the following accident analysis techniques:

- Sequence of events (domino theory)

- Energy transfer theory

- Technique of operations review (TOR) approach

- Change analysis

- Job-safety analysis

▷ Describe system safety, its primary purpose, and its advantages.

▷ Explain how to implement the following loss control techniques for hazard risk:

- Avoidance

- Loss prevention

- Loss reduction

- Separation, duplication, and diversification

# Introduction to Risk Assessment and Treatment

**1**

## OVERVIEW OF RISK ASSESSMENT

The risk assessment process provides information regarding uncertainties that can affect an organization's ability to meet objectives.

Risk assessment helps an organization to define the parameters of risk and to manage uncertainties. The risk assessment process includes risk identification and risk analysis.

### Risk Assessment Defined

Every organization faces **risks** within its operation. These risks may have positive effects, such as meeting or exceeding sales goals, or the negative effect of not meeting established goals. The risk assessment process provides all levels of management with a picture of the risks affecting the organization. Thorough risk assessment enables an organization to effectively manage all aspects of risk and their impact on meeting organizational objectives.

Through **risk management**, an organization can focus on the importance of assessing risk to improve organizational results. Appropriate management of risk can also result in enhanced governance, compliance with legal and regulatory requirements, and better identification of opportunities and threats facing the organization.

Risk can be classified as a hazard risk, an operational risk, a financial risk, or a strategic risk. An organization's size and operation are among the factors that determine the types of risk it faces. See the exhibit "Risk Quadrants."

### Goals of Risk Assessment

The goals of risk assessment are to inform management at all levels of the risks facing an organization and how those risks affect the organization's ability to meet objectives, as well as to identify potential risk treatment options. An organization must consider not only its existing operations but also any emerging threats or opportunities. For example, increased dependence on technology can expose an organization to privacy issues and the need to protect customer data. The steps in the risk assessment process assist in forming a clearer picture of risk and facilitate communication throughout the organization regarding risk.

**Risk**
Uncertainty about outcomes that can be either negative or positive.

**Risk management**
The process of making and implementing decisions that enable an organization to optimize its level of risk.

## Risk Quadrants

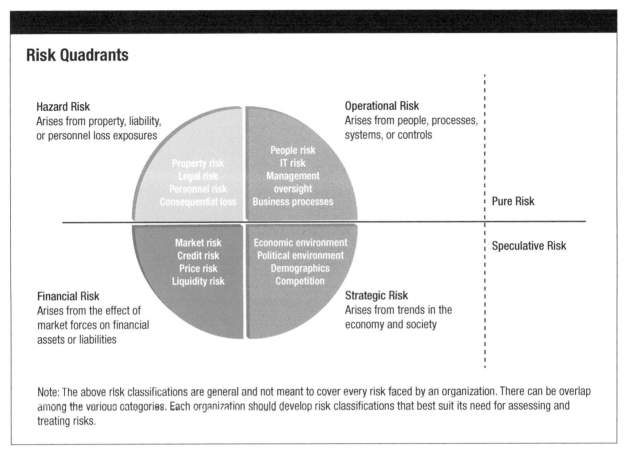

**Hazard Risk**
Arises from property, liability, or personnel loss exposures

Property risk
Legal risk
Personnel risk
Consequential loss

**Operational Risk**
Arises from people, processes, systems, or controls

People risk
IT risk
Management oversight
Business processes

Pure Risk

Speculative Risk

Market risk
Credit risk
Price risk
Liquidity risk

Economic environment
Political environment
Demographics
Competition

**Financial Risk**
Arises from the effect of market forces on financial assets or liabilities

**Strategic Risk**
Arises from trends in the economy and society

Note: The above risk classifications are general and not meant to cover every risk faced by an organization. There can be overlap among the various categories. Each organization should develop risk classifications that best suit its need for assessing and treating risks.

[DA08677]

Risk assessment allows an organization to identify uncertainties and to quantify the upsides and downsides of those uncertainties. Through analysis, the likelihood and consequences of events can be determined, which provide input for the risk treatment decision.

# Risk Assessment Process

The risk assessment process is a major part of the overall risk management process and is conducted within the risk management structure. To be effective, those conducting risk assessment must understand the organization's risk appetite and risk tolerance, as well as their own accountability within the process.

Risk appetite is the total exposed amount that an organization wishes to undertake on the basis of risk-return trade-offs for one or more desired and expected outcomes. Risk tolerance is the amount of uncertainty an organization is prepared to accept in total or, more narrowly, within a certain business unit or particular risk category, or for a specific initiative.[1]

It is also important that those involved in the risk assessment process understand the tools and techniques available for assessing and treating risk. These tools and techniques vary based on the needs of an organization and can be qualitative or quantitative. They include questionnaires, checklists, cause-and-effect analysis, and failure analysis. Qualitative methods, such as surveys or interviews, are more subjective and subject to interpretation. Quantitative assessments are objective and based on numerical data and calculations. For example, quantitative assessments include evaluation of actual sales data from one quarter to the next or trended loss information. Generally, the most effective approach is to use a combination of both qualitative and quantitative methods to provide broader risk assessment results.

Risk assessment approaches are either top down or bottom up. Top-down assessments involve senior management and/or the organization's board of directors and focus on strategic issues that could affect the organization's ability to meet objectives. Such assessments identify major risks that affect the entire organization. Bottom-up assessments are conducted at the business level and are more operational in nature. For example, a division manager may identify risks that affect the ability to meet day-to-day objectives—such as employee injuries or interruptions to operations—and analyze their significance. The results of these approaches must be integrated to provide a comprehensive risk assessment.

Risk identification and risk analysis are two steps in the enterprise-wide risk management process. See the exhibit "Enterprise Risk Management Process Model."

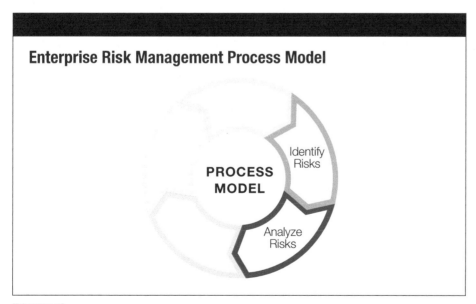

**Enterprise Risk Management Process Model**

[DA08717_8]

# Risk Identification

Risk identification involves reviewing all aspects of the internal and external environments to identify events that could either improve or inhibit the organization's achievement of objectives. It is important at this step to uncover a complete inventory of possible risks to avoid the consequences arising from an unidentified risk in the future.

As part of risk identification, all risk sources and risk exposures should be examined to determine the potential financial consequences. For each risk that is identified, possible controls should be considered for mitigation purposes.

# Risk Analysis

Risk analysis entails investigating the identified risks to make decisions regarding whether risk treatment is needed and which techniques should be used.

**Risk map**

A template depicting the likelihood and potential impact/consequences of risks.

Risk analysis considers the causes and sources of risk, as well as positive and negative impacts and the likelihood of those impacts. A **risk map**, also referred to as a risk matrix, can be used to evaluate risk analysis results. One event may result in multiple types of impact, and each variation must be evaluated. Another important consideration is any interrelation between risks that could increase the impacts of any events or provide an offset of the impacts of one risk against another. At the risk analysis step, the probabilities of various impacts must also be estimated, with an emphasis on those risks with the highest probability.

## *Apply Your Knowledge*

The chief executive officer and senior management team for a large, global food distribution conglomerate are part of a risk assessment initiative with the corporation. Describe the types of strategic risks this group would consider and identify which approach to risk assessment would be used at this management level.

*Feedback:* Strategic risks arise from trends in the economy and in society and include consideration of the economic and political environments within the countries in which they do business. The team should also consider demographics and competition. When risk assessment is undertaken by senior managers, it follows a top-down approach.

After risks are identified and analyzed, the organization would need to decide on appropriate risk treatment techniques. Its ultimate decision would be based on the organization's objectives and risk appetite.

# CATEGORIES OF RISK IDENTIFICATION AND ANALYSIS TECHNIQUES

Many types of techniques are available to identify and analyze risks. The technique used depends on the nature of the risk, the amount of data available, and other factors. Multiple techniques may be used throughout the risk identification and analysis process.

Risk identification and analysis techniques may include these:

- Questionnaires and checklists
- Workshops
- Cause-and-effect analysis
- Failure analysis
- Future states analysis
- Strategy analysis
- Emerging technologies and smart products

This is a representative list of techniques; however, other categories are available, depending on the specific nature of the risk in question. See the exhibit "Categories of Risk Identification and Analysis Techniques."

## Questionnaires and Checklists

Questionnaires and checklists are some of the easiest risk identification techniques to use. For example, an insurance coverage checklist can be used to obtain details and information on the current insurance program. A questionnaire can be used to identify various risks within an organization's operation. These techniques are often used as either a starting point in the risk identification process or a summary when other, more complex techniques have been used.

One disadvantage of questionnaires and checklists is that they do not produce quantitative results. Another disadvantage is that, because of the format of these techniques, not all risks may be identified, and potential problems may be overlooked.

## Workshops

Workshops can be effective in identifying key risks and in determining the likelihood and impact of various events. A facilitator may lead discussions during a workshop and take the group through the process of identifying and analyzing risks that could prevent an organization from meeting its objectives.

Such workshops allow multiple departments, business units, and stakeholders to contribute, which results in not only a broader view of risk but also a shared understanding of issues facing other departments within the organization.

## Categories of Risk Identification and Analysis Techniques

| Category | Examples |
| --- | --- |
| Questionnaires and Checklists | Risk analysis questionnaires |
| | Insurance coverage checklists |
| Workshops | Brainstorming |
| | Delphi |
| Cause-and-Effect Analysis | 5 Whys |
| | Fishbone (Ishikawa) Diagram |
| Failure Analysis | Hazard and operability studies (HAZOP) |
| | Fault tree analysis (FTA) |
| | Failure mode and effects analysis (FMEA) |
| Future States Analysis | Scenario analysis |
| | Monte Carlo simulation |
| Strategy Analysis | SWOT analysis |
| | PEST analysis |
| Emerging Technologies and Smart Products | Sensors |
| | RFID tags |
| | Wearables |
| | Supply chain management |

[DA12631]

When multiple perspectives are considered in the risk assessment, the results are usually more thorough and comprehensive.

One potential disadvantage of workshops is that the opinion of senior management may take precedence over that of other stakeholders. Participants at all levels must feel comfortable sharing their observations and resist conceding to senior management's viewpoints.

Brainstorming is another technique that can be used as part of a workshop or independently. This technique can be used to identify and analyze risks facing the organization. An advantage of brainstorming is that all ideas are encouraged, leading to a more creative approach.

The Delphi technique is a form of brainstorming that relies on a panel of experts to reach a consensus opinion on an issue. A team is formed to select the panel and monitor the process. The team sends the experts a semistructured questionnaire, which the experts respond to anonymously. The team then collates the panel's responses and sends a summary report to the panel. This process is continued until a consensus opinion is reached. The advantages of this approach include a wider range of opinions, gained because of respondents' anonymity, and the ability to use widely dispersed experts because the panel does not meet in person. A possible disadvantage is that the process can be time-consuming. This technique is used to address issues that are of moderate complexity, and it produces qualitative data.

# Cause-and-Effect Analysis

Cause-and-effect analysis identifies the possible causes of an event or problem. This technique uses a formal approach to examine all possible causes and sub-causes of a given issue. The analysis uses a template that graphically illustrates all the causes and their effects. Such analysis is most often used when trying to determine the root cause of a problem or to examine interrelations within a specific process that produce an unintended result.

Two approaches to cause-and-effect analysis include the fishbone diagram and the 5 Whys technique.

With a fishbone diagram, the effect or problem being analyzed, such as an increase in a particular type of loss, is the starting point for analysis. From there, various causes are identified on the diagram, which resembles a fish skeleton, and further examined to isolate a root cause.

The 5 Whys approach is similar: the problem is stated first, and then the root cause is identified by continuing to ask why (often five times, although it may be less or more than five). The 5 Whys approach is often used in conjunction with a fishbone diagram to generate causes that contribute to the problem being considered.

These techniques are used to examine problems that are relatively simple to construct. One disadvantage is that participants may stop the process before all underlying causes have been identified and examined. This can result in a failure to accurately uncover the true root cause of the issue under analysis.

# Failure Analysis

Failure analysis techniques focus on identifying the causes of failure to prevent recurrences. Failures can include not meeting established sales or production goals, equipment breakdown, or physical losses to buildings or inventory. These are examples of techniques that fall under this category:

- Hazard and operability studies (HAZOP)
- Fault tree analysis (FTA)
- Failure mode and effects analysis (FMEA)

## Hazard and Operability Studies

The HAZOP technique is an intensive, time-consuming process used to solve complex problems. It uses a team of specialists from different operational areas to study a process or procedure and examine how failures may result in a hazard. An important feature is the use of guide words that are appropriate for the process under consideration. For example, the terms "more" and "less" could be chosen to identify deviations that are higher or lower than expectations. The team studies the process and provides documentation of its results. This documentation includes specific plans for treating the risks identified in the study.

HAZOP is often used in manufacturing and processing operations to examine the process and identify potential hazards that could result in direct physical damage, injury to employees, or other failures.

## Fault Tree Analysis

The FTA technique identifies a specific event, referred to as the top event, and then analyzes factors that contribute to it. For example, an organization could identify a catastrophic fire at its main location as the top event. The potential causes of failure and factors contributing to the top event, such as a malfunctioning sprinkler system, are then identified and evaluated. The display of causes for the event can be used to develop methods for reducing the likelihood and consequences of that event.

The construction of the fault tree includes symbols that graphically represent the logical progression of causal factors from the top event. FTA provides a means to systematically examine problems.

## Failure Mode and Effects Analysis

FMEA examines the components within a system or process to identify possible modes of failure and how each affects the system or processes. This technique can also analyze the probability and potential severity of failures. FMEA can be used to improve processes at the design stage and to identify the effect of human error within the system.

FMEA uses a team approach to examine the process and identify potential failure modes at each step. Every element of the process is analyzed to determine where failures might occur and to identify the consequences of these failures. Where failure points are identified, the design should be modified to compensate for failures. FMEA produces qualitative output and is used for problems of moderate complexity. The team could extend the process to categorize failure modes based on their criticality. Criticality analysis is generally accomplished by assigning a risk priority number. In this case, the process is called failure mode, effects, and criticality analysis.

## Future States Analysis

Future states analysis techniques seek to determine what risks may develop in the future. Scenario analysis is used to examine how the current environment may be influenced by emerging developments, such as new technology or new competitors in the market. Using this approach, a team forms and considers changes or major trends; then it develops various scenarios and possible outcomes related to these changes. Based on these outcomes, the team can identify, analyze, and evaluate risks.

A Monte Carlo simulation uses random variables, such as gross domestic product and competitor price levels, to simulate a range of outcomes—for example, levels of product demand. It is based on a random sampling of the variables. This technique is used to evaluate risks arising from a broad scope of situations. The computer model samples the random variables hundreds or thousands of times to produce a distribution of various outcomes. Based on several risk assessment decisions, the Monte Carlo technique uses statistical analysis to calculate possible outcomes and the probability of each.

# Strategy Analysis

Risk assessment can also be conducted as part of an organization's strategic planning process, which sets the organization's overall vision, mission, and goals. At the corporate level, this planning is long range and spans a three- to five-year period. It is important to identify, analyze, and evaluate the potential risks related to the organization's strategy.

A widely used strategy analysis technique is a SWOT (strengths, weaknesses, opportunities, and threats) analysis. This analysis starts with an internal evaluation of the organization's strengths and weaknesses and is followed by an evaluation of the opportunities and threats in the external environment. This external evaluation considers economic, social, political, and technological factors, as well as competitors, customers, and suppliers. See the exhibit "SWOT Analysis Table."

A related technique is a PEST (political, economic, social, and technological) analysis, which is sometimes used to identify the opportunities and threats within a SWOT analysis. A PEST analysis examines the organization's external macroenvironment. For example, it would consider economic factors such as growth rates, interest rates, inflation, and other factors that affect the organization's business strategy.

Risk assessment should be closely aligned with the organization's strategic planning process to identify uncertainties that would affect the organization's ability to meet its objectives. The risks identified within a strategy analysis can be further evaluated using other risk identification and analysis techniques.

---

## Apply Your Knowledge

A technology organization is undertaking a strategic review of its manufacturing operations. Currently, it has two plants in the United States and one plant in Asia. The manufacturing costs are 20 percent lower at the Asian plant, but production disruptions have been caused by earthquakes and typhoons.

## SWOT Analysis Table

| | Strengths | Weaknesses |
|---|---|---|
| Internal | List assets, competencies, or attributes that enhance competitiveness | List lacking assets, competencies, or attributes that diminish competitiveness |
| Internal | Prioritize based on the quality of the strength and the relative importance of the strength | Prioritize based on the seriousness of the weakness and the relative importance of the weakness |
| | Opportunities | Threats |
| External | List conditions that could be exploited to create a competitive advantage | List conditions that diminish competitive advantage |
| External | Prioritize based on the potential of exploiting the opportunities | Prioritize based on the seriousness and probability of occurrence |
| | Note strengths that can be paired with opportunities as areas of competitive advantage | Note weaknesses that can be paired with threats as risks to be avoided |

[DA03626]

Additionally, distribution costs have increased by 10 percent. The organization is expanding its product line and will need to build another plant. It is considering whether to locate the new plant in Asia. Using a SWOT analysis, identify the strengths and weaknesses of building the new facility in Asia.

*Feedback:* The strengths include lower manufacturing costs and the organization's established presence in Asia. The weaknesses include possible production disruptions caused by natural catastrophes and higher distribution costs.

**Sensor**

A device that detects and measures stimuli in its environment.

**Radio frequency identification (RFID) tag**

A transponder that communicates with an antenna and transceiver (together called the reader) using radio frequency identification.

# Emerging Technologies and Smart Products

Emerging technologies are being incorporated into smart products and operations that identify and assess risk. These smart products and operations complement and enhance other techniques by supplying large amounts of current, relevant data. For example, the data collected by workers' smart helmets and safety vests may be used in a failure analysis discussion or to confirm strengths, weaknesses, opportunities, or threats as part of a SWOT analysis. And emerging technologies may facilitate a future states analysis by more accurately identifying anticipated trends and scenarios.

Emerging technologies and smart products and operations can provide real-time, dynamic risk identification and assessment. For example, **sensors** and **radio frequency identification (RFID) tags** connected to wireless sensor networks can capture many types of vital information, including environmental conditions, worker health and safety, incomplete shipments, temperature, and humidity levels. This information can be further analyzed using algorithms based on **artificial intelligence** or **computer vision** to identify conditions such as unanticipated earthquake activity, workers' elevated anxiety levels, lost inventory, or a factory's suddenly harmful air quality.

**Artificial intelligence (AI)**
The ability of machines to simulate human intelligence.

**Computer vision**
A technology that simulates human vision.

Although these technologies, products, and operations do not replace other risk identification and analysis techniques, they do overcome some of the shortcomings of the other techniques. For example, they are able to explore a vast number of possible outcomes based on large data sets that they can analyze quickly and accurately. Through the use of artificial intelligence, these outcomes may even be based on simulated human thoughts and inferences.

These technologies and smart products and operations enable organizations to discover risk scenarios, infer critical risk insights, and quickly respond to the risks they have identified and assessed. Advancements in sensors and data analytics, as well as an increasing number of organizations engaging in networked ecosystems, are furthering the use of emerging technology to manage areas such as supply chain risk, cyber risk, controls testing, and internal auditing. As smart devices and controls become more pervasive, their use as risk identification and assessment techniques will grow accordingly.

## RISK TREATMENT

Risk treatment decisions are based on the results of a risk assessment.

The assessment includes identifying and analyzing an organization's various risks. See the exhibit "Enterprise Risk Management Process Model."

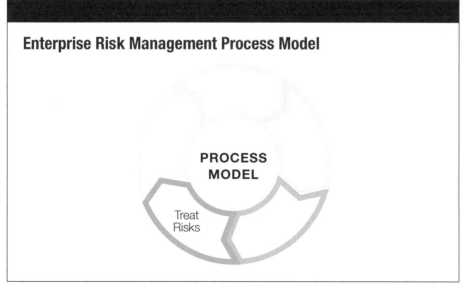

**Enterprise Risk Management Process Model**

PROCESS MODEL

Treat Risks

[DA08717_6]

Available risk treatment techniques include these:

- Avoid the risk
- Modify the likelihood and/or impact of the risk
- Transfer the risk
- Retain the risk
- Exploit the risk

The appropriate treatment can be achieved by using the risk treatment process to select the appropriate risk treatment techniques.

## Risk Treatment Process

Risk treatment involves making decisions based on the outcome of the risk identification and analysis. For risks identified as needing treatment, specific options must be selected to modify them. Treatment options will vary, and the negative or positive effects of the uncertainty on the organization should be considered. The goal of risk treatment is to modify identified risks to assist the organization in meeting its objectives.

**Residual risk**

Risk remaining after actions to alter the risk's likelihood or impact.

The risk treatment process is continuous and entails examining each risk treatment option (or combination of options) in terms of whether it leads to a tolerable level of **residual risk**. It also involves selecting and implementing a risk treatment option or options, and measuring the effectiveness of each option selected.

Risk treatment techniques are not mutually exclusive, and many risks require a combination of techniques. The risk treatment plan should indicate risk priorities and the order in which chosen techniques will be implemented. Review of risk treatment plans as part of overall monitoring of the risk management process is important. Risks may change based on changes in the organization's operation or on environmental factors, such as economic conditions or legal and regulatory requirements. Previous risk treatment decisions may no longer be valid, and implemented controls may no longer be effective. Furthermore, emerging risks—such as those arising from new technology or the acquisition of a new business unit—must be identified and assessed. The risk treatment process should also include a cost-benefit analysis to assess whether the benefits of the chosen treatment option outweigh the related costs.

The risk treatment plan should document the process and designate the chosen risk treatment options as well as people responsible for implementing the plan. The plan should also include a timetable for implementing the risk treatment options and for monitoring and reviewing the established plan.

# Risk Treatment Techniques

Risk treatment techniques apply to hazard, operational, financial, and strategic risks. In general, available risk treatment options fall into the categories of avoidance, modification, transfer, retention, or exploitation. Because **speculative risks** can result in both negative and positive consequences, the organization must consider a range of risk treatment techniques or a combination of techniques to manage negative and positive outcomes. For **pure risks**, the focus of risk treatment is on managing negative outcomes.

For events that appear to have primarily positive potential outcomes, such as a major competitor leaving the market, treatment would focus on exploiting the risk by maximizing expected gains. Techniques would include modifying the likelihood of an event to increase the opportunity to meet objectives while also considering treatment options for potential negative outcomes.

In some cases, risk **avoidance** is an appropriate option; when considering it, organizations must take into account any opportunity costs of not accepting a particular risk. See the exhibit "Risk Treatment Techniques."

**Speculative risk**
A chance of loss, no loss, or gain.

**Pure risk**
A chance of loss or no loss, but no chance of gain.

**Avoidance**
A technique that involves ceasing or never undertaking an activity so that the possibility of future gains or losses occurring from that activity is eliminated.

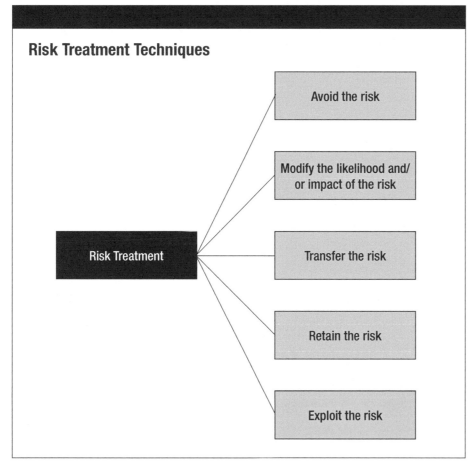

[DA08744]

**Loss prevention**

A risk control technique that reduces the frequency of a particular loss.

**Loss reduction**

A risk control technique that reduces the severity of a particular loss.

**Retention**

A risk financing technique that involves assumption of risk in which gains and losses are retained within the organization.

Identified risks can also be treated by modifying the likelihood and/or impact of events resulting in positive or negative outcomes. For hazard risks, modifying the likelihood of events focuses on **loss prevention** efforts to reduce overall loss frequency. Techniques designed to modify the impact of events recognize that not all negative outcomes can be avoided, but that the financial consequences of these events can be decreased. Techniques such as sprinkler systems in buildings or driver training for commercial truck operators are **loss reduction** efforts aimed at reducing the severity of losses. An organization can use contingency plans to modify the consequences of an operational risk, such as a disruption in its supply chain resulting from a permanent or temporary loss of a major supplier of raw materials.

Risks can be transferred, or shared, through contractual arrangements or joint ventures with other organizations. Outsourcing is a method of risk sharing that can be used to transfer noncritical operations and their related risks to another organization. For hazard risks, insurance is the primary technique used to transfer risk. Contractual risk transfers (noninsurance), such as hedging or other contractual agreements, can be used to transfer financial consequences of risks to another party or organization.

Risk **retention** is used for residual risk after other treatment techniques have been considered. Retention is often used in combination with risk modification and transfer. Because unplanned retention of unidentified risks can result in catastrophic loss to an organization, risk retention should be used for risks that have been identified and analyzed so that the organization clearly understands the risks that are being retained. Organizations may also actively take or increase their risk to exploit an opportunity.

## *Apply Your Knowledge*

An organization has just completed an extensive risk management review for its operations. As part of this effort, it has established a risk treatment plan. Explain why the organization should monitor this plan periodically going forward.

*Feedback:* The organization should periodically monitor the risk treatment plan because the organization's operations, economic conditions, or legal and regulatory requirements may change. The current risk treatment plan may become invalid, and previously implemented controls may become ineffective.

# TRADITIONAL ACCIDENT ANALYSIS TECHNIQUES

Accident analysis techniques assist risk management professionals in determining possible causes of accidents to help select appropriate risk control techniques.

Many people have studied accident causation to provide a framework for analyzing the cause or causes of a particular accident. By analyzing the causes of past accidents, risk management professionals can select and implement risk control techniques to prevent future accidents, or to reduce the losses associated with accidents that do occur.

## Accident Causation

Accidents can have many causes, and understanding the causes of past accidents is important to preventing future accidents. Often, the focus of accident causation centers on either an unsafe act or an unsafe condition. However, the cause of an accident is more complicated, and multiple actions are needed for an accident to occur. One accident causation approach states that accidents have a direct cause, which is usually an unplanned release of energy that cannot be safely absorbed by a person or an object. Unsafe acts or conditions are either indirect or underlying causes of the accident, with poor management, safety policy, and personal or environmental factors as the basic causes of most accidents. Risk management professionals must take a comprehensive approach when examining the causes of potential accidents to uncover these multiple layers that contribute to losses. See the exhibit "Accident Causation."

## Accident Analysis Techniques

These five theories or approaches to understanding accident causation include elements of direct, indirect, and basic causes of accidents:

- Sequence of events (domino theory)
- Energy transfer theory
- The technique of operations review (TOR) approach
- Change analysis
- Job safety analysis

These theories and approaches illustrate how to analyze accidents from different perspectives. No one theory or approach is necessarily the best or applicable to all situations. However, the risk management professional can use these theories and approaches as tools to help in the analysis of accident causation.

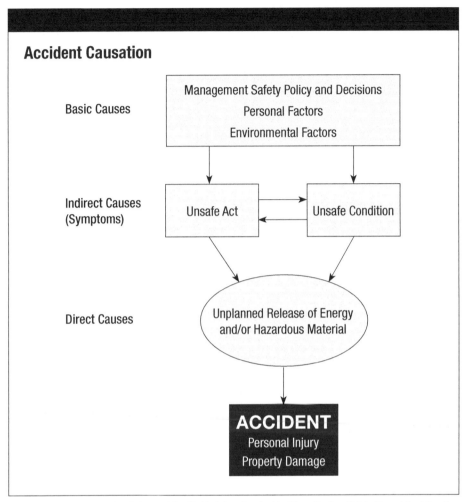

**Accident Causation**

U.S. Department of Labor, Mine Safety and Health Administration, Accident Investigation, Safety Manual No. 10, p. 2. [DA08748]

## Sequence of Events (Domino Theory)

**Domino theory**

An accident causation theory that presumes that accidents are the end result of a chain of accident factors.

The sequence of events theory, also known as the **domino theory**, was developed by H.W. Heinrich, a leading industrial safety engineer. He believed that the chain of accident factors consisted of these:

1. Ancestry and social environment
2. Fault of person
3. An unsafe act and/or a mechanical or physical hazard
4. The accident itself
5. The resulting injury

The exhibit explains these factors. Heinrich described each of the five accident factors as a domino, emphasizing that every accident sequence begins with a negative ancestry or social environment for a person and ends with an injury or illness. He added that removing any of the four dominoes preceding the injury or illness will prevent that injury or illness. Removal of the third domino, the unsafe act and/or mechanical or physical hazard, is usually the best way to break the accident sequence and prevent injury or illness. See the exhibit "Sequence of Events (Domino Theory)."

## Sequence of Events (Domino Theory)

| Accident Factors | Explanation of Factors |
| --- | --- |
| 1. Ancestry and social environment | Ancestry includes inherited psychological disorders. |
| | Dysfunctional social environment can form unsafe character traits and may impede learning. |
| | Both ancestry and social environment can cause faults of person. |
| 2. Fault of person | Faults of person can include impulsiveness, violent temper, nervousness, and resistance to accept safe practices, all of which can cause unsafe acts to occur and/or mechanical or physical hazards to exist. |
| 3. Unsafe act and/or mechanical or physical hazard | Unsafe acts can include improper use of a machine or equipment, such as ignoring lockout tag out safe operating procedures or carelessly overextending a ladder. |
| | Mechanical or physical hazards can include slippery floors and inadequate ventilation which can result in an accident. |
| 4. Accident | An occurrence that causes an injury. |
| 5. Injury or illness | Trauma to the body caused by an accident. |

[DA08749]

Heinrich believed that unsafe human acts (such as the improper use of a machine) are far more common than unsafe conditions (such as a defect in a machine). Therefore, correcting unsafe acts is the most effective method of preventing injuries or illnesses. Most of Heinrich's predecessors in industrial accident prevention stressed unsafe conditions rather than unsafe acts and concentrated on designing safe machines and surroundings.

Because of its emphasis on human fault, the domino theory is most applicable to situations within human control. This theory, therefore, has limited applicability to accidents caused by natural disasters. Although to some extent it is within the control of people to protect themselves and their property from a natural disaster such as a hurricane, preventing the cause of the accident is not within their control. However, the domino theory is well-suited to accidents caused by human carelessness.

## Energy Transfer Theory

**Energy transfer theory**

An approach to accident causation that views accidents as energy that is released and that affects objects, including living things, in amounts or at rates that the objects cannot tolerate.

The **energy transfer theory** was developed by Dr. William Haddon Jr., an expert in public health and the first president of the Insurance Institute for Highway Safety. According to Haddon, the basic cause of accidents is energy out of control. The approach ("strategies") for preventing accidents or reducing the resulting harm focuses on controlling released energy and/or reducing the harm caused by that energy. The ten basic strategies of the energy transfer theory are:[2]

1.   Prevent the marshaling of the energy by eliminating the production of high-powered vehicles

2.   Reduce the amount of energy marshaled by limiting the speed of vehicles

3.   Prevent the release of built-up energy by keeping elevators from falling or reckless drivers from having access to automobiles

4.   Modify the rate or spatial distribution of the release of energy by reducing the slope of ski trails or installing explosion-relieving walls

5.   Separate, in space or in time, the energy being released from a susceptible structure by establishing separate lanes for pedestrian and vehicular traffic or by controlling the time interval between landings and takeoffs at airports

6.   Interpose a physical barrier between the energy and the susceptible structure by requiring fire doors in public buildings or requiring workers to wear protective clothing

7.   Modify the contact surface or basic structure that can be affected by installing breakaway highway light poles or by requiring front and side airbags in automobiles to cushion occupants' impact

8.   Strengthen the susceptible structure that might be damaged by the energy by requiring special building construction in earthquake zones or building codes that require hand rails on stairwells to be able to withstand the weight of multiple users at once

9.   Move rapidly to detect and evaluate damage and to counter its continuation or spread by giving first aid or protecting property in imminent danger of fire

10.  Take long-term action (after the emergency period) to reduce further damage by rehabilitating injured persons or salvaging damaged property

## Technique of Operations Review (TOR) Approach

**Technique of operations review (TOR)**

An approach to accident causation that views the cause of accidents to be a result of management's shortcomings.

Another approach to accident causation is the **technique of operations review (TOR)**, which focuses on ineffective management. Regarding workplace accidents, Dan Petersen, a well-known safety consultant, stated this:

> Root causes often relate to the management system. They may be due to management's policies and procedures, supervision and its effectiveness, training…. Some root causes could be a lack of inspection procedures, a lack of management policy, poor definition of responsibilities (supervisors did not know they were responsible…), and a lack of supervisory or employee training.[3]

This view of the root causes of accidents led Petersen to establish five basic principles of risk control:

- An unsafe act, an unsafe condition, and an accident are all symptoms of something wrong in the management system.
- Certain circumstances, unless identified and controlled, will produce severe injuries.
- Safety should be managed like any other organizational function, with management setting achievable goals and planning, organizing, leading, and controlling to achieve them.
- Management must specify procedures for accountability if safety efforts are to be effective.
- The function of safety is to locate and define the operational errors that allow accidents to occur.

Although Petersen's approach focuses particularly on industrial work injuries and illnesses, his approach is applicable to any accident causing a property, personnel, liability, or net income loss.

Developed by D.A. Weaver and endorsed by Petersen, TOR identifies particular faults of an organization's management and groups these faults into categories such as inadequate coaching, failure to take responsibility, unclear authority, and inadequate supervision, among others.

The TOR approach helps identify accident causes and suggests corrective actions. In the TOR approach, managers must recognize their own (or their colleagues' or subordinates') faults and correct them. Removing these management faults will eliminate most, if not all, accidents.

## Change Analysis

**Change analysis** is an approach to analyzing the cause of accidents. It asks a series of "what if" questions and projects the consequences for each of the changes and for all feasible combinations of change. For example, suppose an automobile manufacturer is considering using hybrid gas and electric engines instead of gas-powered engines for its automobiles. Risk management professionals can ask how the change will affect the safety of the drivers, the employees assembling the automobiles, the operators of service stations, and perhaps the general public.

Change analysis
An analysis that projects the effects a given system change is likely to have on an existing system.

As another illustration, risk management professionals might join the Human Resources Department in asking, "If the company changes to a flextime arrangement that allows employees to have a workweek consisting of four, ten-hour days, what may happen to the frequency or severity of automobile or train accidents that our employees suffer while commuting?"

Change analysis can also apply to various combinations of changes in systems. To illustrate, the automobile manufacturer considering the hybrid gas and electric engine option may recognize that an automobile's safe performance depends partially on the automobile's weight. Change analysis can evaluate the safety implications of switching from gasoline to hybrid engines, changing the weight of the vehicles, and using various combinations of weight changes and hybrid engine options. This analysis may reveal that a particular combination of engine options and weight changes is safer than any engine option or weight change alone.

## Job Safety Analysis

**Job safety analysis (JSA)**

An analysis that dissects a repetitive task, whether performed by a person or machine, to determine potential hazards if each action is not performed.

Another approach to analyzing the cause of accidents is **job safety analysis (JSA)**. This technique is one of the most universally applicable and versatile. Each job (activity or operation) is broken down into individual sequential steps. Hazards associated with each step are identified, controls are defined, and responsibility for implementing each is assigned (provided that the added benefit of the safety procedure outweighs its costs). JSA applies best to repetitive human tasks performed in an environment sufficiently stable to allow most hazards to be foreseen. Repetitive tasks and person/machine systems are so common that JSA is applicable in almost every case in which a person must act safely to avoid causing bodily injury or property damage.

# SYSTEM SAFETY ANALYSIS

System safety is a discipline that originated within the United States Department of Defense, where it was first used in the design, manufacture, and deployment of the Minuteman nuclear missile systems. Because of its success, system safety was soon adopted by the entire aerospace industry and gradually by the petrochemical and power generation industries.

Organizations can be viewed as systems. Many aspects of organizations, such as their machinery, organizational structures, transportation networks, production processes, and services, can also be viewed as systems. A primary duty of all risk management professionals is to keep these systems operating safely and effectively.

## System Safety Defined

**System safety**

A safety engineering technique also used as an approach to accident causation that considers the mutual effects of the interrelated elements of a system on one another throughout the system's life cycle.

**System safety** analysis looks at an organization as a whole to identify potential sources of losses. An accident occurs when a component of a system malfunctions. System safety predicts how these malfunctions might occur so that appropriate action can be taken either to prevent the failure or to reduce its consequences. It also provides a framework for investigating accidents that have already occurred.

System safety relies on a number of specific techniques for identifying and analyzing hazards and for determining how these hazards can lead to system failures and accidents. These techniques can estimate the probability of particular kinds of breakdowns (based on the probabilities of all the events that produce the breakdown) and suggest cost-effective ways of preventing these system failures.

The system safety approach differs from traditional accident causation approaches that focus on unsafe acts or conditions. In the traditional approach, once these conditions are identified, controls are applied to avoid future accidents.

# The Concept of a System

By understanding the features of systems, risk management professionals can be more effective at protecting the integrity and reliability of any system. All systems have these four features:

- Components
- Purpose
- Environment
- Life cycle

# Components

The first feature of a system that a risk management professional needs to understand is its components. Because systems vary, care must be taken to describe the components of systems in ways that are broad enough to include all the system's aspects yet sufficiently specific to be meaningful.

One system component is its physical elements, which deserve special attention because any impairment of a physical element can jeopardize the system's ability to perform. Accidental impairments have traditionally been a risk management or safety department responsibility.

Other forms of impairment (for example, deterioration or technological obsolescence) have been the responsibility of other managers. The system approach eliminates this distinction. Consequently, system safety requires the risk management professional to consider the impairment of all of the systems' physical elements.

Virtually all systems consist of subsystems. Any organization is a subsystem within its industry. The subsystem concept is essential to effective loss control. Operating even the largest system reliably can be jeopardized when a single, deeply layered subsystem fails.

Subsystems can be layered within one another. For example, payroll processing is a sub-subsystem within the organization's accounting subsystem. Regardless of how deeply layered, all systems are typically also subsystems. For example, a single pressure relief valve on one tank is a subsystem within the larger system of a petrochemical complex.

An organization's risk management professional must understand what all the organization's systems and subsystems are, how they interact, and how the failure of any subsystem can endanger other subsystems and systems (including the entire organization).

Systems are powered or moved by energy sources. For example, electricity is required to operate an organization's computer systems, and fuel is required to move products from manufacturer to distributor. However, energy can also be a source of substantial risk and can cause great harm when released uncontrollably.

A risk management professional must protect the integrity of an organization's systems by ensuring the controlled application of energy and the intended movement of a system's physical elements. To do this, a risk management professional must protect the ability of a system's parts to move as planned, ensure a reliable source of energy to power the organization's systems when needed, and guard against this energy's escaping and causing harm.

## Purpose

The second feature of a system that a risk management professional needs to understand is its purpose. Every system has at least one purpose. For example, a fire detection/suppression system must protect a structure and its contents against a particular type of fire. Another illustration is that a food product container must protect the food from temperature extremes and provide the consumer with product information.

To assess the adequacy of a system's components, risk management professionals must know the purpose of those components. For example, each physical element must be sufficiently strong and properly adapted to its purpose, including unintended but foreseeable purposes. The energy sources must be sufficient but not excessive for powering the system. Finally, the subsystems must support the purpose of the overriding system.

## Environment

The third feature of a system that a risk management professional must understand is the system's environment. Every system operates in an environment that affects (and is affected by) it. Within this environment, a system fulfills its purpose. Environments are typically aspects of larger systems of which the system in question is a subsystem.

Environments can be classified according to how broadly one is considering them:

- The immediate physical environment includes temperature, illumination, pressure, walking/working surfaces, and so on. Systems may be limited in their ability to perform effectively under extreme physical environmental conditions.
- The organizational (management) environment includes the policies and procedures that govern the interaction of the system's physical elements. This environment determines whether a clear definition of authority and

responsibility exists within the organization, management's commitment to safety, and employee empowerment to raise issues and stop or refuse to work if a hazardous condition is detected.

- The socioeconomic/legal environment includes social norms and conventions; safety, environmental, and transportation laws and regulations; and local, national, and global economic considerations.

## Life Cycle

The fourth feature of a system that a risk management professional must consider is the life cycle. Just as systems exist in many types of environments, they also exist over time. System safety recognizes five phases in the life cycle of any system. The system approach to safety applies differently to each of these life cycle phases. See the exhibit "Phases of the Life Cycle."

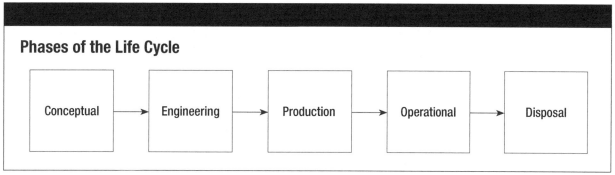

**Phases of the Life Cycle**

Conceptual → Engineering → Production → Operational → Disposal

[DA08729]

A system-oriented approach designs each product or process so that its disposal or obsolescence creates the minimum amount of hazardous waste or environmental harm. Ideally, raw materials can be recycled efficiently, and the replacement system can be readily implemented. Once a risk management professional has identified and is familiar with the features of organizational systems, he or she can apply appropriate system safety analysis techniques to those systems.

At the **conceptual phase**, the more that hazards are managed or designed out of the system, the less the system will need to rely on protective equipment and special procedures in the operational phase to reduce the chances of human error. In the **engineering phase**, the system progresses, and a prototype is created. The precise dimensions, specifications, and procedures are tested for full-scale use. Safety design features, such as machine guards or a fire detection/suppression system, also become integral parts of the system during this phase.

Because the **production phase** (or developmental phase) involves creating the system according to the dimensions, specifications, and procedures determined in a prior phase, most of the system safety opportunities occur in other

**Conceptual phase**
A phase in the life of a system when the basic purpose and preliminary design of the system are formulated.

**Engineering phase**
A phase in the life of a system when the system's design is constructed and prototypes are tested.

**Production phase**
A phase in the life of a system when the actual system is created.

**Operational phase**

A phase in the life of a system when the system is implemented.

**Disposal phase**

A phase in the life of a system when the system reaches the end of its useful life and is disposed of.

phases. In the **operational phase** (or deployment phase), when the system is fully functional, safety features built into the system during the earlier phases must be maintained. For example, fire detection/suppression systems must be supervised, fire doors must remain closed, and periodic fire drills must be conducted to keep personnel trained in emergency procedures. Opportunities for adding safety options in the operational phase are not as numerous (or are much more costly) as in the earlier phases. These opportunities are more limited because the system's basic features have already been implemented and are therefore harder to change. The **disposal phase** (or termination phase) is the final phase of a system's life cycle. Its importance has been driven largely by environmental concerns.

## System Safety Example

To illustrate how system safety can help prevent system failures or identify causes of failures that have already occurred, consider an accident that a computer manufacturer might experience. Suppose that the brakes on one of the manufacturer's delivery trucks fail while the truck is transporting a shipment of Internet servers to a customer, thus preventing delivery by a specified contract date. See the exhibit "Systems Safety Example."

---

**Systems Safety Example**

The failure of the brakes on the delivery truck can be viewed within these systems:

- The brake mechanism itself, consisting only of its mechanical parts
- The brake system for the truck, including the brake mechanism, the driver's foot on the brake pedal, and the truck tires on the highway
- The driver/vehicle/highway system that transports the Internet servers
- The transportation system (truck, rail, ship, or air) through which the computer manufacturer delivers its products to customers
- The computer manufacturer's overall management system
- The overall economic and legal systems of the U.S.

[DA08728]

---

A system safety approach allows a risk management professional to view the accident from the perspectives of many different systems. Each system suggests different ways in which the accident might occur and ways in which the frequency or severity of such accidents could be reduced.

The table illustrates the systems that can be analyzed and examples of loss control techniques related to each system for the truck in the previous example. This illustration indicates three advantages of applying system safety to loss control programs. See the exhibit "Loss Control Techniques for Each System."

## Loss Control Techniques for Each System

| System/Component | Possible Loss Control Technique |
|---|---|
| Braking system | Purchase better parts components/parts or replace them more often |
| Truck's brake system | Purchase trucks that use a more reliable brake system design |
| Driver/vehicle/highway system | Improve fleet management |
| Manufacturer's transportation system | Find a more reliable way to transport goods to customers |
| Manufacturer's overall management system | Focus senior management's attention on transportation/fleet safety |
| U.S. economic and legal systems | Revise the manufacturer's contracts of sale to allow for delays caused by specified types of accidents |

[DA08730]

# System Safety Advantages

The delivery truck example indicates three advantages of applying system safety to loss control programs. First, by considering how an accident impairs various systems, risk management professionals can follow an orderly process for developing a range of loss control measures that improve the reliability of interrelated systems. Second, because systems differ in scope, risk management professionals can use system safety analysis to enlist the cooperation of many people inside and outside the organization. In the delivery truck case, these people could be included:

- The computer manufacturer's purchasing personnel (responsible for buying and maintaining trucks with adequate braking systems)
- The drivers of the trucks
- The manufacturer's senior management (responsible for coordinating the work of all departments)
- Legal experts (responsible for reviewing contracts with customers)

Finally, by using a system safety approach, risk management professionals can reduce accident frequency and severity by defining and preventing events that lead to a particular type of accident.

# LOSS CONTROL TECHNIQUES FOR HAZARD RISK

Hazard risks are pure risks that arise from property, liability, or personnel loss exposures and are generally the subject of insurance. Once the causes of potential or past losses arising from hazard risk have been determined, loss control techniques must be selected and implemented to prevent future accidents and to reduce their effects.

Loss control techniques include these:

- Avoidance
- Loss prevention
- Loss reduction
- Separation, duplication, and diversification

Each of these loss control techniques can employ many different loss control measures.

## Avoidance

**Avoidance**

A risk control technique that involves ceasing or never undertaking an activity so that the possibility of a future loss occurring from that activity is eliminated.

**Avoidance** is a loss control technique that involves ceasing or choosing not to undertake an activity so that the possibility of future losses occurring from that activity is eliminated. Suffering a loss from a particular loss exposure is impossible when that exposure is avoided. Therefore, risk management professionals reduce the probability of loss to zero when they eliminate or decide not to undertake a particular activity. An avoided loss exposure requires no further loss control or risk financing measures. However, even though avoidance can eliminate future loss exposures, it cannot eliminate past ones. For example, a manufacturer that stopped making a defective product is still liable for losses caused by the products it manufactured and distributed in the past.

Some loss exposures can be avoided. For example, a manufacturer that is located on an island and is concerned about the weakened condition of the one bridge that trucks use to carry its merchandise to market may want to avoid the loss exposure of losing a shipment in a bridge collapse. The company can avoid this exposure by transporting its merchandise by boat. Using boats helps the company avoid exposing trucks to a possible bridge collapse, but it also exposes its shipments to boating accidents. This example illustrates how avoiding one loss exposure often creates another.

If this company's primary concern is exposing its merchandise to damage while in transit, boats might not be better than trucks. The only ways the manufacturer can avoid the loss exposure altogether are by not transporting to the mainland or by moving its manufacturing operations to the mainland.

Even if it took one of those actions, the manufacturer would likely face other transit loss exposures because products must be shipped to wholesalers and retailers. Despite its inherent difficulties, avoidance should be considered when the expected value of the losses from an activity outweighs the expected benefits of that activity. For example, a toy manufacturer might decide not to produce a particular toy because the cost of the products liability claims would outweigh the revenue from its sale, no matter how cautious the manufacturer might be in producing and marketing the toy.

Also, avoidance has limited applications. Many loss exposures are automatically created and cannot be avoided. For example, all organizations have personnel loss exposures. They cannot be avoided because they are a fact of the organization's existence. Similarly, the only way to avoid all types of property loss is to possess no property whatsoever. Therefore, avoidance is not a feasible loss control technique for most loss exposures.

## Loss Prevention

Loss prevention is a loss control technique that reduces the frequency of a particular loss without necessarily affecting loss severity. It differs from avoidance because loss prevention does not eliminate all chance of loss. Loss prevention is also distinct from loss reduction because loss reduction focuses on reducing loss severity, not loss frequency. In practice, risk management professionals might combine loss prevention and loss reduction—for example, when a highway speed limit is lowered. That particular measure can reduce the number of automobile accidents (frequency)—because drivers have more time to react to dangerous situations—and the seriousness of accidents (severity), because accidents tend to be less severe when they occur at lower speeds.

Generally, a loss prevention measure is implemented before an accident occurs to break the sequence of events that lead to the accident. Breaking the sequence should prevent the accident from occurring or at least make it less likely.

Because of the close link between accident causation and loss prevention, determining effective loss prevention measures usually requires carefully studying how particular accidents are caused. For example, according to Heinrich's domino theory, most workplace injury accidents result from a chain of events that includes an unsafe act or an unsafe mechanical or physical hazard. Therefore, work-safety efforts have focused on trying to eliminate specific unsafe acts or conditions. As another example, fire safety engineers consider the fire triangle, which includes three elements (fuel, oxygen, and heat) that must all be present for fire to occur. Consequently, preventing fire-related accidents requires removing at least one of the three elements of the fire triangle.

## Loss Reduction

Loss reduction is a loss control technique that reduces the severity of a particular loss. What loss prevention does for the frequency of losses, loss reduction does for the severity of losses. To assess loss reduction opportunities, risk management professionals must assume that an accident has occurred and then consider what could have been done, either before or after the accident, to reduce the size or extent of the resulting loss.

The two broad categories of loss reduction measures are pre-loss measures (applied before the loss occurs) and post-loss measures (applied after the loss occurs). Pre-loss measures to reduce loss severity can also reduce loss frequency (for example, driving ambulances at lower speeds in nonemergency situations). Pre-loss measures generally reduce the amount of property damage or the number of people suffering loss from a single event.

Post-loss measures typically focus on emergency procedures, salvage operations, rehabilitation activities, or legal defenses to halt the spread or to counter the effects of loss. For example, erecting firewalls to limit damage from a fire is a pre-loss measure; activating a fire detection/suppression system is a post-loss measure.

Many loss reduction measures are suggested by the energy transfer theory. For example, reducing the amount of energy marshaled, modifying the rate or spatial distribution of the energy's transfer, modifying the impaired contact surface or structure, and strengthening a weak structure are all pre-loss measures of loss reduction. Similarly, the final two energy transfer strategies— rapidly detecting and evaluating damage to counter its spread, and taking long-term action to reduce further damage—are post-loss measures for loss reduction. Some loss reduction measures, such as setting a maximum speed limit for automobiles, may also reduce loss frequency, making them appropriate examples of loss prevention. The dual purpose of these measures illustrates the importance of carefully tracing and distinguishing among the various effects of a particular loss control technique.

## Separation, Duplication, and Diversification

**Separation**
A risk control technique that isolates loss exposures from one another to minimize the adverse effect of a single loss.

**Separation** is a loss control technique that disperses a particular asset or activity over several locations and regularly relies on that asset or activity as part of the organization's resources. Separation of exposure units can reduce an organization's dependence on a single asset, activity, or person, making individual losses smaller. Two examples are dividing existing inventory between two separate warehouses or manufacturing a component in two separate plants. Separation is appropriate if an organization can operate with only a portion of these separate units intact. If one unit suffers a total loss, the portion of the assets or operations in the other unit must be sufficient for operations to continue. Each of the separated units is normally kept in daily use.

**Duplication**
A risk control technique that uses backups, spares, or copies of critical property, information, or capabilities and keeps them in reserve.

**Duplication** of exposure units is a loss control technique that uses backups, spares, or copies of critical property, information, or capabilities and keeps them in reserve. These duplicates are not used unless the primary asset is damaged or destroyed. Like separation, duplication can reduce an organization's dependence on a single asset, activity, or person, making individual losses smaller. The distinction between separation and duplication is how often the organization will be relying on the asset or activity. Duplication is appropriate if an entire asset or activity is so important that the consequence of its loss justifies the expense and time of maintaining the duplicate. An example of duplication is maintaining duplicate accounting records.

**Diversification** of exposure units is a loss control technique that spreads loss exposures over numerous projects, products, markets, or regions. Diversification prevents a single event or series of events from destroying a large percentage of the organization's assets. For example, by an organization's entering into different geographic markets, if one market becomes too competitive, the other markets may still generate enough profit for the organization to continue operations. (Because diversification deals primarily with business risk, the remainder of this section discusses only separation and duplication.)

Even though separation and duplication both deal with hazard risk, they are distinct from one another, and both are distinct from other loss reduction measures. These five points need to be considered for separation and duplication to be implemented effectively:

- Unlike other loss control techniques, neither separation nor duplication attempts to reduce the severity of loss to a single unit. Each unit might still be subject to total loss, but each unit is less significant to the organization than the sum of the combined units.

- The intent of both separation and duplication is to reduce the severity of an individual loss, but they could have differing effects on loss frequency. Using two distantly separate warehouses instead of one might increase loss frequency because now two units are exposed to loss. Duplication, however, is likely to only slightly increase loss frequency because the duplicated unit is kept in reserve and is not as exposed to loss as is the primary unit. For example, a duplicate vehicle is presumably garaged and is not as vulnerable to highway accidents as is the primary vehicle.

- Duplication is likely to reduce the average expected annual loss from a given risk exposure because duplication reduces loss severity while only slightly increasing loss frequency.

- Separation may decrease the average expected loss. Much depends on whether the reduction in loss severity from separation outweighs any related increase in loss frequency.

- The net result of the increase in the number of loss exposures and reduction in severity per loss exposure is that losses tend to be more predictable, especially if the number of exposure units is large enough for the law of large numbers to be applied.

Both separation and duplication tend to be expensive and sometimes impractical loss management techniques. Separation, in particular, is seldom undertaken for its own sake but is usually a by-product of another management decision. For example, few organizations build a second warehouse

**Diversification**
A risk control technique that spreads loss exposures over numerous projects, products, markets, or regions.

simply to reduce the severity of losses to the first warehouse. However, if an organization is considering building a second warehouse to expand production, the risk management benefits of a second warehouse can strengthen the argument in favor of the expansion.

In contrast, duplication is often prompted by risk management considerations. Senior management recognizes the importance of a particular asset or activity and is willing to invest in duplicating it so as not to be without this essential element of its operations. Duplicate records, spare machinery parts, and cross-training employees are typical risk management safeguards.

For cost reasons, separation of exposure units (keeping all units in daily use) typically has a more practical application than does duplication of exposure units (with which standby units remain idle except during emergencies).

Opportunities for separation include these:

- Maintaining several warehouses at different locations to store inventory rather than maintaining an entire inventory at one location.

- Operating trucks with only partial loads, which requires 5 or 10 percent more trucks than are necessary. This provides excess capacity if part of the fleet becomes disabled or requires maintenance, in which case the remaining portion of the fleet would operate at full capacity.

- Equipping each of several facilities to perform a variety of operations so that the firm's operations can be maintained if one facility temporarily shuts down.

Opportunities for duplication include these:

- Maintaining duplicates of accounting records and other valuable documents in a safe location for use only if the original documents are damaged or destroyed.

- Keeping an inventory of spare machinery parts or even spare machines for use when the primary ones are unusable for any reason.

- Entering into a mutual aid pact with similar organizations to use one another's facilities or equipment such as computers, printing presses, and refrigerated storage when facilities or equipment are damaged or otherwise unavailable.

# SUMMARY

Risk assessment is a process designed to identify and analyze the risks that face an organization. These risks can have a positive or negative effect on the organization's ability to meet objectives. The results of risk assessments form the basis of an organization's risk response and treatment decisions.

Several categories of risk identification and analysis techniques can be used to identify, analyze, and evaluate risks. They include questionnaires and checklists, workshops, cause-and-effect analysis, failure analysis, future states analysis, strategy analysis, and emerging technologies and smart products. Several of these techniques are often used throughout the risk identification and analysis process.

The risk treatment process involves assessing specific risk treatment options to determine whether residual risks are tolerable to an organization. Risk treatment techniques include avoiding risk, modifying the likelihood and/or impact, transferring the risk, retaining the risk, and exploiting the risk. These techniques can be applied to hazard, operational, financial, and strategic risks.

The choice of a specific risk management technique depends, in part, on the assumptions made about how accidents are caused, prevented, or made less severe. Because different sets of assumptions imply different causes (some primarily unsafe human acts and others unsafe conditions), differing theories of accident causation suggest distinct ways of removing those accident causes.

Many aspects of organizations can be viewed as systems. A primary duty of risk management professionals is to keep these systems operating safely and effectively. However, in all organizations, accidents will occur. The primary purpose of using system safety analysis is to address potential system failures before a loss and to provide a framework for investigating accidents that have already occurred.

Loss control is one way to treat loss exposures. Loss control techniques reduce accident frequency and severity through avoidance, loss prevention, loss reduction, separation, duplication, and diversification.

# ASSIGNMENT NOTES

1.  Risk and Insurance Management Society, "Exploring Risk Appetite and Risk Tolerance," RIMS Executive Report, 2012, www.rims.org/resources/ERM/Documents/RIMS_Exploring_Risk_Appetite_Risk_Tolerance_0412.pdf (accessed June 1, 2012).

2.  William Haddon Jr., MD, "On the Escape of Tigers," American Journal of Public Health and the Nation's Health, December 1970, pp. 2229–2234.

3.  Dan Petersen, Techniques of Safety Management: A Systems Approach, 4th ed. (Des Plaines, Ill.: American Society of Safety Engineers, 2003), pp. 28–29.

# Root Cause Analysis

## Educational Objectives

After learning the content of this assignment, you should be able to:

▷ Describe root cause analysis and the steps in the root cause analysis process.

▷ Explain how an organization can use failure mode and effects analysis (FMEA) to assess and mitigate risk.

▷ Explain how an organization can use fault tree analysis (FTA) to determine the causes of a risk event.

▷ Explain how an organization can use a "5 Whys" analysis and fishbone (Ishikawa) diagram to determine the causes of a risk event.

# Root Cause Analysis

## INTRODUCTION TO ROOT CAUSE ANALYSIS

Determination of an accident's root cause allows organizations to discern the cause of a harmful event and prevent such events from recurring.

When an accident occurs in the workplace, the cause may initially appear obvious. For example, if a customer slips on a restaurant floor, a cursory examination might reveal that the wet floor is the cause. A more thorough analysis, however, would focus on why the floor was wet. It would explore whether an employee failed to follow procedures that called for only mopping floors before and after hours, whether the employee was properly trained, and so forth. Determining the answers to these and other questions leads to the **root cause** of the accident. This can help restaurant management implement procedural changes to prevent future customer slips.

Events that affect the safety of an organization's workplace, its employees' health, the environment, or its product's quality, reliability, and production are of concern to risk managers and an organization's management. **Root cause analysis (RCA)** is used to determine the underlying cause of a harmful event.

## The Nature of Root Cause Analysis

Root causes have four basic characteristics:

- A root cause is expressed as a specific underlying cause, not as a generalization. For example, "Employee did not follow directions" cannot be the root cause of an accident. The RCA would address why the employee did not follow directions. As another example, identifying operator error or equipment failure as a root cause of an event is not sufficient because management cannot address such vague causes. The root cause of such an event should be expressed as something specific, such as "operator removed machine guard."

- A root cause can be reasonably identified. In the machine guard example, it would be necessary to know why the operator removed the machine guard. Was it because it was not working properly? Did the supervisor demand faster production and the guard hampered that? Did the employee want to get the work done faster so he could leave work early? Answers to these and other questions help identify the root cause.

**Root cause**

The event or circumstance that directly leads to an occurrence.

**Root cause analysis (RCA)**

A systematic procedure that uses the results of the other analysis techniques to identify the predominant cause of the accident.

- A root cause must be expressed as something that can be modified. For example, weather conditions or an earthquake could not be considered root causes because such events are beyond human control. In the machine guard example, the root cause could conceivably be maintenance of the machine or personnel problems. If an employee was injured because a lightning strike caused a power failure, the lightning strike could not be considered a root cause because management cannot control the weather. However, the root cause could be the absence of a backup generator.

- A root cause must produce effective recommendations for prevention of future accidents that stem from the root cause. Identifying and mitigating the actions, inactions, conditions, or behaviors that caused a harmful event can prevent reoccurrence of the event. By addressing the root cause of a problem, risk managers can help prevent future incidents.

Harmful events generally are associated with one of three basic causes of loss: physical, human, or organizational. Physical cause is defined as a failure of a tangible or material item, such as a vital part on a manufacturer's production line breaking. When human error or inaction lies at the root of an accident, it is considered to be a human cause of loss (for example, the maintenance department did not perform the proper maintenance on the manufacturer's production line). Organizational causes of loss stem from faulty systems, processes, or policies (such as procedures that do not make it clear which maintenance employee is responsible for checking and maintaining the manufacturer's production line). See the exhibit "Root Cause Analysis Approaches."

---

### Root Cause Analysis Approaches

Root cause analysis (RCA) encompasses a variety of tools, philosophies, and processes. There are several broadly defined RCA approaches, identified according to their basic approach or field of origin:

- Safety-based RCA originated from accident analysis and occupational safety and health.

- Production-based RCA evolved from quality control procedures for industrial manufacturing.

- Process-based RCA is similar to production-based RCA, but it also includes business processes.

- Failure-based RCA stems from failure analysis and is used primarily in engineering and maintenance.

- Systems-based RCA combines these four approaches with change management, risk management, and systems analysis concepts.

---

[DA08696]

# Steps in the Root Cause Analysis Process

The RCA process is a systematic way to determine root cause. See the exhibit "Steps in the Root Cause Analysis Process."

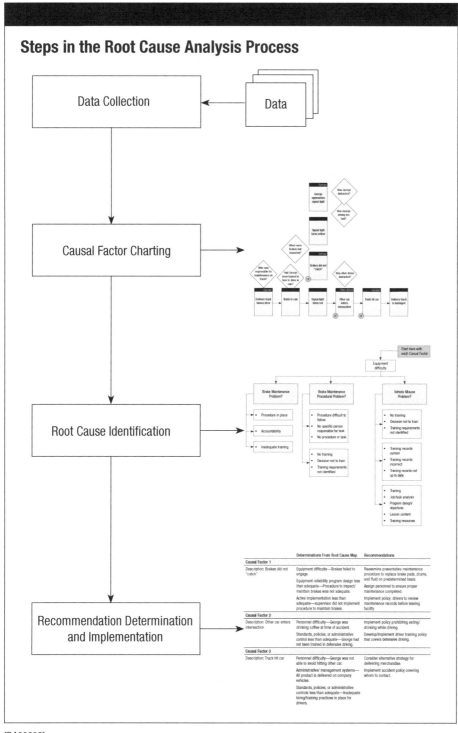

[DA08692]

The first step in the RCA process is data collection. Root causes associated with an event cannot be identified without complete information about the surrounding circumstances, facts, and causes.

**Causal factors**

The agents that directly result in one event causing another.

The second step in the process is **causal factors** charting. This provides the structure to organize and analyze the data gathered during the investigation. It also helps to identify gaps and deficiencies in knowledge as the investigation progresses. Usually, the most readily apparent causal factor is given the most attention during the charting process, but more than one causal factor can be associated with an event. For example, an employee is injured on a manufacturer's production line. Was the injury a result of lax maintenance, the employee removing a machine guard, inadequate training, or all of these?

Step three of the RCA process is root cause identification. Mapping or flow-charting can help determine the underlying reason(s) for each causal factor identified in step two. For example, if equipment difficulty is identified as a causal factor, the map or flowchart is used to identify whether the difficulty was caused by equipment design, reliability, installation, misuse, or some other cause (in which case additional flowcharting is used until the causal factor is determined).

Step four of the RCA process is recommendation determination and implementation. After a root cause has been identified, attainable recommendations for preventing its recurrence are then generated. It is important to implement these attainable recommendations for two reasons. First, if they are not implemented, the effort necessary to perform the RCA process has been wasted. Second, the event(s) that caused the RCA to be performed is likely to occur again. The recommendations determined by the RCA process should be tracked to completion.

RCA is typically used after an event has occurred. However, it also can be used to predict events that could harm the organization. By using RCA in this fashion, organizations can learn to solve problems before they become major events, rather than just reacting to them as they occur.

## Root Cause Analysis Example

George drives a delivery truck for New Space furniture store. He was recently hired by New Space but previously worked in the same role for another furniture store. While making a delivery on a rainy afternoon, he encountered a yellow traffic light at an intersection. He applied the truck's brakes, but, according to George's statement, they failed to "catch." His truck slid through the intersection after the light turned red, striking another vehicle. The delivery truck sustained a dented front fender and flat tire. The other vehicle sustained greater damage and was declared a total loss by the driver's insurance company. Both drivers were uninjured. The risk manager for New Space must determine the causal factor(s) and the root cause(s) associated with George's accident.

The first step is to collect data by taking statements from George, the other driver, witnesses, and first responders. They investigated the accident scene to determine road conditions. The delivery truck brakes were examined by a mechanic to determine if they were functioning properly.

The next step is to chart the causal factors. By starting with what is known to be true, investigators can work backward to determine the causal factors. See the exhibit "Causal Factor (CF) Charting."

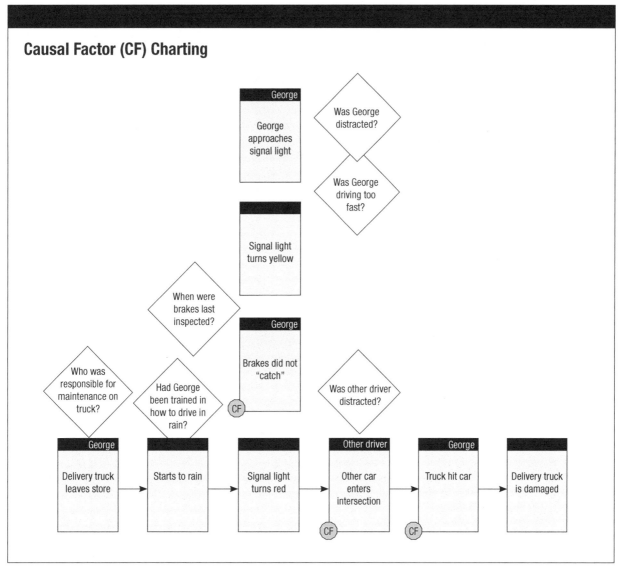

**Causal Factor (CF) Charting**

[DA08693]

After all causal factors have been identified, root causes are investigated. Each causal factor is inserted into a root cause map to determine its root cause. See the exhibit "Root Cause Mapping."

## Root Cause Mapping

Start here with each Casual Factor

Equipment difficulty

**Brake Maintenance Problem?**

- Procedure in place
- Accountability
- Inadequate training

**Brake Maintenance Procedural Problem?**

- Procedure difficult to follow
- No specific person responsible for task
- No procedure or task

- No training
- Decision not to train
- Training requirements not identified

**Vehicle Misuse Problem?**

- No training
- Decision not to train
- Training requirements not identified

- Training records system
- Training records incorrect
- Training records not up to date

- Training
- Job/task analysis
- Program design/ objectives
- Lesson content
- Training resources

[DA08694]

The fourth step in the process is to develop recommendations that management can implement to prevent the event from recurring. See the exhibit "Root Cause Summary Table."

## Root Cause Summary Table

|  | Determinations From Root Cause Map | Recommendations |
|---|---|---|
| **Causal Factor 1** | | |
| Description: Brakes did not "catch" | Equipment difficulty—Brakes failed to engage. | Reexamine preventative maintenance procedure to replace brake pads, drums, and fluid on predetermined basis. |
| | Equipment reliability program design less than adequate—Procedure to inspect/maintain brakes was not adequate. | Assign personnel to ensure proper maintenance completed. |
| | Active implementation less than adequate—Supervisor did not implement procedure to maintain brakes. | Implement policy—Drivers to review maintenance records before leaving facility. |
| **Causal Factor 2** | | |
| Description: Other car enters intersection | Personnel difficulty—George was drinking coffee at time of accident. | Implement policy prohibiting eating/drinking while driving. |
| | Standards, policies, or administrative control less than adequate—George had not been trained in defensive driving. | Develop/implement driver training policy that covers defensive driving. |
| **Causal Factor 3** | | |
| Description: Truck hit car | Personnel difficulty—George was not able to avoid hitting other car. | Consider alternative strategy for delivering merchandise. |
| | Administrative/management systems—All product is delivered on company vehicles. | Implement accident policy covering whom to contact. |
| | Standards, policies, or administrative controls less than adequate—Inadequate hiring/training practices in place for drivers. | |

[DA08695]

# FAILURE MODE AND EFFECTS ANALYSIS (FMEA)

An organization can use failure mode and effects analysis (FMEA) to prioritize its risks and maximize its risk control resources.

**Failure mode and effects analysis (FMEA)** is a root cause analysis technique used predominately in product development and operations management. Its objective is to identify **failure modes** and perform **effects analysis**.

Determining a failure mode's effect on a process requires identifying the effect's location in the system under analysis. FMEA identifies a system's **indenture levels** for this purpose. For example, a system's first indenture level

**Failure mode and effects analysis (FMEA)**

An analysis that reverses the direction of reasoning in fault tree analysis by starting with causes and branching out to consequences.

**Failure mode**

The manner in which a perceived or actual defect in an item, process, or design occurs.

**Effects analysis**

The study of a failure's consequences to determine a risk event's root cause(s).

**Indenture level**

An item's relative complexity within an assembly, system, or function.

**Local effect**

The consequence of a failure mode on the operation, function, or status of the specific item or system level under analysis.

**Next-higher-level effect**

The consequence of a failure mode on the operation, function, or status of the items in the indenture level immediately above the indenture level under analysis.

**End effect**

The consequence of a failure mode on the operation, function, or status of the highest indenture level.

(Level 1) is the system itself. The next indenture level (Level 2) represents the system segments, with the prime items designated as Level 3. Level 4 represents subsystems, components are at Level 5, subassemblies or circuit cards are at Level 6, and parts are at Level 7.

A failure mode with an effect on the same level that is being analyzed produces a **local effect**. A failure mode that affects the next-higher level produces a **next-higher-level effect**; one that affects the highest indenture level produces an **end effect**.

FMEA's primary goal is to ensure customer safety and production of quality products through these outputs:

- Improvement in the design of procedures and processes
- Minimization or elimination of design characteristics that contribute to failure
- Development of system requirements that reduce the likelihood of failures
- Identification of human error modes and their effects
- Development of systems to track and manage potential future design problems

FMEA may be applied to services as well as products and processes. These are examples of types of FMEA:

- Concept—used in the early design stages to analyze systems or subsystems
- Design—used to analyze products prior to production
- Process—used in manufacturing and assembly processes
- Equipment—used to analyze machinery and equipment design before purchase
- Service—used in service industry processes before release to determine impact on customers
- System—used in global system functions
- Software—used for software functions

## Steps in the FMEA Process

Ideally conducted by teams as opposed to an individual, FMEA is used in the design stage to avoid future failures and subsequently for process control. Essentially, it can be used to prevent a harmful event or reduce its severity. See the exhibit "Steps in the FMEA Process."

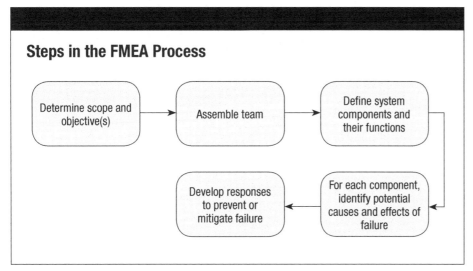

**Steps in the FMEA Process**

Determine scope and objective(s) → Assemble team → Define system components and their functions → For each component, identify potential causes and effects of failure → Develop responses to prevent or mitigate failure

[DA08788]

FMEA can be followed by a **criticality analysis**. These four categories of failures are used in criticality analysis:

- Category 1—failure resulting in excessive unscheduled maintenance
- Category 2—failure resulting in delay or loss of operational availability
- Category 3—failure resulting in potential mission failure
- Category 4—failure resulting in potential loss of life

For example, an explosion caused by defective static controls aboard a truck may be classified as a Category 4 failure, while the driver's temporary illness may be classified as a Category 1 or 2 failure. These categories can be used either subjectively to establish priorities among hazards and their controls or objectively to measure how a risk management professional can alter the expected criticality of a system failure.

One method used to perform a criticality analysis is the calculation of a **risk priority number (RPN)** for each identified failure. RPN determines the relative risk of a particular FMEA item. These are its components:

- Consequence rankings (C)—rate the severity of the effect of the failure
- Occurrence rankings (O)—rate the likelihood that the failure will occur (failure rate)
- Detection rankings (D)—rate the likelihood that the failure will not be detected before it reaches the customer

The rankings for consequence, occurrence, and detection are usually on a one-to-five or one-to-ten scale, depending on the criteria for the organization and process. The highest number on the scale is assigned to the most severe, most likely to occur, or hardest to detect events. See the exhibit "Typical Criteria for the Rankings of Consequence, Occurrence, and Detection."

**Criticality analysis**

An analysis that identifies the critical components of a system and ranks the severity of losing each component.

**Risk priority number (RPN)**

The product of rankings for consequence, occurrence, and detection used to identify critical failure modes when assessing risk within a design or process.

## Typical Criteria for the Rankings of Consequence, Occurrence, and Detection

**Consequence**

| 1 | 2 | 3 | 4 | 5 | 6 | 7 | 8 | 9 | 10 |

No effect                        Moderate
                          (most customers annoyed)

Very high and hazardous
(product inoperative,
customers angered)

**Occurrence**

| 1 | 2 | 3 | 4 | 5 | 6 | 7 | 8 | 9 | 10 |

No known                      Moderate
occurrences              (occasional failures)

Very high and hazardous
(failure almost certain)

**Detection**

| 1 | 2 | 3 | 4 | 5 | 6 | 7 | 8 | 9 | 10 |

All faults                       Moderate
caught on test

Fault will be passed to
customer undetected

[DA08789]

**Criticality**

A product of the risk priority number elements of consequence and occurrence used to determine the relative risk of a failure mode and effects analysis item.

To calculate the RPN, the rankings for consequences, occurrences, and detection are multiplied. The resulting product is then compared with RPNs associated with other failures. The failure associated with the highest RPN usually is addressed first. However, the failure associated with the highest RPN is not always the most critical. That is, it may not necessarily have the greatest **criticality**. See the exhibit "Criticality Example."

Once the most critical failures have been identified, the team or risk management professional should develop a plan of action and implement it by assigning specific actions (remedies) to specific personnel. The remedies should include eliminating the failure mode, minimizing the severity (consequences), reducing the occurrence, and improving detection. After remedies have been applied, revised RPNs can be calculated to determine their effectiveness.

## Criticality Example

C = Consequence rankings

O = Occurrence rankings

D = Detection rankings

| C | × | O | × | D | = | RPN |
|---|---|---|---|---|---|-----|
| 10 | | 10 | | 2 | | 200 |
| 3 | | 10 | | 10 | | 300 |

While the second RPN is higher, the first would require more immediate attention because it has consequence (10) and criticality (10 × 10 = 100) numbers that are far greater than the second. As a general rule, any RPN with a high C-value should be given top priority; any C × O combination that results in a high number is given next priority. C × O, severity of the failure mode consequences times the probability of occurrence, represents how critical that failure is to the failure of the entire system or process (the criticality of the failure).

[DA08790]

# FMEA Example

A vending machine company performed an FMEA on individual soda vending machines in various parts of the city. The team performing the FMEA noticed that RPN and criticality prioritized causes of failure were different. According to RPN, "Machine out of sodas" and "Not enough change in machine" were the top two risks. Criticality ranked "Malfunction in money dispensing mechanism" and "Correct change light malfunction" as the most critical.

The organization found that it only took either a high consequence or occurrence along with a high detection rating to generate a high RPN. Because criticality does not include the detection rating, it returned different priorities. The team would need to use its experience and judgment to determine appropriate priorities for action. See the exhibit "FMEA Example."

## FMEA Example

| Function | Potential Failure Mode | Potential Effect(s) of Failure | C | Potential Cause(s) of Failure | O | Current Process Controls | D | R P N | C R I T |
|---|---|---|---|---|---|---|---|---|---|
| Dispense soda when correct amount of money is inserted in machine | Does not dispense soda | Customer very annoyed | 6 | Machine out of sodas | 7 | On regular delivery route | 9 | 378 | 42 |
| | | Discrepancy in machine tallying system | | Malfunction in soda dispensing mechanism | 2 | On regular delivery route | 9 | 108 | 12 |
| | | | | Power outage | 2 | None | 10 | 120 | 12 |
| | Gives too much change | Discrepancy in machine tallying system | 7 | Malfunction in money dispensing mechanism | 7 | Alert to company | 4 | 196 | 49 |
| | | Loss of property/ expense for repairs | | Damage to machine by customer/ vandalism | 2 | None | 10 | 140 | 14 |
| | Gives too little/no change | Customer dissatisfied | 6 | Change stuck together | 2 | Alert to company | 5 | 60 | 12 |
| | | Discrepancy in machine tallying system | | "Correct change" light malfunction | 8 | Alert to company | 6 | 288 | 48 |
| | | | | Not enough change in machine | 5 | None | 10 | 300 | 30 |

[DA08791]

# Advantages and Disadvantages

These are the advantages of using FMEA:

- It is widely applicable to many different system modes.
- When used early in the design phase, it can reduce costly equipment modifications.
- It can improve the quality, reliability, and safety of a product or process, as well as improve an organization's image and competitiveness by possibly reducing scrap in production.
- It emphasizes problem prevention by identifying problems early in the process and eliminating potential failure modes.

These are the disadvantages associated with FMEA:

- When used as a top-down tool, FMEA may only identify major failure modes in a system.
- Other analysis methods might be better suited for this type of analysis. When used as a bottom-up tool, it can complement other methods, such as **fault tree analysis (FTA)**, and identify more failure modes resulting in top-level symptoms.
- Analyzing complex multilayered systems can be difficult and tedious with FMEA, and studies that are not adequately controlled and focused can be time-consuming and costly.

**Fault tree analysis (FTA)**
An analysis that takes a particular system failure and traces the events leading to the system failure backwards in time.

# FAULT TREE ANALYSIS (FTA)

Fault tree analysis is a tool risk management professionals can use to determine the underlying causes of a risk event.

Fault tree analysis (FTA) uses the deductive method of moving from the general to the specific to examine conditions that may have led to or influenced a risk event. It can be used to identify potential accidents and to predict the most likely system failures. FTA identifies various ways of "breaking" the fault tree; that is, it interrupts the sequence of events leading to system failure so that the failure itself can be prevented.

## The Nature of Fault Tree Analysis (FTA)

The "Fault Tree for Hand Injury to Press Operator" exhibit depicts a fault tree for a harmful event. This harmful event (the injury) appears at the top of the fault tree, and the events necessary to produce it appear as branches. This is known as the fault tree's top event. The tree's branches are connected by "and" gates (shaped like beehives) and "or" gates (shaped like fish tails). These gates represent the causal relationships between events, which are depicted as rectangles within the tree. For example, the "and" gate directly below the injury found in rectangle A indicates that event A can occur only if all four events in rectangles B, C, D, and E occur first. If any one of those four events does not occur, the hand injury to the press operator also cannot occur. See the exhibit "Fault Tree for Hand Injury to Press Operator."

In contrast, an "or" gate signifies that any one of the events leading to the gate is sufficient to cause that event. For example, the operator's hand will be under the die (rectangle C) either if the operator is arranging a piece under the die (rectangle H) or if the operator is inattentive or distracted (rectangle I). To break a fault tree at an "or" gate, none of the events below the gate can be allowed to occur. In this example, to prevent the operator's hand from being under the die, the operator must remain alert and must always use some tool (other than his or her hands) to arrange pieces under the die.

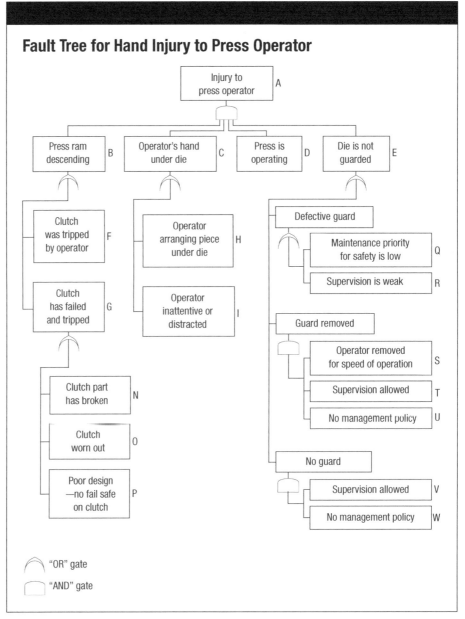

**Fault Tree for Hand Injury to Press Operator**

Source: Dan Peterson, Techniques of Safety Management: A Systems Approach, 4th edition (Des Plaines, Ill.: American Society of Safety Engineers, 2003), p. 161. [DA01461]

# Adding Probabilities to a Fault Tree

A fault tree also can be used to calculate the probability of the risk event if the probabilities of the causal events are known. An "and" gate requires calculating the joint probability that all the events immediately below it will occur. If the probabilities of events in rectangles S, T, and U of the "Fault Tree for Hand Injury to Press Operator" exhibit are .15, .20, and .30, respectively, then the probability of the guard being removed may be calculated in this manner:

$$p(S \text{ and } T \text{ and } U) = p(S) \times p(T) \times p(U)$$

$$= .15 \times .20 \times .30$$

$$= .009$$

An "or" gate requires calculating the probability that any one or more of the events directly below it will occur. This probability is also the probability that the chain of events will proceed through that gate to the next higher branch of the tree, bringing the harmful event that much closer. The "or" gate connecting rectangles $H$ and $I$ to rectangle $C$ in the exhibit indicates that if the probabilities $H$ and $I$ are .40 and .20, and if these two events are not mutually exclusive, then the probability of one or the other (or both) of them occurring is the sum of the probabilities of either one of them occurring alone minus the probability of their both occurring together. This produces these results:

$$p(H \text{ or } I \text{ or both}) = p(H) + p(I) - p(H \text{ and } I)$$

$$= .40 + .20 - (.40 \times .20)$$

$$= .60 - .08$$

$$= .52$$

## Application to Loss Control

Because fault tree analysis identifies the events leading to a harmful event, it naturally suggests loss prevention measures. The distinctions between "and" and "or" gates provide some guidance in choosing among loss prevention alternatives. For example, in the "Fault Tree for Hand Injury to Press Operator" exhibit, to prevent a clutch from failing (rectangle $G$), all three of the conditions in rectangles $N$, $O$, and $P$ must be prevented because the "or" gate above these three events indicates that any one of them is sufficient to cause a clutch to fail. Conversely, a press will lack a guard (the "No guard" rectangle at the bottom right of the fault tree) only if the conditions in both rectangles $V$ and $W$ exist. Consequently, preventing either one of these two conditions (through active supervision or through a strong management policy on such guards) will prevent the removal of a guard.

To encourage sound loss control decisions, a fault tree must be as complete and accurate as possible. An incomplete fault tree may entirely omit a chain of events that would make loss control measures applied to some other tree branch ineffective. For example, if a branch of events leading directly to the harmful event in rectangle $A$ of the "Fault Tree for Hand Injury to Press Operator" exhibit were unintentionally omitted from the fault tree, then risk control measures to prevent events $B$ through $E$ would not be sufficient to prevent the harmful event represented by rectangle $A$. See the exhibit "Five Steps of Fault Tree Analysis."

---

### Five Steps of Fault Tree Analysis

To ensure that a fault tree includes all necessary and sufficient events and is useful as a risk management tool, risk management professionals should follow five steps:

1. Identify a specific harmful event to construct the fault tree. Be as specific as possible so that events contributing to the failure can be fully described.

2. Diagram, in reverse order, the events that led to the harmful event.

3. Determine whether the events leading to any other event on the fault tree are connected by an "and" gate or by an "or" gate.

4. Evaluate the fault tree to determine possible system improvement.

5. Make suggestions to management about risk control measures that can treat the hazards identified in the fault tree.

---

[DA08707]

# Assumptions and Limitations

To properly use fault tree analysis, risk management professionals must recognize its underlying assumptions:

- All components exist in only one of two conditions—success or failure (operational or not operational).

- Any system component's failure is independent of any other component's failure.

- Each failure has an unchanging probability of occurrence. Moreover, to keep fault tree analysis manageable, many fault trees limit the number of potential causes of failure they examine, perhaps overlooking other causes. However, despite this simplified approach, fault tree analysis can aid in evaluating a harmful event.

The limitations of fault tree analysis also should be recognized:

- If a high degree of certainty does not exist concerning the probabilities of the underlying or base events, the probability of the top event may also be uncertain.

- Important pathways to the top event might not be explored if all causal events are not included in the fault tree.

- Because a fault tree is static, it may need to be reconstructed in the future if circumstances or procedures change.

- Human error is difficult to characterize in a fault tree.

- "Domino effects" or conditional failures are not easily included in a fault tree.

# "5 WHYS" ANALYSIS AND THE FISHBONE DIAGRAM

A team of investigators can use a fishbone, or Ishikawa, diagram to determine the root cause of a risk event. When used with a "5 Whys" analysis, a fishbone diagram also can reveal relationships among the variables in a process or system.

Creating a fishbone diagram is a root cause analysis technique in which a team of investigators brainstorms the causes of a risk event, sorts them into categories, and traces them to their origin. The resulting diagram determines a risk event's underlying cause in an effort to eliminate it, thereby preventing the problem's recurrence. Devised by Kaoru Ishikawa and relying heavily on a 5 Whys root cause analysis, the fishbone diagram is also known as a herringbone diagram, a cause-and-effect diagram, and a Fishikawa diagram.

## 5 Whys Analysis

A 5 Whys analysis is a crucial component of a fishbone diagram's construction. It is a specific root cause analysis technique used primarily for problems involving human factors, such as lack of managerial oversight. After a problem has been identified, asking "why" repeatedly (five times is a general rule) can lead to determination of its ultimate cause. A 5 Whys analysis prevents investigators from relying on potentially erroneous assumptions about the root cause of a problem (for example, that the problem was caused by a shortage of time or resources) and instead traces the problem through a chain of causality to its origin.

### Procedure for Conducting a 5 Whys Analysis

These are the steps in a 5 Whys analysis:

1.  The specific problem under investigation is described completely. (This helps to formalize the problem.)
2.  The investigator asks why that particular problem occurred and determines the answer.
3.  If the answer does not reveal the problem's root cause, the investigator determines why the problem embodied by the determination made in Step 2 occurred.
4.  The investigator repeats the previous two steps until the root cause of the original problem has been determined.

Despite its name, a 5 Whys analysis is not limited to asking why five times. If the root cause is found after the fourth why, then a sufficient number of questions has been asked. If it takes more than five whys, then the analysis should continue until the root cause has been determined.

# 5 Whys Example

The exhibit illustrates how an accident can be traced to its root cause. In practice, a worksheet typically is based on the chain of command within the organization and poses questions at all levels. See the exhibit "5 Whys Analysis of Hand Injury to Press Operator."

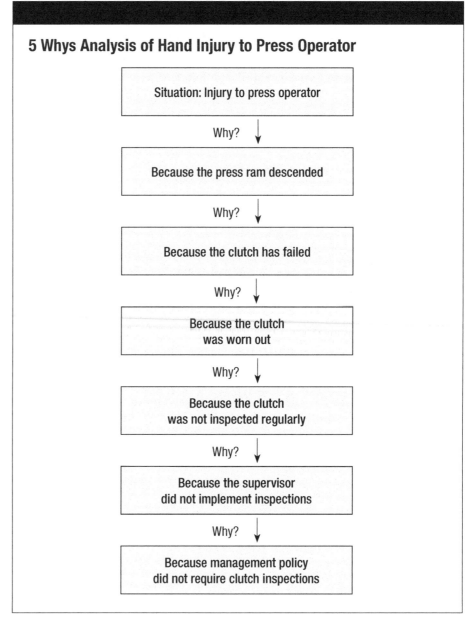

**5 Whys Analysis of Hand Injury to Press Operator**

Situation: Injury to press operator

Why? ↓

Because the press ram descended

Why? ↓

Because the clutch has failed

Why? ↓

Because the clutch was worn out

Why? ↓

Because the clutch was not inspected regularly

Why? ↓

Because the supervisor did not implement inspections

Why? ↓

Because management policy did not require clutch inspections

[DA08708]

The investigator(s) could have stopped at the fourth or fifth why, but doing that would not have determined the root cause of the problem. By the time this analysis reaches the last why, it becomes evident that a broken process or management practice is the accident's root cause. This is a common conclusion of this type of analysis.

## Advantages and Disadvantages of 5 Whys Analysis

These are the advantages of a 5 Whys analysis:

- It can determine the root cause of a problem.
- When several root causes are found, it can help determine the relationship among them.
- It usually does not require statistical analysis or data collection.

These are its disadvantages:

- Investigators tend to stop the analysis after the first determination rather than asking additional questions to discover a problem's root cause.
- Investigators tend to focus on only one answer to each question.
- Organizations sometimes do not help the investigator ask the right why questions.
- An uninformed investigator cannot ask relevant questions.
- Different investigators will discover different causes for the same problem. (This can be an advantage if several root causes exist for the same problem.)

## The Fishbone Diagram

A 5 Whys analysis is the most prevalent method used to fuel the brainstorming sessions that generate the specific causes depicted in a fishbone diagram. As shown in the exhibit, these causes are depicted as diagonal lines (the fish's bones) connected to a horizontal arrow (the fish's spine) that indicates the problem being addressed. See the exhibit "Fishbone Diagram."

**Fishbone Diagram**

Cause                                                                Effect

Machinery          Methods

Manpower          Materials

Problem
being
investigated

[DA08709]

The most frequently used categories are industry- or process-specific and are known by names that signify the first letter of each of the categories within the group. For example, the "6 Ms" group of categories typically is used to determine root causes of problems in manufacturing:

- Machine (technology)—Any equipment or technology involved in completing a job, such as computers, tools, or other machinery
- Method (process)—Requirements that specify how a process is performed (for example, policies, procedures, rules, regulations, and so forth)
- Materials—Information, parts, pens, paper, raw materials, and so forth used to produce the final product (consumables)
- Manpower (physical work)/mindpower (brain work)—Anyone involved in a process who provides physical or mental effort
- Measurement (inspection)—Data generated from a process used to judge the quality of the product
- Milieu/Mother Nature (environment)—Local conditions, such as temperature, time, location, or culture, within which a process operates

The 4 Ms is a simplified version of the 6 Ms that uses only the categories of machine, method, materials, and manpower. Though seldom used, the 8 Ms adds the categories management/money power and maintenance to the 6 Ms. As another example, an organization in the service industry might use the 8 Ps or the 5 Ss. See the exhibit "The 8 Ps and the 5 Ss."

## The 8 Ps and the 5 Ss

| The 8 Ps | The 5 Ss |
| --- | --- |
| • Product or Service | • Surroundings |
| • Price | • Suppliers |
| • Place | • Systems |
| • Promotion/Entertainment | • Skills |
| • People (key person) | • Safety |
| • Process | |
| • Physical Evidence | |
| • Productivity & Quality | |

[DA08710]

## Steps in Developing a Fishbone Diagram

Ideally, when a fishbone diagram is developed, the entire investigative team should be able to view it simultaneously. This facilitates the brainstorming process that is key to revealing all relevant causes. These are the steps the team should follow:

1.  Team agrees on a problem statement.
2.  Facilitator writes statement on the far-right-hand side of the diagram, draws a box or circle around it, and draws a horizontal arrow across the center of the page that points to the statement.
3.  Team brainstorms the major categories of causes of the problem. These categories will depend upon the type and structure of the organization and system under question.
4.  Facilitator depicts the categories of causes as branches emanating from the main arrow. The categories may be common to the industry or specific to the organization.
5.  Team members brainstorm possible specific causes of the problem, using techniques such as the 5 Whys analysis.
6.  Facilitator writes each specific cause as a branch from the appropriate category. Causes can be assigned to any category to which they relate.

7.  For each of the specific causes listed in the previous step, the team again asks, "Why did this happen?" The facilitator writes the sub-causes as branches from the causes. The team continues to ask why to generate deeper levels of causes. As the layers of branches are drawn on the diagram, causal relationships are revealed.

8.  Before moving to the final step, the team should focus on areas of the diagram with the fewest ideas.

9.  Once the team has determined the root cause(s), remedies are developed and implemented to prevent recurrence of the problem described in the original statement.

## Fishbone Diagram Example

Bluebonnet Meat Packing is one of several subsidiaries of a vertically integrated meat producing operation that also owns bovine research laboratories, cattle ranches, and feed yards. During an economic downturn spurred by rising fuel prices, Bluebonnet's management investigates various cost-saving opportunities. One of its major expenses is fuel for the delivery trucks that deliver meat to restaurants, grocery stores, and meat markets.

Bluebonnet gathers a team of employees knowledgeable about the delivery aspect of the business and charges them with finding the root cause that answers the question, "Why is actual gas/diesel mileage so much lower than the original estimates?" The team engages in a 5 Whys analysis and uses a fishbone diagram to chart the results. See the exhibit "Fishbone Diagram for Bluebonnet Meat Packing."

The team uses the 4 Ms for the categories of causes, as it believes that measurement and environment are not relevant to this analysis. It begins by applying the 5 Whys analysis to the machinery category. After exhausting that category, it moves on to methods, manpower, and materials. Then it examines the fishbone diagram to determine causes it might have missed or that fall into more than one category.

The team ultimately determines that the absence of procedures, poor documentation, and lack of funds were some of the root causes of the original problem. In response, the team decides to create procedures and documentation while management hires a consultant to help reorganize the corporate structure, thereby reducing waste and maximizing available funds for purchasing more delivery trucks and hiring and training additional drivers.

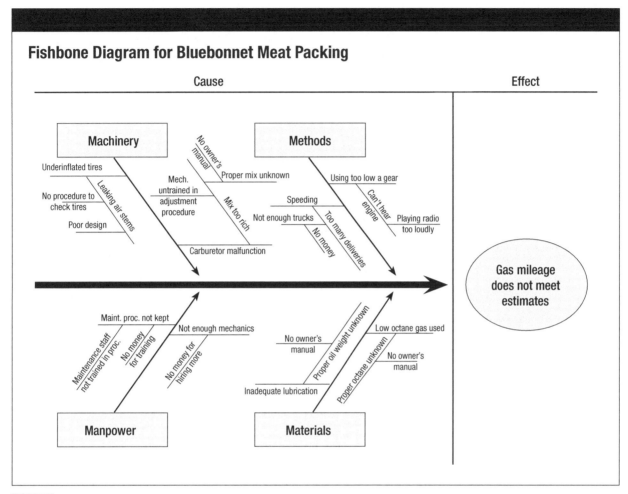

## Fishbone Diagram for Bluebonnet Meat Packing

[DA08711]

# SUMMARY

The root cause analysis process involves four steps:

1.  Data collection
2.  Causal factor charting
3.  Root cause identification
4.  Recommendation determination and implementation

FMEA is a root cause analysis technique used predominantly in product development and operations management. Its ultimate objective is to identify the most critical system failures that can cause the most damaging consequences. Once this is known, a plan of action can be developed and implemented.

FTA traces the events leading to the failure to their underlying causes. When these causes are identified, the risk management professional can determine the probability of their occurrence and apply the loss control techniques that will be most beneficial in preventing the harmful event.

A 5 Whys analysis involves asking the question "why" repeatedly about a problem until its root cause is revealed. It does not require statistical analysis and requires very little, if any, data collection. Best performed by teams of investigators who have a collective knowledge of the process in question, a 5 Whys analysis is instrumental in creating a fishbone (Ishikawa) diagram, which is an analytical tool used by a team of investigators to record all possible causes of a problem.

# 3

# Business Continuity Management

## Educational Objectives

After learning the content of this assignment, you should be able to:

▷ Describe the evolution of business continuity management and its alignment with risk management.

▷ Explain how risk mitigation is achieved through business continuity planning.

▷ Describe the scope and stages of strategic risk redeployment planning.

▷ Explain how risk mitigation is achieved through efficient communication in times of crisis.

▷ Explain how supply chain risk management is used to assess and mitigate risks that could disrupt an organization's flow of goods and services.

▷ Given a scenario involving a supply chain, recommend the risk-appropriate mitigation tools.

# Business Continuity Management | 3

## INTRODUCTION TO BUSINESS CONTINUITY MANAGEMENT

When an organization suffers any level of disruption—from a relatively minor occurrence, such as a market downturn, or a major catastrophic event—its leaders must act to restore normal operations.

An organization can use business continuity management (BCM) to address potential threats to its operations, such as natural disasters, major physical damage to a building, or the loss of a critical supplier. BCM involves examining such threats and establishing an operational plan with contingencies that allow the organization's key operations and critical functions to continue if a disruption occurs. Many organizations call BCM "business resiliency" because continuity planning for risk helps organizations withstand disruptive events and, ultimately, survive.

BCM seeks to minimize the loss of resources essential to an organization's recovery from a disruption in operations. This is accomplished by focusing an organization's efforts on effective pre- and post-loss actions.

## Evolution of BCM

The terms "emergency preparedness," "disaster recovery," and "business continuity" are often used interchangeably. Although the concepts are closely related, they differ in scope and focus, having evolved over the past century as organizations' goals changed from merely surviving a catastrophe to responding to one with resilience.[1]

The roots of BCM are in emergency preparedness and response planning. Such planning developed early in the last century and centered on providing emergency supplies and trained personnel to ensure the safety of both people and an organization's physical assets during and after catastrophes such as hurricanes and fires. Although limited to disasters, emergency preparedness planning helped establish the need for comprehensive planning.

Disaster recovery planning arose from organizations' increasing use of and dependence on technology in the latter part of the last century. Organizations became vulnerable to loss of systems responsible for data management and storage, inventory management, communication, and other critical systems. In response, information technology (IT) departments developed plans for protecting data and equipment and for recovering data. In many organizations, disaster recovery is still considered an IT function. However, as technology became pervasive in nearly all business operational functions, the concept of disaster recovery planning expanded to include planning for the protection and recovery of operational systems in the event of a disaster.

In the broader sense, disaster recovery plans seek to ensure that an effective response occurs amid the confusion and emotional distraction of a disaster. Disaster recovery plans typically focus on actions that can be taken before and immediately after a disaster to ensure the safety of personnel and the viability of future operations.

The concept of BCM developed gradually, as organizations realized that, to plan adequately for recovery after a disaster, they had to look beyond their organizations to other systems on which they depended, including supply and distribution chains. From the emergency preparedness focus on protecting people, buildings, and equipment after a disaster, through the disaster recovery focus on protecting data and technological systems from disaster, BCM expanded to encompass the need to ensure continuing business operations and recovery—not just in the event of a disaster, but in the event of any serious disruption in operations.

Events such as the September 11, 2001, terrorist attacks on the World Trade Center; Hurricane Katrina in the southeastern United States in 2005; and the earthquake, tsunami, and resulting nuclear crisis in Japan in 2011 have reinforced the importance of BCM. Organizations far from those disaster sites felt the effects of when suppliers' and customers' facilities, business data, and financial records were destroyed and supply and distributions channels were disrupted, often at multiple points along the chain. These experiences have expanded the practice and application of BCM, prompted more organizations to adopt or expand their BCM programs, and spurred the development of businesses created solely to provide BCM services for other entities.

## Aligning Business Continuity Management With Risk Management

Some organizations include BCM within the purview of their risk management function. Others separate the roles of business continuity managers and risk managers; they might or might not coordinate their efforts, or they might even compete.

Risk management and BCM are similar in that they both involve planning, organizing, leading, and controlling an organization's resources and activities to achieve a particular result. However, BCM deals primarily with consequences of disruption; its focus on minimizing the results of disruptions to operations means it typically deals with operational risk. In contrast, risk management focuses more broadly on ongoing risk assessment and risk treatment and deals not only with operational risk, but also with hazard risk (property, liability, and personnel loss exposures), financial risk (resulting from the effect of market forces on financial assets or liabilities), and strategic risk (resulting from economic and societal trends).

Organizations that treat BCM and risk management as complementary rather than competing functions can benefit from an integrated approach. For example, risk management's identification of hazard risks and related data can be useful to BCM in determining exposures that could result in operational disruptions, and an effective risk management program can reduce some types of disruptive exposures. To coordinate efforts, organizations should clearly define the roles, responsibilities, and reporting structures of both functions.

## Business Continuity Certifications and Standards

The United States Department of Homeland Security (DHS), created after the September 11, 2001, terrorists attacks on New York City and Washington, D.C., has pressed for voluntary adoption of emergency-preparedness standards by private-sector businesses. DHS has adopted three internationally recognized standards that promote private-sector preparedness, including disaster management, emergency management, and business continuity management:

- ASIS SPC.1-2009, "Organizational Resilience: Security, Preparedness, and Continuity Management Systems"—Developed by ASIS International, an organization that disseminates information about security, this standard emphasizes organizational resilience in emergencies. It provides guidelines for the implementation of policies, objectives, and programs that reinforce organizational resilience through business continuity management.
- British Standard 25999-2:2007, "Business Continuity Management"— Identified as the best practice standard for business continuity, this standard defines requirements for a management systems approach to business continuity.
- National Fire Protection Association 1600:2010, "Standard on Disaster/ Emergency Management and Business Continuity Programs"—This standard focuses on disaster and emergency management and business continuity, including prevention, mitigation, preparedness, response, and recovery from disasters. It aligns with the related disciplines and practices of risk management, security, and loss prevention.

The standards seek to encourage more U.S. organizations to prepare for emergencies. They provide organizations with guidelines for assessing their preparedness for hazards and for developing plans to protect their employees and to ensure recovery and continuity following disasters or other emergencies. DHS's adoption of three different standards allows organizations to choose the standard that most appropriately applies to their particular industry.

Although compliance with the standards is voluntary, an organization that chooses to apply them must commit organizational resources to the endeavor.

If an organization chooses to participate, it develops a preparedness plan under one of the three standards and submits it to a DHS accrediting organization. Certification confirms that the organization's plan complies with the standard chosen. Once an organization is certified, periodic audits are conducted to confirm that its plan continues to comply with the chosen standard.

# BUSINESS CONTINUITY PLANNING

An organization can develop a detailed plan of action to mitigate risk and maintain operations regardless of external and internal events that could otherwise prove disastrous.

Over half of all businesses subjected to a catastrophic event fail immediately. Of those businesses that survive a catastrophe, half fail within two years. While government agencies may not fail immediately, a catastrophe could result in the reassessment of their effectiveness and mission, a change of leadership, or reorganization, leading to further disruption.

The development of a business continuity plan (BCP) is an important component of business continuity management (BCM). A BCP allows an organization to analyze all possible eventualities to determine the critical functions that must continue during a disruption so that the organization survives, recovers, and resumes growth. The development and implementation of a BCP entails seven steps:

1.  Understanding the business
2.  Conducting a business impact analysis (BIA)
3.  Performing a risk assessment
4.  Developing the continuity plan
5.  Implementing the continuity plan
6.  Building a BCM/BCP culture
7.  Maintaining and updating the plan

While BCP and BCM contain the word "business," both terms refer to securing continuity of operations. Thus, applying the concept to other than for-profit entities can be accomplished by considering the "business of the agency" or the "business of the charity," for example. Thus, "business" considers the mission, vision, and strategy of the enterprise in addition to its survival.

## Understanding the Business

To complete a business continuity plan, an organization must first understand all aspects of its business. This includes determining key objectives and how and when they will be met, as well as the internal and external parties involved in achieving them.

Once the organization determines its key objectives (for example, a key objective may be "continuing to manufacture and sell widgets"), it must examine how it uses its facilities, materials supply chain, human resources, communications, information systems, processes, distribution channels, and customers to achieve them. This allows the organization to identify the key processes that will constitute the basis for its BIA.

## Conducting a Business Impact Analysis

An organization conducts a BIA to identify and assess the risks that may affect it. A BIA assesses what events may occur, when they may occur, and how they could affect achievement of key objectives. The BIA also measures the financial and nonfinancial effect of risks and explores organizational vulnerabilities, critical elements in developing strategies to protect organizational resources.

The analysis also distinguishes between critical and noncritical processes. This allows the organization to use the BIA to determine its recovery time objective, which is the time period within which a critical process must be recovered in order for the organization to resume operations after a disruption of operations.

Various international standards, such as ISO 31000:2009, take different approaches or use different terminology for the BIA. In some standards, the BIA and the risk assessment are combined. In other standards, the BIA goes beyond a more traditional risk assessment, which often focuses only on hazard risks and fails to assess the full impact of risk on all aspects of the operation.

## Performing a Risk Assessment

An organization performs a risk assessment to identify and evaluate potential exposures and the probability that certain events will occur. It also indicates how susceptible the organization may be to particular disruptions. This helps the organization prioritize its BCM strategy and risk controls and assists management in making decisions regarding organizational risk appetite. A thorough risk assessment will reveal exposures and can assist in establishing methods for future risk mitigation efforts. Finally, the risk assessment helps the organization determine an action plan.

Assessments can be conducted at various levels. Convergys Corporation, for example, conducts three levels of assessment:[2]

- Enterprise assessment—a global assessment of risks that could affect the enterprise's overall business goals
- Site assessment—an assessment by risk owners at risk centers of risks associated with particular sites or locations or even specific geographies
- Program or project assessments—an assessment of a project's capabilities, resources, and limitations in relationship to a viable recovery strategy

# Developing the Continuity Plan

After it has conducted the BIA and performed a risk assessment to establish recovery time objectives, an organization can begin to develop strategies to maintain critical functions during disruptions. Organizations may use one strategy or a combination of strategies to ensure resiliency:

- Active backup model—The organization establishes a second site that includes all of the necessary production equipment housed at the primary site. Staff may be relocated to the second site if operations are disrupted at the primary site.

- Split operations model—In this model, an organization maintains two or more active sites that are geographically dispersed. Capacity at each site is sufficient to handle total output in the event of a disruption at either site.

- Alternative site model—An organization that uses this strategy maintains a production site and an active backup site that functions as the primary site as needed.

- Contingency model—This strategy involves the organization's developing an alternate way to maintain production, perhaps using manual processes.

All of these strategies involve three levels of planning:[3]

- BCM organizational strategy
- BCM process level strategy
- BCM resource recovery strategy

These planning levels require the organization to examine its basic processes, determine potential points of failure, and create alternate operational methods.

Strategic choices for addressing a disruption of operations include these options:

- An insurance policy—This allows the organization to recover some of its financial losses if it suffers an insurable loss.

- Transfer processing—This entails the organization's entering reciprocal arrangements with another company or division to perform a necessary function in the event of a disruption of operations.

- Termination—With this strategy, an organization ceases production of the affected product or service.

- Loss mitigation—This entails implementation of risk controls and plans to reduce, minimize, or divert any loss.

- Do nothing—If an organization does nothing in the event of a disruption of operations, it absorbs the potential loss. This represents an increase of its risk appetite.

# Implementing the Continuity Plan

Senior management must impress upon the organization that the BCP is integral to its survival and success. The business continuity coordinator (BCC) assists and directs each department in formulating a departmental plan. This ensures that the organization's component parts work effectively for the entire organization.

Each department's plan must include these elements:[4]

- Statement of acceptable level of functioning
- Recovery time objectives, resources needed, and potential failure points
- Tasks and activities required
- Procedures or processes
- Supporting documentation and information
- Structure to support the plan
- Description of division teams—purpose, team members, mission
- Explanation of interdependencies among the various division teams

The BCC presents the drafted BCP to senior management for approval. Once the BCP is approved, the BCC and senior management begin to influence the organization's culture to accept, practice, and maintain the BCP.

# Building a BCM/BCP Culture

Senior management provides the vision statement and support for the BCP. It must also set expectations and objectives for middle management concerning maintenance of departmental plans. See the exhibit "Business Continuity Management (BCM) Encompasses All Divisions."

## Business Continuity Management (BCM) Encompasses All Divisions

| Risk Management | Facilities Management | Human Capital Management | Technology Management |
|---|---|---|---|
| Intellectual Property Management | Reputation Management | Market Share Management | Supply and Distribution Management |

[DA03892]

Staff must be educated on the importance of maintaining the BCP. One way management can achieve this is to hold semiannual exercises in which staff members react to a hypothetical disaster scenario by using the plan to maintain operations. If successful, these exercises may find "holes" in the BCP that need to be addressed. Exercises also provide opportunities to amend the BCP as new processes are introduced and used.

External suppliers and customers should know that the organization has a BCP and be encouraged to provide their own contingency plans. When key suppliers and customers are prepared for a disruption of operations, their relationship with the organization is improved.

## Maintaining and Updating the Plan

Organizational environments, processes, and products change rapidly in today's business environment, and so too should the BCP. A BCP is effective only if it is kept fresh and updated. The BCP should be reviewed in detail and amended as internal or external conditions warrant. Analyzing the written BCP is essential and should be done semiannually or when a significant change has occurred in product line, processes, or management. An organization must also determine how best to store its BCP. Companies often maintain electronic copies of the BCP on a secure server accessible from several locations, while written copies are also maintained by key members of the organization.

Business continuity planning may not be effective in all cases. When an organization's survival is threatened, strategic redeployment planning is required.

## STRATEGIC REDEPLOYMENT PLANNING

Following a business disruption caused by chaotic events, an organization can use strategic redeployment to determine how to resume its business operations and ensure its survival and recovery.

Small disruptions within an organization can develop into major disruptions that jeopardize its survival. During major disruptions, business continuity plans may be insufficient for fully restoring the organization and ensuring its survival. Once a disruption has occurred, management must determine whether existing organizational strategies are still valid and, if not, make necessary strategic adjustments to ensure the organization's survival. When an analysis of the situation reveals that the disruption is due to a chaotic situation, the organization must reorganize its resources. In such cases, strategic redeployment becomes necessary for the organization to determine how to realign itself in order to survive, regain its position in the marketplace, and protect its reputation.

## Strategic Redeployment Planning Stages

A strategic redeployment plan (SRP) is a comprehensive plan for resiliency after a severe disruption. It is designed to bring the organization back from a state of chaos in four stages:

- Emergency stage
- Alternate marketing stage
- Contingency production stage
- Communication stage

The communication stage in strategic redeployment planning has a distinct meaning and context. However, effective, accurate, and timely communication to both internal and external stakeholders is required at all of the stages of strategic redeployment, not just the communication stage.

## Emergency Stage

The emergency stage, sometimes referred to as disaster recovery, starts at the moment of disruption and constitutes the organization's immediate response. This stage is designed to accomplish three objectives:

- Protect people—For example, by contacting emergency authorities, evacuating the area, and warning neighbors
- Protect physical assets—For example, by guarding the site and organizing salvage operations
- Protect reputation—For example, by communicating with all economic stakeholders and maintaining control of all media releases

The emergency stage may include closing and cleaning the facility, recalling products, and meeting with employees and news media to communicate the status of the emergency response.

## Alternate Marketing Stage

The second stage of strategic redeployment requires the organization to evaluate the impact of the disruption on the organization's reputation and market share. The organization must determine whether it needs a new marketing strategy. It must also consider consumer loyalty—will customers remain loyal during the crisis, or will they seek substitute products or services? Will suppliers and subcontractors work with the organization during this interval? Will competitors use the organization's disruption as an opportunity to increase their market share or capture the affected organization's current suppliers? In the alternate marketing stage, no course of action to save the core business or resources should be ruled out, including pulling out of a market or a business. The organization's leadership should set up a center of operations or data room where reliable data and business intelligence information are available for testing various scenarios.

Some organizations may use a color-coded approach at this stage, using "red," "yellow," or "green" to denote the level of disruption. Green indicates that the current strategy should be maintained.

A new marketing strategy developed during this stage may determine, at a minimum, whether the organization will maintain production of its traditional products and services. For instance, the organization may decide that a limited output of products or services should be continued for supplying certain customer segments. Yellow coding may be used to designate such intermediate situations.

If the organization decides to discontinue low-priority products or services, it must analyze the ultimate effect of discontinuance on the organization and on any synergies associated with those products or services. The organization must also evaluate the loss of revenue from current and potential customers of these products or services.

In instances in which the current strategy cannot be maintained and a new marketing strategy is needed, red coding can indicate the need for a radical alteration to the business model or even its complete replacement. In this case, the organization must consider substitutions for the current products or services; what synergies may be created; what resources are needed; and, ultimately, how to restore desired goals and outcomes.

## Contingency Production Stage

The analysis completed in the alternate marketing stage leads to the contingency production stage. At this stage, any downtime for the organization must be minimized. The organization must decide what products or services it will provide depending on the facilities available and whether its technology and machinery are adequate. It must also consider its supply chain with respect to the quality and cost of resources needed and determine whether the product packaging must be adapted for a new product. Other considerations during this stage include the availability of transportation and of routes to distribute products and services.

## Communication Stage

The sole objective of the communication stage is to preserve or enhance stakeholders' trust and confidence in the organization. This stage begins when a disruption has occurred and is initially referred to as crisis communication. When the organization's production and reputation have been restored, the crisis communication becomes post-crisis communication. To meet the objectives of crisis and post-crisis communication, the organization must identify and address the concerns and expectations of all internal and external stakeholders, including these four basic concerns:

- Safety and security of all stakeholders
- Transparency in all of management's decisions
- Clarity and consistency in communications
- Perceived lack of trust in management and the organization

The key to effective communication in a time of disruption is a good relationship with the news media, established before any crisis. The organization must maintain a permanent link with the media so that when a crisis occurs, it can leverage the goodwill created in normal times. To achieve clarity and consistency, information released to the media must echo the information provided to employees. The organization must keep open channels of communication with local authorities and industry associations. Employees need up-to-date information as soon as it is practical. Keeping employees, customers, suppliers, and other stakeholders well informed during a crisis will not only prevent defection to competitors, but also strengthen loyalty and rebuild trust in the organization.

## Conditions for Success

Strategic redeployment requires attention to the increasing concerns of internal and external stakeholders. If an organization fails to protect its reputation before a disruption, it may not survive the disruption. The manner in which the organization interacts with internal and external stakeholders determines its credibility in the marketplace. Successful redeployment is an organization-wide effort.

Depending on the nature of the crisis, an SRP may not always involve major changes for an organization. In some dire circumstances, however, the plan may be drastic and may involve major changes that take an organization in a new direction.

## CRISIS COMMUNICATION

An organization's ability to communicate plans and activities to stakeholders during a crisis is critical to overcoming the situation and contributes to the success of any redeployment strategy.

Consider this scenario: Smoke is billowing out of the fourth, fifth, and sixth floors of a building. Firefighters, police, and emergency medical technicians dart into the building and back to their rapid-response vehicles. Employees rush out of the building. Some are covered in soot, coughing, or screaming for co-workers, while several are brought out on stretchers. The news media are on the scene, reporting live and questioning distraught employees. Executives'

cell phones start ringing as calls come in from members of the board of directors, key clients and suppliers, and the press.

This situation has clearly triggered reactions from many stakeholders, as well as from the media. This is the instant that the organization must begin to manage the crisis and protect its reputation. Crisis management, properly handled, can help mitigate organizational risk on several levels. Communication is a key element in managing a crisis.

## Mitigating Risk Through Crisis Communication

Risk management is a complex system based on a web of relationships among internal and external stakeholders. Good risk management practices should be embedded within the organization and include all financial partners, suppliers, customers, and other stakeholders. This is particularly true in times of crisis.

When an organization implements its crisis management plan, its prime objective is to survive the crisis event. Survival depends on the organization's speedy return to normal operations—brought about by proper continuity, contingency, or disaster recovery planning—and the successful implementation of its strategic redeployment plan. Although crisis management includes several vital components, the quality of an organization's crisis communication is essential to its resiliency.

## Stakeholder Communications

Crisis communication begins before any threats have materialized; it involves establishing a baseline of trust with all stakeholders. Every stakeholder must believe that management will competently handle and resolve any crisis. When a crisis occurs, the organization's message must be candid, address the prominent issues, and engage all stakeholders in order to be effective in restoring and maintaining stakeholders' trust. As part of its crisis communication plan, the organization should maintain an open dialogue with the media (press, television, and radio).

Additionally, effective communication that conveys to various stakeholders that the organization has considered all risks helps engender trust. A theme emphasizing corporate involvement in safety and security should underlie such messages. Communications must also demonstrate that senior management is committed to maintaining an environment of transparency in its decision making. All crisis communications must be consistent and tailored to specific audiences. To maintain stakeholders' trust in the organization and its management, the messages must embody corporate integrity and authenticity.

Communication with different stakeholder groups continues after the immediate crisis. The organization will operate differently and face both threats and opportunities differently after a crisis. It is important for the organization to examine and carefully select various communication tools for use with internal and external stakeholders in order to analyze the specific concerns of the stakeholders, provide the solution, and speak the stakeholders' language.

## Internal Stakeholders

Internal stakeholders' individual needs must be acknowledged. Employees must be informed continuously, especially regarding how the crisis will affect their jobs and working conditions. New safety concerns may emerge and will need to be addressed. This can be done through meetings, displays of visual aids in the workplace, hands-on training, and the organization's intranet site.

Unit and operational managers must be made aware of ongoing risks. Their assistance in training and maintaining attentiveness to potential risks is crucial to the plan's success. Because risk management is a key responsibility of line managers, managers must be held accountable for specific aspects of the crisis management plan.

Stockholders must be informed of all steps taken to manage, mitigate, and even prevent future crises. Communicating organizational health in the annual report and during quarterly meetings is imperative. Senior management must report major trends and pending claims as well as demonstrate corporate resilience. The board of directors must also be informed regularly about strategic exposures, governance issues, and long-term resilience.

## External Stakeholders

In addition to communicating with internal stakeholders, the organization must keep external stakeholders informed. Suppliers must be notified of procedures for scheduled deliveries during the period of disruption and of how the organization will make required payments. Maintaining goodwill with suppliers during a crisis will help them work with the post-crisis organization, which is a critical component of the organization's resilience.

Customers should be assured of the organization's continuity and safety. A sound communication plan can help build trust and maintain consumer loyalty during the period of recovery.

Public officials and local authorities must be informed of the organization's efforts to ensure public safety and health and to demonstrate its commitment to the community. Statutory compliance must be monitored and reported. Other external stakeholders include local associations and special interest groups, which should be informed of the organization's recuperation efforts immediately after a crisis and as part of an ongoing effort to maintain strong relationships with these groups.

The media can be leveraged to transmit information to many internal and external stakeholders. Press releases and interviews on health, safety, and financial progress can help restore and retain marketplace confidence.

Every communication from the organization must be truthful. Risk managers must speak clearly and honestly about current conditions, known risks, and potential risks. The organization must manage and monitor its communication with every stakeholder.

## Benefits of Crisis Communication

Regular communication before and throughout a crisis will improve relationships between the organization and its internal and external stakeholders. Good communication will create an open and truthful environment that encourages future investments in the organization and continues to provide it with favorable access to capital. As a long-term result of effective communication, the organization will be able to attract and retain the most talented employees because it has preserved its reputation post crisis. Externally, this reputation will help the organization to continue to build relationships with new and existing suppliers and customers.

Protection of the organization's reputation through good crisis communication reduces barriers to the development of new markets. A successful and well-communicated crisis management plan will promote trust in the organization's products and services. As a result, the organization may be able to gain a competitive advantage based on its reputation and its stringent attention to managing past, current, and potential risks. Additionally, a well-communicated and well-executed crisis management plan may help to minimize litigation arising from the crisis event.

## SUPPLY CHAIN RISK MANAGEMENT

Market globalization and outsourcing for economic efficiency have substantially increased interdependencies between events and the production of goods and services in different regions and industries.

Supply chains may be viewed as branches of a tree connected to one another through a common trunk. A disruption in the availability of one good or service may have far-reaching effects on an organization, including, in the short term, inability to deliver on contractual promises and, in the long term, destruction of shareholder value.

Supply chain risk management entails assessing and mitigating all the threats that might interrupt the normal flow of goods and services from and to an organization's stakeholders. When applied to the production of goods, supply chain risk management encompasses managing the volatility related to producing, transporting, and storing goods, as well as managing the distribution channels from the initial raw materials to the final consumer product. Disruptions in an organization's production affect its immediate financial condition and may damage its brand reputation irreparably.

When applied to services, supply chain risk management encompasses managing the volatility associated with delivering the service to its end users, taking into consideration all the components of the value chain. Organizations must identify the risks and opportunities within supply chains and balance efficiency and best practices against vulnerability to disruptions. Supply chain risk management visibility has increased with the introduction of ISO 28000: *Supply Chain Security Management Requirements.*

## Threats and Opportunities Inherent in Supply Chains

An organization must assess supply chain risk by examining both internal and external exposures and vulnerabilities. Internal exposures and vulnerabilities include these:

- Production location—Facilities may be vulnerable to natural disaster, manmade disaster, or terrorism.
- Production bottlenecks—Production may depend on a key machine or material; a malfunction or breakdown in the machine would slow or halt production.
- Information technology—The data center may be vulnerable, information backup may be unavailable, or staff may fail to follow restoration protocols.
- Infrastructure—Damage to infrastructure can impede or halt production altogether.
- Strikes or other employment issues—Production may cease, inventory cannot be moved, and orders are not filled.
- Machinery breakdown—Production may stall, or a critical backup in production may occur, while new parts (or new machines) are ordered and installed.

External exposures and vulnerabilities include these:

- Third-party suppliers—Disruption in production from the supplier could undermine an organization's ability to generate its product and to satisfy customer demand.
- Sole-source suppliers—Disruption in supply when only one supplier of goods is available will reduce or potentially shut down an organization's ability to produce and satisfy customer demand.
- Single source supplier—Disruptions in supply can also occur when an organization chooses to rely on only one supplier, even when multiple suppliers are available.
- Change in demand level—Incremental or substantial changes in demand because of changes in customer taste or to competition can cause over- or under production. If demand is not accurately forecasted, market reputation could be damaged.

- Financial risks—Increases in the cost of materials or transportation charges will cause costs to rise. Organizations may not be able to pass on increased costs because of consumer preferences, prior contracts, and competition. Exchange rate fluctuations may cause increases in materials costs and may also reduce the attractiveness of the product in overseas markets.

- Geopolitical environment—Imports and exports may be affected by government regulation or taxation. Unstable governments increase the chance of nationalization of an organization's overseas assets.

- Natural or manmade catastrophes—Storms, earthquakes, volcanic eruptions, and other natural disasters can damage an organization's facilities or interfere with its transportation routes. Pandemics may interrupt an organization's activities if too few employees are available to work. Terrorist activity can disrupt normal supply and distribution channels for extended periods.

- Merger of a key supplier with a competitor—Changes in ownership of key suppliers can affect the price of materials and the availability of supplies.

Organizations can also assess supply chains to uncover potential opportunities that may include these:

- Inventory and storage costs can be reduced by using the supply chain for just-in-time deliveries and work processes.

- Improvements in technology can be leveraged to improve process efficiencies.

- Supplier relationships can be improved to build positive relationships that strengthen communication and minimize potential supply chain disruptions.

## Balance Between Efficiency and Vulnerability to Disruptions

Once an organization assesses potential risks of disruption in its supply chain, it must determine how it will defend its production processes, distribution channels, and market reputation. It also should examine various options to maintain production efficiency, as well as test and consider its ability to accurately forecast demand for materials, labor, and sales. Flexibility in supply sources as well as product design can help balance efficiency against potential disruptions.

The business impact analysis of a supply chain disruption must take into account all the components of a potential loss, such as loss of net revenues, increased costs, and any mitigation costs. If the organization determines that a potential disruption would have little or no impact on the flow of revenues, it may choose not to consider such a disruption in its business continuity plan. To ensure continuity, the organization must thoroughly analyze the short-, medium-, and long-term consequences of any threat or disruption. Such consequences could include potential downgrades by a financial rating agency and/or legal requirements in foreign countries to ensure continuity for industries deemed vital in that jurisdiction.

## Supply Chain Best Practices

The organization must periodically assess its supply chain and establish best practices for various disruption scenarios. This assessment requires a multidisciplinary team of managers to prioritize potential risks and determine disruption timing and recovery time. As it analyzes each type of disruption, the team should consider various responses. The response to each situation should depend on the likelihood and impact (the level and duration) of the potential disruption.

Based on this review, the team will establish best practices and then take action as needed. Such action includes the regular use of dry-running and updating the business continuity plan on a regular basis as conditions change. See the exhibit "Supply Chain Best Practices and Mitigation Techniques."

## Supply Chain Best Practices and Mitigation Techniques

| Internal Disruption | Best Practices/Mitigation |
|---|---|
| Production location | Diversify locations |
| Production bottlenecks | Redesign product or production process to reduce or eliminate bottlenecks |
| IT and infrastructure failures | Maintain appropriate backup protocols, redundant systems, and maintenance |
| Strikes or employment issues | Maintain and educate staff on proper human resource management |
| Machinery breakdown | Maintain spare parts or establish changeover processes |

| External Disruption | Best Practices/Mitigation |
|---|---|
| Third-party/single suppliers | Diversify suppliers, contract carefully, maintain ongoing dialogue with suppliers |
| Sole-source supplier | Consult with the supplier to mitigate some of the risks (expand to several production sites) and/or design technological innovations |
| Change in demand | Monitor and forecast changes in competition and environment |
| Financial risks | Legal contracts to provide protection for some risk, insurance contracts for others, and monitoring the environment to identify emerging financial trends that could affect costs |
| Geopolitical environment | Understand and monitor the political environments in which the organization operates |
| Natural or manmade catastrophes | Maintain and update the business continuity plan |
| Merger of a key supplier | Diversify suppliers, contract carefully, and maintain ongoing dialogue with suppliers |

[DA03893]

# MITIGATING SUPPLY CHAIN RISK

The twenty-first-century consumer can choose goods and services provided by vendors throughout the global market. A breakdown in one link of the supply chain can have disastrous results for an organization. Every organization must prepare for a disruption in order to keep its goods and services flowing to its consumers.

When an organization analyzes its supply chain to determine and recommend risk mitigation tools, it is important to understand these concepts:

- Cascading disruption—seemingly unrelated events that can cause major disruptions
- Supply chain management—the development of sound relationships and diversity among suppliers
- Business resiliency planning—the development of plans that prepare the organization to respond to disruptions

To determine appropriate mitigation tools, an organization should analyze the companies with which it has a business relationship to identify potential dependencies. The organization must then determine how to mitigate the immediate damage that would result from each exposure and select methods to reduce future risk.

The purpose of this analysis is to determine apparent exposures and the impact of losses related to those exposures and to consider possible alternatives to mitigate losses.

## Case Facts

Bakeries, Inc., manufactures organic whole-grain sesame bread and crackers. The company purchases its ingredients—whole-grain flour, sugar, eggs, canola oil, and sesame seeds—from organic farms and processors. Bakeries' whole-grain flour is processed by Mille Company, which Bakeries uses exclusively. The products are sold to high-end retail stores specializing in organic foods.

Bakeries is the sole supplier of sesame bread and crackers to Health Foods, a regional high-end wholesome food specialty shop. Health Foods operates on a 3 percent margin, and Bakeries, Inc., products constitute 35 percent of the shop's retail sales.

Originally privately owned, Mille Company has 300 employees. The company culture was built on the premise of providing organic alternatives to the public. Management actively solicited employee feedback on its products and processes and encouraged employee involvement. Three months ago, however, Mille Company was sold to a large food manufacturer. Rather than continue with the existing culture and corporate environment, new management began making production changes to increase the organization's bottom line. Several of the organic farms supplying wheat to Mille Company were unable to increase their production quickly enough to meet the levels demanded by the new corporate owners. Contracts were not renewed, and the new Mille organization began mixing nonorganic grain with organic grain to lower costs and increase supplies. A disgruntled employee reported Mille Company to the Food and Drug Administration (FDA).

The FDA investigated Mille Company, and the results of the investigation were made public. As a result of this investigation, Mille was required to cease branding its flour as "organic." Enraged consumer groups sued Mille Company for product fraud and fraudulent advertising.

Bakeries, Inc., was unable to locate an immediate alternate source of whole-grain flour, and its production subsequently decreased by 60 percent. Canceling its contract with Mille Company required three months' notice, and cancellation within the contract period would result in a penalty. Bakeries, Inc., also missed its production goals by 40 percent and was unable to fulfill its contract with Health Foods.

Health Foods lost profits and customers and sued Bakeries, Inc., for breach of contract and false advertising. Bakeries, in turn, sued Mille Company, citing the same causes of action, along with an additional one: products liability.

## Case Analysis Tools

Analyzing exposures and determining appropriate risk mitigation tools for the three organizations involved in this scenario requires analysis of this information:

- Supply chain elements
- Relationships between elements
- Existing contractual arrangements
- Available mitigation tools

## Overview of Analysis

Analyzing an organization and its supply chains to develop risk mitigation tools involves a series of steps. Following these steps will assist all three organizations in effectively uncovering potential solutions:

- Identify the exposures and types of risk for each company independently
- Determine co-dependencies between each company
- Analyze the exposures and determine how each company can avoid or mitigate losses to these exposures

### Exposure Identification

The first step in developing supply chain risk mitigation tools is to identify exposures. An organization begins this process by examining the upstream and downstream flow of materials to identify the entities involved. A business continuity plan can be a valuable resource in this process. The exclusive relationship Bakeries, Inc., has with Mille Company to purchase all the organic flour it needs creates the potential for Bakeries' overdependence on a single supplier. Bakeries' contract with Mille Company specifies that Mille must deliver organically grown and processed flour. It also requires Bakeries to give Mille Company three months' notice if it wants to change the tonnage of flour purchased or, if it fails to give such notice, pay a monetary penalty to

Mille Company. When negotiating this contract, which is favorable to Mille Company, Bakeries, Inc., failed to insist on inclusion of a renegotiation clause if ownership of Mille Company changed. Further, Bakeries, Inc., had no contingency plan in place to address problems that could occur with production at Mille Company. Bakeries, Inc., also neglected to monitor the organizational changes at Mille Company.

Bakeries supplies its products to only one company—Health Foods. Bakeries' failure to deliver contracted products to Health Foods jeopardizes not only Bakeries' future sales but also its survival. Because Health Foods can purchase similar products from other manufacturers, there is a good possibility that Bakeries will not recover its previous market share.

Defending the company in litigation will be costly, further straining Bakeries' shrinking profits. Failure to deliver its product and the resulting negative publicity can cause a major disruption for Bakeries, Inc. With production and sales decreased by 60 percent, Bakeries may not survive. See the exhibit "Bakeries, Inc.: Manufacturer of Whole-Grain Organic Products."

### Bakeries, Inc.: Manufacturer of Whole-Grain Organic Products

| Exposure | Type of Risk |
| --- | --- |
| One key supplier | Financial |
| Unbalanced customer base | Financial |
| Litigation—Mille Company and Healthy Foods | Financial/Reputation |
| Reputation | Financial/Reputation |
| Survival | Financial/Reputation |

[DA03894]

Mille Company, purchased by a large corporation, is undergoing internal cultural changes. Seeking to increase profits and production, the new management at Mille Company is improperly handling the need for an increased grain supply. It has no quality assurance program in place and may have purchased nonorganically grown wheat in order to produce the quantities required. Employees, who are already unhappy due to changes in the organization, noticed that the wheat purchased for processing had not been organically grown and made this fact public.

FDA involvement will be costly to the organization because every shipment of wheat purchased must now be scrutinized. Flour production has decreased, and Mille Company is unable to adhere to its production and delivery schedules. Mille Company is receiving negative media coverage, and several consumer groups are launching independent investigations.

Wheat farms supplying Mille Company are coming under investigation regarding their farming methods. Many customers are canceling their orders to avoid being tainted by the negative publicity. Consumer trust is at an all-time low.

Breach of contract litigation is also expensive. The new corporate parent is forced to defend Mille Company but may ultimately decide to close the facility. See the exhibit "Mille Company: Processes Whole-Grain Organic Flour and Sells It to Bakeries, Inc.."

## Mille Company: Processes Whole-Grain Organic Flour and Sells It to Bakeries, Inc.

| Exposure | Type of Risk |
| --- | --- |
| New management and culture—employee risk | Social/Political/Legal |
| Broad number of questionable suppliers | Financial |
| FDA investigation | Legal/Reputation/Ethical |
| Small market | Financial |
| Reputation | Financial/Reputation/Social |
| Litigation | Financial/Reputation |
| Survival | Financial/Reputation |

[DA03895]

Health Foods has contracted with Bakeries, Inc., as a supplier of sesame bread and crackers, which account for 35 percent of Health Foods' profits. Health Foods does not have another supplier for these products immediately available. Customers wishing to purchase these products are finding alternative sources, notably a large grocery chain. Sales of other products have also dropped due to decreased customer visits to Health Foods. Selling products reputed to be inorganic is tarnishing the company's reputation. Health Foods' management believes its only option is to sue Bakeries, Inc., for breach of contract and faulty advertising. See the exhibit "Healthy Foods: Retail Chain Selling Organic Baked Foods Supplied by Bakeries, Inc.."

## Determination of Co-Dependencies

Once the individual exposures have been identified, the co-dependencies between the organizations must be determined.

Specific organic farmers are contractually bound to deliver organically grown wheat to Mille Company. Mille Company contracts for a certain tonnage and reserves the right to purchase additional wheat. The farmers agree to grow the

**Healthy Foods: Retail Chain Selling Organic Baked Foods Supplied by Bakeries, Inc.**

| Exposure | Type of Risk |
|---|---|
| One key supplier | Financial |
| Customer loyalty | Reputation/Financial |
| Reputation | Financial/Reputation |
| Litigation | Financial/Reputation |

[DA03896]

wheat using only organic methods, and any violation of this agreement voids the contract.

Mille Company processes the wheat using no additives or preservatives. The company supplies flour to Bakeries, Inc., based on a delivery schedule outlined in the contract. Mille Company is the exclusive supplier to Bakeries, Inc., which must give Mille three months' notice if the contracted amount is to be changed. Bakeries, Inc., is tied to Mille Company by contract and by reputation.

Using the flour it receives from Mille Company, Bakeries produces the whole-grain organic sesame bread and crackers sold at Health Foods' store. Based on the amount of product sold to Health Foods, it is Bakeries' principal customer. Failure to supply product on time to Health Foods constitutes a breach of contract that can drive Bakeries out of business. See the exhibit "Organizational Co-Dependencies."

## Organizational Co-Dependencies

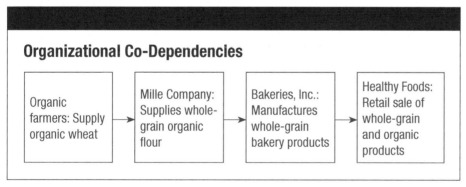

[DA03901]

## Analysis of Exposures

With the information resulting from identification of exposures and co-dependencies, the exposures are then analyzed to determine how each company can avoid or mitigate losses. Mitigation plans are based on the analysis of the exposures and co-dependencies between the supply chain elements. Mitigation plans, which establish strategies in advance of a disruption, are an important part of any business continuity plan.

Bakeries, Inc., is in crisis due to its broken supply chain. It needs to quickly find a substitute supplier of organic flour in order to resume baking operations. Concerns that other products it has sold may also have nonorganic components should be addressed with all stakeholders. Communication with customers is critical to the company's survival. Bakeries may need to increase production of other products to keep its operations going and to offset losses arising from its sesame bread and crackers line.

Mitigation plans for Bakeries, Inc., include these:

- Find a new source of organic flour
- Communicate to its business partners the steps it is taking to ensure that the products sold are truly organic
- Communicate those same steps to customers
- Use buffer inventory
- Use hold-harmless agreements to its advantage
- Review existing business continuity plan

Mille Company must communicate with its business partners and the public. If the FDA's allegations are untrue, Mille Company must salvage—and may even rebuild—its reputation as quickly as possible. Cooperation with the FDA investigation will expedite the end of the crisis.

Mille Company may choose to increase its advertising when the FDA issues its report. Depending on the veracity of the allegation, Mille Company may need to redesign its business plan. The company is in crisis because of a failure to meld organizational cultures. Internal communication must be handled as carefully as external communication.

Mitigation plans for Mille Company include these:

- Cooperate with FDA investigation
- Repair employee relations by improving communications
- Communicate with customers
- Redefine its business plan

Health Foods lost valuable inventory items and needs to find an alternate supplier to lure customers back. Its reputation may be damaged, and it must find ways to communicate with the public to regain consumer trust.

Mitigation plans for Health Foods include these:

- Obtain new bakery product suppliers
- Increase advertising
- Regain customer trust

The root cause of this disruption was the change of ownership of one company, Mille Company. The company's new management did not handle the change of culture well, incurring employee anger and ultimately a costly investigation and scandal.

Bakeries, Inc., did not foresee that a change in its supplier's ownership and culture could affect its business. The disruption in its supply caused a loss in revenue, increased costs due to litigation, and a damaged reputation. Bakeries, Inc., failed to maintain close ties with its business partners.

Health Foods is also damaged in this situation. It may find new suppliers of bakery products or be able to increase sales of other products. If not, it may not recover its customer base, and this may be the final circumstance that causes this boutique store to fall victim to a chain store operation. See the exhibit "Case Analysis and Solutions."

## Case Analysis and Solutions

Bakeries, Inc.: Manufacturer of whole-grain/organic bakery products distributed to retail stores

| Exposure | Type of Risk | Potential Solution |
| --- | --- | --- |
| One key supplier | Financial | Diversify/Buffer inventory |
| Small customer base | Financial | Increase advertisement |
| Litigation—Mille Company and Healthy Foods | Financial/Reputation | Renegotiate contracts with hold-harmless clauses |
| Reputation | Financial/Reputation | Communication/Media |
| Survival | Financial/Reputation | Redefine strategy |

Mille Company: Processes whole-grain organic flour, selling to Bakeries, Inc.

| Exposure | Type of Risk | Potential Solution |
| --- | --- | --- |
| New management and culture—employee risk | Social/Political / Legal | Employee meetings/Training/ Change management |
| Broad number of questionable suppliers | Financial | Quality assurance program |
| FDA | Social/Reputation/Ethical | Adhere to all regulations |
| Small market | Financial | Increase consumer awareness/Advertise |
| Reputation | Financial / Reputation/ Social | Communication—use media outlets/Community involvement |
| Litigation | Financial/Reputation | Resolve issues/ Renegotiate contracts |
| Survival | Financial/Reputation | Return to a new simple state |

Healthy Foods: Retailer of whole-grain organic foods supplied by Bakeries, Inc.

| Exposure | Type of Risk | Potential Solution |
| --- | --- | --- |
| One key supplier | Financial | Diversify |
| Customer loyalty | Financial | Communication/ Advertising |
| Reputation risk | Financial/Reputation | Communication/ Community involvement |
| Litigation | Financial/Reputation | Reevaluate business plan |

These solutions may not be the only viable options. Other solutions could be exercised if justified by the analysis. In addition, specific circumstances and organizational needs or goals may enter into the evaluation, making an alternative action a better option.

[DA03902]

# SUMMARY

An organization can use BCM to address potential threats to its operations. BCM has evolved from emergency preparedness and disaster recovery planning. Although BCM is similar to risk management, the two functions differ in focus and scope. The U.S. Department of Homeland Security has designated three standards of emergency preparedness for private business that address BCM as well as disaster recovery.

BCM is a strategic and operational approach designed to maintain business operations in the event of a catastrophe. Its purpose is to analyze potential risks and determine the most effective solutions the organization may employ to mitigate the risk and resulting damage. An important component of the BCM process is the business continuity plan, which entails these steps:

1.  Understanding the business
2.  Conducting a BIA
3.  Performing a risk assessment
4.  Developing the continuity plan
5.  Implementing the continuity plan
6.  Building a BCM/BCP culture
7.  Maintaining and updating the plan

A strategic redeployment plan is a four-stage plan designed to reinforce an organization's resiliency and allow it to survive and flourish following a crisis. The stages are emergency, alternate marketing, contingency production, and communication. Each stage is designed to protect the organization, its stakeholders, its reputation, and its physical assets.

Communicating in a truthful and transparent way throughout a crisis will mitigate organizational risk and benefit the organization in the short term and the long term. During a crisis, stakeholders must be continually engaged and informed so that their concerns are fully addressed. Providing information will increase trust in management and help protect the organization's reputation, allowing for optimum access to capital, markets, talent, suppliers, and customers.

Organizations must achieve a balance between operational efficiency, cost effectiveness, and vulnerability to potential disruptions. They must also accurately assess risk to their supply chain and predetermine measures and countermeasures to maintain production and market share. When the supply chain is affected, organizations must be able to adjust and adapt quickly. Failure to do so may result in loss of market share and brand recognition as well as a reduced capacity to raise capital.

Developing risk mitigation tools involves a review of operations to identify exposures and risks as well as co-dependencies within the supply chain. This review will form the foundation of a risk mitigation plan.

# ASSIGNMENT NOTES

1.  The material in this section is based partially on Kurt Engemann and Douglas Henderson, *Business Continuity and Risk Management* (Brookfield, Conn.: Rothstein Associates, Inc., 2011), pp. 6–14.

2.  Adapted from an unpublished manuscript, Carol A. Fox and Michael S. Epstein, "Why Is Enterprise Risk Management (ERM) Important for Preparedness?" (Convergys Corporation, 2009).

3.  PAS 56: 2003, Guide to Business Continuity Management, The Business Continuity Institute, March 2003, p. 14.

4.  PAS 56: 2003, Guide to Business Continuity Management, p. 18.

# Direct Your Learning ▶▶

# 4

# Physical Property Risk

## Educational Objectives

After learning the content of this assignment, you should be able to:

▷ Describe various categories of physical property exposed to risk.

▷ Describe the major sources of risk affecting physical property.

▷ Describe the nature of and the pre-loss and post-loss actions appropriate for windstorms, earthquakes, and floods.

▷ Explain how a building's construction and occupancy reduce the likelihood and consequences of fire damage.

▷ Explain how a building's protection and external exposures reduce the likelihood and consequences of fire damage.

▷ Explain how human characteristics, building occupancies, and the Life Safety Code affect the safety of persons exposed to fire in buildings.

▷ Explain how to use various methods to value physical property.

▷ Describe the types of legal interests in physical property.

▷ Given information on a physical property, assess the risk and recommend treatment options for protecting lives and property.

# Physical Property Risk

# 4

## PHYSICAL PROPERTY CATEGORIES

A risk exposure must be assessed—that is, identified and analyzed—before it can be effectively treated. Once assessment occurs, the best techniques to employ in treating the exposure often become apparent.

Assessing property risk sources involves identifying the property exposed to loss. For legal purposes, property is categorized as either real property or personal property.

## Real Property

**Real property** includes land and all structures permanently attached to the land. Examples of real property include buildings, driveways, sidewalks, underground piping, and radio transmitting towers. Risk management professionals often distinguish between land and buildings and other structures when assessing an organization's property risk exposures because insurance coverages generally treat them separately.

Real property (realty)
Tangible property consisting of land, all structures permanently attached to the land, and whatever is growing on the land.

### Land

Unimproved land is land in its natural state without any man-made alterations. Risk management professionals may find determining the proper value of unimproved land challenging because each tract has unique attributes, including these:

- Water (such as a lake, river, creek, spring, or underground water table)
- Mineral resources (such as coal, iron, oil, copper, bauxite, potash, sand, or stone)
- Natural attractions of commercial value (such as a cave, therapeutic spring or pool, historic site, or artifacts)
- Natural forests
- Resident wild animals

The most important factor affecting the value of unimproved land is its location. For example, wooded acreage that may be developed commercially has much greater value if it is located at the intersection of two major roads than if it is isolated.

Sometimes an organization overlooks the value that can be lost by damage to unimproved land because unimproved land is perceived to have little intrinsic value. For example, an organization might purchase a large tract of land for a future need for the organization's facilities. The value of the timber currently on the land that could be destroyed by a forest fire may not have been recognized when the purchase was made. Additionally, an organization's unimproved land might be unsupervised for long periods, thereby making it possible for trespassers to occupy the land or for the land to be subject to unauthorized use, such as waste dumping.

Improved land is land with man-made alterations. Improved land includes buildings and structures as well as crops such as corn, fruit orchards, and planted forests. The presence of these alterations makes it easier to recognize and determine the value of the improved land.

## Buildings and Other Structures

Buildings are permanent structures that have walls and a roof, while other structures are anything that is built or under construction. Examples of buildings and other structures that are permanent improvements when added to real property include:

- Buildings: homes (including trailers on cement slabs), churches, schools, stores, factories, and offices
- Outbuildings: sheds, barns, stables, and greenhouses
- Other structures: hookups to sewer and electrical facilities, roads, fences, and retaining walls

Buildings and other structures can be categorized based on physical characteristics that make them either more or less subject to property risk sources, such as fire. Fire is usually considered the most likely risk source to affect buildings and other structures. Consequently, risk management professionals usually assess a property risk exposure based on the property's susceptibility to fire before considering other potential sources of risk. Construction is a factor in a structure's tendency to be damaged from fire and other sources of risk. For example, a wood-frame building might suffer only minor damage during an earthquake because it is somewhat flexible, while a rigid, fire-resistant steel building is more likely to collapse during the same earthquake.

## Tangible Personal Property

Personal property includes all property other than real property. It can be divided into **tangible personal property** and **intangible personal property**.

Tangible personal property is relatively straightforward for risk management professionals and others in the organization to recognize. Tangible personal property typically falls into one or more of these categories:

- Money and securities
- Accounts receivable records

**Tangible property**
Property that has a physical form.

**Intangible property**
Property that has no physical form.

- Inventory
- Furniture, equipment, or supplies
- Computer equipment and media
- Machinery
- Valuable papers and records
- Mobile equipment

The first category of tangible property is money and securities. This category includes all types of monetary assets, such as cash, bank accounts, certificates of deposit, securities, notes, drafts, and evidence of debt. The magnitude of risk exposure varies widely among organizations. For example, a single supermarket typically has large sums of cash on hand that present a significant exposure. In contrast, a large manufacturer may have a small exposure for cash on hand yet face the possibility of large embezzlement losses over time. By far the most significant source of risk for monetary assets is theft by either employees or outsiders.

The second category of tangible personal property is accounts receivable records. Accounts receivable records show the money currently due and previously collected from customer or client accounts. These records are subject to physical damage, destruction, theft, or fraudulent alteration. If accounts receivable records are damaged or destroyed, an organization may have difficulty reconstructing them and therefore may be unable to collect the amounts due. Even if the organization is able to reproduce these records from underlying data, this may be costly, and therefore the loss can be substantial. However, the risk presented by accounts receivable records can be effectively controlled. Organizations often back up financial data daily and store these backup records in other locations, thereby minimizing the potential property risk exposure.

The third category of tangible personal property is inventory. For a wholesaler or retailer, inventory represents goods ready for sale. For a manufacturer, inventory is usually more specifically defined as raw materials, stock in process, and finished goods. Inventory values can fluctuate widely, so valuation can be difficult. For example, value is added to stock in process at each stage of the production process. Additionally, inventory is subject to a wide range of risk sources, especially as it is moved from one location to another.

The fourth category of tangible personal property is furniture, equipment, or supplies. Examples include much of the contents of office buildings, such as office furniture, typewriters, showcases, counters, office supplies (like stationery and printed forms), manufacturing supplies, and packaging materials. This category of property often consists of many low-value items but can also include expensive equipment that might not be easily replaced if damaged or destroyed. For example, a direct mail company that handles bulk mailing for others would likely have a substantial investment in sorting equipment. Such equipment is usually customized to meet the organization's specifications as well as physically adapted to the organization's facility. Therefore, replacing this equipment would be difficult, time-consuming, and expensive.

The fifth category of tangible personal property is computer equipment and media. This category includes software and data as well as computer hardware, including servers, laptops, and tablets. Computer equipment and media can be subject to damage from excessive heat or moisture. As a result, many computer facilities require a special environmental control system, which itself represents a significant additional property risk exposure. Computers may also be damaged by electrical impulses or power surges.

In addition to risk sources that can cause physical damage to computer equipment, misuse of computer systems can result in property losses. For example, computer fraud by employees or outsiders sometimes involves theft of property. Alternatively, an employee or outsider may try to sabotage computer equipment. Although any computer equipment is exposed to theft, laptop computers and tablets are particularly vulnerable because of their portability.

The sixth category of tangible personal property is machinery. Depending on the nature of the business, an organization may be highly dependent on machinery to produce its products. Some machinery is customized, thereby making it difficult to replace. Machinery can also be categorized as equipment or even computer-controlled equipment. For example, a high-speed printer used at a professional print shop may be both machinery and computer equipment. However, machinery is categorized separately because its significant value warrants separate treatment.

The seventh category of tangible personal property is valuable papers and records. Many organizations rely on this category of physical property. For example, physicians maintain medical histories of their patients; businesses maintain customer lists; and photographers, architects, engineers, and journalists maintain files of their previous work to draw on for current projects. Likewise, risk management professionals also have valuable records needed to accomplish their duties. In some instances, these valuable papers and records are the physical manifestation of intangible property, so while they have a value, they are easier to replace. For example, stock certificates are evidence of ownership in a publicly traded company but can be replaced for a fee if they are destroyed. Because of advances in technology and automation, many valuable records are stored in an electronic format rather than as a physical file.

Assigning a value to valuable papers and records is difficult. Usually, the risk management professional values this property based on the cost to reproduce it, which might be incidental in some instances while excessive in other instances. For example, architectural plans, unless there are other copies available, may cost thousands of dollars to replace. Risk management professionals usually find that it is challenging to determine the cost of reproducing these documents.

The eighth category of tangible personal property is mobile property, including autos, aircraft, boats and ships, and heavy mobile equipment used by contractors. Such property can have extremely large values concentrated in a single item. An airplane, a ship, or a piece of earth-moving equipment can be valued in the millions of dollars. In addition to the sources of risk that can strike other property, mobile property is exposed to special hazards, such as slippery roads or speeding vehicles.

# SOURCES OF PROPERTY RISK

Once the risk management professional has identified property risk exposures, the sources of risk that may affect those risk exposures must be considered.

A property's susceptibility to a source of risk should direct the risk management professional's treatment of that loss exposure. Consequently, categorizing sources of risk can help provide a framework for managing the risk exposures. However, no approach to categorizing sources of risk is completely satisfactory, and some sources could fall into more than one category. See the exhibit "Categories of Risk Sources."

The approach to categorizing these risk sources shown in the exhibit—natural, human, and economic—was chosen because it encompasses most sources of risk that might affect property.

## Natural Risk Sources

Natural risk sources include acts of nature and acts that do not involve human intervention—for example, windstorm, earthquake, and flood. Although natural risk sources encompass natural disasters that affect whole communities, they also include events that affect just one organization, such as a building collapse caused by snow accumulating on the roof. The occurrence of a natural risk source is largely beyond human control. Consequently, risk management has little, if any, effect on reducing the likelihood of an event. However, organizations can implement loss reduction measures to control the consequences of any events.

## Windstorm

**Windstorms** need not be hurricanes or tornadoes to cause significant damage. However, hurricanes, tornadoes, and winter storms are significant sources of catastrophic losses. For example, a February 2010 winter storm with high winds affecting France, Germany, and other European countries caused an insured loss of $2.7 billion U.S.[1]

A hurricane is a severe tropical cyclone, usually accompanied by heavy rains and winds moving at seventy-five miles per hour or more. Tropical storms that form in the Atlantic and Eastern Pacific Oceans are called hurricanes, but tropical storms that form in other parts of the Pacific Ocean are called typhoons or cyclones. Hurricanes are a leading cause of catastrophic loss in

Windstorm
A storm consisting of violent wind capable of causing damage.

## Categories of Risk Sources

**Natural Risk Sources—Acts of nature; no human intervention**

| | | |
|---|---|---|
| Cave-in | Landslide/mudslide | Rot |
| Drought | Lightning | Rust |
| Earthquake | Meteors | Temperature extremes |
| Erosion | Mildew | Tidal waves |
| Evaporation | Mold | Tides |
| Fire | Perils of the air (such as icing and clear-air turbulence) | Uncontrollable vegetation |
| Flood | | Vermin |
| Hail | | Volcanic eruption |
| Humidity extremes | Perils of the sea (such as icebergs, waves, sandbars, and reefs) | Water |
| Ice | | Wind (such as tornadoes, hurricanes, typhoons) |

**Human Risk Sources—Acts of one individual or a small group of individuals**

| | | |
|---|---|---|
| Arson | Industrial contamination | Strikes |
| Chemical leakage | Labor union strikes (direct effects) | Terrorism |
| Collapse | | Theft, forgery, fraud |
| Discrimination | Machinery breakdown | Toppling of high-piled objects |
| Electrical overload | Molten materials | |
| Embezzlement | Pollution (smoke, smog, water, noise) | Vandalism, malicious mischief |
| Explosion | | |
| Expropriation (confiscation) | Power outage | Vibration |
| | Riot | War |
| Fire and smoke of human origin | Sabotage | Water hammer |
| | Shrinkage | |
| Human error | Sonic boom | |

**Economic Risk Sources—Acts of large groups of people who respond to particular conditions**

| | | |
|---|---|---|
| Changes in consumer tastes | Depression (recession) | Stock market declines |
| | Inflation | Technological advances |
| Currency fluctuations | Obsolescence | |

[DA01879]

the United States. For example, in 2005, Hurricane Katrina caused an estimated $41.1 billion in insured losses over six states.[2]

A tornado is a localized and violently destructive windstorm occurring over land and characterized by a funnel-shaped cloud extending toward the ground. Tornadoes form in warm, humid, and unsettled weather and often are the result of thunderstorms and tropical storms. A tornado consists of winds rotating at speeds that can reach up to 300 miles per hour, creating a partial vacuum at the center. When the tornado makes contact with the ground, it draws debris into the circulating air. Tornadoes can occur anywhere in the world; however, U.S. weather conditions result in a significant number of tornadoes each year.

## Earthquake

Although earthquakes can occur throughout the Pacific Rim, destructive seismic events typically affect only a few areas. More earthquakes strike Alaska than any other state, but the loss exposure is most severe in California, where exposed property values are the highest. The 1994 earthquake centered in Northridge, California, caused insured property damage of an estimated $15.3 billion, making it the second costliest earthquake ever for the insurance industry. The costliest earthquake occurred in Japan in March 2011, with insured losses of $30 billion and total losses of over $200 billion.[3]

Earthquakes occur along fault lines, where plates of the earth's surface adjoin one another, at a point called the **earthquake focus**. Seismologists use the Richter scale to measure, by either magnitude or intensity, the energy released by an earthquake at its **epicenter**.

The **Modified Mercalli Intensity Scale** measures intensity—the damage that an earthquake causes to people, property, and the surface of the earth—rather than magnitude. This scale is based on human observation, which is subjective and could make the results imprecise, but the scale can still be a good tool for underwriters to evaluate earthquake loss exposures by looking at past earthquake activity and the extent of damage for an account location.

## Flood

Flood is a rising or overflowing of water onto what is normally dry land. Flooding is a common event in many areas of the world, recurring at regular intervals. Some locations flood every year, and others face unpredictable flood hazards. Floods result from an area's receiving greater precipitation than the land can drain off. In 2010, several floods caused significant damage in Australia ($2.0 billion U.S.), France ($818 million U.S.), and China ($761 million U.S.). See the exhibit "Common Types of Floods."

**Earthquake focus**

The point on an earthquake fault line where the movement of the plates begins.

**Epicenter**

The point on the earth's surface directly above the earthquake focus.

**Modified Mercalli Intensity Scale**

A twelve-level set of descriptions of an earthquake's effects at a specified location, near or far from the earthquake's epicenter.

---

## Common Types of Floods

Seven types of flood are common:

- Riverine floods occur when rivers, streams, and other watercourses rise and overflow their banks. They result from either heavy rainfall or snow melt upstream in their drainage basins.

- Tidal floods result from high tides, frequently driven by high winds offshore, and from tropical storms making landfall or passing closely offshore. They affect bays and the portions of rivers along a coast.

- Wind floods can happen whenever a strong wind holds back part of a large body of water from its normal drainage course and raises the water level. Back bays behind barrier islands are especially susceptible to wind floods. Water that cannot escape through normal channels can flow out of these bays across the barrier islands.

- Rising water levels downstream might prevent drainage upstream, causing a backwater flood. Backwater floods can extend for a substantial distance upstream.

- Ice jams sometimes develop as ice thaws and begins to move downstream. They block the flow of water, causing it to back up and flood upstream areas. If the ice jam breaks suddenly, it can cause flooding downstream.

- Accidental floods are caused by the failure of flood control systems. A dam, levee, wall, or dike might break and cause flooding downstream. Blocked floodgates and spillways cause upstream flooding.

- Man-made topographic changes can also cause floods. For example, instead of being absorbed into the soil, rain water can accumulate on concrete and asphalt parking lots. If storm sewer drains have inadequate capacity or are blocked, water can build up and flood adjacent properties.

[DA07542]

# Fire and Lightning

Fire is the rapid oxidation of combustible material, releasing heat and flame. Slower types of oxidation and other chemical reactions might release heat or cause heat buildup. For insurance purposes, damage to a structure caused by fire includes the damage caused by flame, heat, smoke, and the water used to extinguish the fire. However, damage caused by smoke can be considered a separate risk source. In 2010, fire losses in the U.S. totaled an estimated $19.6 billion, and 482,000 structural fires occurred.[4]

Lightning is a natural electric discharge in the atmosphere. In its flow to the ground, lightning can damage property either by a direct hit, by passing nearby, or by a ground surge. Lightning damage to a building following a direct hit usually consists of shatter or blast-like damage or resulting fire damage. The likelihood of fire damage depends on the combustibility of materials used in the building and the extent of grounding afforded by lightning rods and metal roofs.

## Smoke

Smoke is hot vapor containing fine particles resulting from combustion. Most fires produce smoke, and in many fires the damage caused by the smoke is significant relative to the size of the fire. For example, a small fire in a supermarket could result in a major loss if the supermarket had to destroy its inventory because of health department restrictions on selling smoke-damaged foods. Alternately, a furrier may have to sell its inventory of furs at steep discount to a salvager because the smoke odor would likely be impossible to completely eliminate even with commercial cleaning of the goods. In addition to smoke produced by an unplanned (hostile) fire at the property, smoke damage may be caused by other sources of smoke, such as burning debris, industrial operations, brush fires, and agricultural smudging.

## Water

Water that damages a structure can come from several different sources. For example, water damage can occur when a pipe bursts; when a fracture develops in an appliance, thereby allowing water seepage; and when sewer systems back up through toilets, sinks, and drains. Many commercial structures are protected by sprinkler systems, which can leak if not properly maintained or if damaged. For insurance purposes, damage done by water from sprinkler systems is usually considered a consequence of fire if the sprinklers are activated in response to a fire. However, sprinkler leakage can be a form of water damage.

# Human Risk Sources

Human risk sources encompass deliberate acts of individuals or groups, as well as events that are not deliberate acts but that involve some element of human intervention. Examples include terrorism, vandalism, and explosion. The likelihood and consequences of human risk sources can be managed to some extent by the application of risk control techniques.

## Riot and Civil Commotion

Generally, riot is a violent breach of the peace by three or more persons assembled together and acting with a common intent. A riot need not result from conspiracy; it can be spontaneous. Some states' criminal codes require only two people in order to define the action as a riot, and others require as many as five. The rioters' act or acts must be of an unlawful nature. Riot damage includes fire, breakage, theft, looting, and vandalism.

Civil commotion can be described as an uprising among a mass of people that causes a serious and prolonged disturbance of civil order. Civil commotion and riot are similar, and the two terms include most incidents of civil unrest. Examples of riot and civil commotion are the violent protests at the World

Trade Organization meeting in Seattle in 1999 and the demonstrations in Miami during the Elian Gonzalez custody dispute in 2000.

## Explosion

The most common types of explosion are combustion explosions (ignition of flammable clouds) and pressure explosions (rupture of confined spaces).

A dust explosion is an example of a combustion explosion. Airborne dust, such as that found in grain elevators, can ignite and result in a significant explosion. A boiler explosion is an example of a pressure explosion.

## Vandalism

Vandalism is the willful or malicious destruction or defacement of public or private property. For example, a brick thrown through a storefront window out of spite would be considered vandalism. However, damage done to landscaping by deer would not be considered vandalism because animals are unable to form malicious intent.

## Vehicles

One type of vehicle damage results from physical contact between a vehicle and property; for example, when a delivery truck hits and damages a building's loading dock. Examples of vehicle-related losses in which physical contact does not occur include these:

- A building is damaged by the vibrations from heavily loaded logging trucks running on an adjacent road.
- A vehicle collides with a pole owned by a telephone company, and the pole falls on a building, caving in the roof.
- A chain is attached to a loading dock and to a vehicle, and the vehicle drives away, pulling on the chain, which damages the loading dock.

## Collapse

Collapse is an abrupt falling down or caving in of a building, with the result that the building or any part of the building cannot be occupied for its intended use. Collapse of a structure can be caused by lack of proper maintenance that may result in hidden decay; hidden insect or vermin damage; weight of people or personal property; improper design that allows rain or snow to collect on the roof, which may add more weight than the structure can hold; and the use of defective materials or methods of construction, remodeling, or renovation.

## Crime

Property crimes include burglary, larceny-theft, and arson. Burglary and larceny-theft involve taking property without the owner's consent. Property crimes in the U.S. in 2010 totaled an estimated $9.1 billion. This amount includes $737 million from motor vehicle thefts, $6.1 billion from larceny thefts, and $2.1 billion from burglaries.[5]

**Terrorism** is a form of crime in which individuals or groups may target an organization's property, persons, or activities with the intention of forcing the organization to change or close its business. Terrorism may also involve the deliberate contamination of property through chemical, biological, or radio-active materials, or the destruction of property by bombing or aerial impact. The terrorism risk source has been a growing concern for risk management professionals as political and other issues arise around the globe. A terrorist attack could involve a high-profile political, sports, or monetary event, such as a presidential inauguration, the Olympic Games, or an international trade conference.

**Terrorism**

The use of violence, intimidation, or threats to influence others' behavior, often for a political purpose.

## Economic Risk Sources

A risk management professional should consider economic risk sources in addition to natural and human risk sources. Economic risk sources are caused by acts of large groups of people responding to particular conditions. These risk sources are, therefore, dynamic and typically involve large segments of the population. Economic risk sources stem from changes in market conditions, such as price levels, interest rates, the general economy, or changes in consumer preferences. These risk sources can generate prosperity for those whom they favor but threaten unemployment and recession for others as well as increase or decrease the value of property. Because economic risk sources are generally beyond the effective range of any risk management program, risk management professionals sometimes overlook them.

# WINDSTORM, EARTHQUAKE, AND FLOOD LOSS CONTROL

It is important for organizations to implement disaster recovery plans as a risk control technique to effectively mitigate a disaster loss. A disaster recovery plan must tailor its pre- and post-loss actions to specific risk sources.

Extreme wind conditions are not uncommon, whether it be a coastal hurricane or an inland thunderstorm with or without a tornado accompanying it. Flooding is also not uncommon; but, unlike other natural sources of risk, most flooding occurs after a substantial warning period, which allows time to implement control techniques. Earthquakes are less common but can easily result in a disaster depending on the proximity of the earth movement to an organization's property and personnel. These sources of risk require tailored disaster recovery plans.

# Windstorm

A windstorm is a storm with high winds or violent gusts of wind with little or no rain. Windstorms have different warning periods. Some can be tracked for days, and such storms might allow time for battening exposed windows, anchoring portable outdoor property, evacuating the area, and obtaining disaster supplies. Other storms occur more rapidly and less predictably. These storms might only allow time for finding immediate shelter. Therefore, disaster recovery plans for this source of risk should reflect not only weather conditions but also the difference in warning times.

## Pre-Loss Actions for Windstorm

The greatest threat from windstorm is building damage, such as collapse of roofs and outside structures. Pre-loss actions for windstorm include these:

- Design buildings and outside structures to withstand anticipated wind loads. The design should reflect location conditions in which wind velocities might exceed the average.

- Provide storm shutters and blinds for windows and other openings rated to handle higher wind loads.

- Maintain roof and wall systems, including roof tie-downs, in good repair and provide adequate supports for outside structures.

- Secure materials and equipment located in areas surrounding the facility.

## Post-Loss Actions for Windstorm

Post-loss actions for windstorm include these:

- Use spare construction materials such as plywood panels, tarpaulins, and plastic sheets to temporarily repair damage to buildings and to reduce further loss exposure of the building and equipment to the elements

- Patrol premises to prevent looting or vandalism

# Tornado

**Tornado**

A type of violent windstorm that consists of winds rotating at speeds of up to 300 miles per hour; a partial vacuum develops at the center of the storm (vortex).

A **tornado**, or cyclone, is a rotating column of air in a funnel-shaped vortex. The tornado extends downward from a cloud and rotates at speeds of up to 300 mph. Tornadoes affect most of the continental United States east of the Rocky Mountains with varying degrees of frequency and severity. However, higher frequency areas include the central plains, east central Arkansas, northern Mississippi and Alabama, and central Indiana. According to National Oceanographic and Atmospheric Administration (NOAA) data and other data repositories, central Oklahoma has the highest frequency of tornado activity in the world.

## Pre-Loss Actions for Tornadoes

Nothing can prevent property losses from direct tornado contact. Bodily injury can be reduced by taking shelter. Most constructions are not designed to withstand a tornado's violent winds. Some building designs of reinforced concrete construction have withstood tornado-force winds, but building all structures this way is neither practical nor economical. However, the installation of underground shelters has proven effective as a means of providing a safe place of evacuation.

## Post-Loss Actions for Tornadoes

The severity of the tornado damage may not leave any meaningful post-loss options beyond preserving life and clearing rubble. If the devastation is not total, these are appropriate post-tornado procedures:

- Begin search and rescue process
- Complete temporary repairs to avoid additional property damage
- Proceed with caution near downed power lines
- Start salvage procedures

# Earthquake

An earthquake is a sudden movement of a portion of the earth's surface that is sometimes sufficient to cause property damage, injury, and death. Earthquakes result from volcanic action or the sudden release of geophysical forces that have accumulated along the edges of tectonic plates comprising the earth's crust. Volcanic or tectonic action can occur either above or below sea level. Oceanic earthquakes can cause massive tidal waves or tsunamis that are extremely damaging to coastal areas.

## Pre-Loss Actions for Earthquake

Pre-loss actions to control earthquake causes of loss include these:

- Select an appropriate geographic location
- Design or select earthquake-resistant buildings

Location is a key factor in controlling earthquake damage and injuries for two reasons. First, people and property located farther away from volcanic areas and major geological faults (where earthquakes tend to concentrate) are less likely to experience detectable earthquakes than those located nearer to such areas. Second, at any given distance from an epicenter, people and structures situated on stable earth that can absorb most earthquake shock waves tend to suffer less harm than those located on more unstable ground. Consequently, to modify the likelihood of an earthquake event, selecting an appropriate geographic region and choosing a specific site within that region are crucial to earthquake risk control. Evaluating the earthquake source of risk at a specific site normally requires a detailed geologic analysis.

The design of a building or other structure is another pre-loss action. A building in an earthquake zone should be constructed to ride atop the ground without damage. The two major types of earthquake-resistant construction incorporate either box action design or frame action design.

**Box action design** buildings are stiff and can withstand considerable ground motion. However, their foundations or other anchors can be severed by an intense earthquake. **Frame action design** relies on the building's ability to absorb the energy of the earth movement. Many buildings in earthquake-prone areas incorporate both box and frame action features.

## Post-Loss Actions for Earthquake

Immediate post-loss actions following an earthquake should focus on these areas:

* Take care of both injured and noninjured people
* Take any possible actions to protect damaged buildings and infrastructure from further damage

During and immediately after an earthquake, post-loss actions should focus on caring for the injured, protecting uninjured persons, and safeguarding endangered property. Within the seventy-two hours after a major earthquake, less intense aftershocks typically occur. Weakened buildings, underground piping, and utilities should be reinforced to the extent feasible without endangering persons doing this work. Any buildings that are not designed to withstand earthquake forces should be left temporarily unoccupied, and people should stay clear of areas where additional debris could fall. Also, during aftershocks, people may not want to or be able to return to their homes. Therefore, it might be necessary to provide temporary housing for people until the aftershocks cease. Apart from preventing any imminent additional injury or damage, post-loss restoration efforts should wait until the danger of further earthquake action passes.

## Flood

Inland and coastal areas are subject to flooding from heavy rainfall and melting snow and to tidal surges. Efforts to reduce flood risk exposures have been moderately successful. However, continuous vigilance and planning can help alleviate the dangers presented by these sources of risk.

Oceanic seismic activity can cause a tsunami or tidal wave, which can travel at up to 600 mph in deep water. As a tidal wave enters the coastal shoals, its velocity is greatly reduced, but its wave height increases. Some tidal waves can crest at over 100 feet. Tidal waves occur most frequently in the Pacific Ocean basin.

**Box action design**

Earthquake-resistant construction, used in buildings under three stories tall, that integrates roof and floor diaphragms that can flex to transmit and distribute the forces an earthquake exerts on a structure.

**Frame action design**

Earthquake-resistant construction that relies on the resilience of steel or specially designed reinforced concrete to absorb energy while undergoing considerable distortion and return to their original shapes.

## Pre-Loss Actions for Flood

Though damage from all types of flooding may be extensive, pre-loss actions such as these can prevent property risk exposures resulting from flooding:

- Evaluate location of operations. Flood-prone areas or coastal areas may not be the best location from a risk management perspective.

- Analyze existing structures in flood zones for their ability to withstand normally expected events.

- Use temporary levees (or landscaping that incorporates levee features), shutters for building openings, and barriers.

- Stock disaster supplies, including portable power equipment, to maintain vital utility services.

- Place main electrical service equipment on upper floors of buildings above historical flood stage heights.

Many floods indirectly cause fires that start in electrical shorts, flammable liquids floating on top of the water, and flammable gas escaping from broken piping. Pre-loss actions for minimizing fire loss exposures resulting from floods include these:

- Allow no open flames or electrical wiring that is not waterproof near or in a flood-exposed structure

- Protect flammable gas piping (whether utility or process services) where exposed to mechanical damage and install shutoffs or disconnects above normally expected flood stage heights

- Prevent flood water from entering buildings, either by having no lower-level openings or by covering those openings against water entry

## Post-Loss Actions for Flood

Post loss actions for flood emergencies include these activities once flood waters have receded:

- Complete damage assessment with particular attention to building foundations

- Make temporary repair of any building openings

- Start salvage operations

- Clear all drains of debris

- Clean and inspect all production and electrical equipment prior to restarting

# BUILDING CONSTRUCTION AND OCCUPANCY

There are four primary factors to consider when controlling property risk exposures to buildings and their contents—construction, occupancy, protection, and external environment. Collectively, these are known as "COPE"

factors. When controlling the threat of hostile building fires, two important factors are a building's construction (the C in COPE) and its occupancy (the O in COPE).

Risk management professionals must consider a building's construction and how construction features may affect the likelihood and consequences of fire damage to the building and its contents. An additional factor that risk management professionals should consider is occupancy. The fire hazards in any facility are influenced by the nature of the activity in the building—that is, building occupancy.

# Construction

There are six types of construction:

- Frame
- Joisted masonry
- Noncombustible
- Masonry noncombustible
- Modified fire-resistive
- Fire-resistive

To assess a building's exposure to fire loss, risk management professionals should be familiar with each type of construction. See the exhibit "Distinctive Characteristics of Major Types of Building Construction."

## Frame

**Frame construction**

A class of construction that has load-bearing components made of wood or other combustible materials such as brick or stone veneer.

Many dwellings and small mercantile buildings are **frame construction**, which is more susceptible to fire damage than other construction classes. Despite that fact, this construction type is popular, although its popularity varies by geographic region. Buildings with a single layer of brick (brick veneer) on the walls with combustible floors and a roof supported by wood framing fall under the frame construction category.

## Joisted Masonry

**Joisted masonry construction**

A class of construction that has load-bearing exterior walls made of brick, adobe, concrete, gypsum, stone, tile, or similar materials; that has floors and roofs of combustible materials; and that has a fire-resistance rating of at least one hour.

In **joisted masonry construction**, exterior walls are made of masonry or other noncombustible materials. Other structural components, such as the floors and roof, are usually made of combustible materials.

From a fire risk perspective, joisted masonry construction is usually preferable to frame construction because the severity of loss caused by fire is generally less. However, in a fire of considerable intensity, only the shell (the bare walls) of a building may be left. In such a fire, some significant portion of the walls may even fall, be knocked down if the roof collapses, or be pulled or pushed down by collapsing wooden support beams. Even the bricks can be irreparably damaged by intense and prolonged heat.

## Distinctive Characteristics of Major Types of Building Construction

| Type of Building Construction | Distinctive Characteristics |
| --- | --- |
| Frame | Exterior walls made either of combustible material such as wood or noncombustible material such as brick veneer but that have wall supports, floors, and a roof made of combustible material. |
| Joisted masonry | Self-supporting exterior walls made of masonry such as brick, stone, concrete, hollow concrete block, or other noncombustible materials. Other structural components, such as floors and roof, are usually made of combustible materials such as wood. |
| Noncombustible | Exterior walls, floors, and roof are made of, and supported by, noncombustible materials but with trim and interior walls that may be made of combustible materials. |
| Masonry noncombustible | Exterior walls made of masonry or of fire-resistive materials with a fire-resistive rating of not less than one hour, and floors and roof made of noncombustible materials with noncombustible supports. |
| Modified fire-resistive | Exterior walls, floors, and roof made of masonry or fire-resistive or other noncombustible material with a fire-resistive rating of between one and two hours. |
| Fire-resistive | Exterior walls, floors, and roof made of masonry or other noncombustible material with a fire-resistive rating of at least two hours and a roof with a fire-resistive rating of at least one hour. |

[DA08685]

Heavy timber construction (mill construction) is used mainly in older industrial buildings. It involves heavy timber structural supports and masonry wall construction. Large, solid pieces of wood are extremely difficult to burn. Therefore, a bare wooden beam eight inches by ten inches in diameter ordinarily resists fire damage better than a bare steel beam with the same load-bearing capacity (the ability to support overhead weight). Although the steel beam would not burn, it would warp and twist in a hot fire and lose its strength.

## Noncombustible

Noncombustible construction is a specialized term in fire protection and property insurance. The term is not applied to all buildings of noncom-

**Heavy timber construction (mill construction)**
A type of joisted masonry construction that is considered more fire resistant than typical joisted masonry construction.

**Noncombustible construction**
A class of construction in which the exterior walls, floor, and roof of a building are constructed of, and supported by, metal, gypsum, or other noncombustible materials.

bustible materials—many such buildings fall into the fire-resistive class of construction.

One common type of noncombustible construction is all-metal construction (light metal walls and roof with light metal supports). Although many light noncombustible buildings do not add fuel to fires, the heat resulting from fires that involve the building's contents can damage the building. Its structural members expand, twist, crack, and otherwise deteriorate in such fires, often causing the building to collapse. In addition to the loss of the building, this increases the damage to contents and the threat to human life. Therefore, noncombustible buildings are not necessarily safer than buildings of frame or joisted masonry construction. See the exhibit "Light Noncombustible Building After Fire."

### Light Noncombustible Building After Fire

Photo by Kim Holston [DA08686]

**Masonry noncombustible construction**

Masonry construction or construction that includes exterior walls of fire-resistive construction with a fire-resistance rating of not less than one hour.

**Modified fire-resistive construction**

A class of construction that has exterior walls, floors, and roofs of masonry or other fire-resistive materials with a fire-resistance rating of one to two hours.

**Masonry noncombustible construction** is generally more resistant to fire damage than any of the light noncombustible, joisted masonry, or frame construction types.

## Modified Fire-Resistive

**Modified fire-resistive construction** includes materials such as reinforced concrete and protected structural steel for framing and reinforced concrete or masonry for load-bearing walls. Lighter noncombustible materials may be used in other parts, such as curtain walls that are enclosing but not load bearing. Fire-resistive ratings of materials are determined by standard tests in laboratories. The fire resistance of building materials is commonly rated by testing the materials in furnaces specially designed for subjecting the materials to a standard fire. A one-hour fire-resistive rating means that the materials met a furnace test under which they were able to retain structural integrity without failure for approximately one hour.

## Fire-Resistive

True **fire-resistive construction** provides the most fire protection. Although these building materials resist heat longer than materials used in protected ordinary or noncombustible construction, fire-resistive buildings can still be severely damaged or totally destroyed by fire.

## Fire Divisions

Another construction technique used to decrease the severity of fire losses is a **fire division** in buildings. A fire wall is a floor-to-roof wall made of noncombustible materials and having no open doors, windows, or other spaces through which fire can pass. Doors in fire walls, known as fire doors, are designed to have a fire-resistive rating and remain closed when not in use. This rating is expressed as the length of time the door is expected to hold back fire.

To effectively control fire, risk management professionals should understand how fire divisions work. A well-designed fire division prevents a fire originating outside the division from spreading into the division. Fire can spread both horizontally and vertically. A vertical opening, such as an elevator or a stairwell, is protected when segregated into a separate fire division. Fire divisions can also restrict the spread of fire in large horizontal structures by separating areas either by two independent walls or by one continuous, common masonry wall that divides two adjoining properties.

A fire igniting within a fire division should not spread beyond the division. Conversely, a fire outside a fire division should not penetrate or damage property within the division. Fire walls, fire doors, elevator shafts, and automatic devices are used to close off ventilation.

If a poorly designed building or a series of adjoining buildings has no fire divisions, the entire structure will be vulnerable to a fire. To create a true fire division, the division wall must extend above the roof, creating a parapet, which is essential to prevent fire from spreading along the underside of the roof. For structures with combustible walls, the fire division wall has to be extended beyond the exterior wall to decrease the spread of fire. A **fender wall** can prevent fire spread around the sides of the combustible walls. See the exhibit "Fire Divisions."

**Fire-resistive construction**
A class of construction that has exterior walls, floors, and roofs of masonry or other fire-resistive material with a fire-resistance rating of at least two hours.

**Fire division**
A section of a structure so well protected that fire cannot spread from that section to another, or vice versa.

**Fender wall**
An extension of a fire wall through an outer wall.

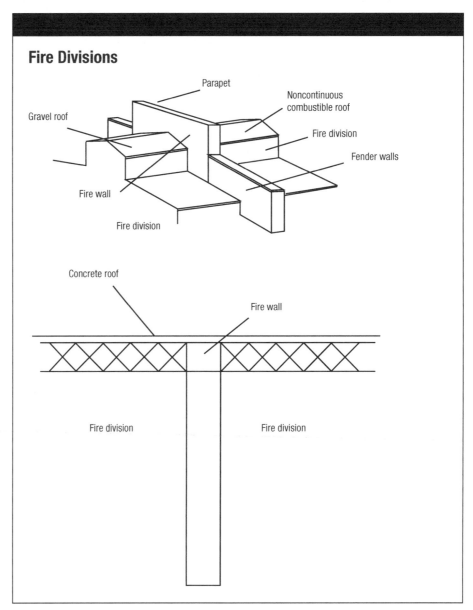

**Fire Divisions**

[DA06380]

# Occupancy

The second factor to consider in regard to controlling the threat of hostile building fires is occupancy. The risk management professional needs to know information about the activities and operations taking place in the building. There are six common types of occupancies:

- Habitational
- Office
- Institutional
- Mercantile

- Service
- Manufacturing

## Habitational

Habitational occupancies include apartments, hotels, motels, and nursing homes. Habitational occupancies are often in the control of someone other than the building owner, so detecting or controlling hazards can be difficult. Often, superior habitational occupancy results when the owner performs most of the building maintenance. Such maintenance demonstrates that the owner cares about the building's condition. In addition, regular maintenance permits the owner regular access to occupant-controlled areas that might have deteriorated because of tenant neglect. Unfavorable conditions can then be corrected.

Habitational occupancies may contain a wide range of potential **ignition sources**. Cooking equipment is the leading cause of habitational occupancy fires. Other common ignition sources include overheated machinery and equipment (for example, clothes dryers, from which fires can spread rapidly because of lint accumulation), malfunctioning appliances, and faulty wiring (electrical equipment).

**Ignition source**
Item, substance, process, or event capable of causing a fire or explosion, such as open flames, sparks, or static electricity.

When analyzing habitational occupancy ignition sources, the risk management professional should ensure that electrical wiring, equipment, and machinery are routinely maintained and inspected. Wiring and electrical equipment should be sufficient to handle a heavy electrical load. It should also adhere to the National Fire Protection Association (NFPA) 70 National Electrical Code®. Because habitational occupancies encompass a wide variety of structures, from skyscrapers to old, converted buildings, the risk management professional should consider that converted buildings might contain renovations that do not meet current building codes. Therefore, older buildings require closer analysis of wiring, heating, and trash disposal systems than do newer structures.[6]

Habitational occupancies, especially those in the hospitality industry, are often affected by fluctuations in the economy. The owner's financial stability correlates directly with the business's vacancy rate. The vacancy rate can be evaluated by comparing it with the average vacancy rate of similar operations in the area.

## Office

Office occupancy is a relatively low-hazard category because materials found in offices are usually of limited combustibility and are relatively less susceptible to damage than those found in other occupancies. Office occupancies can exist in any type of structure and often share a building with other occupancies, such as restaurants or heliports.

The primary ignition sources for fires that originate in office occupancies are faulty or malfunctioning wiring and electrical and lighting equipment. Electrical distribution and lighting equipment fires and intentionally set fires caused more property damage than fires cause by other ignition sources, such as heating equipment and smoking materials.[7]

Computer systems are a consideration for office occupancies and range from highly complex installations to desktop computers. A fire will result in a significant loss, because the equipment is susceptible to damage from heat, fire, corrosive fumes, gases, and smoke. Water used to fight the fire might also damage equipment if the equipment is not dried out immediately. NFPA has established standards for computer installation and wiring.

## Institutional

Institutional occupancies include schools, churches, hospitals, and property owned by governmental entities. Governmental entities often operate habitational properties such as public housing and nursing homes. Institutional occupancies also include special-purpose facilities, such as prisons and police or fire stations. These public entities are often insured through risk retention groups, municipal pools, and other alternative risk-transfer programs.

## Mercantile

Mercantile occupancies include businesses that buy and sell goods and merchandise, such as department stores, clothing stores, hardware stores, specialty shops, and grocery stores, whether wholesale or retail. The combustibility of a mercantile operation's contents varies by the type of stock the store sells. A sporting goods store might stock ammunition and camping-stove fuel, while hardware stores and home centers normally have large quantities of flammables and combustibles, such as paints, varnishes, solvents, lumber, curtains, and wallpaper.

The stock of mercantile occupancies is usually of significant value and is susceptible to fire, smoke, and water damage. Clothing is especially subject to severe loss from smoke and water damage, and a hardware store's stock can rust from the water used in fighting a fire. Because health authorities usually require food exposed to fire and smoke to be withdrawn from sale, a small fire can produce a large loss in this occupancy category.

Although many mercantile occupancies are predominantly smoke free, some permit limited smoking in designated areas. This can represent a significant ignition source. If smoking is allowed on the applicant's or insured's premises, its smoking policy should be assessed to ensure that preventative measures are in place, such as "no smoking" signs and proper ash receptacles, and that housekeeping measures are taken to minimize the potential of smoking-related fires. Steps should also be taken to prevent employees of the mercantile occupancy from smoking, as many smoking-related fires in stores stem from careless employee smoking practices.

## Service

Service occupancies are businesses that perform an activity or a service for the customer rather than create or sell a product. This category includes service businesses such as dry cleaners, auto service stations, barbers, and car washes and contains a diverse assortment of occupancies. The hazards presented by a service occupancy are usually specific to the service being performed. Dry cleaners, for example, have several occupancy hazards. Lint accumulation presents a fire and an explosion hazard, large boilers for the hot water used in cleaning require regular maintenance, irons and presses could serve as ignition sources, and many of the solvents used in dry cleaning are flammable and need to be handled and stored properly.

Overheated electrical equipment is one primary potential ignition source in service industry occupancies, many of which use large machinery and office equipment. For example, although a refrigeration unit might not be thought of as a heat-producing system, the motors generate heat. Motor installations have a grill or screen permitting air circulation, and blockage of that ventilation will cause the motor to run hot.

Service occupancies that use flammable paints, refinishing fluids, and cleaning solvents (for example, repair shops) should use them carefully in a well-ventilated area. Flammable items should be stored in metal, enclosed lockers. Spray painting is another hazardous operation that is often found in repair shops. Shops should be kept clean and ventilated, and spray painting should be done only in an approved spray booth.

## Manufacturers

Manufacturers' operations involve converting raw stock into finished products. The hazards of occupancies in this category vary widely according to the product being manufactured. Each occupancy must be considered and evaluated on its own merits based on any special hazards in that occupancy. For example, a steel manufacturer has blast furnaces, rolling mills, and associated steel processing equipment, while a pasta manufacturer has an extensive drying process that creates a severe dust hazard.

Manufacturing occupancies often require extensive electrical systems to operate production processes. Therefore, the age, type, and condition of the occupancy's wiring should be considered. Also, it is important for it to comply with the National Fire Protection Association (NFPA) 70 National Electrical Code® and to be sufficient to meet the occupancy's electrical needs. Manufacturing occupancies should have planned inspection and preventative maintenance programs in place for all wiring.

Friction is another significant ignition source in manufacturing occupancies. Overheated, inadequately lubricated, or poorly maintained machinery can generate excess heat or friction and become an ignition source. Friction can build up quickly, causing equipment to overheat and igniting combustible parts (such as belts) or nearby materials, vapors, or dust. Proper maintenance and lubrication can control this exposure.

### *Apply Your Knowledge*

A risk management professional is reviewing the plans for a distribution company's new warehouse building. The large, one-story structure contains 100,000 square feet of storage space. Describe how fire divisions in this structure can reduce the likelihood and consequences of fire damage.

*Feedback:* The use of fire divisions, such as fire walls, in such a large structure is important in decreasing the likelihood and consequences of fire damage to the building. Fire divisions will prevent fire originating outside a division from spreading into that division. Also, any fire originating within a division will not spread to other divisions within the building.

# BUILDING PROTECTION AND EXTERNAL EXPOSURES

Internal and external protection is an important factor in controlling fire damage to buildings. When controlling the threat of hostile building fires, another factor to consider is the building's exterior environment. A building's environment presents many hazards for the risk management professional to control.

There are various internal and external (private and public) means of controlling a hostile fire through systems that not only detect a fire and signal authorities inside and outside the organization but also extinguish the flames. A building's environment exposes it to fire from many outside sources, such as fires in neighboring buildings. An organization should evaluate exterior exposures to modify the likelihood and consequences of fire damage to its buildings.

## Internal Fire Protection

The risk control measures for hostile fires fall into two groups— **internal (or private) fire protection** and **external (or public) fire protection**. The two risk control measures for internal fire protection are detection and suppression.

## Detection

Detecting a fire before it has a chance to spread and cause additional damage should be a priority of any internal fire protection system. Two integral parts of every suppression system are fire detection devices, which activate the

**Internal (or private) fire protection**

The action an organization takes to detect and suppress fires striking its own property.

**External (or public) fire protection**

The action fire departments and other public facilities take to safeguard the general public, including organizations, from hostile fire.

system, and alarm devices, which alert an outside fire department or the organization's personnel.

Fire detection devices may be set to respond to heat, rate of temperature increase, smoke, flame, or a combination of these. To be effective, detectors must be properly located; respond to hostile fire but not to extraneous, non-hazardous conditions; and be designed for the structure in which they operate. A detection system must be properly maintained to be effective and also cover all building areas, because fire can occur in any of these areas.

Similar to detection devices, alarm devices must be effective throughout the building so that all personnel in an area can hear or see an activated alarm. In fact, many alarm devices are meant to signal the occurrence of a fire to both off-site fire-suppression personnel and a municipal fire department station.

One of the basic functions of virtually every alarm device is to automatically emit a signal to alert people to take appropriate actions. The five basic types of fire alarms, in terms of where the alarm signal is received, are local alarms, auxiliary alarms, remote alarms, proprietary alarms, and central station alarms. In addition to mechanical or electrical detection devices, security guards, either through a contract service or as the facility's employees, help detect fires.

## Suppression

Once a fire is detected, suppression measures must be initiated to prevent damage, if possible, or to minimize the amount of damage. Internal fire suppression is achieved by using a combination of these risk control measures:

- Automatic fire suppression systems
- Standpipe systems
- Fire extinguishers

**Automatic fire suppression systems** may rely on fire detection devices to detect a hostile fire and on signaling devices to alert personnel on or off the premises. They consist of piping with discharging nozzles or heads, control valves that direct the extinguishing agents, gauges that monitor pressure within the system, and alarm devices that signal when the system becomes operative. Some systems also have other monitoring alarms that signal malfunction so that the systems can be repaired.

Automatic water **sprinkler systems** are fire suppression systems that rely on water supplied from sources such as public water systems; gravity tanks; in-ground tanks; natural bodies of water; or private supplies, such as reservoirs and fire pumps. The water is discharged from one or more sprinkler heads. Discharge occurs when a fire creates sufficient heat to melt or break the sprinkler-head operating mechanism (fusible link). When this mechanism opens, it allows the water to discharge.

**Automatic fire suppression system**

A system that uses water, chemicals, carbon dioxide, and foam as extinguishing agents.

**Sprinkler system**

A system that can detect a fire and suppress it using water or other extinguishants.

**Wet pipe sprinkler systems**

Automatic fire sprinkler systems with pipes that always contain water under pressure, which is released immediately when a sprinkler head opens.

**Dry pipe sprinkler systems**

Automatic fire sprinkler systems with pipes that contain compressed air or another inert gas that holds a valve in the water line shut until an open sprinkler head releases the gas and allows water to flow through the previously dry pipe to the sprinkler head.

**Deluge sprinkler system**

A type of sprinkler system in which all the heads remain permanently open; when activated by a detection system, a deluge valve allows water into the system.

**Preaction sprinkler system**

An automatic fire sprinkler system with automatic and closed-type sprinkler heads connected to a piping system that contains air or nitrogen, with an additional fire detection system that serves the same area as the sprinklers.

**Dry chemical system**

A type of fire suppression system in which finely divided powders are distributed through pipes to nozzles positioned to allow for full distribution over the fire exposure area.

**Wet chemical system**

A type of fire suppression in which wet chemicals suppress a grease- or oil-based fire.

The two basic types of water-based sprinkler systems are **wet-pipe sprinkler systems** and **dry-pipe sprinkler systems**. The advantage of a dry-pipe system is that it can be installed in unheated buildings, because heat is only needed around the dry-pipe valve—and enclosing that valve in noncombustible material and heating the area around the valve provide such heat. However, the dry-pipe system has limitations. Any sprinkler head triggered by fire requires air in the piping to be released first. This action creates a delay and results in more heads operating than in a wet-pipe system under similar conditions.

In addition to basic wet- and dry-pipe sprinkler systems, these types of systems are available:

- **Deluge sprinkler system**—Deluge systems are used in occupancies with severe fuel hazards that could result in a quickly spreading fire. Such occupancies include those in which flammable liquids are stored or used, as well as cooling towers, explosives or ordinance plants, and aircraft hangars. The water supply capacity must be sufficient to accommodate deluge systems, which discharge large quantities of water.

- **Preaction sprinkler system**—These are particularly appropriate for occupancies that would be especially devastated by water damage, such as computer rooms or libraries, and for unheated areas. They combine elements of both wet- and dry-pipe systems. The sprinkler heads have heat-sensing elements, and the pipes are filled with air or nitrogen, either pressurized or nonpressurized. The water is held back by a preaction valve triggered by a separate fire detection system.

- **Dry chemical system**—Underwriters Laboratories recommends that a dry chemical system be used on Class B (flammable liquid) and Class C (electrical equipment) fires. This system is therefore appropriate for loss exposures involving dip tanks, flammable liquid storage, and spray painting. However, when the dry chemicals are discharged, they leave a residue.

- **Wet chemical system**—Wet chemical systems are most often used in kitchens, where fires occur frequently because of heat, waste, and grease. Water is not an appropriate extinguishing agent for areas in which heavy accumulations of grease are common. Wet chemical systems disperse wet chemical extinguishing agents. They should comply with the National Fire Protection Association (NFPA) 17A standard.

- **Carbon dioxide system**—This system stores pressurized liquid carbon dioxide and discharges it as a gas through the system's pipes when a fire occurs. The system is activated by a heat or smoke detector, a fusible link, or manual operation. It may be used in electrical areas and engine rooms.

- **Gas extinguishing system**—This type of system is common in computer rooms or other areas where water damage to sensitive property is a concern or in areas involving flammable liquids or chemicals for which gas extinguishants are more appropriate and effective than water.

- **Foam system**—This kind of system extinguishes fires by smothering them with a foam blanket and separating the fuel from the air (oxygen). The foam blanket also suppresses the release of flammable vapors that can mix with the air. A foam system requires proportioning equipment to mix the foam with water in the required concentration. Foam systems have various commercial and industrial uses, including indoor and outdoor use—for example, aircraft hangers and warehouses.

**Standpipe and hose systems** allow firefighters to operate in a large or high-rise building without having to pull in hoses. They play an especially important role in getting hoses into service on upper floors. Therefore, installing a standpipe system is essential for fire protection in high-rise structures.

One consideration related to standpipe systems is water supply. When no suitable public water supply is available, an adequate private supply must be provided. This can be in the form of a water tower, a standpipe water tank, or a body of ground water with a fire pump and a yard system. A lake or river, if nearby, may suffice. However, an adequate supply of water must be available even during the driest periods of the year. The water source should be large enough to supply at least twice the volume and pressure needed to serve the premises. Risk management professionals considering a private water supply should consult with engineers who specialize in this area.

It is also important for system elements, such as piping, hoses, and hose storage devices, to be inspected at least annually, and some after each use. Some system elements (such as hose storage devices) should be tested annually, and other tests (such as flow tests) are required every five years. The NFPA outlines the standards for inspections, testing, and maintenance.

In addition to automatic fire suppression systems, organizations can use fire extinguishers as fire-fighting devices to control small fires or a fire in its early stages. Each extinguisher should be readily accessible, visible, properly inspected, and appropriate for the combustible material in the area. The NFPA has developed five fire classifications and specifies the type of extinguisher to be used for each. See the exhibit "NFPA Fire Extinguisher Classifications."

In many instances, personnel are untrained in the proper use of an extinguisher. Therefore, education is an important part of risk control. Education includes training on the extinguishers' locations, discharge ranges, capabilities and limitations, and methods of use. For some highly hazardous operations, personnel should have on-the-spot extinguisher training in a controlled-fire setting.

**Carbon dioxide system**
A type of fire suppression system in which carbon dioxide is stored as a liquid under pressure and is discharged as a gas through the pipes of the system to the fire site.

**Gas extinguishing system**
A type of fire suppression that uses gas extinguishing agents, typically halon, carbon dioxide, or environmentally friendly agents, to disrupt the chemical reaction in a fire.

**Foam system**
A chemical foam system that is used in outside areas to smother a fire.

**Standpipe and hose system**
A category of fire suppression equipment that consists of a water main with fire department hose connections inside a building; used in buildings with expansive floor areas and buildings more than four stories tall.

## NFPA Fire Extinguisher Classifications

| Fire Class | Fuel or Heat Source | Type of Suppression Agent |
|---|---|---|
| Class A | Wood, cloth, paper, rubber, many plastics | Relies on the quenching and cooling effects of water or solutions containing a high water content |
| Class B | Flammable liquids, gases, greases | Requires blanketing or smothering |
| Class C | Energized electrical wiring or equipment | Requires a suppression agent that will not conduct electricity; conductive agents present a life safety threat |
| Class D | Combustible metals, such as magnesium, titanium, zirconium, sodium, and potassium | Requires one of a variety of dry powder extinguishing agents; many of these metals react violently with water |
| Class K | Fats and oils used in commercial kitchen cooking appliances | Relies on alkaline mixtures that generate a soapy foam that smothers the fire |

Adapted with permission from NFPA's Fire Protection Handbook®, Copyright ©2008, National Fire Protection Handbook, pp 17-71 to 17-74. [DA07656]

Risk management professionals are often responsible for periodically inspecting and maintaining fire extinguishers for these reasons:

- To determine the maintenance and inspection requirements for each extinguisher
- To ensure that an employee or a qualified outside specialist inspects and maintains the extinguishers
- To check and maintain the extinguisher inspection and maintenance records

*NFPA 10: Standard for Portable Fire Extinguishers* outlines the requirements for fire extinguishers' selection, placement, inspection, and maintenance. The NFPA also provides requirements for regular testing of protection and sprinkler systems.

## External Fire Protection

Risk management professionals should also be familiar with the characteristics of external fire protection to assess its effectiveness. External fire protection—typically experienced through fire departments—offers effective protection only when adequate services and equipment are available. This means that public fire hydrants are reasonably accessible, with adequate water volume and pressure, and that the fire department has appropriate firefighting equipment and personnel.

When working with a public fire department, risk management professionals should consider these factors:

- The distance from the fire department to the organization's property
- The terrain and obstructions that might interfere with the fire department's response (for example, hilly roads, railroad tracks, roads with rush hour traffic, and areas that might be subject to flooding or other natural causes of loss)
- The time it takes for the fire department to respond to a fire

The risk management professional should also take these actions:

- Invite the fire department to review the facility's layout, hazardous operations and storage areas, internal fire protection, and data packet.
- Develop a firefighters' data packet to be retained on the premises at a designated location. The data should include a plot plan of the property and describe the facility's construction, hazardous contents and production operations, fire protection levels, utility shutoff valves, and any other data vital to controlling a fire.
- Designate a liaison between the fire department and the organization to enhance coordination and communication before and during a fire emergency.

## Exterior Environment

Another factor to consider when controlling the threat of hostile building fires is the building's exterior environment. The building's environment presents many hazards for the risk management professional to control, as it exposes the building to fire from many outside sources, such as fires in neighboring buildings. To guard effectively against this exterior exposure, an organization should evaluate and control exterior exposures.

## Evaluating Exterior Exposures

The extent to which a particular building is threatened by fire spreading from the surrounding environment is influenced by characteristics of the neighboring buildings from which the fire may spread.

Construction considerations for neighboring buildings include these:

- Building materials—Construction features, such as whether a building is frame or fire-resistive, influence fire frequency and severity.
- Building height and area—The larger the neighboring building, the greater the fire hazard. The hazard is greater for tall buildings because they allow more intense fires to develop, windblown fire bands travel farther

from tall buildings, and firefighters have greater difficulty reaching the upper floors.

- Wall openings—Preferably, the facing wall of the neighboring building would have no openings. This blank wall can act as a firewall by forcing heat and flames up through the roof. The wall therefore acts as a barrier to diminish the amount of heat that can be radiated from a fire in that building.

A building's occupancy can also affect fire frequency and severity. For example, a woodworking shop or petroleum storage facility usually involves a more hazardous occupancy than a department store. And vacant buildings pose a significant fire hazard because they receive less care. Their stairwells and elevator shafts might provide chimneys through which fire could spread, and any automatic fire detection/suppression (sprinkler) system in them is likely inoperative.

If the neighboring building has protection from an operational automatic suppression system, any fire that occurs in the building should be contained. Other types of fire protection at the neighboring buildings, such as fire detection, signaling devices, and guards, also decrease the probability of fire spreading.

The general maintenance and housekeeping of surrounding property are important variables in assessing the fire hazard from an exterior environment. For example, flammable materials (such as boxes and pallets) that have been left in the space between buildings can be a source of fuel. Some businesses may routinely store flammable materials outside.

## Apply Your Knowledge

A risk management professional is evaluating external exposures surrounding the office building of an organization's headquarters. On one side is a vacant building formerly occupied by a hardware store. On the other side is a fully occupied office building. Describe the factors to consider in evaluating these exposing occupancies.

*Feedback*: The risk management professional would be concerned about the vacant hardware store building. Such buildings generally receive less maintenance, and automatic fire detection and suppression devices, such as alarms and sprinklers, may not be in working order. These factors pose a concern regarding spread of fire to the headquarters building. The occupied office building would be less of a concern, but the risk management professional would still consider construction of the building, its height, and any wall openings between the two buildings that would increase the chance of fire spreading from one to the other.

## Controlling Exterior Exposures

Risk control measures to counter dangerous conditions in the surrounding area and buildings include these:

- Reduce the extent of wall openings facing the exposure. This can be done by closing the wall openings with masonry material, reducing the size of the openings, installing glass blocks for the openings, replacing the existing windows with wired glass windows in noncombustible frames, installing fire shutters on the windows, or installing window sprinkler protection.

- Remove combustible material from the building. This can involve replacing combustible window frames, overhangs, and siding. If the entire wall is combustible, then a new masonry wall may have to be constructed to lessen the ignition potential.

- Clear the area between buildings. If a wall or fence obstructs the area around a building, it is difficult for firefighters to position hoses so that water reaches the building. Brush or debris, such as combustible trash or stacks of pallets of waste paper, creates a ready fuel source that can enable a fire to spread more rapidly. Removing this material slows the spread of fire.

- Construct a freestanding barrier wall between buildings. If the potential fire spread is severe and little can be done to decrease that potential, then constructing a barrier wall may be necessary to absorb heat from the fire.

- Install a water-spray system. A water-spray system has open, directional spray nozzles to soak an exposed building. When used for protection, water-spray systems are usually activated manually.

# LIFE SAFETY

Safeguarding people from fire has grown in importance from a risk control perspective because of the emphasis legislative bodies have placed on health and safety issues and because of the increasing frequency and severity of liability claims.

**Fire safety** and **life safety** consider both the characteristics of people who occupy buildings and the types of building occupancies.

## Human Characteristics

Life safety engineers have identified six characteristics of individuals and groups of individuals that affect susceptibility to injury or death caused by a building fire.

**Fire safety**
The risk control measures used to protect people and property from the adverse effects of hostile fires.

**Life safety**
The portion of fire safety that focuses on the minimum building design, construction, operation, and maintenance requirements necessary to assure occupants of a safe exit from the burning portion of the building.

The four characteristics that affect individuals are:

- Age
- Mobility
- Awareness of the fire
- Knowledge of the building

The two additional characteristics that affect groups of individuals are:

- Density (crowding)
- The extent to which the occupants can be controlled in their response to the fire

The exhibit elaborates on these factors. See the exhibit "Characteristics Affecting Building Occupants' Susceptibility to Fire."

## Characteristics Affecting Building Occupants' Susceptibility to Fire

| Characteristics | Considerations |
| --- | --- |
| Age | Whether occupants are very old or very young (each group has a significantly higher fatality rate because they are less mobile or less aware of a fire) |
| Mobility | Whether occupants who have impaired abilities need special attention (covers those who are physically or mentally disabled, hospitalized, or incarcerated) |
| Awareness of fire | • Whether occupants are awake or asleep<br>• Whether occupants are affected by drugs or alcohol<br>• Whether occupants' attention is affected by diversions such as sporting or entertainment events<br>• Whether occupants in one part of a building are unable to detect a fire in another part of a building |
| Knowledge of building | • Whether occupants have training in fire drills and evacuation procedures<br>• Whether occupants are familiar with the building |
| Density (Crowding) | What number of people are in an enclosed area |
| Control of occupants | • What discipline or control of occupants might exist (for example, school children under a teacher's control or direction)<br>• Whether occupants who are subject to discipline and control are less likely to panic |

[DA01380]

# Building Occupancies

In addition to being affected by human characteristics, life safety is also determined by a building's occupancy (how it is used). Life safety engineers have identified these twelve classes of occupancy and related concerns:[8]

1. Assembly—Generally contains large numbers of people who are unfamiliar with the spaces.
2. Educational—Includes large numbers of young people.
3. Daycare—Contains both young and senior occupants who are supervised by adults other than their relatives or legal guardians.
4. Healthcare—Contains occupants who are incapable of self-preservation and unable to use exits, regardless of the number provided.
5. Ambulatory Healthcare—Similar to healthcare occupancies.
6. Detention and Correctional—House occupants are incapable of self-preservation because of imposed security.
7. Residential—Includes occupants who are asleep for a portion of the time they occupy the building and may be unaware of an incipient fire that could trap them before egress occurs. Such occupancies include dwellings, rooming houses, hotels, dormitories, and apartment buildings.
8. Residential Board and Care—Provides sleeping accommodations where residents also receive personal care services by caretakers who live with them.
9. Mercantile—Contains large numbers of people who gather in a space that is relatively unfamiliar to them and often also contains sizable quantities of combustible contents.
10. Business—Generally has a lower occupant density than mercantile occupancies, and the occupants are usually more familiar with their surroundings.
11. Industrial—Exposes occupants to a wide range of processes and materials of varying hazard.
12. Storage—Relatively low human occupancy in comparison to building size and characterized by varied hazards associated with the materials stored.

The occupancy classes are relevant to life safety because, for example, each of them has certain features that affect safe exit from a building. Therefore, life safety risk control techniques and specific measures are determined jointly by the characteristics of the people in the building (the occupants) and what the building is used for (the occupancy).

# Life Safety Code

By considering the general characteristics of both building occupants and occupancy, safety engineers have developed specific fire safety standards for buildings. These standards are codified in the Life Safety Code® published by the National Fire Protection Association (NFPA).

The standards are also incorporated explicitly, or by reference, into the statutes and ordinances of most United States localities. Therefore, compliance with applicable provisions of the Life Safety Code is usually a legal requirement. Failing to comply is not only a breach of an ordinance (resulting in fines and other penalties) but can also indicate negligence in failing to adequately safeguard others. Consequently, not complying with the Life Safety Code increases the likelihood not only of property and personnel losses but also of liability losses.

An important function of every organization's risk management professional is complying with the provisions of the Life Safety Code (or local ordinances) for the building(s) the organization owns or occupies. Although these provisions are detailed and vary significantly among classes of occupancy and types of building structure, risk management professionals should be familiar with the fundamental requirements.

The Life Safety Code requires that every building or structure should use these loss reduction risk control measures:[9]

- Construct, arrange, equip, maintain, and operate buildings and structures to avoid undue danger to the lives and safety of occupants. (Dangers include fire, smoke, fumes, or resulting panic.)
- Provide a sufficient number of exits so that occupants can promptly escape in case of fire or other emergency.
- Design exits so that they do not rely on any one single safeguard. Provide additional safeguards, such as fire extinguishers and sprinklers, in case any single safeguard fails.
- Provide the appropriate kind, number, location, and capacity of exits. (To determine what is appropriate for a building or structure, consider the occupancy, number of persons exposed to a fire cause of loss, the fire protection available, and the height and type of construction.)
- Arrange and maintain exits to provide free and unobstructed egress from all parts of the building or structure while occupied. (No lock or fastening should prevent free escape.)
- Make exits clearly visible or conspicuously indicate the route to the exit so that every physically and mentally capable occupant can determine the direction of escape.
- Arrange and clearly mark doorways or passages that do not lead to exits so that occupants do not become confused. Make every effort to avoid having occupants mistakenly travel to dead-end points.
- Provide a minimum of two means of egress wherever occupants could be endangered by attempting to escape through a single means of egress blocked by fire or smoke.
- Arrange separate means of egress to reduce the possibility that more than one could become impassable at the same time.
- Incorporate adequate and reliable lighting for exits.

- Install fire alarms that alert occupants to danger and that facilitate orderly fire-exit drills.
- Enclose or protect vertical exits and other vertical openings between floors to protect occupants while exiting and to prevent the spread of fire, smoke, or fumes.

# VALUING PHYSICAL PROPERTY

Once a risk management professional has identified a property exposed to loss, he or she needs to determine the value of that property.

Organizations value their property in various ways depending on the purpose of the valuation. For example, the market value of an item of property may differ from the value recorded in the organization's financial statements. These are some of the typical approaches to valuing property:

- Book value
- Replacement cost
- Market value
- Economic value

Organizations normally own a considerable amount of property, making it difficult to track the values of all but the most significant items. Additionally, valuing property is a time-consuming task, and the determined values are usually relevant for only a limited time because the value of property changes.

Similar problems arise when historical costs are used to value inventory. Historical cost accounting values inventory based on what it cost to acquire the inventory. However, if the inventory is destroyed and needs to be replaced, the value represented by the historical cost may be insufficient.

## Book Value

An asset's **book value** is calculated on the accounting assumption that a portion of that asset's useful life has expired. Generally, a long-term asset's book value is lower than its market value because inflation increases the market value while depreciation decreases the book value. Consequently, risk management professionals do not rely on book value for valuing property. However, a property's book value may serve as a starting point in determining an accurate value.

**Book value (net depreciated value)**
An asset's historical cost minus accumulated depreciation.

The book value of property is based on its **historical cost**. Financial statements use the historical cost method for most assets. However, this does not mean that the financial statements simply show the original cost of those assets. For example, for a piece of real estate, the historical cost includes the building's total original purchase price, including the value of the land it occupies, plus real estate commissions, closing costs, and any other legitimate business expenses attributable to that purchase. Any capital improvements to

**Historical cost**
The original cost of a property.

the building are added to the original purchase price as funds are expended. For example, if an organization originally purchased its building ten years ago for $250,000 (including closing costs) and spends $5,000 to reroof the building, the historical cost is $255,000.

# Replacement Cost

**Replacement cost**

The cost to repair or replace property using new materials of like kind and quality with no deduction for depreciation.

**Replacement cost** can be used to value buildings and personal property. Generally, a risk management professional depends on qualified property appraisers to estimate replacement cost.

## Buildings

A building's replacement cost is the cost of constructing a new building to replace an existing building that has been damaged or destroyed. Construction costs to replace a building can be estimated with a high degree of accuracy. Appraisers may use a simplified method, often called the unit-cost method of appraisal, in which average local costs are applied on a square or cubic-footage basis to estimate replacement costs. A more detailed method uses the segregated costs, which adds average local costs for each major building element to obtain a more precise estimate of the building's replacement cost.

The most accurate way to determine a building's replacement cost is to ascertain the cost to construct the building from scratch. This involves recognizing costs such as those for architect services, site preparation, and building permits (although it may not be necessary to obtain building permits because the building is being replaced, not built new).

Some buildings might have little economic value but very high replacement costs. That is particularly true of construction styles featuring large and ornate structures as well as structures specifically designed for uses that are obsolete because of technological advances. For example, Airbus's introduction of the A380 with a seven-story tall tail created the need for hangars to be built to larger specifications.

## Personal Property

The risk management professional often finds replacement cost the appropriate basis for valuing personal property because, in the event of damage or destruction, the property may have to be replaced for operations to resume. Although estimating the replacement cost of personal property is usually not as difficult as for buildings, it can be more time consuming and require more specialized knowledge because many separate items of property can be involved in one loss exposure.

Valuing an organization's personal property begins by tracking an inventory of all furniture, fixtures, equipment, vehicles, supplies, and other tangible property that the organization owns or uses at each of its facilities. This inventory may be developed from several sources, including purchase records, values reported on insurance policies, personal inspections, and discussions with the organization's personnel.

The next step in the valuation process is to determine how to establish property replacement cost. Replacement cost differs depending on the type of business: manufacturer, wholesaler, or retailer. Every damaged or destroyed piece of inventory could be valued at its production cost (for the manufacturer), its purchase price from the manufacturer (for the wholesaler), or its purchase price from the wholesaler (for the retailer). The production costs or purchase prices that are relevant for the manufacturer, wholesaler, or retailer are the current costs or prices that are required to replace the inventory. The time of replacement could be some time after the inventory suffered the loss. For example, if the event that damaged the inventory also severely damaged the premises and forced temporary closure, lost inventory may not be replaced until the facilities are reopened. At that time, the cost of replacing the inventory could be quite different from the costs or prices at the time the loss occurred.

## Functional Replacement Cost

Risk management professionals use **functional replacement cost** when valuing property that is easily affected by technological changes. For example, an organization may network all of its computers through a server that it purchased several years ago. When purchased, the server was the latest model, but now it is technically obsolete (although it continues to perform its essential functions). Consequently, that model is no longer produced. The risk management professional therefore has to consider the cost of a server that is available in the current market and that can perform the necessary functions. This need not be the latest model.

**Functional replacement cost**
The cost of replacing damaged property with similar property that performs the same function but might not be identical to the damaged property.

## Market Value

Unlike some of the valuation standards previously discussed, **market value** may be more appropriate in risk management because property that must be replaced will usually be replaced at the going price in today's marketplace.

Perhaps the most appropriate use of market value is for valuing products that are relatively indistinguishable from one another, such as agricultural products, oil, or precious metals. These nonspecialized products are considered commodities and are traded as such on organized exchanges. Consequently, these products have a determinable daily market value. For the risk management professional, market value at the date of loss usually is the most appropriate valuation standard for such property. For example, if the grain in a warehouse is lost in a fire, the measure of that loss is the market value of the grain on the date of the fire.

Risk management professionals tend to use market value for other assets as well. For example, the valuation of automobiles is typically at "Blue Book."

**Market value**
The price at which a particular piece of property could be sold on the open market by an unrelated buyer and seller.

This refers to the Kelley Blue Book, available online, which lists various makes and models of automobiles and the accessories that affect their price and states a wholesale and retail value for each kind of car based on market conditions. Other online services also offer vehicle values by type, mileage, condition, and zip code.

# Economic Value

**Economic value**
The amount that property is worth based on the ability of the property to produce income.

**Economic value** is not affected by the cost of the property or the expense that would be incurred to repair or replace it. For risk management purposes, economic value can be relevant in measuring property risk exposures for real or personal property that the organization would not replace if it became damaged or destroyed. This is true because economic value focuses on the effect that the loss of the property would have on the organization's future income and, therefore, the property's contribution to the organization's overall value and net worth.

Assume, for example, that a particular metal stamping machine generates an annual output that has an income value of $10,000 after deducting all expenses. If this machine has an expected remaining life of ten years, its economic value is the present value of $10,000 received annually over each of the next ten years. This present value is likely to be significantly less than $100,000 ($10,000 × 10 years) because of the effect of the time value of money.

Another example of economic value at risk of loss is the leasehold value of a rental property. A portion of a property's value to its owner/landlord consists of its economic value—that is, the present value of the future rental income for which it could be rented in the existing rental market. To secure the economic value, the owner/landlord must relinquish occupancy (or possession) of the rented property during the period for which the tenant has rented it. Relinquishing this right of present occupancy to secure a rental income tends to reduce the value of the landlord's ownership but also tends to increase the landlord's economic value interest. For the landlord, the total value of property becomes the total of the values of the ownership interest and the economic value interest.

## *Apply Your Knowledge*

Parker International operates call centers that support several retailers. The company is located in a building that was constructed one year ago. Parker's state-of-the-art automated call system and related technology provide the company with a competitive advantage over similar types of businesses. How would Parker's risk management professional value the company's physical property?

*Feedback:* Parker's risk management professional could use several methods to establish the value of physical property. The book value or the historical cost of the building would be relevant because the building is only one year old with a low depreciation factor. The most appropriate method for the building would be replacement cost, which may require the services of qualified appraisers. Replacement cost would also be appropriate for personal property such as furniture, fixtures, and equipment. For the automated call system, the risk manager may consider using functional replacement cost. Although the current technology is state-of-the-art, it may quickly become obsolete, and newer technology may actually be less costly to replace in the future.

# LEGAL INTERESTS IN PHYSICAL PROPERTY

The type of legal interest an organization holds in physical property determines the extent to which the organization is harmed if the property is damaged or destroyed.

In order to select the appropriate risk management technique, a risk management professional needs to understand the types of legal interests that the organization holds in the property in question. Legal interests in physical property can be categorized in these ways:

- Ownership interest
- Secured creditor's interest
- Seller's and buyer's interest
- Bailee's interest
- Landlord's interest
- Tenant's interest

## Ownership Interest

An ownership interest refers to how much of a property someone owns. A physical property owner suffers a loss to the extent of that ownership interest when that property is damaged or destroyed. Property can be owned by an individual or an organization in its entirety, or it can be owned jointly with others.

## Secured Creditor's Interest

A **secured creditor** is a creditor who has a right to reclaim property for which a loan was extended. For example, an organization may have borrowed money from a bank to purchase its fleet of trucks. If the organization defaults on its repayments to the bank, the bank can take possession of the trucks. A secured creditor's rights are superior to those of nonsecured creditors who must make a general claim against the individual or organization that defaulted. A secured

**Secured creditor**
A creditor who has a right to reclaim property for which a loan was extended.

creditor usually retains the property's title and stands to lose the outstanding loan balance if the property is stolen, damaged, or destroyed.

## Seller's and Buyer's Interest

When someone buys property, the terms of sale stipulate when the physical property's title is transferred from the seller to the buyer. When transferred, the seller relinquishes, and the buyer acquires, an interest in the property rights that are the subject of the sales contract. Particularly for personal property, the time of title transfer must be specified so that the seller's and buyer's interests can be adequately protected, usually through insurance.

If the property being bought and sold needs to be shipped from seller to buyer, the risk management professionals for both the seller and the buyer must understand which party has the loss exposure for the property while it is in transit. If, as is often the case, the property has been paid for before it is shipped, the buyer has the loss exposure during transit because the title shifted to the buyer when the purchase price was paid, unless otherwise stipulated. If, however, the buyer makes less than full payment, both parties must be concerned with the consequences of a loss while the property is in transit. Sometimes the entity transporting the property assumes responsibility for safekeeping the property while it is in transit. In this case, neither the buyer nor the seller is responsible for the loss exposure during transit; they can rely on the transporting entity for loss indemnification.

## Bailee's Interest

**Bailee**

The party temporarily possessing the personal property in a bailment.

**Bailor**

The owner of the personal property in a bailment.

**Bailment contract**

A contract that requires the bailee to keep the property in safekeeping for a specific purpose and then to return the property to the bailor when the purpose has been fulfilled.

A **bailee** is a person or entity who receives physical property from another (the **bailor**) under a bailment contract. A **bailment contract** requires the bailee to keep the property in safekeeping for a specific purpose and then to return the property to the bailor when the purpose has been fulfilled. Bailments frequently arise in business transactions involving repair, storage, or transport of personal property. For example, an organization may regularly rotate its fleet of delivery vans through an auto repair shop for routine maintenance, thereby creating a bailment.

A bailee assumes responsibility for the reasonable care of the property in its care, custody, or control. If the property is damaged or destroyed, the bailee is responsible for its replacement. Although a bailee's obligation is a liability loss exposure, the extent of that exposure is limited to the property's value. Consequently, risk management professionals who address bailee interests often treat them more as property loss exposures rather than liability loss exposures.

Warehouses and common carriers (those that are available to the general public as carriers for hire) have specific statutory and other legal duties as bailees of the property entrusted to them. Therefore, the risk management professionals for common carriers and warehouses should determine the degree of care legally imposed on them and the financial extent of their obligations to replace property damaged while in their custody. Unless otherwise provided by statute or the common carrier's bill of lading (the contract between the parties that also limits the common carrier's liability), the carrier is responsible for the full value of property transported. However, under a limited bill of lading, a common carrier may limit its liability for property damage to a lower specified dollar amount.

State laws might also limit the liability of other bailees. For example, hotels and motels in most states benefit from innkeepers' statutes that limit their liability for their guests' property to a specified amount per person or per family.

## Landlord's Interest

The owner of real or personal property (the landlord) may choose to rent or lease it to another (the tenant) for specific periods in exchange for rent that the tenant pays to the landlord. The terms of the rental contract should determine responsibility if the rented property is damaged or destroyed. The risk management professional needs to be aware of the retention or transfer of any legal liabilities. Similarly to bailment, although a landlord's obligations are a liability loss exposure, the risk management professional will also consider the property loss exposures.

## Tenant's Interest

Tenants do not own the property they use, but they can have legally protected interests in the occupancy of that property for the length of the lease. They also have an obligation to return that property when their right to use it has expired. A tenant's rights and obligations depend on the terms of the lease (or rental) agreement. If there is no lease agreement, a tenant is usually not liable under common law for damage to a lessor's property. If there is a lease agreement, the agreement defines the rights and obligations of the tenant and the lessor. (The obligations assumed under the terms of a lease contract are legal liability exposures.)

Apart from this liability exposure, a tenant can have a property interest (known as a tenant's leasehold interest) in rented property when the fair market value of the tenant's rights under a lease is greater than the rent that the tenant is paying. That leasehold interest can be lost if the rented property becomes unusable or if the lessor has the right to terminate the lease.

Tenants occupying leased premises also have a property interest in improvements and betterments that they make. Improvements and betterments are alterations to premises made by a tenant that make it more useful for the tenant's purposes, increase the value of the property, and become part of the leased structure. For example, if a restaurateur constructs an internal wall to separate the kitchen from the dining area, this would be considered an improvement. A distinguishing feature of improvements and betterments is that they are intended to remain permanently attached to the portion of the building that the tenant occupies.

**Trade fixtures**

Fixtures and equipment that may be attached to a building during a tenant's occupancy, with the intention that they be removed when the tenant leaves.

Fixtures and equipment that may be attached to the building during the tenant's occupancy, with the intention that they be removed when the tenant leaves, are known as **trade fixtures**. Trade fixtures are usually treated as personal property. If, for example, a toy store was located in a leased building, all of the shelving and other fixtures it had installed in the building would be considered personal property. Typically, if a building having any of these trade fixtures is damaged, the landlord is obligated to restore only the structure, not the trade fixtures. Unless the lease specifies otherwise, the trade fixtures are considered the property of the tenant. Most leases state that the landlord is not responsible for any damage to the property of the tenant.

# ASSESSING AND TREATING PHYSICAL PROPERTY RISK

Knowing how to apply risk assessment of physical property to the facts of a case is an important skill. By carefully considering the facts provided and answering the Knowledge to Action questions, this activity should help you make the transition from knowing risk assessment considerations to knowing how to apply that knowledge.

## Case Facts

East Side Productions is a theater company that presents live plays throughout the year. The company owns a large historic building on a waterfront property in a major city. East Side Productions presents five productions per year, including dramas and musicals. The company offers a subscription program, and individual tickets may also be purchased for events. You are the risk management professional for this organization and are assessing the physical property risk.

When answering the questions in this case-based activity, consider only the information supported by the facts of the case and any recommended tools.

## Overview of Steps

Protecting lives and property involves these two steps:

- Risk assessment
- Risk treatment

# Risk Assessment

Risk assessment includes risk identification and risk analysis. The risk management professional begins by identifying the theater's property that is exposed to loss.

## Knowledge to Action

All of these are categorized as real property, EXCEPT:

a. Land
b. Buildings
c. Driveways
d. Inventory

*Feedback:* d. Inventory is categorized as personal property, not real property.

In addition to real property, all personal property must be identified.

## Knowledge to Action

Describe the categories of tangible personal property for East Side Productions.

*Feedback:* The primary category of personal property for this theater operation is furniture, equipment, or supplies. This would include theater seating, furniture in offices, and lighting equipment, as well as any costumes and props used for productions throughout the year. This category of personal property requires special attention, as it may be difficult to replace.

Additional categories include money, such as ticket receipts and accounts receivable. The risk management professional should also consider any computer equipment owned or leased by East Side. Another category of personal property that should be considered is valuable papers and records. These could include business records, any scripts used in production, and historical records and photographs.

The risk management professional must also determine the values of the building and personal property for East Side.

## Knowledge to Action

Explain why it might be difficult to establish a replacement cost for East Side's building.

*Feedback:* Although East Side's building may be older and of relatively little economic value, it may have a high replacement cost. Many historic structures have ornate features and very detailed architectural finishes, which would be costly to replace in the event the building is damaged or destroyed by fire or another risk source.

Once all physical property exposed to risk has been identified, the risk management professional should consider the sources of risk that may affect the identified risk exposures.

### Knowledge to Action

Which one of these risk sources is categorized as a natural risk?

a.   Explosion

b.   Riot

c.   Earthquake

d.   Collapse

*Feedback: c.* Earthquake is categorized as a natural risk source.

## Risk Treatment

A key risk treatment technique for physical property is to change the likelihood and/or consequences of an event that damages the property or injures its occupants. The risk management professional is concerned about the theater's waterfront location and the potential for flood damage to the building and contents.

### Knowledge to Action

Describe the pre-loss actions the risk management professional should implement to reduce the likelihood and/or consequences of a flood that damages East Side's building.

*Feedback:* The risk management professional should implement these pre-loss actions:

• Analyze the existing structure for its ability to withstand expected flood events

• Use temporary levees and shutters for building openings

- Stock disaster supplies, such as portable power equipment, to maintain vital utility service after a flood event
- Place main electrical service equipment on upper floors above historical flood stage heights

The risk management professional must also review life safety considerations and the characteristics that affect injury or death to occupants of the building resulting from fire.

### Knowledge to Action

Explain how the age and mobility of occupants can affect their susceptibility to injury in the event of a fire in the theater building.

*Feedback:* Very old or very young occupants have higher fatality rates in building fires because they may be less mobile or less aware of a fire. Any occupants with mobility issues, such as physical or mental disabilities, will need special attention to protect them in the event of a fire.

Internal fire protection is an important factor that affects the likelihood and consequences of fire damage.

### Knowledge to Action

Which of the following is an important detection device that should be installed in the theater?

a. Standpipe systems
b. Fire extinguishers
c. Alarm devices
d. Dry pipe systems

*Feedback: c.* Alarm devices are an important detection device that should be installed to alert outside fire departments and East Side employees.

# SUMMARY

Property values exposed to loss fall into two broad categories: real property and personal property. Real property includes land and all structures permanently attached to the land. Risk management professionals often distinguish between land, both unimproved and improved, and buildings and other structures when assessing an organization's property risk exposures. Personal property includes all property other than real property.

The risk management professional should consider the risk sources that may affect identified property risk exposures. Categorizing risk sources can provide a framework for managing those risk exposures. Although no approach to categorizing risk sources is completely satisfactory, categorizing according to natural, human, or economic factors encompasses most risk sources that might affect property.

An impending natural disaster loss requires that appropriate pre- and post-loss actions be taken to ensure the organization's survival and continuing operating efficiency. Disaster recovery plans should be developed for wind, earthquake, and flood risk sources.

Each construction type, whether frame, joisted masonry, noncombustible, masonry noncombustible, modified fire resistive, or fire resistive, has different characteristics. The materials used in the building's construction directly affect its ability to resist a fire. Another factor that must be considered when evaluating the likelihood and consequences of fire damage to buildings is the occupancy, or the activities being conducted within the building.

Some basic risk control measures to modify the likelihood and consequence of fire damage are designing appropriate internal and external fire protection systems, including detection and suppression, and decreasing hazards from the surrounding environment, such as nearby buildings or other structures in which a fire could start and spread to an organization's property.

It is important to know the minimum building design requirements for adequate fire safety. Many of these requirements focus on ensuring that a building has enough exits and that they are properly located and clearly visible.

Risk management professionals need to value the organization's property so that the magnitude of a property loss can be considered as part of risk assessment. Organizations normally own a significant amount of property, making it difficult to track the values of all but the most significant items. Typical approaches to valuing property include book value, replacement cost, market value, and economic value.

Risk management professionals must identify the organization's legal interest in physical property. This means to what extent, if at all, the organization is harmed if property is damaged or destroyed. These are legal interests in property loss exposures that an organization may have:

- Ownership interest
- Secured creditor's interest
- Seller's and buyer's interest
- Bailee's interest

- Landlord's interest
- Tenant's interest

You should now understand how to assess a physical property risk and recommend treatment options for protecting lives and property.

## ASSIGNMENT NOTES

1.  Insurance Information Institute, The III Insurance Fact Book 2012 (New York: Insurance Information Institute, 2012), p. 123.

2.  The III Insurance Fact Book 2012, p. 133.

3.  The III Insurance Fact Book 2005, p. 126.

4.  The III Insurance Fact Book 2012, p. 144.

5.  The III Insurance Fact Book 2012, p. 149.

6.  "Hotels, Motels and Conference Centers," Best's Underwriting Guide, April 2003, www3.ambest.com/buglcem/htmlReport.asp?NewRep=1&repID=137&T= 4&C=A&M=0URatingID=2252766&altsrc=1 (accessed January 26, 2011).

7.  Ben Evarts, "U.S. Structure Fires in Office Properties," National Fire Protection Association, November 2010, www.nfpa.org/assets/files/PDF/OfficeFactSheet.pdf (accessed February 1, 2011).

8.  Reprinted with permission from NFPA 101®-2012, Life Safety Code®, copyright 2011 (Quincy, Mass.: National Fire Protection Association, 2012), pp. 120-145. This reprinted material is not the complete and official position of the NFPA on the referenced subject, which is represented only by the standard in its entirety.

9.  Reprinted with permission from NFPA 101®-2012, Life Safety Code®, copyright 2011 (Quincy, Mass.: National Fire Protection Association, 2012), pp. 40-43. This reprinted material is not the complete and official position of the NFPA on the referenced subject, which is represented only by the standard in its entirety.

# Segment B

# Direct Your Learning ▶▶

# 5

# Intellectual Property and Reputation Risk

## Educational Objectives

After learning the content of this assignment, you should be able to:

▷ Describe the nature of and types of intellectual property protection.

▷ Describe the features of copyrights and risk control measures for copyright loss exposures.

▷ Describe the features of trademarks and risk control measures for trademark loss exposures.

▷ Describe the features of patents and risk control measures for patent loss exposures.

▷ Describe the features of trade secrets and risk control methods for trade secret loss exposures.

▷ Describe the importance of and methods for valuing intellectual property.

▷ Describe each of the following with regard to reputation risk:

- Reputation as a key asset

- Key risk sources

- Systemic approach to managing reputation risk

- Implementation of risk management for reputation risk

# Intellectual Property and Reputation Risk

# 5

## INTRODUCTION TO INTELLECTUAL PROPERTY RISK

Intellectual property is many organizations' most critical asset. Yet, because it is often intangible and its worth can be difficult to quantify, it is frequently misunderstood, economically undervalued, and unprotected.

**Intellectual property** includes a wide range of products—from fiction, music, designs, and graphic art, to product names, service organization names, mechanical and electronic inventions, processes, formulas, and software programs. It derives its value from the right of its owner to exclude others from using it. If its owner could not legally require others to refrain from using the property or to provide compensation in exchange for its use, ownership of the property would have little economic value.

**Intellectual property**
The product of human intelligence that has economic value.

Protection of an organization's intellectual property often is the risk management professional's responsibility. Therefore, risk management professionals should be familiar with intellectual property protection strategies. Another reason intellectual property is important to the risk management professional is the liability loss exposure constituted by inadvertent **infringement**. Lawsuits claiming infringement are expensive to defend. Being able to recognize the intellectual property rights of another and avoid an infringement lawsuit can be the most cost-effective intellectual property risk control measure possible.

**Infringement**
The unauthorized use of an individual's intellectual property.

## Nature of Intellectual Property Protection

In the United States, intellectual property is protected by a body of law—statutes, regulations, and case law—that helps to define ownership of a piece of intellectual property and ownership rights. This body of law gives intellectual property owners the right to enforce their rights in courts of law. Intellectual property owners historically have enforced their rights through civil suits, although criminal suits are increasingly common. As technology makes it increasingly easy for information and ideas—the essence of intellectual property—to pass unfettered between parties around the globe, risk management professionals must be aware of the intellectual property protections offered throughout the world.

Under a variety of treaties, most countries offer reciprocal rights of protection to U.S. intellectual property that is used abroad. However, there are notable exceptions, including Thailand and Malaysia, that are not signatories to the

Patent Cooperation Treaty. Knowing which countries will enforce which type of intellectual property protection can affect the geographical market an organization may want to enter.

One of the more prominent treaties regarding intellectual property rights is the Berne Convention, which governs copyrights in most countries. International patents are widely recognized because of the Paris Convention and the Patent Cooperation Treaty. The Paris Convention was the first major international treaty designed to help people of one country obtain protection in other countries for their intellectual creations in the form of industrial property rights.

## Types of Intellectual Property Protection

There are four common types of protection for intellectual property. Although these types of protection can overlap, they each serve a different purpose to the intellectual property owner.

A copyright is the legal right granted by a governmental entity to a person or organization for a period of years to exclusively own and control an original written document, piece of music, software, or other form of expression. It is the most prevalent type of intellectual property protection. However, copyright laws do not protect the ideas and underlying concepts of an expressive work. Such laws only protect the literal form that the expressive work takes.

A trademark is the legal right granted by a governmental entity to an organization to exclusively own and control a distinctive design or set of words that legally identifies a product or service as belonging to that organization. Trademark owners also have some international rights under the Paris Convention. The intent of a trademark is to create a distinction of the products or services that the organization provides in the minds of its customers. This protection can last indefinitely, provided the trademark is maintained by its owner. For example, in the United States, a registered trademark's owner must file for renewal from the United States Patent and Trademark Office (USPTO) before the end of the sixth year after the registration date and at regular intervals subsequently.

A patent is the legal right granted by a governmental entity to an inventor or applicant for a limited period to exclusively own and control a new, useful, and nonobvious invention. How long the inventor retains the exclusive right depends on the kind of patent.

A trade secret is a practice, method, process, design, or other information used confidentially by an organization to maintain a competitive advantage. Protection applies if the information was improperly disclosed to or acquired by a competitor and if the owner took reasonable precautions to keep it secret. Trade secrets can last indefinitely. Trade secrets receive international protection under the General Agreement on Tariffs and Trade (GATT). See the exhibit "How Intellectual Property Protection Methods Overlap."

---

### How Intellectual Property Protection Methods Overlap

**Trade Secret and Copyright**

An original work of expression can be protected as a trade secret and also as a copyright up until the time it is published. Trade secret protection arises from actions the owner takes to keep the work secret for purposes of obtaining an economic advantage over competitors. Copyright protection automatically applies to any work of expression when it becomes fixed in a tangible medium. Obviously, once a work of expression is published, it is no longer secret and therefore loses protection as a trade secret. However, copyright protection continues.

**Trade Secret and Patent**

An owner can pursue a patent application and at the same time assert that the invention is a trade secret. However, the moment a patent is published, the invention's trade secret protection is lost because the invention will be fully disclosed as an issued patent for the patent's protection to be viable. Because of this full disclosure, some organizations elect not to apply for a patent and rather to maintain the invention as a trade secret. Another consideration is that a trade secret can be maintained indefinitely, while a patent has a limited life span.

**Copyright and Patent**

Copyright law protects the expression of an idea but not the idea itself. A patent is intended to protect the idea itself but not how the idea is expressed. A common example of the overlap is computer software, which can simultaneously have both copyright and patent protection. A copyright protects the literal expression, which includes the program's structure, sequence, and organization. A patent protects the program's innovative approach to solving a problem. Because patent protection is not restricted to how the program is expressed, it provides broader protection than a copyright, but it is also harder to obtain and has a shorter lifespan.

[DA08660]

# COPYRIGHTS

Of all the types of intellectual property protection, copyright is probably the best known.

Copyright automatically applies to all types of original expression, whether the expression is authored in the form of words, musical notes, sculpture, video, or lines of source code in a computer program. Copyright protection covers expressions such as literary works, sculpture, graphic art, choreography, music, songs, and computer programs.

## Copyright Features

The important features of copyright are creation, ownership, and duration.

## Copyright Creation

A copyright is created when a work meets three criteria:

- The work must be original. It cannot be copied from another source.
- The work must be fixed in a tangible medium of expression that is permanently recorded. This could be in any manner of forms, such as paper, videotape or audiotape, or digital media.
- The work must have some degree of creativity. No set rule governs what constitutes enough creativity.

Once these three criteria are met, the work automatically obtains basic copyright protection.

## Copyright Ownership

When a work is created by an organization's employee, it is important to determine whether the organization or the employee owns the copyright. Ownership of a copyright creates value for an organization. Therefore, copyright ownership must be determined to help establish the values exposed to loss and to ensure the organization owns what it believes it owns.

Copyrights are generally owned by the person (author) who created the work. However, three exceptions apply:

1. When the work was created in the course of the author's employment. In that case, the copyright is owned by the employer.
2. When the work was created on commission. If the author acted as an independent contractor when creating the work under a written agreement with the commissioning party, the copyright is then owned by the commissioning party.
3. When the author sells the copyright.

The first two exceptions to the copyright ownership rule, works created in the course of the author's employment and works created on commission, are often referred to as **work for hire**. An example of a work for hire is when an author is commissioned by a movie studio to write a script for use in a movie.

**Work for hire**

A term that applies to two exceptions to the copyright ownership rule: works created in the course of the author's employment and works created on commission.

## Copyright Duration

The duration of copyright protection depends on when the work was originally created. A work that is created (fixed in tangible form for the first time) on or after January 1, 1978, is automatically protected from the moment of its creation and is ordinarily given a term that lasts for the author's life plus an additional seventy years after the author's death.

In the case of a joint work prepared by two or more authors, the term lasts for seventy years after the last surviving author's death. For works made for hire, and for anonymous works, the duration of copyright is ninety-five years from publication or 120 years from creation, whichever is shorter.

# Risk Control Measures for Copyright Loss Exposures

After establishing that copyright exists and understanding the features of such copyright, the risk management professional must determine the appropriate risk control measures to apply.

These are risk control measures that can be used for copyright loss exposures:

- Notice
- Registration
- Restrictive covenants
- Responses to anticipated defenses
- Licensing agreements

## Notice

To control copyright infringement exposures, many copyright owners have chosen to place a copyright notice on their published works. The notice takes the form of the symbol ©, followed by the year in which the work was published and the name of the copyright owner. Once this notice is placed on a published work, any party that copies the work without permission cannot claim lack of knowledge of the copyright, which makes it easier for the copyright owner to collect damages. An innocent infringer normally does not have to pay any damages to the copyright owner beyond the reasonable economic value of the work's use. Any infringer, whether innocent or not, will be ordered to cease the infringement.

Copyright laws are meant to apply to internet use as well as traditional print. However, once a work is posted on a Web site, it can be copied by millions of users in many different countries, even if the copying is illegal. This presents a difficult challenge from a risk management perspective because often there is no practical way to reassert control over the work so that copyrights can be meaningfully enforced.

One way of providing copyright notice for work published on the internet is digital watermarking. Digital watermarking software embeds information about the copyright owner into an organization's video, audio, or graphics files. This watermark can reveal things such as the copyright owner's address, terms of use, copyright date, and so forth. Watermarks are unremovable and unalterable.

Risk management professionals should also assess the possible copyright infringement by their own companies. Companies can infringe on another's copyright, whether or not intentionally, by broadcasting or publishing, either in print or on the internet, material that contains copyrighted material.

## Registration

Copyright protection comes into existence the moment a work is expressed in a tangible medium. However, this only entitles the copyright owner to the basic protections under common law (law from judicial decisions). To obtain the full protection under the law and more significant monetary damages under the applicable statute, a copyright owner should register the work with the United States Copyright Office.

The registration process is simple. Copyright owners file a form with two samples of the published work with the U.S. Copyright Office along with a modest fee. The registration must be filed within three months of the date the work is first published or before the infringement occurred. For a writing to be considered a published work does not require widespread circulation among the reading public. Being categorized in a library that is open to the public is sufficient.

Copyright owners gain several benefits from registering their work. First, registration provides reasonable, if not indisputable, evidence of ownership rights. Second, registration allows the copyright owner to collect statutory damages (up to $100,000 plus attorneys' fees) without having to prove actual monetary harm.

## Restrictive Covenants

Many companies attempt to control copyright infringement loss exposures by drafting and enforcing restrictive covenants. In this context, a restrictive covenant is any provision, clause, or agreement that, on termination of employment or contract, restricts the post-termination activities of the employee or contracting party.

Being a legally binding contract, a restrictive covenant provides an additional claim that an organization can assert when its copyrights are infringed upon. If enforced, restrictive covenants help to reduce the likelihood of copyright infringement. Counsel should be used to draft restrictive covenants to ensure compliance with laws of a particular jurisdiction.

## Responses to Anticipated Defenses

**Laches**

The legal term for waiting too long to assert a legal right.

In some situations, alleged infringers do not deny they copied the works, only that copyright owners waited too long to claim infringement. The legal term for waiting too long to assert a legal right is called **laches**. Counsel can help the risk management professional determine if the copyright protection has actually been lost because of such a delay. If the infringement was hidden or difficult to discover, some courts allow additional time to bring an infringement claim. Although the copyright owner has no duty to actively search out infringers, the copyright owner must act in a timely manner once an infringement has been discovered.

Copyright infringers can claim their infringement was for the purposes of teaching, research, scholarship, criticism, or journalism. These purposes have been recognized by some courts as legitimate, "fair use" exceptions to copyright protection. However, these purposes are only defenses, not rights. Therefore, an infringer who relies on this defense does not know a court will agree that the use was fair until the court upholds the defense. Most infringers do not want to take this risk and cease their activities voluntarily when asked. To avoid an infringement claim entirely, the party wanting to use the work should obtain permission from the copyright owner before doing so.

The innocent infringement defense allows parties who admittedly but unintentionally infringed upon the copyrights of an organization or individual to cease their activity and pay only the economic value of the material they used. This defense is less likely to be successful if the copyright owner has provided the copyright notice that was previously discussed. Innocent infringement often arises when the copyrighted material's use has been authorized. For example, the owner of copyrighted material may give an innocent infringer the right to use its material in the infringer's initial publication but not in subsequent derivative works.

## Licensing Agreements

Copyright owners can grant permission to others to use their copyrighted material. The permission usually takes the form of a licensing agreement. Because the licensor (copyright owner) usually specifies the exact material to be used, the type of use allowed, and the duration of the license, the licensor controls the loss exposure.

An honest difference of opinion can exist about the extent of a license granted by the copyright owner to a party who paid to use the work. For example, if the license was ambiguous about how long or what purposes the work could be used for, the party who paid for the license could argue that the license agreement should be interpreted in his or her favor. Careful drafting of the license agreement can prevent this defense from expanding the use of the copyright owner's work beyond the scope intended.

# TRADEMARKS

Organizations use trademarks to protect their intellectual property.

Trademarks (also called marks) are used by organizations to differentiate their products from their competitors'. A trademark can be a distinctive word (for example, "Nike"), phrase (for example, Nike's "Just Do It"), logo (for example, the Nike "swoosh"), or other marketing device. An organization hopes its customers will associate its trademark with the organization.

When an organization emulates another organization by copying its trademark, it is taking advantage, whether intentionally or not, of the reputation that the other organization has earned. To prevent this unfair result, state, federal, and international laws can be used to penalize an organization that copies a trademark if the trademark's owner has used the proper measures to control the loss exposure.

A trademark should not be confused with a **servicemark** or **trade dress**, even though both generally have the same characteristics and follow the same rules as trademarks.

**Servicemark**

A way that an organization can differentiate its services from those of its competitors.

**Trade dress**

The total image of a product or service that allows the product or service to be distinguished from its competition in the marketplace.

# Features of Trademarks

Trademarks, servicemarks, and trade dress share these important features:

- Categories
- Creation
- Duration

## Categories

These are the four trademark categories, listed in decreasing order of the extent to which they provide protection from infringement by competitors:

- Arbitrary mark
- Fanciful mark
- Suggestive mark
- Descriptive mark

An arbitrary mark is a word or phrase that appears to have been used randomly. These marks are considered memorable because of their random nature. For example, Hush Puppy shoes is an arbitrary mark in relation to the product it sells. Because it is surprising and original, it stands out. These qualities provide the highest degree of trademark protection possible, which means an organization that is seeking help from a court to prevent another from using its mark has a lower burden of proof to be successful. A fanciful mark is a word or phrase that conjures up an image that is imaginative. For example, the phrase "pillow walker," when used to describe a brand of shoe, would be a fanciful mark. A suggestive mark is one that implies certain product qualities. An example is Bite-No-More insect repellent. A descriptive mark describes the product. Examples are Scenic Landscaping or Luxury Limo Service. In each of the examples, the name emphasizes a product feature rather than distinguishing the product from its competitors.

Not every trademark receives the protection of trademark law. If a mark is generic, in that it describes the type of product rather than the brand, it is not covered by federal statute. For example, "color television" is not protected because it describes the product itself. People's names are also not entitled to protection under trademark law, unless the name becomes well-known through use or advertising. McDonald's and Campbell's are examples of surnames that have become trademarks. Likewise, a trade name or the name of a business are not considered trademarks unless they are used in the marketplace to identify a product produced by the business. An example of this is the Dixie Cup Company.

## Creation

A risk management professional should be able to recognize which assets can be protected by trademark law. Trademarks are created when the mark is first used on a product or in product marketing. The business that first uses the mark is considered to be the mark's owner. There are two requirements for trademark creation. The first is that the mark must be distinctive. The second is that the trademark's owner must be the first to use the trademark.

The first requirement, that the trademark be distinctive, is satisfied if it is memorable because it is unique or unusual (making it inherently distinctive) or if it is ordinary but over time has become well-known to the general public. A trademark is distinctive if it is one of these:

- Unique symbol or logo
- Fabricated word (for example, Wal-Mart)
- Word that is unexpected in the context it is used (for example, Payroll Factory)
- Word that creates a fanciful image (for example, Spring Meadow Ice Cream)
- Word that describes a product's qualities (for example, Slim Fast Diet Shake)

Generally, if a word used to describe a product is not distinctive, such as A-1 Auto, then a trademark is not created. An exception to that rule is when the organization has used the word to describe the product for so long that a substantial percentage of the general public associates the word with the product—for example, McDonald's. Common words that have become associated by the general public with a product because of long-term usage are said to have acquired a secondary meaning. Trademarks with a secondary meaning qualify as being distinctive.

The second requirement of trademark creation is that the owner of the trademark must be the first to introduce the mark into the stream of commerce. This is accomplished by attaching the trademark to a product being sold or by using it in product marketing. Generally, the first to use the trademark in this way owns it. An exception to the rule occurs when another party files an intent-to-use trademark application with the United States Patent and Trademark Office (USPTO). The date the intent-to-use application is filed becomes the date of first use, provided the applicant attaches the trademark to the product or uses it in product marketing within a specified time period and follows up by registering the trademark.

## Duration

A trademark that has been entered on the USPTO Principal Register is protected for ten years (or twenty years if registered before November 16, 1989). The registration can last indefinitely, provided it is renewed every ten years. Trademark protection can continue indefinitely without registration. However, it is considerably more difficult to defend.

# Risk Control Measures for Trademark Loss Exposures

Risk management professionals should identify all trademarks and service-marks that their organizations use and ensure that each is properly protected. These risk control measures can be used for trademark and servicemark loss exposures:

- Notice
- Registration
- Searches and watches
- Licensing agreements
- Restrictive covenants
- Enforcement of rights

## Notice

The trademark owner can obtain additional protection under the law by registering the trademark with the USPTO. Once registered on the principal register, the mark should be shown with the symbol ®, to put all on notice that the mark is registered. Until registered on the principal register, TM should be used with the mark. Failure to show the mark with ® or TM can hinder the owner's action against an infringer. Claiming trademark ownership is also possible by filing an intent-to-use registration with the USPTO.

## Registration

The symbol ® can be used only if the trademark has been registered with the USPTO. If the mark has been registered and the symbol is not used, then much of the protection that would normally be gained by registration is lost.

Registering a mark has two advantages. First, it creates a presumption, even if it is rebuttable, that the party doing the registering is the owner. Second, registration creates a nationwide notice, not just notice in the local market where the party is currently operating.

Because registered marks have a shorter protection period than copyrights, the risk management professional should create a list of the registered marks to diary the marks' ten-year renewal dates. To facilitate the registration process, internal controls should be in place to document when the mark was first used in the stream of commerce. Likewise, documentation of the mark's continuous use must be maintained. If the mark's owner fails to continuously use the mark, then someone else may claim it was abandoned. If a court agrees, the mark's owner loses the ability to prevent the other party from using it.

It should be noted that not all trademark registrations are granted trademark status. A problem that could occur in the registration process is that some other party has registered the mark.

## Searches and Watches

Before a trademark registration is attempted and periodically thereafter, a search should be done to determine if someone else has a similar trademark or servicemark or has applied for a similar mark. A professional search-and-watch firm can do this. These firms can alert subscribers to potentially conflicting trademark applications and registrations when they are published for opposition and cancellation purposes throughout the world.

## Licensing Agreements

Licensing agreements should be carefully drafted before allowing anyone else to use an organization's mark. These agreements should address quality control issues if the mark is to be used on a product other than the trademark owner's own products. Additionally, the agreement should limit the liability of the organization that owns the mark if the licensee fails to meet quality standards.

## Restrictive Covenants

Restrictive covenants can be used to protect trademarks in much the same way they are used to protect copyrights. By agreeing to a restrictive covenant, if the other party were to infringe upon a trademark right of the organization, that organization has the additional protection created by the agreement.

The organization can assert that the other party is not an innocent infringer because it acknowledged, per the restrictive covenant, the existence of the trademark right. Further, it promised it would not infringe upon it. The promise, if broken, allows a breach of agreement action to be brought against the infringing party. The type and amount of damages may even be agreed upon in advance in the event an infringement has been found to have occurred. The parties may also agree to binding arbitration, thereby avoiding the expense of litigation. Each of these agreements within a restrictive covenant can simplify an organization's efforts to prevent further infringement and to recover from an infringement.

## Enforcement of Rights

Infringers should be dealt with in a timely manner with a cease-and-desist letter or notification of intent to sue. Any applications for a similar mark should be handled by filing oppositions to the mark with the USPTO. If the infringement continues or if the USPTO fails to act, more aggressive action may be required. Counsel may need to be retained to assert available legal remedies.

# PATENTS

A patent is a commonly used type of intellectual property protection.

A patent is a legal protection and a right granted by the United States government that gives its owner the ability to control who makes, uses, sells, or imports for sale his or her invention for a limited period. The length of that time period depends on the category of patent granted.

## Features of Patents

The three types of patents are utility, design, and plant. See the exhibit "Categories of Patent Protection."

### Categories of Patent Protection

| Type of Patent | Examples |
|---|---|
| 1  Utility | Machine<br>Article of manufacturing<br>Chemical compound<br>Process or method |
| 2.  Design | Ornamental features of a product |
| 3.  Plant | New biological asexually reproducing plant |

[DA01409]

A utility patent is a patent issued for an invention or a process that has some utility or usefulness. The invention does not have to be marketable to qualify for a patent, but the invention must work. A design patent is a patent issued for a design that is new or innovative or that is ornamental or aesthetic in nature. For example, a bottle shape would qualify for a design patent if the shape was new and did not affect the bottle's functionality. A plant patent is a patent issued for a biological asexually reproducing plant that is new. An example is the Sugraone grapevine used in wine production.

Each country has its own standards regarding what is patentable and how long a patent will last. An inventor can apply individually to each country in which he or she would like to have a patent or file an international application that covers many countries. Inventors need permission from the United

States Patent and Trademark Office (USPTO) to file for a patent in another country for an invention they have patented in the U.S. Failure to secure such permission can result in forfeiture of U.S. patent protection.

An invention does not automatically receive a U.S. patent. To be eligible to receive a U.S. patent, an invention must be new, useful, and nonobvious. Nonobvious means that the invention displays a level of innovation or produces results that are unexpected when compared with previous developments in that area (prior art). Also, the invention must be nonobvious to someone with ordinary skill in the applicable field. For example, a new dental tool would have to be nonobvious to other members of the dental profession in order to receive a patent. The inventor (or the inventor's employer) must file an application with the USPTO. The patent application explains how to make and use the invention and explains how or why the invention is different from other similar items. While patent applications may be filed by an individual or organization, many patent applications are filed by attorneys. Before filing a patent application, a patent search should be performed to determine if similar inventions already exist. A patent attorney or a patent search service may be employed to perform this search. Alternatively, a search can be done manually at the USPTO or online. Although it is not necessary to perform a search before filing a patent application, if a search is performed, then the results must be disclosed in the patent application.

Upon receiving a patent application, the USPTO publishes the application. The application is published eighteen months after filing. Before publication, the USPTO performs various administrative tasks, including assigning an application number, reviewing the application for completeness, assigning the application to an examiner, and adding the application to the USPTO database.

Once the application is published, third parties can submit information to the examiner about prior art. Many companies and inventors use monitoring firms to watch the newly published applications in order to protect their own patents or to object to a patent application. The examiner begins the review process sometime after the application's publication. Generally, the entire process, from initial application to the patent issuance, takes approximately three years. During this three-year period, the invention can be marked as "patent pending." Falsely marking a product as patent pending is a federal offense.

Examiners conduct their own searches for prior art and review the results of the applicant's search. They then review an invention to determine if it is new, useful, and nonobvious. After the review is concluded, the examiner may allow the entire patent as claimed, allow some claims in the application and reject others, or may reject the entire application. Rejection of some claims or the entire application is usually because the claims in the application do not distinguish the invention from prior art, the claims are anticipated (meaning they are not novel or obvious in view of the known prior art), or the claims are indefinite (meaning they do not really explain the invention).

If the patent application is allowed (accepted), the inventor receives a "ribbon copy" of the document bestowing the patent. To maintain the patent in force, the inventor or patent owner must pay regular maintenance fees until the patent expires. If the patent application is rejected in whole or in part, the USPTO issues an "Office Action" letter explaining the reasons for the rejection. The inventor (or the inventor's patent attorney) can reply to the Office Action letter by amending the rejected claims or by explaining why the rejection is improper. The examiner then reviews the amended claims and explanations. If persuaded, the examiner allows the claims and issues a patent. If the claims are rejected again, the inventor can appeal to the Board of Patent Appeals and Interferences. If the board rejects the application, the inventor's only recourse is to file a lawsuit against the USPTO in federal court.

If the patent application is rejected or the patent has expired, either because of the statutory time limit or for failure to maintain it, the invention enters the public domain. This means that the inventor cannot prohibit anyone from using it.

Patent applications must be filed in the inventor's name. The patent inventor owns the patent rights but may assign them to another party at any time. Inventors who sign "invent for hire" agreements with their employer often do this. Therefore, while the patent application may list the inventor, it may also show the employer as assignee of the rights.

The duration of patent rights depends on the type of patent, but in all cases is less than the duration of copyrights. These are the durations of the three types of U.S. patents:

- Utility patent—Twenty years from application date. A utility patent's practical life is approximately seventeen years because it takes about three years from the time it is first filed for a utility patent to be issued.
- Design patent—Fourteen years from date of issuance.
- Plant patent—Seventeen years from date of issuance.

A patent may expire if abandoned, which can occur if the owner of a patent fails to make a timely response to any request of the USPTO, such as paying the required maintenance fee when due.

## Risk Control Measures for Patent Loss Exposures

Obtaining a patent is only the first step in controlling patent loss exposures. The patent must be maintained with periodic payments to the USPTO. Patent owners must be diligent in looking for infringers, and once an infringer is discovered, be timely in asserting their rights. Likewise, the patent owners must be diligent in ensuring that they do not infringe on the work of others.

Patent owners must also be willing to defend against infringement claims. These risk control measures can be used for patent loss exposures:

- Notice
- Licensing agreements
- Restrictive covenants
- Freedom to operate search

While a patent application is pending, the invention should be marked as patent pending. Once the patent has been issued, the invention should be marked with a patent number. If the invention is marked with a patent number or as patent pending, a presumption of notice exists. This is important when dealing with infringement cases because it means that an infringer cannot claim the infringement was unintentional. Willful or intentional infringement entitles the patent owner to treble damages (three times the amount the judge or jury finds to be owed) and attorney's fees. If an invention is not marked, the infringer can claim the infringement was unintentional. Consequently, damages may amount to a reasonable royalty or provable loss.

Patents are often sold or licensed to others who can manufacture the invention. Language should be included in the sale agreement or licensing agreement that transfers the risk of infringement claims to the buyer or licensee. Likewise, when licensing or buying someone else's patent, the risk should be transferred to the seller or licensor. This language is the holdharmless language that is found in many contracts.

Some of the most technically demanding methods of protecting patents concern work for hire, hire to invent, and confidentiality agreements with employees. Any work for hire or hire to invent employment contract is typically drawn up by counsel. When the reason for the employment is a specific project (work for hire) or a specific invention (hire to invent), additional safeguards must be included in the contract. These agreements or restrictive covenants must be clear about the rights the employee will retain and the circumstances under which they will be retained.

The employment contract should define items of intellectual property, (copyright, patent, or trade secret) that are covered by the agreement. The agreement should require full disclosure of any discoveries, inventions, improvements, or ideas, whether patentable or not, that the employee makes or conceives during work hours using materials, funds, or facilities supplied by the employer. The agreement should specify whether prior inventions are included in the agreement and should include confidentiality and nondisclosure language. The agreement may also include a provision in which the employee agrees not to use patents or trade secrets belonging to others in the course of the employee's employment. In the event of an infringement claim against the employer, this provision helps show that the employer was not willfully infringing.

These agreements should be used with all new hires who will have access to intellectual property. Current employees should also be asked to sign such an agreement, if their positions warrant it.

In addition to protecting against infringement of their own patents, organizations need to protect against patent infringement allegations made against them. One risk control measure to prevent infringement allegations is to perform a freedom to operate search. A freedom to operate search reviews prior art and current patent applications to ensure that an invention currently under development does not infringe an existing patent. If the search reveals a pending patent of interest, the inventor must assess the potential effect that the pending patent, if allowed, could have on the invention under development.

One way to protect against willful infringement allegations is to get a reasoned opinion from an intellectual property attorney that an invention does not infringe on existing patents. While the inventor may still be found to be infringing, such infringement would not be willful. This is important in assessing damages.

# TRADE SECRETS

If an organization takes reasonable steps to ensure the confidentiality of information about an invention it has devised, the invention can attain the status of a trade secret.

**Reverse engineering**

A process used to discover trade secrets by taking them apart.

A trade secret can be anything that gives its owner an advantage over competitors and that is treated as secret. Not every invention lends itself to trade secret classification. If an invention's secret can be deduced by **reverse engineering**, then the item is better protected by a patent. For example, if a golf ball can be cut open to determine what the secret core is, it is better to protect it with a patent.

However, if a new type of protective coating is invented for frying pans and the secret chemical cannot be detected in the final product, maintaining this chemical as a trade secret is a good alternative.

## Features of Trade Secrets

A trade secret is created automatically—that is, without a formal application process. In fact, no mechanism exists to officially designate an invention, an idea, or a process as a trade secret. Therefore, this determination is often made by the courts. The starting point for the determination is whether the information regarding the invention, idea, or process has value and whether the information has really been treated as a secret. Courts answer questions to determine trade secret status:

- How well is the secret known outside the business that owns the secret?
- How much of the secret is disclosed to employees of the business that owns the secret?
- What steps are taken to guard the secret?
- What is the secret's commercial value?
- How difficult would it be for someone else to acquire or duplicate the secret?

A trade secret remains in force for as long as the secret can be maintained.

Once a trade secret is no longer commercially valuable, its owner may not want to continue efforts to maintain the secrecy.

An example of how a trade secret is terminated when it is no longer a secret involves a consortium of entertainment and technology companies known as DVD CCA. The consortium had sued the publisher of a computer program that allowed users to view DVDs using computers running the Linux operating system. DVD CCA withdrew the suit when it conceded the program had been available on hundreds of Web sites for four years and therefore was no longer a secret.

## Trade Secret Loss Exposures

Several loss exposures are associated with trade secrets. The most obvious is that another entity might honestly recreate an organization's secret invention, process, or method and get it patented. In such an instance, the organization that was relying on trade secret protection alone would lose that protection. Similarly, the trade secret might be stolen or simply disclosed as a result of negligence. If the secret is stolen, then a court could decide whether it was in fact a trade secret and, if so, prevent the thief from using it and require the thief to pay monetary damages.

## Risk Control Measures for Trade Secret Loss Exposures

Because no formal process exists for designating something as a trade secret, the risk control measures associated with trade secret loss exposures focus on maintaining secrecy. Whether something is a trade secret often depends on the risk control measures used to keep the secret confidential.

These are some of the risk control measures that can be used to ensure information confidentiality:

- Disclose the information only to those employees who need to know the information to perform their jobs
- Require a sign-in or similar security measure to gain access to the area where the secret information is used or maintained
- Control any documentation regarding the secret by using a safe, a "confidential" stamp, or a burn bag (a bag used to burn documents that are meant to be kept secret, in lieu of using a shredder)
- Require employees to sign a restrictive covenant in the form of a nondisclosure or confidentiality agreement

Having employees maintain a trade secret's confidentiality is difficult because of the constantly changing status of employment and relationships with employees. Trade secrets can be protected with confidentiality agreements and employment contracts. A risk management professional may decide that these types of agreements should be drawn up by an attorney with specific expertise in this area of law. A confidentiality agreement between an employer and an employee should define the nature and limits of the information to be covered by the agreement, as well as what efforts the employee must make to protect the confidentiality of the information. Having new hires sign confidentiality agreements is particularly important. Requiring existing employees to sign such agreements is often more difficult. Similarly, a nondisclosure agreement can be signed between parties who want to collaborate on a project. Such an agreement would contain language similar to the confidentiality agreement between employer and employee.

# VALUING INTELLECTUAL PROPERTY

Unlike traditional forms of tangible property, intellectual property is not easily inventoried or quantified. However, it is among many organizations' most valuable commodities.

An organization's intellectual property often provides its greatest distinction from its competitors and the most durable impression in the minds of its customers. A fast-food restaurant's "secret recipe," a decades-old brand name that is part of everyone's vocabulary, a unique device, or a client list, for example, can resonate more powerfully in the marketplace than any advertising campaign or corporate strategy. In many instances, an organization stripped of the distinction its intellectual property provides loses much of its value.

An organization can safeguard some of its intellectual property through copyright, trademark, patent, or trade secret protection. But because the essence of intellectual property is information and ideas, protecting all of it is challenging, as is assigning it a specific value. However, doing so is vital to managing the risk associated with intellectual property. There are several intellectual property valuation methodologies.

# Reasons for Valuing Intellectual Property

The importance of intellectual property to an organization's identity, market share, competitive strategies, and overall worth make determining its value essential. These are some of the specific reasons why intellectual property must be properly appraised:

- Even intellectual property that has been protected through copyright, trademark, patent, or trade secret protection is still vulnerable to infringement by third parties, particularly as technology makes it increasingly easy for intellectual property to be stored, transferred, and transmitted around the world. When it is faced with unauthorized use of intellectual property, an organization must quantify the resulting damage in order to recover. The property's monetary value is a necessary part of such quantification and any related litigation.

- As with a tangible commodity, an organization can generate revenue with its intellectual property by selling it or licensing its use. An accurately appraised piece of intellectual property maximizes its profit potential.

- Acquiring intellectual property is frequently the primary goal in mergers and acquisitions. An entity's worth in such transactions may be largely determined by the true value of its intellectual property. The intellectual property's value may be affected by the extent to which the target organization has sold or licensed it, how well the property is protected, and the nature of the target organization's ownership of the property, all of which could affect the merger or acquisition.

- If an organization pursues financing, securitization, or other means of acquiring capital, the value of its intellectual property, which may be substantial, could be a source of collateral.

- Because it is considered an intangible asset, intellectual property's accounting and taxation treatment differs from other types of assets.

- The value of a piece of intellectual property may be used to determine the proportion of risk management resources that should be devoted to it.

# Valuation Methodologies

These are the most frequently used of the wide variety of intellectual property valuation methodologies:

- The fair market value approach is the valuation method used by most formal intellectual property valuation reports as well as the standard recognized by the Internal Revenue Service and most courts. It assigns to a piece of intellectual property the value it would have on the open market were it to change hands between a willing buyer and a willing seller. This is also referred to as market value.[1]

- The income approach is the most prevalent intellectual property valuation method. It assigns a current value to a piece of intellectual property based on the discounted cash flows the property would generate over its useful life. The income approach is the most effective approach for risk management purposes because its formula can incorporate a number of risk factors.[2] For example, the discount rate can be increased when considering different types of risk that potentially affect the intellectual property's value, such as technology or regulatory risk. Also, the income approach examines various scenarios under which threats to the value of intellectual property could lower its income potential, leading to the prioritization of resources to protect it.

- The cost approach assigns a value to a piece of intellectual property based on the amount the organization invested in its creation and development. This method assumes that no other entity would pay more for the intellectual property than it would cost to create it.

# REPUTATION RISK

Managing an organization's tangible assets is one aspect of risk management; however, in an enterprise-wide approach to risk, intangible assets, which can often represent more than one-half to three-quarters of a company's total value, should also be managed.

**Reputation**

An intangible asset, a key determinant of future business prospects, resulting from a collection of perceptions and opinions, past and present, about an organization that resides in the consciousness of its stakeholders.

**Reputation** is an intangible asset that relates to an organization's goals and values, results from the behaviors and opinions of its stakeholders (stakeholder perception), and grows over time. It is the comparison between stakeholders' experience and their expectations and is the pillar of the organization's legitimacy or social license to operate. An organization maintains a good reputation when it meets or exceeds stakeholder expectations.[3]

For an organization to maintain a good reputation, it must earn and retain the trust and confidence of its key stakeholders. Additionally, a good reputation can differentiate one organization from another, thus creating a competitive advantage, or, in the case of a government agency, greater effectiveness and efficiency of its service to the community. While a good reputation is built over time, good can turn to bad in an instant of poor decision making. An organization that fails to meet stakeholder expectations risks earning a bad reputation. A bad reputation can cost an organization its stakeholders and even threaten the viability of the enterprise as a going concern.

Any event or scenario that could benefit or damage an organization's reputation presents risk to reputation. Successfully managing risk to reputation requires an understanding of these important concepts:

- Reputation as a key asset
- Key risk sources
- Systemic approach to managing reputation risk
- Implementation of risk management for reputation risk

# Reputation as a Key Asset

Reputation is a key asset to an organization because of its intrinsic, intangible value (its goodwill reserve or reputational equity) and because of its potential to generate (or erode) future value. The value of some intangible assets, such as trademarks and licenses, is quantifiable. Reputation, however, is not quantified on a company's financial statements as an intangible asset. Nonetheless, it is a key asset whose value is based on the beliefs of its stakeholders. For example, an organization's reputation might facilitate the recruitment of high-potential employees, who will, in turn, enhance the organization's value over time.

Managing risk to an organization's "reputation asset" involves managing stakeholder expectations and understanding that reputation is subject to both threats and opportunities. An organization should identify its key stakeholders and prioritize them in terms of relative importance because stakeholders' expectations and perceptions vary by enterprise. For example, a financial services organization might have government regulators as a key stakeholder, whereas a commercial builder might not. Conversely, a commercial builder might have its raw material suppliers (lumber, steel) as key stakeholders, whereas a financial services organization would not. As another example, a department of defense has many contractors and engineers as stakeholders, while a public health organization has many medical providers as stakeholders.

Additionally, the perspectives of each of these organizations' key stakeholders differ. For example, the builder's lumber supplier might have an expectation of a steady flow of product orders. A steady flow of product orders keeps the stakeholder satisfied and might minimize the need for a high level of communication as long as the stakeholder remains the lumber supplier of choice. Alternatively, the financial services company's government regulator stakeholders play a major role in daily business operations and might require frequent interactions to ensure their expectations are being met.

Stakeholders can be classified as internal—for example, an organization's management, executive board, and employees—and external, such as shareholders, customers, suppliers, regulators, governmental entities, and so forth.

A power/interest matrix can be used to capture the broad range of an organization's stakeholders and prioritize their importance. For example, a matrix may be applied to a scenario in which a garment maker has an exclusive contract with a major retailer as its sales arm (high power/high interest in the quality of the garment maker's reputation for quality and value). According to the matrix, the garment maker would want to expend maximum effort to maintain its reputation for quality and value with the major retailer. Conversely, the garment maker's zipper supplier may have no power and little interest in the garment maker's reputation. Thus, the garment maker may expend minimal efforts to maintain its reputation with the zipper manufacturer. See the exhibit "Power/Interest Matrix for Prioritizing Stakeholders."

## Power/Interest Matrix for Prioritizing Stakeholders

| Interest | | Low Power | High Power |
|---|---|---|---|
| **High** | | Keep Informed | Maximum Efforts |
| **Low** | | Minimum Efforts | Keep Satisfied |
| | | Low | High |
| | | **Power** | |

[DA03844]

# Key Risk Sources

Risks to an organization, such as legal and regulatory noncompliance, unethical behavior on the part of the board of directors or senior management, or the filing of major lawsuits, can threaten reputation as a key asset. However, when examining risk to reputation, organizations often consider only the downside, or threats that could adversely affect the company. The upside of risk—leveraging opportunities to enhance reputation—should also be considered. For example, shifts in the competitive marketplace or uncertainty surrounding environmental concerns could create opportunities for companies to focus on more profitable areas or to gain a competitive advantage by developing "green" technologies or alternatives.

In fact, leading companies search for ways to exploit risk and seek to maximize the positive consequences of risk and the respective probabilities of successfully achieving gains. Procter & Gamble (P&G), a well-known multinational company, established its five sustainability strategies with specific, measurable goals in key areas.[4] As a direct result of this risk-exploitation strategy, P&G has received numerous environmental awards that strengthen its brand reputation among its customers. Such recognition also contributes to product innovations that help to improve P&G's financial and reputational results.

Key sources of risks to reputation must be identified in order for an organization to protect—or take advantage of—its reputation. A number of global business surveys have consistently identified key drivers of reputation that then become the sources of risk to reputation.

An organization should consider how each of the key drivers interacts with its stakeholders. For example, if an organization identifies "the community" as one of its stakeholders, that stakeholder group would drive corporate social responsibility as a possible risk to reputation. See the exhibit "Key Drivers of Reputation and Sources of Risk."

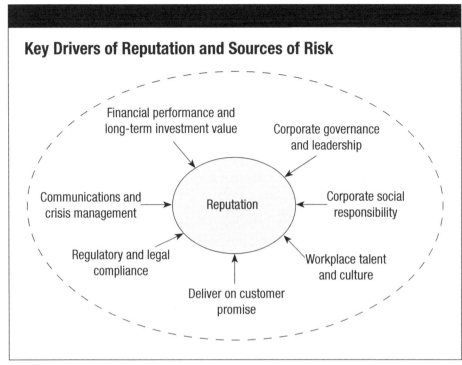

**Key Drivers of Reputation and Sources of Risk**

Source: Adapted from Galliard, Hindson, Louisot, and Rayner, "Managing Reputational Risk," an unpublished research article written in 2009. [DA03847]

# Systemic Approach to Managing Reputation Risk

An organization continually interacts with its stakeholders, its environment (internal and external), and its resources. All of these elements should be considered from a systemic, holistic perspective to determine, as they interact with the organization and with each other, what risk they present to reputation.

A systemic approach to risk to reputation can be examined by studying "The Essential Triangle," the mechanism of reputation, and the potential negative impact on reputation.

An organization is a dynamic combination of interactions among the organization itself, its message, and its stakeholders' expectations, known as "The Essential Triangle."[5] Reputation can be either enhanced or damaged as a consequence of these interactions.

In a systemic approach, the organization is considered within the context of a complex combination of available resources. Stakeholders have expectations regarding how these resources should be managed. The organization must work to gain the trust of stakeholders and assure them that resources are being integrated and optimized. Many organizations use transparent business practices and good governance to achieve this goal. For instance, a company could have a communication policy that includes periodic messages to shareholders about decision making, partnering, and acquisitions. The message that the organization transmits to its stakeholders is vitally important, especially concerning its business plans, its values, and its goals. The relationship between the communication and stakeholders' expectations can either enhance or damage the organization's reputation.

A systemic approach to risk to reputation also involves carefully managing the organization's interactions with the general public, its stakeholders, and its employees. The mechanism of reputation, or how the organization interacts with and communicates its message to its stakeholders on an everyday basis, can be expressed by grouping the key drivers of reputation around three ethical dimensions: goals and missions, rules (laws and regulations), and values (internal forces).

The organization should ask certain questions that apply to the driver/dimension intersects, such as, "Are our daily business activities aligned with our corporate goals and mission?" "Are we compliant with (or do we exceed) current rules and regulations?" "Are our stated values or internal forces consistent with our strategic plan?" An organization's senior management is responsible for clearly setting the appropriate tone at the top.

By examining the mechanism of reputation through the key drivers of risk and several ethical dimensions, an organization reveals its risks to reputation when its message does not match expectations. For example, risk to reputation could occur as a result of discrepancies between the organization's employees or between its departments, between the organization's activities and its strategic plan, or between the organization's message and its stakeholders' expectations. See the exhibit "Mechanism of Reputation: Key Drivers and Dimensions."

The experiences that a number of organizations have had in recent years with reputation risk have been well-documented by the business and news media. For example, as it was revealed that particular banks were burdened with a poor real-estate loan portfolio or had invested in mortgage-backed derivatives, those banks saw large numbers of customers withdraw their deposits. Some banks became insolvent as a result. When news broke that certain automobile manufacturers were in dire financial circumstances, those manufacturers saw their new-car sales virtually cease because potential buyers were not confident that new-car warranties would be honored or that other services would be available if the manufacturer became insolvent. See the exhibit "Manage Risk to Reputation: Cases (Johnson & Johnson)."

By considering two well-publicized cases of reputational risk management and the experiences of the companies involved, lessons learned are developed.[6] Three factors are common to both cases cited: the companies quickly recognized that they had a risk to reputation, they rapidly made important decisions to manage the risk, and the companies' leadership and culture played key roles in successfully managing the risk. These factors are common not only to the companies discussed but also to the many other enterprises that have successfully managed risk to reputation during a crisis. Nor are risks

# Mechanism of Reputation: Key Drivers and Dimensions

|  | Dimensions | |
| Goals and Missions | Rules (Laws and Regulations) | Values (Internal Forces) |
| --- | --- | --- |
| **Financial Performance and Long-Term Investment Value**<br><br>• Does the company have a consistent record of financial performance?<br><br>• Does the company have good investment potential?<br><br>• Which stakeholders are most linked to financial performance? | **Corporate Governance and Leadership**<br><br>• Do the board of directors and senior management set an appropriate tone at the top?<br><br>• Does the business plan include a compelling vision and mission?<br><br>• Are the proper strategies in place, together with employees who are equipped with the competencies required to deliver on the business plan? | **Delivering on Customer Promise**<br><br>• Does the company have a consistent record of delivering high-quality, fairly priced products and services?<br><br>• Is the company a market leader in innovation?<br><br>• Is confidential customer information kept secure?<br><br>• How responsive is the company's customer service department? |
|  | **Corporate Social Responsibility**<br><br>• Is the company viewed by its stakeholders as a good corporate citizen?<br><br>• Do the company's actions reflect its stakeholders' long-term interests?<br><br>• Does the company minimize the negative impact and maximize the positive impact of its business activities on the environment and society? | **Workplace Talent and Culture**<br><br>• Does the company recruit, hire, train, and develop high-quality employees?<br><br>• How well does the company treat its employees?<br><br>• Does the organization's corporate culture inspire employees to take pride in their work and in the business, and to give their maximum effort? |
|  | **Regulatory and Legal Compliance**<br><br>• Is the company viewed by its stakeholders and by the general public as law-abiding?<br><br>• Does the company strive to comply with the spirit of laws and regulations rather than meet minimally acceptable requirements?<br><br>• Is the company compliant with its internal policies and procedures? | **Communications and Crisis Management**<br><br>• Does the company have a robust communications plan designed to manage stakeholder expectations?<br><br>• Is the company transparent in its business activities, and does it clearly communicate decisions and implications of decisions to stakeholders?<br><br>• Does the company not only have a crisis management plan but also engage in crisis scenario planning? |

Key Drivers

[DA03851]

## Manage Risk to Reputation: Cases (Johnson & Johnson)

| Johnson & Johnson | | |
|---|---|---|
| Johnson & Johnson (J&J), founded more than 100 years ago, is a global leader in consumer healthcare, developing and manufacturing medical devices, consumer healthcare products, and pharmaceuticals. The company's credo, defining its core values, was developed in the 1940s by Robert Wood Johnson, chairman, a member of J&J's founding family. The credo challenges J&J to place the needs and well-being of the people it serves first. | | |
| **The Event:** Tylenol product recall. Seven people died in September 1982 after consuming the painkilling drug. | Recognition | Authorities determined that certain bottles of Tylenol contained cyanide-laced capsules. The information caused a panic across the United States. At the time, Tylenol represented 17 percent of J&J's profits. Copycat cases of product tampering ensued, and hospitals admitted many patients who suspected they had been poisoned. |
| | | Of 270 total cases of suspected product tampering, the Food and Drug Administration estimated only about thirty-six of the cases were a result of verifiable product tampering. J&J was not responsible for the product tampering (the criminals are still at large). Still, the company recognized that it needed to assume responsibility and act quickly to protect the public—turning to its credo. |
| | Decision Making | Guided by its credo, J&J decided to take an extremely proactive approach to the Tylenol poisonings. It implemented an immediate nationwide Tylenol product recall, ceased Tylenol product advertising, and subsequently revolutionized the product packaging industry and regained consumer confidence by reintroducing Tylenol with tamper-resistant packaging. |
| | Leadership and Culture | J&J's top management, leading by example and following the company credo, placed consumer safety first, ahead of any concerns about any effect on profit. Although J&J had crisis management plans, the extent of the Tylenol disaster far exceeded any existing plan. Instead, J&J and its CEO turned to the company's organizational culture and business philosophy, believing that if they remained true to their primary responsibility of protecting customers, the business would once again thrive. |
| **The Outcome:** J&J continues to be a global leader in its business segments. | J&J recognized the severity of the risk, immediately acted to respond to it, and successfully navigated the crisis because of the strength and values of its leadership and culture. Although its reputation was temporarily damaged as a consequence of the Tylenol poisonings, it used extensive marketing, promotional, and communications campaigns to regain consumer confidence. Additionally, the threat to reputation was turned into an opportunity as J&J innovated tamper-resistant packaging. J&J's holistic approach to crisis management preserved and even enhanced its reputation. | |

[DA03852]

to reputation confined to the for-profit realm. Following Hurricane Katrina, many governmental institutions' reputations were enhanced by their response to the disaster, and others' reputations were sullied, resulting in leadership and legislated changes. Charitable organizations' reputations have been harmed by revelations of excessive executive compensation and by lack of transparency in the distribution of their benefits and services. See the exhibit "Manage Risk to Reputation: Cases (Mattel)."

## Implementation of Risk Management for Reputation Risk

Organizations can implement risk management for risk to reputation by following several risk management principles that must be viewed holistically, implemented actively, and monitored:[7]

- Identify, evaluate, and prioritize reputational risks—Identify key drivers of risk to reputation, evaluate the tangible consequences of the increase or decrease in reputation as an asset, and prioritize accordingly. For example, poor corporate governance can lead to ethical breaches. Depending on the organization, the subsequent impact of the breach on reputation can cause a decrease in stock price, a wholesale withdrawal of bank deposits, criminal investigations, regulatory investigations, or a financial-ratings downgrade.

- Develop and implement risk responses—The appropriate response to a risk affecting reputation is contingent on the source of the risk (for example, sources could be a recently acquired company, supply chain practices, or revised regulatory requirements), whether the risk is a threat or an opportunity, the exposure relative to the organization's risk appetite (risk assessments regarding whether an exposure is acceptable or unacceptable differ among organizations), whether the risk is treatable, and the cost of treatment. Risk responses should be implemented in ways that address the gap between the message communicated by the organization and stakeholders' expectations.

- Monitor and report—After risks to reputation have been identified, evaluated, and prioritized and risk responses designed and implemented, risks should be continually monitored by management, who should constantly be on guard for early risk detection so that immediate corrective action can be taken when required. Additionally, any changes in risk should be reported to the appropriate parties, whether internal or external to the organization, so that timely responses can be implemented.

When implementing risk management for risk to reputation, roles and responsibilities must be clearly defined. This begins with the importance of the chief executive officer (CEO) and board of directors in managing the organization's risk to reputation, but ultimately all of the organization's stakeholders play a role. For instance, the company's audit function can assure the board and

## Manage Risk to Reputation: Cases (Mattel)

| Mattel |
|---|
| Mattel, formed in the United States post-World War II, is today the largest manufacturer of children's toys in the world, with over 25,000 employees worldwide. Mattel has a formalized, highly structured approach to corporate responsibility and in the 1990s established its Global Manufacturing Principles (GMPs), which clearly state the desired product standards to which it aspires. |

| | | |
|---|---|---|
| **The Event:** Within the span of three weeks in the summer of 2007, Mattel suffered two major product recalls: one because of lead paint on toys, traced to vendors in China (lead paint has been banned in the U.S. in toys since the 1970s), and a second recall because of powerful magnets that could detach from toys and be deadly if swallowed. | Recognition | Lead paint, poisonous if swallowed, was discovered on more than eighty different Mattel product lines. Mattel immediately launched an investigation into the problem and at the same time initiated a product recall. As a result of the lead paint investigation, Mattel discovered a design flaw in various products using small, powerful magnets that could be extremely harmful if detached from the toys and swallowed. A recall was announced on those products as well. |
| | | Mattel recognized that it needed to act immediately to retain parents' trust and confidence. The lead paint recall was global and affected more than 1.5 million total items. The company was able to trace the source of the lead paint to specific times, locations, and vendors. Because the company was unable to make the same determinations with toys containing the problem magnets, it recognized that it needed to take a stance that would respond to its stakeholders' concerns, and so it recalled all products with the defect dating back to 2002: over 17 million toys. |
| | | Mattel also understood that, despite its GMPs, it had supply chain failure in China. Mattel recognized that it had to quickly remedy its magnet design flaw. |
| | Decision Making | Mattel took an extremely proactive approach to its multiple risks to reputation and business viability. Mattel has a global crisis management and communication strategy that it immediately implemented. Mattel's CEO assumed immediate, personal control over the crises, making clear to Mattel's management that they would do the "right thing." Mattel decided to be as transparent as possible, providing plentiful information about the recalls to concerned parents by holding press conferences and scheduling television appearances. Additionally, Mattel used the Internet, posting information on high-traffic sites designed to spread the word to key opinion leaders. |
| | Leadership and Culture | The message Mattel communicated to the public, its stakeholders, and especially parents was that the company assumed responsibility for the crisis, was committed to remedial actions and policies, would continue to communicate the status of changes, and would improve its products through better supply chain and product design controls. Mattel's CEO confronted the crisis directly, and the company did not attempt to hide the problem, blame others, or react slowly. Rather, it immediately dealt with the problem, made corrections to its GMPs, and strengthened its ethical standards. |
| **The Outcome:** Despite the cost of the product recalls and a depressed global economy reducing consumer spending, the Mattel brand rebounded from the crisis, and Mattel today retains its strong global position. | While Mattel terminated the contracts with some of its Chinese vendors as a result of the lead paint contamination, it implemented vigorous supply chain management using a GMP unit that grew to 500 employees after the crises. Vendors must now meet or exceed specific product specifications, and outputs are routinely audited to ensure compliance. Design changes were also made to Mattel products as a result of the magnet-related recall; magnets were subsequently encased in plastic to keep them attached to the products. Mattel's leadership reassured parents around the world with full-page newspaper advertisements outlining the critical steps it took to repair the damage done—part of an ongoing media campaign that focuses on GMP standards and corporate accountability. | |

senior management that the company's risk management program is effectively implemented.

Barriers to successfully managing risk to reputation are rooted in a lack of clarity, resources, or awareness. For example, some organizations place a low value on reputation as an asset, choosing to focus instead on tangible assets, while others are simply unaware of reputation's true value. However, a reputation carefully protected and built over time can provide the reputational equity required to help organizations navigate the inevitable gaps that will occur between stakeholders' experiences and expectations.

Organizations must also prepare managers at all operational levels to effectively respond to disruptions as they occur.

# SUMMARY

The economic value of intellectual property is derived from its owner's right to control its use. These are the four common types of protection for intellectual property:

- Copyrights
- Trademarks
- Patents
- Trade secrets

Copyrights protect all types of original expression. To be protected by a copyright, the work must be original, fixed in a tangible means of expression, and show some degree of creativity. A copyright is usually owned by the author who created the work.

The important features of copyright are creation, ownership, and duration.

A trademark is a device used to distinguish a product from its competition. A servicemark is used to distinguish an organization's services from its competition. The important features of trademarks are categories, creation, and duration. Risk control measures for trademarks include registering all trademarks, servicemarks, logos, domain names, and graphics and designating them either with the TM or ®. In addition, periodic searches of the USPTO databases should be made to see if an application for similar trademark or servicemark has been made.

Obtaining a patent gives the inventor of a new, useful, and nonobvious invention the right to that invention's exclusive use for a limited time period. The important features of patents are categories, creation, ownership, and duration. The three categories of patents are a utility patent, a design patent, and a plant patent. These risk control measures can be used for patent loss exposures:

- Notice
- Licensing agreements
- Restrictive covenants
- Freedom to operate search

A trade secret can be anything that gives its owner an advantage over competitors and that is treated as secret. The important features of trade secrets are creation and duration. A trade secret cannot be formally declared. To create a trade secret and to maintain a competitive edge, an owner takes reasonable precautions to keep the information secret. Whether something is a trade secret is often left to the courts to decide. Trade secrets endure as long as they are kept a secret. Therefore, the inventor or owner must implement risk control measures to ensure the information secrecy such as limited disclosure, limited access, and restrictive covenants.

Intellectual property is among many organizations' most valuable assets. An organization can legally protect its intellectual property, but it must also accurately appraise its value. Reasons an organization should assign value to its intellectual property include recovering adequate damages in the event of third-party infringement, pricing it for sale or licensing, valuing in the event of a merger or acquisition, obtaining financing, accounting and tax treatment, and determining the amount of risk management resources that should be devoted to it. Prevalent intellectual property valuation methods include the fair market value approach, the income approach, and the cost approach.

Any event or scenario that could benefit or damage an organization's reputation presents risk to reputation. Successfully managing risk to reputation requires an understanding of these important concepts:

- Reputation as a key asset
- Key risk sources
- Systemic approach to managing reputation risk
- Implementation of risk management for reputation risk

## ASSIGNMENT NOTES

1.  Daryl Martin and David Drews, "Intellectual Property Valuation Techniques," www.ipmetrics.net/IPVT.pdf (accessed March 8, 2012).

2.  David Bradford, "Intellectual Property Risk Management: IP Valuation and Protection," www.advisen.com/downloads/IP_)Value_Protect.pdf (accessed March 8, 2012).

3.  This discussion is adapted from "Managing Reputational Risk," an unpublished research article written in 2009 by Sophie Gaultier Gaillard, Alex Hindson, Jean-Paul Louisot, and Jenny Rayner.

4. "Procter & Gamble Deepens Corporate Commitment to Sustainability," March 26, 2009, www.pg.com/news/sustainability_goals.shtml (accessed July 30, 2009).

5. Adapted from Gaillard, Hindson, Louisot, and Rayner.

6. R. Knight and D. Pretty, The Impact of Catastrophes on Shareholder Value, Oxford Executive Research Briefings (Oxford: Templeton College, University of Oxford, 1997).

7. This three-step process, reflecting the process proposed in the ISO 31000:2009 standard, covers the six steps of risk management found in a traditional risk management approach.

# Legal and Regulatory Risk

## Educational Objectives

After learning the content of this assignment, you should be able to:

▷ Explain how civil law, criminal law, and regulation form the basis for legal and regulatory risk.

▷ Describe the consequences of legal and regulatory risk to an organization.

▷ Explain how each of the following is used to treat legal and regulatory risk:

- Avoidance
- Modification of an event's likelihood
- Modification of an event's consequences

▷ Describe the characteristics of these predominant legal systems:

- Civil law (including Roman-French, German, and Scandinavian)
- Common law
- East Asian
- Hindu
- Islamic
- Socialist-Communist

▷ Distinguish between public international law and private international law.

▷ Describe the legal foundations and the general scope of each of the following commercial liability loss exposures:

- Premises and operations liability
- Products and completed operations liability
- Automobile liability
- Workers compensation and employers liability

# 6

## Educational Objectives, continued

▷ Given information on an organization's legal and regulatory risk exposures, assess the risk and recommend treatment options for modifying the likelihood and/or consequences.

# Legal and Regulatory Risk

**6**

## BASIS FOR LEGAL AND REGULATORY RISK

Legal and regulatory risk includes uncertainties regarding the financial consequences of legal actions against an organization or noncompliance with statutes and regulations. Legal systems and regulatory requirements vary from one country to another.

The law recognizes that every person or entity has legal interests that are protected by civil law, criminal law, and regulation. Violating one of those interests is the basis for legal and regulatory risk.

The major bases of legal and regulatory risk fall into these categories:

- Torts
- Contracts
- Statutes and regulations

## Criminal and Civil Law

Criminal law is a classification of law that applies to acts that society deems so harmful to the public welfare that government is responsible for prosecuting and punishing the perpetrators. This body of law defines offenses; regulates the investigating, charging, and trying of accused offenders; and establishes punishments for convicted offenders. Civil law is a classification of law that applies to legal matters not governed by criminal law and that protects rights and provides remedies for breaches of duties owed to others. Civil law applies to all legal matters that are not crimes and involve private rights.

Society uses criminal law to prescribe a standard of conduct to which all citizens must adhere. A crime can be major (such as murder) or minor (such as a traffic violation). A felony is a major crime involving long-term punishment. A minor crime, or misdemeanor, is punishable by a monetary fine or short-term imprisonment. Summary offenses are crimes that are not felonies or misdemeanors under state law and that usually result in monetary fines rather than imprisonment.

Civil law protects rights and provides remedies for breaches of duty other than crimes. In a civil action, the injured party usually requests reimbursement, in the form of monetary damages, for harm. Written laws, such as statutes and ordinances, specify the nature of crimes and their punishments. Unlike civil law, under which an individual victim can file charges, in criminal law the government decides whether it is in society's best interests to press charges and to prosecute on society's behalf.

In some cases, a single act can constitute both a civil wrong and a crime. For example, a commercial truck driver causes the death of another driver as the result of a traffic accident. Law enforcement authorities may charge the driver with vehicular homicide, a criminal act. The driver and the trucking company may also be subject to civil action by the estate of the deceased party for medical bills, funeral expenses, loss of support, and other damages allowed by law.

# Torts

**Tort**

A wrongful act or an omission, other than a crime or a breach of contract, that invades a legally protected right.

The remedy for a **tort** is usually monetary damages. An organization is liable for any tort it commits through its agents, which can include employees; subordinates; associates; directors and officers; anyone using the organization's property with its permission; and anyone, including volunteers in some situations, acting on the organization's behalf. If its agents commit torts, an organization is generally subject to the same liability as are the individual agents. See the exhibit "Legal Risk—An Example."

---

### Legal Risk—An Example

Traditionally, due to cultural differences, litigation in Japan has been used less frequently than in other parts of the world. However, litigation rates have been increasing there in recent decades. One example is the lawsuits arising from the failure of the Fukushima nuclear power plant following the March 2011 earthquake in Japan. Several hotels and other hospitality-related businesses have filed suits against the utility that operated Fukushima. These suits seek damages for lost business as a result of the power plant failure and concerns about radioactive contamination in the area surrounding the plant. Such actions are a source of legal risk for the power plant operator.

---

[DA08625]

The wrongful acts that constitute torts fall into three categories:

*   Negligence
*   Intentional torts
*   Strict liability torts

# Negligence

Negligence is an unintentional tort. In other words, the wrongdoer (tortfeasor) did not intend the action or the consequences. Instead, the tortfeasor exposed others to unreasonable danger by failing to exercise the duty of care the law requires under the circumstances. The legal responsibility and standard of care established by the law are what a reasonably prudent person would do in similar circumstances. Negligence can be the result of carelessness, ignorance, or accidents.

## Intentional Torts

Intentional torts are actions or omissions that the tortfeasor intended, although the consequences of such actions may not necessarily be intended. Examples of legal interests that can be violated by intentional torts include these:

- Physical safety of one's person is an interest that can be violated by intentional torts such as assault or battery.
- Personal freedom of movement is an interest that can be violated by intentional torts such as false imprisonment.
- Protection of property is an interest that can be infringed on by intentional torts such as trespass, nuisance, or conversion.
- Security of reputation is an interest that can be infringed on by intentional torts such as libel or slander.
- Personal privacy is an interest that can be infringed on by intentional torts such as invasion of privacy.
- Economic freedom is an interest that can be infringed on by intentional torts such as false advertising, harassing or intimidating competitors or their customers, or any other action that a court determines exceeds the limits of fair competition.

## Strict Liability Torts

Strict liability does not require negligence or intent to harm. Strict liability torts typically arise when an organization engages in certain activities that are considered ultrahazardous or that involve product liability cases. Examples of ultrahazardous activities are blasting, harboring wild or dangerous animals, or manufacturing or selling certain hazardous products.

## Contracts

Both businesses and individuals form contracts, which are legally enforceable agreements between two or more parties. A contract may be as simple as the sale of a garden hose or as complex as the sale of an entire organization. Contracts establish the responsibilities of each party involved in the contract. A party that fails to comply with the contract's terms is said to have breached the contract. Individuals and businesses can become liable based on the contract's terms or based on the terms that can be inferred from the contract, known as implied warranties.

## Requirements for Enforceability

For a contract to be enforceable, four basic requirements must be met:

- Agreement (including offer and acceptance)—One party makes an offer that the other party accepts. Both parties must mutually understand and agree on the critical terms of the offer and the agreement.
- Consideration—Each party gives up something of value. Commonly, one party exchanges money for the other party's promise to perform some activity.
- Capacity to contract—The parties must have the legal ability to enter into contracts. A contracting party who is not of legal age, sane, or sober does not have the capacity to enter into a contract.
- Legal purpose—The contract must have a legal purpose and must not be opposed to public policy.

## Types of Contracts

**Express contract**

A contract whose terms and intentions are explicitly stated.

**Implied contract**

A contract whose terms and intentions are indicated by the actions of the parties to the contract and the surrounding circumstances.

**Valid contract**

A contract that meets all of the requirements to be enforceable.

**Void contract**

An agreement that, despite the parties' intentions, never reaches contract status and is therefore not legally enforceable or binding.

**Voidable contract**

A contract that one of the parties can reject (avoid) based on some circumstance surrounding its execution.

**Unenforceable contract**

A contract that is a valid contract but that because of a technical defect cannot be enforced.

Contracts may be **express contracts** or **implied contracts**. If a woman drives her car into a repair facility and asks the owner to fix it, and the garage owner agrees to do so, an implied contract is formed. The garage owner has agreed to use reasonable means to repair the car, and the woman has agreed to pay a reasonable price for the services. Of course, a good business practice would be for the garage owner to form an express contract with the woman that states the estimated cost of repairs. This would avoid controversy over the interpretation and enforcement of the implied contract.

A **valid contract** is one that meets all of the requirements to be enforceable. A **void contract** is not a contract because it lacks one or more of the requirements of a contract, such as agreement, consideration, capacity to contract, or legal purpose. Therefore, it is not legally enforceable and is without legal effect. A contract to commit a crime, for example, is void and unenforceable because it is for an unlawful purpose. Contracts involving fraud or material misrepresentations are **voidable contracts**.

Minors can form contracts, but the contracts are voidable. Some contracts are **unenforceable contracts**, such as an oral contract to sell land. Such a contract could possess all of the elements of a contract but be unenforceable because the law requires real estate contracts to be in writing.

## Statutes and Regulations

In addition to torts and contracts, statutes can impose legal liability on an organization. Statutes are created by federal, state, provincial, or territorial governments and often modify the duties owed to others. In fact, violating the duties imposed by a statute may be used as evidence that the organization breached the duty of care owed to another. Violating a statute also imposes legal liability on an organization regardless of whether the organization committed any tort or assumed any liability under a contract. Statutes are also the basis for most criminal laws.

Examples of statutes that impose legal liability on an organization are tax laws, mail and wire fraud laws, antitrust laws, racketeering laws, and anti-discrimination laws. They also include corporate governance laws such as the Sarbanes-Oxley Public Company Reform and Investor Protection Act of 2002 (Sarbanes-Oxley) in the United States. Sarbanes-Oxley, which applies to publicly traded organizations, requires the principal executive officer and principal financial officer to certify that they have reviewed the corporation's quarterly and annual financial statements. Furthermore, the law requires that the officers certify that the report contains no untrue statements and fairly presents the corporation's financial conditions. These requirements represent a significant source of legal risk for the organization. Similar laws are J-SOX in Japan, the Financial Security Law of France, and the German Corporate Governance Code.

Statutes often do not include all the details necessary for an individual or an organization to abide by the law. To provide these details, governments authorize certain agencies to create regulations. For example, in the U.S., the Environmental Protection Agency (EPA) is authorized to issue regulations for laws protecting the environment. A regulation issued by the EPA might specify the acceptable level of a specific pollutant that complies with the Clean Air Act.

The issuance and enforcement of regulations vary in different regions of the world. For example, the European Union passed trade regulations that ban the import of pirated or counterfeit goods to the member countries. These regulations are binding as law for each of the members. This body of laws continues to grow, and many large organizations have full-time staff whose sole responsibility is to keep the organization in compliance with the applicable statutes.

## Apply Your Knowledge

Describe the types of activities that can result in strict liability torts.

*Feedback*: Strict liability torts typically arise when an organization engages in certain activities that are considered ultrahazardous or that involve product liability cases. Examples of ultrahazardous activities are blasting, harboring wild or dangerous animals, or manufacturing or selling certain hazardous products.

# LEGAL AND REGULATORY RISK CONSEQUENCES

The financial and other consequences of legal and regulatory risk can be catastrophic for an organization.

These are among the consequences of legal and regulatory risk to an organization:

- Monetary damages
- Defense costs
- Indirect losses
- Specific performance or injunction

## Monetary Damages

The consequence of many criminal acts is incarceration for a specified period of time. Criminal acts can also result in monetary consequences, such as fines.

**Compensatory damages**

A payment awarded by a court to reimburse a victim for actual harm.

**Special damages**

A form of compensatory damages that awards a sum of money for specific, identifiable expenses associated with the injured person's loss, such as medical expenses or lost wages.

**General damages**

A monetary award to compensate a victim for losses, such as pain and suffering, that does not involve specific, measurable expenses.

**Punitive damages (exemplary damages)**

A payment awarded by a court to punish a defendant for a reckless, malicious, or deceitful act to deter similar conduct; the award need not bear any relation to a party's actual damages.

Failure to comply with statutes and regulations can also result in penalties and fines. For example, under the Sarbanes-Oxley Public Company Reform and Investor Protection Act of 2002 (Sarbanes-Oxley), bonuses or incentive compensation paid to CEOs or CFOs must be repaid if their organizations are determined to have been involved in misconduct requiring a restatement of financial reports. The Dodd-Frank Wall Street Reform and Consumer Protection Act contains similar provisions for repayment of incentive-based compensation of executive officers because of noncompliance with securities laws. Such provisions are often referred to as "clawbacks."

Frequently, a wrongdoer in a civil suit will have to pay compensatory and noncompensatory monetary damages awarded by a court. **Compensatory damages** indemnify those who incurred losses because of a breach of legal responsibility. The two types of compensatory damages are **special damages** and **general damages**.

Courts may also award a sum of money in excess of the amount necessary to indemnify a party for losses. Sometimes called **punitive damages (exemplary damages)**, the purpose of these damages is to modify the wrongdoer's behavior and to set an example so the behavior is discouraged. The amount awarded is intended to be proportionate to the defendant's total assets. However, the amount can be large because a lesser amount might be an insignificant loss that would fail to modify behavior.

Alternatively, before a court verdict is reached, the wrongdoer and the claimant may reach an out-of-court settlement involving payment. Correspondingly, a wrongdoer convicted of a crime may have to pay a fine. The money to pay for these verdicts, settlements, or fines is the basis of the legal or regulatory risk for an organization at fault.

# Defense Costs

When an organization faces a civil suit or criminal charge, it must investigate the circumstances and prepare a legal defense. Investigation and defense costs can be the most expensive liability loss for organizations. Cases often require many hours of investigation and legal work to avoid, refute, or mitigate the charges.

Many cases are so technical that expert witnesses are required. Both parties in a technical case typically use expert witnesses, whose fees can be significant. Even the cost of reproducing pertinent documents or obtaining witnesses can be significant. Beyond the substantial legal fees, the defendant is usually responsible for paying all costs imposed by the court, including jury fees, filing fees, and premiums on court bonds.

Even if an organization has not committed a legal wrong, it can suffer a liability loss in the form of defense costs. A claimant might, for any reason, file an unfounded claim against an organization. This creates a liability loss because the organization must spend money to respond to the claim.

# Indirect Losses

As a consequence of the direct liability losses, several other net income losses are possible because of the filing of a claim against an organization. For example, having a director or an officer of a corporation face a criminal indictment, whether or not it results in a conviction, can cause substantial harm to a corporation's reputation. A loss of reputation eventually results in loss of revenue or market share.

The subprime mortgage crisis in the United States saw several lenders required to pay monetary damages to customers who were charged unfairly high interest rates or excessive loan fees. As a result of the negative publicity surrounding such actions, many of these mortgage companies either were acquired by other firms or went out of business. Such additional indirect costs can be weighted several times higher than the direct loss costs.

# Specific Performance or Injunction

In a breach of contract claim, a court might order **specific performance**. For example, a construction firm might have breached a contract by failing to erect a structure. A court may order the construction firm to complete the structure specified in the contract.

A court can also order a party to refrain from engaging in a particular activity. This is called an **injunction**. For example, a firm might burn construction waste, thereby spreading noxious fumes to adjoining properties and making the occupants ill. A court may prohibit the firm from burning its rubbish at the construction site.

**Specific performance**

A court-ordered equitable remedy requiring a party to perform a certain act, often—but not always—as a result of breach of a contract.

**Injunction**

A court-ordered equitable remedy requiring a party to act or refrain from acting.

Both specific performance and injunction can result in financial consequences because of associated attorneys' fees and court costs.

# MODIFYING LEGAL AND REGULATORY RISK

Legal and regulatory risk is categorized as hazard risk arising from liability risk exposures.

## Overview of the Procedure

The potential negative aspects of legal and regulatory risk can be treated in these ways:

- Risk avoidance
- Modifying the likelihood of an event
- Modifying the consequences of an event

These are not the only treatment options for legal and regulatory risk. For some situations, risk sharing (transfer) or retaining the risk may be appropriate.

## Risk Avoidance

There are two types of avoidance: stopping a current activity or never starting the activity. When an organization stops a current activity, the probability of any future liability is zero. However, the organization may continue to experience liability claims from previous activities. For example, a manufacturer that stopped making a defective product is still liable for losses caused by the products it manufactured and distributed in the past.

When an organization decides not to undertake an activity, it will not experience any liability claims related to that activity. Avoidance is usually used only in high probability-high severity situations. Although this risk treatment technique does reduce to zero the likelihood of the loss occurring, it is frequently a last resort because when an organization does not engage in the activity, it can never obtain the potential rewards. In other words, using avoidance as a risk treatment technique prevents liability losses, but also prevents any possibility of gain from the activity.

## Modifying the Likelihood of an Event

Modifying the likelihood of an event arising from legal and regulatory risk is often called loss prevention by some risk management professionals. This risk treatment method can be applied to these bases of legal and regulatory risk:

- Torts
- Contracts
- Statutes

## Modifying the Likelihood of Tort Liability

The risk management professional can consider contractual removal or limitation of tort liability and hazard control as a means of modifying the likelihood of litigation against an organization.

One way to prevent the likelihood of litigation is by removing or limiting the organization's legal obligations to others. Several different clauses can be added to contracts to remove or limit liability, including these:

- Waivers—A known right can be voluntarily relinquished through a waiver. For example, for a subcontractor to win a bid for a construction contract from a general contractor, the general contractor may require the subcontractor to obtain a written waiver of the subcontractor's insurer's right of subrogation.

- Hold-harmless agreements—These are contractual provisions by which one party (the indemnitor) agrees to assume the liability of a second party (the indemnitee). Hold-harmless agreements are commonly found in leases that require tenants to hold landlords harmless from claims made by third parties who are injured by the tenants' negligence. Construction contracts also contain hold-harmless agreements.

- Exculpatory agreements—These contractual provisions enable a party to avoid liability for negligence or a wrongful act. The participant in an activity signs a "release of liability" agreement for activities specified in the contract. For example, Jim is a risk management professional employed by a dude ranch that allows tourists to ride horses around the ranch's surrounding area. Laurie pays the ranch owner so she can ride a horse there, and Jim has Laurie sign a contract releasing the owner from any liability associated with her riding the horse. Under the exculpatory agreement in the contract, Laurie agrees not to sue the ranch owner for any injuries she might sustain, even those resulting from the owner's or an agent of the owner's negligence. The exculpatory agreement relieves the owner and the owner's agents of liability to Laurie.

- Unilateral notices—Liability can be limited if unilateral notices are posted so that they are physically apparent, expressed in language the other party understands (which is a concern if the other party does not speak the language used), and reasonable in extent (not forever or applicable to every possible risk). However, the lack of mutual consent, or absence of a freely bargained exchange of values, also limits the legal effectiveness of unilateral notices such as signs posted on walls, notices on backs of ticket stubs, or limitations on product warranties.

**Hazard** control is another method to modify the likelihood of legal risk. Hazard control involves implementing risk control measures that eliminate or reduce hazards. A key aspect of risk control for tort liability is hazard control for the risk exposures covered under an insurance policy, such as premises and operations, products, and completed operations. The specific hazards related to these liability risk exposures vary by organization.

**Hazard**

A condition that increases the frequency or severity of a loss.

For premises and operations, these are the risk control areas of particular concern to a risk management professional:

- Parking lots
- Building entrances and exits
- Walking surfaces
- Merchandise displays and counters
- Escalators, elevators, and stairways

Proper maintenance and housekeeping in these areas can reduce the chance of injury and subsequent litigation.

The products and completed operations liability risk exposure varies by the type of product manufactured, distributed, or sold; or by the type of operation completed. However, there are sound general risk control measures that organizations should consider regardless of the type of product or completed operation. These include proper design and testing of products, quality control, and clear instructions or technical manuals.

## Modifying the Likelihood of Contractual Liability

Organizations enter into a variety of contractual agreements that subject the organization to a wide range of legal responsibilities. Examples include leases, purchase orders, sales contracts, shipping agreements, exculpatory agreements, and hold-harmless agreements.

A primary measure to reduce the likelihood for contractual liability is to have most if not all contracts reviewed by counsel, preferably before they are signed. In addition, contractual liability can be prevented through other measures, such as using written contracts rather than oral contracts that rely on memory and word of mouth. This is true even in long-term business relationships. Care must be taken when committing an agreement to writing that the contract accurately reflects the intentions of both parties. Terms that are vague or ambiguous may be used against the party who drafted the agreement.

## Modifying the Likelihood of Statutory Liability

Risk management professionals can help prevent statutory liability by understanding statutory compliance requirements applicable to their organizations. This understanding can be gained from information acquired from several sources. One source is internal experts who are knowledgeable about statutory requirements. If the organization does not have such persons on staff, it may turn to an external expert or consultant with this expertise. Another source is trade associations, which often provide training courses to educate their members about compliance issues. Additionally, legal libraries, both physical and online, can provide the needed information.

Once this information is obtained, these same sources may help determine how to fulfill the statutory obligations. Once a plan is devised about how to fulfill those obligations, responsibility must be assigned to ensure that the organization stays in compliance. The risk management professional must be vigilant in monitoring the activities of those assigned with compliance responsibilities.

Compliance with corporate governance statutes must be directed by senior management and the corporate board of directors. Directors and officers must place the interests of the corporation above their own and must be alert for signs that this standard is not being met. A board of directors cannot be a rubber stamp for management; it must maintain its independence and devote sufficient time and resources to understanding the firm's operations. Open, clear, and concise communication among directors and officers is an important factor in preventing or reducing losses. Directors and officers must have a clear understanding of the corporation's charter and bylaws, as well as securities laws and antitrust laws, and they must avoid taking actions that would violate any of these. Executive compensation packages should provide incentives for long-term results to reduce the likelihood of noncompliance with regulations and promote ethical decision making.

A corporate code of conduct is also an important technique to modify the likelihood of statutory liability. This code provides all employees with the organization's mission and commitment to ethical behavior and outlines applicable policies and the importance of regulatory compliance. In global organizations, the code of conduct must reflect the various legal and regulatory environments of all of the jurisdictions in which the organization conducts business. For example, several retail companies have been criticized for using child labor in overseas factories that produce goods for the United States market. Corporate codes of conduct for such companies vary regarding this issue with some companies indicating a minimum age for employees while others forbid hiring children regardless of jurisdiction. Other codes state only that the organization must comply with the applicable local laws regarding minimum age of employment.[1]

## Modifying the Consequences of an Event

In addition to risk avoidance and modifying the likelihood of an event, risk treatment involves modifying the consequences of an event. For hazard risk, this risk treatment technique is often referred to as loss reduction. The purpose of this technique is to decrease the severity or effect of an organization's losses. As with modifying the likelihood of an event, modifying the consequences of an event can be applied to these bases of legal and regulatory risk:

- Torts
- Contracts
- Statutes

## Modifying the Consequences of Tort Liability

Two methods to modify the consequences of tort liability are the development of defenses and participation in settlement negotiations.

Developing defenses is an important step in the litigation process. The risk management professional should rely on legal counsel's expertise to develop the most effective defense strategy. However, the risk management professional should be aware of the advantages and implications of these five widely used defenses:

**Privilege**
A rule of law allowing a person to refuse to disclose confidential communications.

- Legal **privilege**—In certain situations, an organization's actions do invade others' legally protected interests and do cause harm, but those actions are legally excused because the organization has the right to invade another's interests to promote or protect one's own, greater interests. In resolving conflicts, common law establishes priorities among competing rights, particularly regarding actions that would otherwise constitute torts. For example, the law generally places more importance on protecting persons than on protecting property and more importance on preserving peace and order than on protecting privacy.

**Immunity**
A defense that, in certain instances, shields organizations or persons from liability.

- **Immunity**—Certain entities, such as governments and governmental officials, charities, young children, and the insane, have traditionally not been subject to lawsuits arising out of contract and tort law. Generally, children and the insane are incapable of the intent or lack the mental abilities usually presumed by legal liability. Governments and their officials have immunity when conducting regulatory activities so agents of the state can act without fear of legal retribution. Charities may be immune from suit so that their resources, largely donated for humanitarian purposes, will not be drained.

**Comparative negligence**
A common-law principle that requires both parties to a loss to share the financial burden of the bodily injury or property damage according to their respective degrees of fault.

- **Comparative negligence**—The degree of the defendant's and plaintiff's negligence may affect the court decision, the size of the verdict, or the severity of the punishment. In most cases, the responsibility may be proportionally shared between the plaintiff and defendant.

**Last clear chance doctrine**
A defense to negligence that holds the party who has the last clear chance to avoid harm and fails to do so solely responsible for the harm.

- **Last clear chance doctrine**—In some instances, the injured party had the ability to avoid loss or injury, but chose to act in a manner that did not avoid risk. For example, a pedestrian crossing a street at a red light may have the last clear chance to observe traffic and step out of harm's way, so the driver of the vehicle that strikes the pedestrian could be relieved of some, if not all, of the fault for causing the injury.

- Assumption of risk—If the plaintiff had a sufficient understanding of the risk and, as a reasonably prudent person, voluntarily accepted the risk, the plaintiff is considered to be in complete control of his or her actions. The defendant should not be held liable for the plaintiff's damages. While no one has perfect information, a plaintiff can argue that the defendant had superior knowledge and failed to disclose the complete risks to the plaintiff.

Another method to modify the consequences of tort liability is participating in settlement negotiations. An organization's risk management professional (and perhaps, for major claims, its senior management) should take an active interest in lawsuit negotiations. Before a final verdict, settlement negotiations might offer opportunities to resolve the suit more favorably than would the court. Therefore, regardless of whether any negotiations are handled by the organization's or by the insurer's legal counsel, the organization's risk management professional or other responsible executive should advise the lawyers in designing or appraising the acceptability of various settlement offers. Without such guidance, the attorneys might fail to recognize or might reject a possibly advantageous settlement offer.

The organization's role in these settlement negotiations is to participate in, advise, and guide. However, the attorneys should ultimately direct the settlement negotiations. If the suit is not covered by insurance, the organization's own legal counsel should direct the negotiations. If an insurance policy applies, this policy will almost always give the insurer the right to control the litigation, including settlement negotiations. In either case, however, the organization's risk management professional and/or senior management should ensure that counsel is aware of the organization's goals in any settlement and should be available to assist in settlement negotiations.

## Modifying the Consequences of Contractual Liability

Measures that can be taken to reduce the loss associated with contractual liability include these:

- Select a favorable jurisdiction—Usually, a clause negotiated into a contract specifies which state's law will govern the contract's interpretation. If the contractual parties are domiciled in the same state, that state's law applies.

- Include limits of liability—This measure tries to anticipate legal claims and to limit an organization's legal responsibility. The limit can range from zero to a specified amount.

- Include a liquidated damages provision—This provision limits the amount for which one party might otherwise be liable. These agreements are usually entered into before either party begins to perform under the contract.

- Include a valuation clause—A valuation clause can be included in a contract for the transportation or bailment of property to specify the valuation of the property in the event that it is lost, stolen, or damaged.

- Evaluate duty to mitigate—The party that claims the other party breached the contract still has a duty to mitigate or use good faith efforts to reduce the severity of its losses. As a defense, the breaching party can claim that the nonbreaching party failed to fulfill this duty to mitigate and therefore suffered greater loss than was necessary.

## Modifying the Consequences of Statutory Liability

Few defenses are available to an organization to reduce the fine or penalty it faces when it violates a statute, which is why most organizations work diligently to prevent violations. A defense commonly pled by organizations in these cases is that the statute was unconstitutional or was too vague or ambiguous to be enforceable. If the statute has already been tested on this defense and upheld by a higher court, it will likely not be effective.

### *Apply Your Knowledge*

The risk management professional for a manufacturer of power tools is reviewing the organization's products liability risk exposures. Describe the risk control measures the organization can use to modify the likelihood of tort liability related to injuries caused by its products.

*Feedback:* These risk control measures should be considered to modify the likelihood of tort liability:

- Proper design of power tools to avoid misuse or injury
- Testing of all products during production and prior to distribution
- Implement quality control procedures
- Provide clear instructions or manuals for the proper use of the power tools

# LEGAL SYSTEMS

Although no two countries have identical legal systems, many nations share legal approaches and concepts. Additionally, some countries classified within one system have incorporated legal concepts found traditionally within other systems. This section provides information about the development of different legal systems to give insurance professionals a basic understanding of the differences they might encounter in the international legal environment.

In a majority of countries, the legal systems fall into these two major categories:

- Civil-law system
- Common-law system

The civil-law tradition developed within these three distinct subsystems:

- Roman (and French)
- German
- Scandinavian (Nordic)

Other predominant legal systems include the East Asian, Hindu, Islamic, and Socialist-Communist systems.

# Civil Law

Civil law, or Roman-Germanic law, uses comprehensive codes and statutes to form the backbone of a legal system. This system relies heavily on legal scholars to develop and interpret the law. The civil-law system is the most influential system in the world. More countries use its subsystems, in one form or another, than any other legal system.

It is the dominant legal system of western Europe, almost all of Latin America, and parts of Africa and Asia. Additionally, the civil-law system can be found in parts of some traditionally common-law countries (for example, Louisiana in the United States, Quebec in Canada, and Puerto Rico). However, these legal systems can vary a great deal from one country to another in their legal institutions, processes, and rules.

In the civil-law system, a judge is a civil servant whose function is to find the correct legislative provision within a written code of statutes and apply it to the facts presented in a case. Judges perform little interpretation of a code, and their opinions do not determine their thought processes on legal issues.

The civil-law courts usually are divided into two or more separate sets, each with its own jurisdiction over different issues, with a different hierarchy, judiciary, and procedures.

The typical civil-law case usually is divided into these three stages:

- The preliminary stage involves submission of pleadings and appointment of a hearing judge.
- At the evidence stage, a hearing judge takes evidence and prepares a written summary of the proceedings.
- At the decision stage, the presiding judge decides the case based on the record provided by the hearing judge, the counsels' briefs, and arguments.

The civil law system does not have the common-law system's jury trial; instead, a series of isolated meetings, written communications, motions, and rulings help decide the case. Civil-law countries have varying time frames for these events; some countries' procedures proceed very quickly, and others proceed very slowly.

## Roman-French Law

The French civil code of 1804 consolidated the contrasting concepts of law by decree and law by custom. Although a magistrate is the final arbiter of a private law dispute, a court can rely on appointed experts, who have wide-ranging powers to investigate and present evidence to support an opinion rendered by a court. A magistrate usually will not reject an expert's opinion.

However, in France and Italy, a party can appeal a primary court's opinion, although courts in those countries tend to have extremely heavy backlogs. Under these circumstances, the examination of detailed factual or legal issues can be difficult because, with the passage of time, memories fade and some witnesses become difficult to find.

The French civil code was the basis for codes in the Netherlands, Italy, Portugal, and Spain. Haiti also adopted the French Code, and Bolivia and Chile adopted it for the most part. In turn, Ecuador, Uruguay, Argentina, and Colombia used the Chilean code as the model for their own legal systems. Puerto Rico and the Philippines used the Spanish code as their legal systems' model.

## German Law

Germany's location in the center of Europe has greatly influenced its political and social history. Many scholars consider the German civil law system as the most developed and influential of all the civil-law subsystems.

The German private law, or *Bürgerliches Gesetzbuch* (BGB), is the civil code that took effect in 1900. Unlike the French code, which was designed for laypersons to read, the BGB was developed for legal professionals to read and was too technical for laypersons. The German civil law influenced the U.S. legal education system; the American Law Institute's (ALI) restatements, or authoritative treatises, on law; and the development of the Uniform Commercial Code (UCC).

The original German code emphasized the rights of people to enter into contracts freely and dealt with the enforceability of all kinds of contracts. Similarly, the German code requires a finding of fault on the part of a wrongdoer in a tort suit. Although some elements of those concepts still exist, the availability of insurance as a risk- and damage-spreading mechanism has caused the German code to expand individual obligations and potential culpability.

Compensation for damages without culpability has effectively created a "cradle-to-grave" safety net as part of a wide social compact in Germany. For example, German statutes grant compensation for certain types of accidents, regardless of culpability, including railway, traffic, aircraft, electrical, gas, and nuclear power station accidents.

The German and Swiss codes, along with the French code, influenced code developments in Brazil, Mexico, precommunist China, and Peru. Additionally, Japan used the German code in the development of its own code, and Turkey used the similar Swiss code in developing its legal system.

## Scandinavian Law

The Scandinavian (Nordic) legal system is both a civil-law system and an independent system. The legal systems in the Scandinavian countries are based neither on large bodies of codified regulations, like those of the French and German systems, nor on case (common) law.

The Scandinavian legal systems evolved from a long-established history of customary law. Elements of law by decree developed as a result of Germanic and Russian influences. Additionally, the Scandinavian countries have codified historical business practices as statutes. In tort law, as distinguished from contracts, damages contain a punitive element beyond just and fair compensation.

The development of a virtually distinct legal system in Scandinavian countries resulted from the historically close links among those countries. For example, Finland was part of Sweden for hundreds of years until it became part of Russia, then eventually gained independence. Norway, now independent, was part of Denmark.

## Common Law

In the common-law legal system, a judge interprets the facts of a case, examines precedents (prior judicial rulings in similar cases), and makes a decision based on the facts in the current case. Precedents are guides, not rigid frameworks for all decisions. This system tends to be fact-intensive, relying on the judge's reasoning for a final decision.

England and most of the former British colonial countries, including Australia, Canada, India, and the U.S., use the common-law system. Japan's law combines the civil- and common-law systems, particularly relating to corporate law, which resulted from U.S. influence in post-World War II Japan. East Asian legal systems also influenced Japan's legal system. Other examples of blended common-law systems are Canada and the U.S. Both the province of Quebec and the state of Louisiana have state legal systems based on French civil law.

## East Asian Law

East Asian countries have a common background profoundly influencing their legal developments over the centuries. China has a dominant presence in East Asia. Although both Korea and Japan have different legal systems, they both reflect the Chinese influence.

Until the 19th century, Japan's civil code was based on the developing German civil code. However, this imported legal code did not supplant the local customary law already existing in Japan. Even today, a tradition of informal compromise, contrasted with individual parties' asserting their rights in negotiations, remains a strong characteristic of the East Asian countries' approach to contract disputes. Japan today has relatively few attorneys, judges, and lawsuits.

Other Asian countries have relied on both civil and common law to varying degrees. French colonialism influenced the legal systems of the southeast Asian countries Laos, Cambodia, and Vietnam for many years. By contrast, England's common-law system influenced the legal systems of Singapore,

Malaysia, and Brunei. U.S. influence was prevalent in post-World War II Japan and in the Philippines after the Spanish-American War.

# Hindu Law

Hinduism provides religious and philosophical rules in India and some surrounding countries. The Hindu legal system is perhaps the oldest in the world. The customs and laws of Hinduism have applied separately and distinctly to the members of four major caste groups: Brahmans (priests), Kshatriyas (warriors), Vaishyas (tradesmen), and Sudras (servants and artisans). Movement from one caste to another historically was not permitted, even with professional or political success, although laws have attempted to eliminate the rigid caste system. Legislation in India has voided all the rules of the caste system when they conflict with social justice.

By the early 1800s, most of India was under the control of the British, whose policy in settling colonies was to retain existing law, allowing Hindu law to become the official system for the Hindu population. The effect of British rule on Hindu law was the development of legislation, the judiciary, and the legal education system. A statutory code of commercial, criminal, and civil procedure has replaced the Hindu law of contracts and property. However, India's legal system still reflects remnants of the caste system.

# Islamic Law

The Islamic legal system is used in countries whose citizens are almost entirely followers of the Islamic religion. This legal system is based on the foundations of the *Book of the Qur'an* (*Koran*) and includes almost all of the countries of the Middle East and northern Africa, southern Asia, southeastern Europe, and parts of southeast Asia.

More Islamic countries are members of the United Nations than countries whose majorities follow any other religion. Islam is the second most prevalent religion in the world, with approximately 1.2 billion followers.

With the end of World War I and the collapse of the Ottoman Empire, Europeans regained control of most of the territories that Islamic warriors had captured in previous centuries. In the decades following World War II, many Islamic peoples attempted to gain their independence, often from European countries. Internal debates, still ongoing, centered on whether states should be theocracies or secular states that follow Islamic law.

The primary system of law within the Islamic countries is the *Shari'ah*, with a secondary system of jurisprudence called the *fiqh*. The *Shari'ah* consists of the two primary sources of Islamic law from which all legal principles derive, the *Qur'an* and the *Sunnah*. The *fiqh*, or Islamic jurisprudence, is the process of applying *Shari'ah* principles to both real or hypothetical cases.

The *Qur'an*, the highest source of law within Islam, gives followers of Islam the authority to make law and render opinions. The *Sunnah* forms a second tier of the *Shari'ah* and mandates the standard of conduct people are to follow to comply with the *Qur'an*.

The *Qur'an* is a religious book, not a legal code or book of law, but it serves as the foundation for the Islamic legal system. It contains specific precepts about ethics, crime, business transactions, domestic relations, inheritance, and war. The *Qur'an* differs from a code of law in that it does not mention the legal consequences of the disregard of its rules.

The *faqh* refers to the body of laws developed from the *Shari'ah*. Five schools of *faqh* (*faqh madhhabs*) exist today. Four are within the *Sunni* sect of Islam. The fifth school is within the *Shai* (*Shiite* or *Shiah*) sect of Islam. At times, conflict has divided the different *faqh madhhabs*. Identifying with a different school or attempting to change affiliation can be considered heresy. Additionally, at times judges prohibit intermarriage between the different *faqh madhhabs*.

Approximately 90 percent of all Muslims identify themselves as *Sunni*, with the balance being *Shai*. The *Shai* live primarily in Iran, southern Iraq, Syria, and Lebanon and believe that the leader of the Islamic religion should be a direct descendant of Muhammad. *Sunni* Muslims do not have this requirement. A significant difference between *Shai* and *Sunni* is that *Shais* also believe that individual reasoning (*ijtihad*) is a legitimate source of Islamic law.

## Socialist-Communist Law

The socialist system originated with the Marxist overthrow of czarist Russia in the October Revolution in 1917, which created the Soviet Union. Before the revolution, Russia was a civil-law country.

The result of the Marxist takeover was the imposition of socialist ideology over the civil-law system that already existed. The central idea of the system was the emphasis on the state's interest over that of individuals. Russia developed new codes that reflected the Marxist ideas that the laws should serve the interests of socialism.

Private-sector business legal principles, such as contracts, commercial law, torts, property, and bankruptcy, are of little use within a socialist system. Public law replaces private-sector legal principles. For example, because the government owns all property and production, all contract law is public. In a socialist country, the socialist political party controls and influences the entire legal system, including the courts. All decisions from the courts, although independent in nature, are subject to party control or revision.

Western civil- and common-law systems heavily influenced the law in Russia. Asian socialist-communist countries discovered problems applying the Soviet-style legal principles in their societies. The communist People's Republic of China, for example, abandoned the legal principles introduced to them by the Soviets and developed a more informal system more similar to East Asian traditions.

With the fall of the Soviet bloc in the 1990s, former eastern European bloc countries abandoned the socialist-communist legal system in favor of a civil-law system. Many changes were profound, with legislatures endorsing basic free market principles. The actual changes varied by country. Today, Russia is a civil-law country. However, the Russian government often changes the legal applications of civil law with regard to individuals and businesses.

Several other communist-ruled or communist-influenced countries, such as Cuba, North Korea, Vietnam, and the People's Republic of China, still use the Soviet-based legal system. The People's Republic of China now permits a private economy and has adopted it as part of the Constitution of the People's Congress. China's dominant constitutional principles still require observance of socialist doctrine. China also has adopted civil-law type of codification, the General Principles of Civil Law, and is developing an ever more extensive codification.

# INTERNATIONAL LAW

In any legal dispute arising between parties from different countries, public and private international law must be considered.

Those resolving international disputes between individuals or corporations first apply any applicable public international law, such as an international treaty, that governs the dispute. If no international treaty applies, then any relevant laws of the involved countries are applied to the dispute in accordance with the principles of private international law.

## Public International Law

**Public international law**
A law that concerns the interrelation of nation states and that is governed by treaties and other international agreements.

**Public international law** concerns the interrelation of nation states and is governed by treaties and other international agreements.

International treaties agreed to by a business's country of origin govern some international business transactions. These treaties may be between two countries, or they may be multilateral treaties among many countries.

The North American Free Trade Agreement (NAFTA) is a trilateral treaty governing all business interactions involving Canada, Mexico, and the U.S. Other treaties, such as the World Trade Organization's General Agreement of Tariffs and Trade (GATT), involve more than one hundred countries as signatories.

These international agreements affect member countries by requiring that they amend their national laws to comply with the agreements' requirements. For example, countries that signed GATT agreed to adjust their tariff rates on imported goods from other GATT member countries. However, these agreements are not limited to trade and tariffs. For example, NAFTA includes investment provisions, and the World Trade Organization's Trade-Related Aspects of Intellectual Property Rights Agreement ensures that the laws of member countries set basic standards for the protection of intellectual property.

# Private International Law

**Private international law** involves disputes between individuals or corporations in different countries and is also referred to as conflicts of law. It involves questions about which laws apply in settling the disputes and how they apply. It determines which jurisdiction's law applies to the business transaction in question, which country's court hears a dispute, and whether other countries will enforce the foreign decision.

In any legal dispute arising between parties from different countries, these two issues must be considered:

*   Whether a court in one country will recognize the decision of another country's court
*   Whether a court has the right to hear the legal dispute

The first issue is referred to as comity, the practice by which one country recognizes, within its own territory or in its courts, another country's institutions. Comity can also apply to the rights and privileges acquired by a citizen in a country. Many experts believe that comity is the basis for all private international law.

The second issue is referred to as jurisdiction. Just as in domestic cases, one of the basic questions of international law is whether a court has the right (jurisdiction) to preside over a particular case.

More specifically, courts in international cases must determine whether they have jurisdiction over the person or entity (*in personam* jurisdiction) and over the subject matter (*in res* jurisdiction) and if they have jurisdiction to render the particular judgment in the case.

In international cases, personal jurisdiction is based on whether the person or entity is present in the country or has committed the act in question in that country.

A significant issue frequently arising in international law is whether one country's courts have jurisdiction over either another country's citizen or a corporation with its place of business in another country. Jurisdictional issues are increasing in importance and complexity as governments try to control the increase in international business.

For example, one country's jurisdiction over Internet commerce originating in another country raises complex jurisdictional questions. Other cases involving jurisdictional issues include the U.S.'s attempt to prevent U.S. residents

**Private international law**

A law that involves disputes between individuals or corporations in different countries.

from purchasing prescription drugs from other countries, China's claim to all Chinese-language domain names and its blocking of certain Web sites, and some European courts' claiming authority over Web sites from outside their countries' borders.

# COMMERCIAL LIABILITY LOSS EXPOSURES

Every commercial entity is exposed to liability loss because of a wide variety of conditions or situations that can result in a claim or suit being made against the entity by someone seeking damages or some other remedy permitted by law. To correctly identify, evaluate, and manage an organization's liability loss exposures, one must understand how these exposures are categorized and the legal foundations of each category.

Commercial liability loss exposures can be categorized in many ways, depending in part on the purpose of the categorization. The exhibit depicts a broad categorization that reflects insurance practices. See the exhibit "Major Categories of Commercial Liability Loss Exposures."

---

### Major Categories of Commercial Liability Loss Exposures

- Premises and operations liability
- Products and completed operations liability
- Automobile liability
- Workers compensation and employers liability
- Management liability
- Professional liability
- Environmental liability
- Marine liability
- Aircraft liability
- Cyber liability

---

[DA12641]

Only the first four categories are discussed here:

- Premises and operations liability
- Products and completed operations liability
- Automobile liability
- Workers compensation and employers liability

An organization faces many legal risks. "Commercial liability loss exposures" form the basis of legal risks that can be covered by an insurance policy. The terms "premises and operations liability" and "products and completed operations liability" are terms used in insurance policies to describe the coverage provided for specific types of liability loss exposures.

## Premises and Operations Liability Loss Exposure

The premises and operations **liability loss** exposure relates to liability arising from bodily injury or property damage caused either by an accident that occurs on an organization's owned, leased, or rented premises or by an accident that arises out of the organization's ongoing (as opposed to completed) operations but occurs away from the premises. An organization's liability for such accidents is usually based on negligence—that is, the organization's failure to exercise the appropriate degree of care owed to some person under the circumstances.

Under the common law, owners and occupiers of land owe different duties of care to others on the premises, depending on their reasons for being on the premises. For example, an owner or occupier would owe a greater degree of care to a business guest or a customer than to an adult trespasser. Many jurisdictions have abandoned these common-law rules in favor of a reasonable care standard for owners and occupiers that applies under the circumstances to anyone who might be on the premises.

In some cases, premises and operations liability can be based on strict liability. For example, a blasting contractor could be held strictly liable for unintentional damage to buildings near the blasting operations. It can also apply to liability assumed by a land owner or occupier under hold-harmless agreements in contracts such as leases of premises, maintenance agreements, and construction contracts.

The premises and operations liability **loss exposure** includes bodily injury or property damage claims arising out of the use of mobile equipment (such as bulldozers and cranes). However, liability arising from the ownership, maintenance, or use of automobiles is treated as a distinct loss exposure, as is watercraft (vessel) liability and aircraft liability. Liability for employee injury or illness, whether based on obligations under workers compensation laws or based on common-law principles, is also regarded as a distinct loss exposure.

## Products and Completed Operations Liability Loss Exposure

Liability for products and liability for completed operations are often treated as components of one loss exposure. However, products liability and completed operations liability each have distinguishing characteristics.

**Liability loss**

Any loss that a person or an organization sustains as a result of a claim or suit against that person or organization by someone seeking damages or some other remedy permitted by law.

**Loss exposure**

Any condition or situation that presents a possibility of loss, whether or not an actual loss occurs.

## Products Liability

Products liability arises out of the manufacture, distribution, or sale of an unsafe, dangerous, or defective product and the failure of the manufacturer, distributor, or retailer to meet its legal duties to the user or consumer of the product.

Products liability lawsuits may be based on a variety of recovery theories, including negligence, misrepresentation, fraud, deceit, and breach of warranty. In negligence actions for products liability, the plaintiff must prove that the defendant failed to take reasonable care in the design, manufacture, distribution, or sale of the article that caused the injury.

Since the 1960s, many products liability lawsuits have been based on strict liability in tort. In contrast to negligence actions, under strict liability in tort, the conduct of the manufacturer, distributor, or retailer is irrelevant, and the focus is on the safety of the product itself. The plaintiff must prove three elements:

- The product was defective when it left the manufacturer's or supplier's custody or control.
- The defective condition made the product unreasonably dangerous.
- The defective product was the proximate cause of the plaintiff's injury.

Although products liability actions based on strict liability in tort are typically directed at the manufacturer of the defective product, the plaintiff can seek damages from any entity that qualifies as a seller, including a distributor or retailer.

## Completed Operations Liability

Completed operations liability is the legal responsibility of a contractor, repairer, or other entity for bodily injury or property damage arising out of the entity's completed work, as in these examples:

- Several months after a heating contractor installed a new boiler in an apartment building, the boiler exploded because the contractor had installed it negligently. The explosion damaged the apartment building and injured a tenant. Both the building owner and the tenant sued the contractor for damages.
- A family was hosting a picnic in their backyard. A wooden deck completed a few weeks earlier by a contractor collapsed under some guests, who were injured. They sued the decking contractor for damages.
- A repair shop overhauled a production machine belonging to a manufacturer. After the machine was returned to service, it malfunctioned and injured an employee of the manufacturer. The employee sued the repair shop for damages.

Under the common-law accepted work doctrine, a contractor could not be held liable for negligent performance of completed work once the owner had

accepted the work. Over time, courts formulated several exceptions to this
doctrine, holding contractors liable even after the work was accepted if the
contractor knew of a danger or deliberately concealed a defect in the completed work. Eventually, many courts abandoned the accepted work doctrine
altogether and permitted a right of action to anyone injured through the
contractor's negligence. Some courts have even applied the strict liability in
tort rule in much the same way as in holding the product manufacturer liable
to the ultimate consumer or user.

## Automobile Liability Loss Exposure

Automobile liability is legal responsibility for bodily injury or property damage
arising out of the ownership, maintenance, or use of automobiles.

Under the common law, ownership of an auto does not in itself make the
owner liable for injury or damage caused by someone else's negligent operation of the vehicle. However, many states have passed laws making an auto
owner liable for damages arising from any person's operation of the auto with
the owner's express or implied permission.

Auto liability loss can also arise from negligent maintenance of a commercial
auto. For example, negligent servicing of brakes, tires, or steering apparatus
may be the proximate cause of a truck's running into another vehicle.

Anyone who is injured or whose property is damaged as a result of the negligent use of an auto has a right of action against the operator. In addition, any
person or organization legally responsible for the operator's conduct can be
held jointly liable. For example, an employer can be held jointly liable for its
employee's negligent operation of an auto during the course of employment.
However, when an employee substantially deviates from the scope of employment, the employer is not usually liable. For example, if a truck driver deviates
from a prescribed route in order to spend the night at the home of a relative,
the employer would not be responsible for an accident that occurs while the
driver is on the way to the relative's home.

## Liability for Operation by Others

A person who negligently furnishes a defective auto to another person may be
held liable to a third person injured as a proximate result of the defect. Some
courts have recognized an exception to the general rule in cases involving a
used auto sold "as is," on the theory that the buyer understands (or can reasonably be expected to understand) that the used auto has not been inspected
for defects and should be inspected by the buyer before being put into use.

Similarly, a person who negligently entrusts an auto to a person who is
unskilled in its operation or otherwise incompetent to operate it may be held
directly liable for resulting injuries. To establish liability for negligent entrust-
ment, the plaintiff must show that the party entrusting the vehicle knew or
should have known of the driver's incompetence, inexperience, or reckless
tendencies.

## Auto No-Fault Laws

The goal of auto no-fault laws is to provide stated benefits for all persons injured in auto accidents without a need to prove fault. In the United States, nearly half the states have some form of no-fault system in operation.

Provisions in the no-fault laws vary widely. About half of the no-fault states preserve the tort system but require insurers to offer, or require all auto registrants to purchase, personal injury protection (PIP) insurance that provides specified first-party benefits for medical expenses, loss of income, or death resulting from auto accidents. These states are said to have "add-on" no-fault plans.

The remaining states have "modified" no-fault plans that restrict the right to sue for torts in motor vehicle cases and require all auto registrants to purchase specified PIP benefits. Some of the states in this category have a "verbal threshold" that defines the seriousness of the injuries (for example, total or partial loss of a bodily member or bodily function, permanent disability or disfigurement, or death) beyond which the right to sue is allowed. The remaining states with modified no-fault plans set a monetary damages threshold that, if exceeded, allows auto accident victims to sue.

A few of the no-fault states give auto owners the choice to either retain the right to sue or to accept some limitations on their right to sue. Those who accept limitations on their right to sue are charged lower auto liability insurance premiums.

Because the right to sue is not entirely eliminated, organizations that use autos still should obtain auto liability insurance or adopt some other risk management technique for handling their auto liability loss exposure. In addition, each state has either an auto financial responsibility law or a compulsory liability insurance law requiring motorists to carry minimum amounts of auto liability insurance.

## Workers Compensation and Employers Liability Loss Exposure

An employer's responsibility to pay claims under workers compensation statutes is a common example of liability imposed by statute. In the context of this discussion, the term "workers compensation statutes" includes the various state workers compensation statutes as well as federal statutes, such as the U.S. Longshore and Harbor Workers' Compensation Act, that have essentially the same effect as the state laws with regard to certain classes of employees.

In addition to payments required by workers compensation statutes, an employer may also be held liable for occupational injuries or illnesses of its employees as a result of either tort suits or hold-harmless agreements to which the employer is a party.

## Employees' Tort Suits Against Employers

The typical workers compensation statute is intended to provide an "exclusive remedy" for occupational injury or illness to all employees subject to the law. Exclusive remedy means that the only remedy available to an injured employee under workers compensation is to recover, on a no-fault basis, the benefits required by the applicable statute.

In practice, various exceptions, such as these, may allow a covered employee (or a spouse or family members) to make a tort claim against the employer:

- Claims for employee injury caused intentionally by the employer
- Claims by the employee's spouse for loss of consortium as a result of employee injury caused by the employer's negligence or other torts
- Claims for injury resulting from the employer's negligence or torts while acting in some capacity other than employer

Workers compensation statutes exempt some types of employees—for example, farm workers, domestic workers, occasional laborers, real estate agents, and employees who are members of the employer's own family. These employees retain the right to make tort claims against their employers for occupational injury or illness resulting from the employer's wrongful acts or omissions.

## Hold-Harmless Agreements

An employer's liability for the injuries of employees can also be assumed under contract. An employer who agrees to indemnify another party against certain types of claims may be agreeing (sometimes unknowingly) to indemnify the other party for claims made by the employer's own employees against the other party. See the exhibit "Liability for Employee Injury Assumed Under Contract."

---

### Liability for Employee Injury Assumed Under Contract

Miguel, a building contractor, agreed in his construction contract with Emma to indemnify her for any bodily injury or property damage claims made against her in connection with his work at her premises.

Carl, one of Miguel's employees, was injured because of a dangerous condition at the building site for which Emma was responsible. Although he was eligible for workers compensation benefits, Carl made a negligence claim against Emma because he believed that the damages recoverable in a tort suit would be greater than workers compensation benefits. Workers compensation statutes do not prohibit covered employees from suing persons other than their employers for occupational injuries or diseases.

Apart from his regular workers compensation obligations, Miguel was legally obligated by contract to indemnify Emma for damages resulting from Carl's suit. This case illustrates how an employer (or the employer's insurer) can end up paying for injury to the insured's own employee despite the fact that workers compensation is considered to be the exclusive remedy for on-the-job injuries of employees.

---

[DA04741]

# ASSESSING AND TREATING LEGAL AND REGULATORY RISK

Knowing how to apply legal and regulatory risk assessment to the facts of a case is an important skill. By carefully considering the facts provided and answering the Knowledge to Action questions, this activity should help you make the transition from knowing risk assessment considerations to knowing how to apply that knowledge.

## Case Facts

You are the risk management professional for a property development company that owns several large shopping malls and two hotels. You are in the process of renegotiating the liability insurance program that is due for renewal in three months. As part of this process, you must assess the organization's legal and regulatory risk and determine risk treatment options.

## Overview of Steps

Your work includes these two steps:

- Risk assessment
- Risk treatment

# Risk Assessment

Risk assessment includes risk identification and risk analysis. As part of risk identification, the risk management professional should consider the causes and sources of risk.

## *Knowledge to Action*

Which one of these sources of legal liability includes wrongful acts classified as torts?

a.  Contracts

b.  Statutes

c.  Negligence

d.  Regulations

*Feedback:* c. Negligence is the source of legal liability that includes the wrongful acts classified as torts.

The risk management professional should also identify commercial liability loss exposures. The organization can be held financially responsible for injuries to individuals or organizations for liability arising from these loss exposures.

## *Knowledge to Action*

Describe the premises and operations liability loss exposure for this property development company.

*Feedback:* The premises and operations liability loss exposure relates to liability from bodily injury or property damage caused by an accident that occurs on the organization's owned, leased, or rented premises. The organization's liability is usually based on its failure to exercise the appropriate degree of care owed to others.

The property management company contracts with a security firm to handle all security matters at its malls and hotels.

## *Knowledge to Action*

Describe the requirements for a contract to be enforceable.

*Feedback:* These are the four basic requirements for an enforceable contract:

•   Agreement—One party makes an offer that the other party accepts.

•   Consideration—Each party gives up something of value.

- Capacity to contract—The parties must have the legal ability to enter into contracts.
- Legal purpose—The contract must have a legal purpose.

---

As part of risk analysis, the risk management professional should consider the consequences of risk events.

---

### Knowledge to Action

A customer trips getting on an escalator at one of the malls owned and operated by this property development company. The customer suffers significant injuries and initiates a civil suit against the company.

Describe the types of monetary damages the company may have to pay if found negligent in this case.

*Feedback:* A wrongdoer in a civil case will have to pay compensatory damages to the injured customer. Compensatory damages include special damages for expenses such as medical costs or lost wages and general damages for losses such as pain and suffering.

---

## Risk Treatment

Risk treatment involves considering ways to modify the consequences of identified risks. The likelihood of litigation can be modified through contractual limitation of tort liability.

---

### Knowledge to Action

Explain how the property development company could use hold-harmless agreements to remove or limit liability from its tenants.

*Feedback:* The property development company could use hold-harmless agreements in the leases with stores and other tenants in the malls. Such agreements would require these tenants to hold the property management company harmless from claims made by third parties who are injured by the tenants' negligence—for example, if a customer in a restaurant within the mall were to be injured as the result of falling on a spill that had not been cleaned up by restaurant staff. The property management company's liability would be limited related to the customer's injuries based on the hold-harmless agreement.

---

Hazard control is another method to modify the likelihood of legal risks. It involves implementing risk control measures within the operation.

## Knowledge to Action

Describe some of the risk control areas that would be of particular concern to the risk management professional for the two hotel operations.

*Feedback:* For the hotels, the risk management professional would consider housekeeping and maintenance in the parking lots, building exits and entrances, and all walking surfaces. Stairways, elevators, and escalators are another risk control area to be considered.

---

The property management company enters into many contracts throughout the year, and the risk management professional is considering measures to reduce the consequences of contractual liability.

---

## Knowledge to Action

Which one of the following is a measure that can be taken to reduce the loss associated with contractual liability?

a. Comparative negligence

b. Legal privilege

c. Risk avoidance

d. Liquidated damages provision

*Feedback:* d. A liquidated damages provision limits the amount for which the management company might otherwise be held liable.

---

Another area of concern for the risk management professional is compliance with statutes and regulations in the various jurisdictions where the organization operates.

---

## Knowledge to Action

Describe the measures the risk management professional should take to assist the organization in modifying the likelihood of statutory liability.

*Feedback:* To modify the likelihood of statutory liability, the risk management professional must understand the statutory compliance requirements that apply to the shopping mall and hotel operations. Internal experts or external consultants can assist with this process. Legal libraries can also provide information on statutory requirements.

---

# SUMMARY

Torts, contracts, statutes, and regulations form the basis of legal and regulatory risk. The financial consequences of litigation, breach of contract, or non-compliance with laws and regulations can be a substantial source of risk to an organization.

The consequences of legal and regulatory risk to an organization can take several forms, such as monetary damages, defense costs, indirect losses, and specific performance or injunction.

Risk avoidance, modifying the likelihood, and modifying the consequences are risk treatment methods for legal and regulatory risk. These methods can be applied to torts, contracts, and statutes.

Countries share legal approaches and concepts, which can be grouped into predominant families of law. In general, countries adopt legal systems that are either civil-law systems or common-law systems.

International law comprises public international law, which governs the interaction of nation states, and private international law, which governs disputes between individuals or corporations in different countries.

Liability loss exposures can be categorized in many ways that reflect insurance practices. Such categories include these:

- Premises and operations liability
- Products and completed operations liability
- Automobile liability
- Workers compensation and employers liability

You should now understand how to assess an organization's legal and regulatory risk exposures and recommend treatment options for modifying the likelihood and consequences of those risks.

# ASSIGNMENT NOTE

1. Corporate Codes of Conduct, International Labour Organization, www.actrav.itcilo.org/actrav-english/telearn/global/ilo/code/main.htm (accessed February 9, 2012).

# Direct Your Learning ▶▶

# 7

# Management Liability and Human Resource Risk

## Educational Objectives

After learning the content of this assignment, you should be able to:

▷ Describe the liability loss exposures of a corporation's directors and officers, with specific reference to their responsibilities and duties and the types of suits that may be made against them.

▷ Describe the major types of claims associated with employment practices liability (EPL) loss exposures.

▷ Describe the legal foundations for fiduciary liability loss exposures, with specific reference to the Employee Retirement Income Security Act (ERISA) and the duties of employee benefit plan fiduciaries.

▷ Describe the following personnel causes of loss:

- Work-related injury and illness
- Retirement and resignation
- Work-related violence

▷ Explain how the following methods help risk managers assess personnel loss exposures:

- Risk assessment questionnaires
- Loss histories
- Other records and documents
- Flowcharts and organizational charts
- Personal inspections
- Expertise within and beyond the organization

▶▶

# 7

▷ Explain how the following risk control techniques can be used to mitigate losses arising from work-related injury and illness:

- Avoidance

- Loss prevention

- Loss reduction

- Separation and duplication

# Management Liability and Human Resource Risk

# 7

## DIRECTORS AND OFFICERS LIABILITY LOSS EXPOSURES

Both large and small corporations invite outstanding business, academic, and social leaders to join their boards to provide the benefit of their experience, advice, and contacts. The risk of being sued based on participation as a board member is a serious concern both for the prospective directors and the corporations.

It is important for risk managers and insurance professionals to be able to identify and analyze directors and officers (D&O) liability loss exposures. This requires an understanding of the role of directors and officers in corporations and the types of suits made against them. Because these suits can have wide-ranging consequences for corporations, as well as for the directors and officers who serve on their boards, risk control should be a key aspect in the management of these exposures.

## Corporations and the Role of Directors and Officers

A corporation is owned by its stockholders but controlled by its board of directors. The directors (sometimes called trustees) may be major stockholders and executive officers of the corporation, but directors also usually include outside business or social leaders who often have little financial stake in the corporation. A corporation's directors are elected by its stockholders in accordance with the corporation's bylaws (the rules by which a corporation governs itself).

The board of directors establishes corporate policy, makes major business and financial decisions, and appoints the corporation's executive officers (such as the chief executive officer, president, secretary, and treasurer) to manage the corporation's daily operations. The executive officers are not necessarily the only employees who are officers of the corporation. The corporation's bylaws may specify that employees above a certain rank or holding certain positions are also considered to be officers of the corporation.

Other types of entities have similar directors and officers. These other types of entities include public bodies, not-for-profit organizations, trusts, limited liability companies, and limited partnerships. Although the titles of the officials may differ, their duties are very similar to those of corporate directors and officers.

# Major Responsibilities and Duties of Directors and Officers

When directors and officers fail to fulfill their responsibilities and duties as required under the law, they can be held liable for losses that result. The major responsibilities of corporate directors include these:

- Establishing the corporation's basic goals and broad policies
- Electing or appointing the corporate officers, advising them, approving their actions, and auditing their performance
- Safeguarding and approving changes in the corporation's assets
- Approving important financial matters and ensuring that proper annual and interim reports are given to stockholders
- Delegating special powers to others to sign contracts, open bank accounts, sign checks, issue stock, obtain loans, and conduct any activities that may require board approval
- Maintaining, revising, and enforcing the corporate charter and bylaws
- Perpetuating a competent board by conducting regular elections and filling interim vacancies with qualified persons
- Fulfilling their fiduciary duties to the corporation and its stockholders

The fiduciary relationship is the most important aspect of the corporation in analyzing D&O liability loss exposures. In addition to performing specific functions, directors and officers occupy a position of trust for stockholders, the board of directors, and the general public. Breach of **fiduciary duty** is a common basis for claims against directors and officers. Directors' and officers' fiduciary duties include the duty of care, the duty of loyalty, the duty of disclosure, and the duty of obedience.

**Fiduciary duty**
The duty to act in the best interests of another.

## Duty of Care

Directors and officers have the duty of care (also called the duty of diligence) when performing their corporate functions. They are considered to have met their duty of care if they meet these standards:

- Act in good faith and in a manner they reasonably believe to be in the corporation's best interests
- Discharge their responsibilities with informed judgment and a degree of care that a person in a similar position would believe to be reasonable under similar circumstances

In applying the concept of the general duty to exercise reasonable care, courts have held that directors and officers are not guarantors of the enterprise's profitability. Nor are directors required to have special business skills. Instead, courts grant directors broad discretion under the **business judgment rule**. Directors and officers are not liable for honest mistakes of judgment even if the result is a financial loss, provided they acted reasonably.

**Business judgment rule**
A legal rule that provides that a director will not be personally liable for a decision involving business judgment, provided the director made an informed decision and acted in good faith.

However, directors and officers can face claims that their actions do not fall within the protection of the business judgment rule. For example, a claimant might allege that the directors did not use reasonable care in making a decision that resulted in a financial loss to the corporation, that they did not use reasonable care in reviewing financial statements, and other similar allegations.

Directors and officers have a duty to keep themselves informed of the facts and other matters required to make prudent business decisions. At a minimum, directors and officers have a duty to attend board meetings and meetings of the committees on which they serve. Many large, for-profit corporations pay their directors substantial fees to participate in board and committee meetings.

## Duty of Loyalty

Directors and officers have the general duty of undivided loyalty to the corporations they serve. Accordingly, directors and officers cannot usurp business opportunities that properly belong to the corporation. For the same reason, directors and officers cannot own or operate businesses that compete with the corporation.

Because directors (and sometimes officers) obtain their positions by the vote or consent of the stockholders, they also owe a duty of loyalty to the stockholders. Under the common law and the Securities and Exchange Act of 1934, no director or officer (or any other person) may use "insider information" to buy or sell stock of the corporation, whether the information was obtained directly or from others.

Moreover, section 16(b) of the Securities and Exchange Act of 1934 requires directors and officers of a corporation to disgorge back to the company any profit realized from sale of the corporation's stock within six months of its purchase, whether or not they had insider information.

## Duty of Disclosure

Directors and officers have the general duty to disclose material facts to all persons who have a right to know such facts and would not otherwise be able to obtain them. For example, directors and officers have a duty to make public disclosures of facts that are material to stockholders, bondholders, and potential investors in the securities of the corporation.

However, there are certain matters that directors and officers must keep confidential. Normally, directors are not authorized to act as spokespersons for the corporation. In addition, directors and officers must refrain from discussing confidential or market-sensitive matters with others, including family members and colleagues.

### Duty of Obedience

Some authorities include a duty of obedience (that is, obedience to the law) in the list of duties of directors and officers. Directors and officers are required to perform their duties according to federal and state law as well as the terms of the corporate charter.

## Types of Suits Made Against Directors and Officers

When various stakeholders in a corporation believe they have suffered financial or other types of harm, they may take legal action against the corporation's directors or officers. The activities of an organization that may give rise to a perception of harm are varied. A typical example is a suit by investors when a corporation's stock price drops significantly. Another example is a suit against a charity that sells an old building used to house the homeless and replaces it with a modern facility. Persons who believe that the old building was adequate might sue the directors for wasting the charity's assets.

Suits made against directors and officers are generally classified as either derivative suits or nonderivative suits. Another type of suit is a class action suit.

### Derivative Suits

A derivative suit is a lawsuit brought by one or more shareholders in the name of the corporation. Any damages recovered go directly to the corporation, not to the plaintiff-stockholder(s). However, successful plaintiffs are often awarded the expenses incurred in bringing the suit, including attorney fees. To be successful, the plaintiff-stockholders normally must establish that the defendants' conduct was outside the permissible boundaries of sound management practice, including the business judgment rule.

### Nonderivative Suits

Nonderivative suits against directors and officers are not made in the name of the corporation. Customers, competitors, employees, creditors, governmental entities, or other persons outside the corporation may initiate such suits. Stockholders who suffer harm may also bring nonderivative suits in their own names as opposed to suing in the corporation's name.

Nonderivative suits typically name specific directors or officers and the corporate entity as co-defendants. The plaintiff must show that an injury or injustice resulted from wrongful acts or omissions of directors and/or officers. Examples are suits for violations of legislative statutes; failure to fulfill legal duties; and intentional, unfair, or harmful conduct.

These are examples of common allegations made against directors and officers in nonderivative suits:

- Providing false or inadequate disclosure in connection with stock issuance
- Making or permitting false entries in the corporate books and records

- Preparing and signing false documents filed with regulatory authorities
- Failing to correct inaccurate statements within a prospectus issued by the corporation
- Failing to review annual financial statements and monitor corporate affairs
- Missing an opportunity for expansion, acquisition, or sale of the corporation

## Class Actions

A class action (or class action lawsuit) is a lawsuit in which one person or a small group of people represents the interests of an entire class of people in litigation. Many class actions against directors and officers are based on wrongful acts related to securities. A typical securities class action lawsuit commonly makes one or more of these allegations:

- The corporation's public statements (usually either in the corporation's communications with securities analysts or in its periodic reports to stockholders or to the Securities and Exchange Commission) contained material misrepresentations or omissions.
- The alleged misrepresentations or omissions artificially inflated the corporation's stock price.
- While the stock price was artificially inflated, insiders profitably sold their personal holdings in the corporation's stock. Following the completion of insider sales, the corporation's stock price dropped sharply.

The Class-Action Fairness Act of 2005 expanded federal jurisdiction over class actions with additional oversight of attorney fees in this type of suit.

## Indemnification of Directors and Officers

Under the common law, corporate directors and officers who have successfully defended against a derivative suit have the right to indemnification from the corporation to reimburse them for expenses they have paid to defend against the suit. However, defense costs and the amount of time required to prepare an adequate defense can be devastating. Accordingly, corporations in many situations make payment to settle claims against their directors and officers. The result is that the suit is terminated with no determination of wrongdoing. In such situations, the common law is not clear whether directors and officers are entitled to indemnification. The rationale is that a wrongdoing insider cannot justifiably be reimbursed by the same party that the wrongdoer's misconduct harmed. Some early cases even denied indemnification for successful defense because the expenditure of corporate funds would not benefit the corporation and would therefore be **ultra vires**.

As a result of the confusion surrounding directors' and officers' common-law right to corporate indemnification, state legislatures enacted statutes granting

**Ultra vires**

An act of a corporation that exceeds its chartered powers.

directors and officers the right to indemnification. Some of the statutes permit indemnification, while others require it. Some of the indemnification statutes are "exclusive" in that they authorize indemnification only to the extent provided by the statute. Other statutes permit directors and officers to benefit from any of the rights to which they may be entitled under any bylaw, agreement, vote of stockholders, or otherwise.

Determining what rules apply is a matter for competent legal advice. As added protection for directors and officers, some authorities recommend that indemnification wording in corporate charters and bylaws require indemnification, not just permit it, and require corporations to reimburse directors and officers for defense costs as they are incurred rather than when the case is resolved.

In most states, for indemnification to be allowed, the corporation must have adopted some form of contractual provision that sets guidelines for reimbursement. This provision—which can be incorporated in the bylaws, a corporate resolution, or another written agreement, such as an employment contract—can obligate the corporation to indemnify the corporate official as long as the requisite standard of conduct is in accord with the statute. Under the laws of some states, corporations can adopt provisions that indemnification will be denied only when the director's or officer's act or omission constitutes gross negligence or willful misconduct.

A related problem for directors and officers is funding defense costs before settlement. Indemnification is retrospective—that is, it occurs after the suit has been concluded. Defense costs can amount to hundreds of thousands, even millions, of dollars. Directors and officers generally want and need advances to cover these expenses before settlement. Most statutes provide that corporations may include provisions for advancing expenses.

Such advances are generally paid subject to the agreement that they will be refunded by the director or officer ultimately found not to be entitled to indemnification. However, agreements to refund advances can be difficult or impossible to enforce. Moreover, a provision of the Sarbanes-Oxley Act of 2002 prohibits corporations from making most kinds of loans to officers or directors. Some authorities view advancing defense costs as a prohibited loan under Sarbanes-Oxley.

## Controlling D&O Liability Loss Exposures

Claims against corporate directors and officers can create significant defense and settlement costs. Perhaps even more serious consequences are the amounts of time that key executives must devote to defending against the claims and the potential loss of reputation for the corporation. Although D&O liability insurance can transfer some of the financial risk of these suits, it cannot restore a corporation's reputation. Loss of a corporation's reputation can damage customer relationships, hinder access to the capital markets, and make it difficult to attract highly qualified executives. Therefore, risk control should be a central part of the management of D&O loss exposures. See the exhibit "Risk Control for D&O Liability Exposures."

## Risk Control for D&O Liability Exposures

These are potential pillars for a risk control program for an organization's D&O liability loss exposures:

- Adhering to the requirements of the Sarbanes-Oxley Public Company Reform and Investor Protection Act of 2002 (Sarbanes-Oxley)

- Establishing the independence of a corporation's board of directors

- Providing opportunities that encourage open, clear, and concise communication among directors and officers

- Ensuring that directors and officers fully understand the organization's operations, corporate charter and bylaws, and securities and antitrust laws

[DA06612]

# EMPLOYMENT PRACTICES LIABILITY LOSS EXPOSURES

Legislation has greatly expanded the basis for employment-related discrimination claims.

Employers face employment practices liability (EPL) loss exposures under a variety of federal and state laws. The first significant law in this area was the Civil Rights Act of 1964, which prohibits discrimination by employers. The act was amended in 1991 to include additional recoveries and to allow jury trial in discrimination cases.

Many states and even some local governments have employment-related laws that are broader than the federal laws. Although these laws can create EPL loss exposures, not all violations of them are covered by EPL insurance. In fact, EPL policies specifically exclude violations of some of these laws. Nevertheless, risk managers must be alert to the loss exposures created by these laws and develop strategies for handling both insurable and uninsurable loss exposures. See the exhibit "Laws Affecting Employment Practices Liability (EPL) Loss Exposures."

These are the major types of EPL claims:

- Discrimination claims
- Wrongful termination claims
- Sexual harassment claims
- Retaliation claims
- Other types of EPL claims

These classifications are not mutually exclusive. An employee may allege that a particular situation involves more than one employment-related offense.

## Laws Affecting Employment Practices Liability (EPL) Loss Exposures

| Name of Statute | What the Statute Does |
| --- | --- |
| Title VII of the Civil Rights Act of 1964 | Prohibits discrimination by employers based on color, race, religion, sex, or national origin. In 1978, the law was amended to bar discrimination on the basis of pregnancy, childbirth, or related medical conditions. The law applies to all employers with fifteen or more employees. |
| Civil Rights Act of 1991 | Amends Title VII of the Civil Rights Act of 1964. Depending on the size of the employer, the law authorizes damage awards up to $300,000 in lawsuits for intentional gender discrimination and racial discrimination in employment and allows a claimant the right to demand a jury trial. |
| Age Discrimination in Employment Act (ADEA) | Prohibits discrimination against individuals age forty or older based solely on their age. ADEA applies to employers with twenty or more employees. Amended in 1990 by the Older Workers Benefit Protection Act (OWBPA), which prohibits employers from denying benefits to older employees. |
| Americans with Disabilities Act (ADA) | Prohibits discrimination against disabled persons and requires an employer to make reasonable accommodations in the workplace for disabled employees. This law currently applies to employers with fifteen or more employees. |
| Family and Medical Leave Act (FMLA) | Requires that all employers with fifty or more employees provide up to twelve weeks of unpaid leave in any twelve-month period to care for a newborn, adopted, or fostered child or to care for themselves or a child, spouse, or parent with a serious illness. Amended in 1998 by the National Defense Authorization Act to provide new military family leave entitlements. |
| Fair Labor Standards Act (FLSA) | Establishes minimum wage and overtime rates and regulates the employment of children. This law applies to employers with at least two employees engaged in interstate commerce and a business volume of over $500,000 per year. |
| Worker Adjustment and Retraining Notification Act (WARN) | Requires employers to provide notice sixty days in advance of covered plant closings and mass layoffs. |
| Consolidated Omnibus Budget Reconciliation Act (COBRA) | Gives workers and their families who lose their health benefits the right to choose to continue group health benefits provided by their group health plan for limited periods of time under certain circumstances. |
| Employee Retirement Income Security Act (ERISA) | Sets minimum standards for most voluntarily established pension and benefit plans. |

[DA04876]

# Discrimination Claims

Discrimination does not have to be intentional to be unlawful. Many firms that do not consciously discriminate against individuals based on race, sex, religion, or other grounds nevertheless run afoul of the antidiscrimination rules developed to implement federal and local laws. Problems may arise because of the differences between overt discrimination, disparate treatment, and disparate impact:[1]

- Overt discrimination (also called intentional discrimination) is a specific, observable action that discriminates against a person or class of persons. An example of overt discrimination is refusal to interview job applicants of a certain race.

- Disparate treatment (also called unequal or differential treatment) is unfavorable or unfair treatment of someone in comparison to how similar individuals are treated. Disparate treatment occurs, for example, if female employees are regularly reprimanded for returning late from lunch but male employees who also return late are not.

- Disparate impact (also called discrimination by effect or adverse impact) is the application of personnel policies to all applicants or employees that have the effect of denying employment or advancement to members of protected classes. For example, requiring that all employees be more than five feet, ten inches tall will have a disparate impact because many more men than women exceed that height. Such a requirement eliminates more women than men from the pool of eligible employees. Unless the requirement is necessary for performance of the job, it is a violation of the law.

# Wrongful Termination Claims

Wrongful termination of employment accounts for the majority of cases of alleged wrongful employment practices. Wrongful termination includes "constructive discharge." Constructive discharge means employees who resign because of unendurable conditions can, if allegations are proved, be treated as if their employment had been terminated by the employer. See the exhibit "Equal Employment Opportunity Commission."

Many wrongful termination claims involve charges of discrimination, but it is possible to bring them for reasons other than discrimination. Traditionally, the legal doctrine of "employment at will" has allowed employers or employees to terminate the private employment relationship with or without cause at any time.

Several states base an exception to employment at will on the theory of implied contract. Under this theory, an employer's oral or written representations to employees regarding job security or disciplinary procedures are held to create a contract of employment even though no written contract exists.

---

### Equal Employment Opportunity Commission

The Equal Employment Opportunity Commission (EEOC) is an independent commission that plays an important role in workplace discrimination claims.

The EEOC was created by the Civil Rights Act of 1964. Originally, its function was to define acts of employment discrimination and to attempt to mitigate their effects by education and conciliation. In 1972, Congress gave the EEOC authority to sue nongovernmental employers, unions, and employment agencies. The EEOC could file suits based on pattern or practice, and Title VII coverage was expanded to include the federal government and state and local governments, as well as educational institutions.

Persons who believe that their employment rights have been violated may file charges of discrimination with the EEOC. In addition, an individual, organization, or agency may file a charge on behalf of another person to protect the aggrieved person's identity. If the charge also involves a state or local law, the EEOC "dual files" with the state or local agency, and vice versa.

The EEOC notifies the employer when a charge of discrimination has been filed against it with the EEOC. The EEOC can investigate and determine whether reasonable cause exists to believe discrimination occurred. The employer may opt to resolve a charge through mediation or settlement. The EEOC can ask for copies of personnel policies, the complainant's personnel files, the personnel files of other individuals, and other relevant information. An EEOC investigator is allowed to conduct interviews of nonmanagement-level employees without the employer's presence or permission.

The charge may be dismissed by the EEOC if it believes no basis exists for proceeding with further investigation. Employees do not have to submit a complaint to the EEOC to sue their employers, and dismissal of a complaint by the EEOC is not a bar to a suit by the employee.

---

[DA04877]

When this doctrine was first established, many courts held that statements in employee handbooks could create an implied contract, absent any clear and express statements reinforcing employment-at-will status.[2] In a typical case, an employee cited an employee handbook provision stating the employees would be discharged only for "just cause." The court found that such wording created an implied contract that the employee would not be arbitrarily fired.[3] Most employers have modified the wording in their employee handbooks to avoid these types of claims.

Courts in a minority of states hold that employment at will is subject to a covenant of good faith. Under this doctrine, just cause for discharge is required even when the employer has made no specific promise to limit discharges to just-cause circumstances. Terminations made in bad faith or motivated by malice are also prohibited.[4]

## Sexual Harassment Claims

The basis for sexual harassment EPL claims developed mainly in the last decades of the twentieth century. In 1980, the Equal Employment Opportunity Commission (EEOC) issued its "Guidelines on Discrimination Because of Sex," which defines sexual harassment as "unwelcome sexual advances...when submission to such conduct is made either explicitly or implicitly a term or condition of an individual's employment."

Some sexual harassment claims are based on the allegation that the employer created a hostile work environment. A hostile work environment exists when an employee is subjected to sexual harassment that is so severe or pervasive that it alters the conditions of his or her employment and creates an abusive working environment.

To prevail in a claim of hostile work environment, an employee generally must prove all of these facts:

- The employee is a member of a protected class.
- The employee was subjected to unwelcome harassment based on the protected characteristic.
- The harassment affected a term or condition of employment.
- The employer knew or should have known about the harassment and failed to take prompt remedial action.

Claims of hostile work environment initially were recognized in the context of sex discrimination, but they have since been recognized in other contexts, such as discrimination because of race or disability. Isolated incidents are insufficient to establish a hostile work environment. In determining whether a workplace is a hostile work environment, courts consider such relevant factors as the frequency of the discriminatory conduct, its severity, and whether it unreasonably interferes with the employee's work performance. See the exhibit "Controlling Employment Practices Liability (EPL) Loss Exposures."

## Retaliation Claims

EPL claims can arise from an employer's alleged retaliation for an employee's legitimate act. The number of retaliation claims filed each year with the EEOC has steadily increased since the mid-1990s. In the first decade of the twenty-first century, the most common grounds for discrimination claims were retaliation and racial discrimination, followed by gender discrimination.[5]

Retaliation claims may be combined with claims of discrimination based on race, gender, age, or another protected classification. Retaliation claims are also brought by employees who, for example, allege that they were discharged because they filed a workers compensation claim; testified against the employer in a legislative or court hearing; or were "whistleblowers," who are protected by many federal and state laws.

---

### Controlling Employment Practices Liability (EPL) Loss Exposures

Organizations can take actions such as these to reduce the frequency and severity of potential EPL claims:

- Establish hiring practices that comply with standards set forth by federal, state, and local regulations and laws.

- Word employee handbooks clearly and concisely to document the company's policies and procedures, including employment-at-will status.

- Provide all employees with a formal policy regarding sexual harassment and discrimination, and document their receipt. Review the policy and update it as needed.

- Permanently post and distribute all EEOC documents, as well as state and local compliance documents.

- Conduct employee performance reviews at least annually, and initiate interim reviews to correct unacceptable behavior.

- Follow a carefully documented termination procedure, and exercise special care when handling terminations.

- Conduct exit interviews and carefully document them.

- Promptly investigate all allegations of harassment or discrimination.

---

Joseph G. Jarret, "Reducing Employment Practices Liability," Risk Management, September 2003, p. 20. [DA06675]

## Other Types of EPL Claims

In recent years, employees have made EPL claims that do not fall within the context of discrimination, wrongful termination, sexual harassment, or retaliation.

For example, costly litigation has ensued after firms have closed plants or otherwise discharged large numbers of employees at one time. In 1988, Congress enacted the Worker Adjustment and Retraining Notification Act (WARN) to mitigate some of the effects of mass layoffs.

Another example is class action lawsuits on behalf of employees who allege that they did not receive overtime compensation. Such claims have resulted in substantial awards. The majority of the claims involve improperly categorizing employees as "exempt" rather than "nonexempt." An exempt employee, such as a supervisory or management-level employee, is not entitled to overtime wages, whereas an employer must pay overtime wages to nonexempt employees.

Employee claims have also arisen from objectionable email or website material sent by other employees.

## ☑ Reality Check

**Discrimination Cases Related to Overtime Pay**

In recent years, numerous class action lawsuits have been filed by pharmaceutical company sales representatives demanding overtime pay. The plaintiffs allege that they are misclassified as sales personnel when they do not actually make sales. Under the Federal Fair Labor Standards Act, sales personnel are classified as exempt employees—that is, salaried employees who are not entitled to overtime pay. The plaintiffs allege the nature of their work entitles them to overtime pay.

In a 2010 case,* an appeals court found for the plaintiffs. The court said the representatives do not sell drugs to physicians but provide them with information about the benefits of particular drugs and encourage them to prescribe those products. The court concluded, "[W]here the employee promotes a pharmaceutical product to a physician but can transfer to the physician nothing more than free samples and cannot lawfully transfer ownership of any quantity of the drug in exchange of anything of value, cannot lawfully take an order for its purchase, and cannot lawfully even obtain from the physician a binding commitment to prescribe it, we conclude that...the employee has not in any sense, within the meaning of the statute or the regulations, made a sale."

* In re Novartis Wage and Hour Litigation, 611 F.3d 141 (2010). [DA06676]

# FIDUCIARY LIABILITY LOSS EXPOSURES

Fiduciary liability loss exposures arise mainly out of the possibility that beneficiaries of an employee benefit plan (such as active employees or retirees) may make a claim against the plan officials (or fiduciaries) for breach of their fiduciary duties.

Fiduciary liability claims, once rare, are no longer either rare, nor are they insignificant. Under defined contribution retirement plans, such as profit-sharing and 401(k) plans, the size of an employee's benefit depends on the plan's earnings. In some cases, employee retirement plans that were heavily invested in company stock lost millions of dollars in value, and aggrieved plan participants filed class action fiduciary liability lawsuits against the fiduciaries of these plans.

Several topics are important for those who seek to identify and analyze fiduciary liability loss exposures:

- The Employee Retirement Income Security Act (ERISA)
- The duties and liabilities of employee benefit plan fiduciaries
- The Health Insurance Portability and Accountability Act of 1996 (HIPAA)

The exhibit contains examples of how three different companies had to deal with a fiduciary breach of responsibility. See the exhibit "Fiduciary Liability Claims."

---

### Fiduciary Liability Claims

One of the first cases in the new era of fiduciary liability claims was a class action against Rite-Aid Corp. The class bringing suit was composed of employees who participated in Rite-Aid's defined contribution retirement plans. Attorneys for the class charged that corporate executives knew that the outlook for Rite-Aid's stock was below average but nevertheless invested a portion of the plan's assets in the company's stock. In 2001, Rite-Aid settled with its employees for $67.7 million.[6]

In 2004, insurers paid $85 million under two of Enron's fiduciary liability policies to settle fiduciary liability claims against Enron's board of directors and members of administrative committees. The claims alleged that the directors and administrators imprudently approved or failed to prevent investing in Enron's own stock.[7]

Later that year, MCI, part of WorldCom, settled similar claims with its employees for $46.8 million, with insurers paying about half of the settlement. Former WorldCom CEO Bernard Ebbers contributed an additional $4 million to the settlement.[8] Insurers were inundated with similar claims involving other firms.

---

[DA04881]

# ERISA

ERISA is the federal law that governs retirement and other benefit plans. It was enacted in response to abuses and underfunding in many benefit plans uncovered by congressional hearings following the insolvency of several leading corporations.

ERISA applies, with only a few exceptions, to everyone involved with the employee benefit plans of employers engaged in interstate commerce or subject to federal minimum wage law. (Federal, state, and local governmental bodies are specifically exempted from ERISA. Religious organizations are exempt from some of the provisions of the law.)

Despite the word "retirement" in the official title of the act, ERISA applies to all types and sizes of employee benefit plans. Plans subject to ERISA range from a customized retirement plan for thousands of employees, having its own trustees, actuaries, and investment advisers, to a group health insurance policy for a small business. The latter plan is basically only a contract between the employer and the insurer. An employee benefit does not have to be called a plan, or declared to be a plan, or filed with or approved by anyone, for it to be a plan subject to ERISA. It only has to be some kind of agreement or arrangement made in advance to provide employee benefits.

Violators of ERISA are subject to penalties such as fines and loss of favorable tax status. Of particular importance to insurance and risk management professionals are the duties and liabilities imposed on plan fiduciaries.

# Duties and Liabilities of Employee Benefit Plan Fiduciaries

A fiduciary duty can be defined in general terms as the duty to act for someone else's benefit. Under ERISA, practically anyone whose role in employee benefits involves discretionary control or judgment in the design, administration, funding, or management of a benefit plan or in the management of its assets is a fiduciary.

Each fiduciary of an employee benefit plan has the specific duties pertaining to the particular function that the fiduciary is performing under the plan and a general duty to act solely in the interest of plan participants, to abide by the relevant dictates of plan documents, and to avoid acting in ways that are expressly prohibited by ERISA.

## Specific Duties

The duties of a plan fiduciary are comparable to those of a corporate director:

- Loyalty—A fiduciary's actions must be solely in the best interests of the plan and all of its participants and beneficiaries.
- Prudence—A fiduciary must carry out his or her duties with the care, skill, prudence, and diligence of a prudent person familiar with such matters. ERISA spells out the "prudent person" rule: a fiduciary must act with the care, diligence, and skill that would be exercised by a reasonably prudent person in the same or similar circumstances. For instance, a fiduciary who undertakes activities requiring specialized skills, such as investment of plan assets, will be held to the standard of care applicable to professional persons who perform such activities.
- Diversification—A fiduciary must ensure that the plan's investments are sufficiently diversified to minimize the risk of large losses.
- Adherence—A fiduciary must act according to the plan documents and applicable law. If the plan document is not in compliance with the law, the fiduciaries must follow the law and bring the plan document into compliance.

## Standards and Liability

These duties imply a relatively high standard of care. The duty of loyalty may present difficult issues for fiduciaries who also are officers, directors, or employees of the employer that sponsors the plan. They cannot take the potential effect on the employer into consideration when making a decision as a prudent independent fiduciary.

If a fiduciary breaches a duty and the breach causes loss to a benefit plan, the fiduciary is personally liable to the plan for the full amount of the loss. Additionally, the guilty fiduciary might also be subject to a fine and an action for monetary damages brought by an aggrieved plan participant. A fiduciary may be liable for the breach of a duty by another fiduciary if the first fiduciary knowingly participates in the breach, conceals it, or makes no attempt to correct it.

An employer may be held vicariously liable for breaches of fiduciary duty committed by its employees or agents. The vicariously liable employer might be able to recover its share of the damages from the employee or agent.

Related to fiduciary liability loss exposures are the loss exposures arising from negligent counseling or administering in connection with employee benefit plans.

## HIPAA

ERISA was amended by the Health Insurance Portability and Accountability Act of 1996 (HIPAA). Plans sponsored by employers with more than fifty employees are subject to HIPAA. In brief, HIPAA accomplishes four major objectives:

- Sets standards for health insurance "portability" by providing credit against preexisting condition exclusion periods for prior health coverage
- Limits exclusions for preexisting medical conditions
- Prohibits discrimination in enrollment and in premiums charged to employees and their dependents based on health-related factors
- Improves disclosure about group health plans

Of particular concern from an insurance point of view, HIPAA calls for the protection of employee medical information and subjects the employer and fiduciaries to penalties for failure to comply.

## TYPES OF PERSONNEL LOSSES

Risk management professionals must be aware of the causes of loss that can affect the contributions of an organization's personnel.

Personnel loss exposures have physical and psychological consequences that can lower employee productivity. Prevalent personnel causes of loss include these:

- Work-related injury and illness
- Retirement and resignation
- Work-related violence

# Work-Related Injury and Illness

Workplace disabilities have traditionally been categorized as those resulting from work-related injuries and illnesses. Although the precise distinction between an injury and an illness is not always clear, injuries are usually caused by an external physical force exerting stress on the human body, resulting in some externally manifested injury such as a laceration, a fracture, a contusion, or an amputation. By contrast, an illness usually develops more slowly as the result of some organic or inorganic agent being absorbed, ingested, inhaled, or injected that impairs a function of a body. Thus, a slip and fall or a pulled muscle can cause an injury, while an infection, radiation poisoning, or asbestos exposure can cause an illness.

In workplace settings, the distinction between injury and illness is relevant because the types of risk controls often applied to reducing the frequency or severity of particular disabilities depend on whether those disabilities arise from sudden external events (considered injuries) or from prolonged exposure to harmful conditions or from a sudden harmful condition that does not immediately manifest itself (considered illnesses).

## Injury Causes of Loss

The majority of work-related injury causes of loss in manufacturing and retail businesses fall under these general categories:

- Machinery and equipment use—Machinery and equipment use includes all mechanical devices that employees use or contact on the job. This can include production equipment, such as presses, saws, filling machines, packaging equipment, conveyor belts, and materials-handling equipment, as well as hand tools like screwdrivers, hammers, and drills.

- Materials handling—Materials handling—that is, all activities associated with moving material around the workplace—includes raw material, components, work-in-process, and finished goods. Because these materials can be heavy, bulky, and awkward to move, their potential for causing injury is considerable. For example, a significant problem associated with materials handling is back injuries.

- Vehicle fleet operations—Vehicle fleet operations present acute physical causes of loss to drivers and passengers.

- Physical conditions of premises—The physical conditions of premises factor includes land and buildings. If floors, steps, and other walking surfaces are not properly maintained, they can cause injuries from slipping or tripping. A risk management professional must consider the four interdependent elements of construction, occupancy, protection, and external exposures (COPE) when evaluating the premises conditions.

## Illness Causes of Loss

Unlike the sudden nature of injury causes of loss, illness causes of loss are often the result of prolonged exposure to chemical, biological, ergonomic, and physical forces.

For example, long-term exposure to low-level radiation can cause illness. Illness can also result from a sudden event that causes the illness to manifest over time. For example, a brief but high dose of radiation or exposure to asbestos may manifest years later as cancer. Illness causes of loss are not only the concern of manufacturing and retailing businesses, but to all types of businesses, including service industries. Worksite causes of loss likely to produce disabling illnesses include these:

- Long-term chemical exposures—Long-term chemical exposures are different from sudden chemical exposures such as splashes, spills, and acute ingestion. They are prolonged, lower-dose exposures that pose illness causes of loss. Chemicals enter the body through three modes of entry: ingestion—when employees eat, drink, or smoke in work areas where toxic chemicals are used; absorption—when chemicals enter the bloodstream by penetrating the skin; and inhalation—when contaminants in gases, vapors, or particles of dust, smoke, or mist are inhaled.

- Noise levels—Noise levels that are excessive can result in premature hearing loss. The key determinants of whether the exposure is harmful are the sound level; the length of exposure; the sound's frequency distribution; and whether the sound pattern is continuous, intermittent, or a series of impact (pounding) sounds.

- Ergonomic stress—Ergonomic stress is the physical stress on joints, bones, muscles, and nerves and the stress created by environmental factors such as lighting, glare, noise, color, and temperature. Ergonomics applies scientific disciplines like physiology, anatomy, biology, and engineering to improve the fit between people and their jobs. Ergonomic problems range from an employee performing a lifting task in an awkward (and thus hazardous) position to that same employee sitting in an uncomfortable chair or being exposed to screen glare for long periods.

- Radiation—Radiation occurs in two forms: ionizing and nonionizing. Ionizing radiation is produced by x-rays and gamma, alpha, and beta radiation from radioactive materials. Nonionizing radiation is produced by microwaves, radio waves, visible light, infrared light, and ultraviolet (UV) light. Microwaves, infrared light, and radio frequency radiation can cause overheating and burns at close distances. Industrial lasers can also cause injury because they emit highly concentrated visible light, making eye damage a particular concern.

- Temperature extremes—Temperature extremes are harmful because people must maintain a constant internal body temperature. Straining the body's automatic temperature regulators to adjust for conditions that are persistently too hot or too cold endangers a person's productivity and health. Consequently, protecting the health and productivity of employees requires protecting them from extreme temperatures.

- Poor air quality—Poor air quality results when the humidity, oxygen content, cleanliness, movement, and ionization (static electricity) of air in a workplace is substandard. Air is subject to pollution by toxic or otherwise harmful substances that can either enter a building from the outside or originate within the building. Indoor air quality (IAQ) has become a highly complex and controversial health issue. The unhealthy air or other environmental factors in many commercial and other public buildings have been said to cause "sick building syndrome." Sick building syndrome has many diverse and individualized symptoms.

## Retirement and Resignation

When an employee retires or resigns, the human resource potential of an organization is temporarily reduced. The extent of this productivity loss depends on how quickly the employee can be replaced. Key personnel are difficult to replace because they perform a critical service for the organization. For example, the resignation of a vice president who has specialized institutional knowledge of an organization's finances could result in a greater loss than the resignation of a line employee.

When an employee retires or resigns, the loss to the organization is the future value that the individual would have provided the organization. Replacing the employee reduces the organization's loss severity. However, until the replacement reaches the level of proficiency of the employee who retired or resigned, the organization will not operate at the same level of productivity.

Employees leave organizations for a variety of reasons, only some of which are within an employer's control. An employee may leave to start a business or because a better position was offered elsewhere. The employee may move to another town for personal reasons or be dissatisfied in the current job for various reasons that may not be controllable by the employer. Controllable causes of dissatisfaction are those that may be resolved with a cost-effective or feasible change, such as shifting the employee to a new position or assigning new responsibilities.

An organization should be concerned when the frequency of employee departures increases. Determining the cause of these departures is essential because it may indicate problems within the workplace. For example, a worker who is poorly treated by a manager may find the work environment intolerable and resign. When this occurs, a risk management professional needs to determine whether this is an isolated incident or if other workers have similar impressions of the manager. Problems may be identified with an exit interview with the departing employee. Exit interviews can reveal whether other workers have resigned for similar reasons. The issue may be with just one manager or may be prevalent throughout the division or company.

Another consideration is whether the manager's behavior may have been illegal. Can the employee claim mistreatment because of discrimination based on gender, age, race, or a disability? If this is the case, the organization may be liable under various federal and state laws. Aside from the immediate short-term loss of the productivity of the individual employee who leaves, there is also the long-term potential of a more severe loss exposure with employment liability.

# Work-Related Violence

These are two prevalent types of work-related violence:

- Workplace violence—Workplace violence includes any type of violence or threat of violence that occurs in the work environment, including physical and verbal assaults, threats, coercion, and intimidation.
- Kidnap and ransom—Kidnap and ransom is a loss exposure that organizations are likely to face if they operate in a high-risk overseas location that is not subject to the kinds of security measures used in the United States.

## Workplace Violence

A violent workplace may cause employees to be fearful or depressed, resulting in reduced productivity and increased rates of absenteeism, disability, and resignation. Workplace violence can occur despite an employer's best efforts to comply with its duty to provide a safe working environment. This duty includes protecting employees from both physical violence and mental harm caused by employees, customers, and other people they come in contact with during their working hours.

Employees who handle money and/or deal directly with the public are particularly vulnerable to violence in the workplace. This can occur more frequently when they work in small groups or late at night. For example, convenience stores, which are generally open late at night, are frequently the target of armed robbers.

The consequences of workplace violence are potentially severe. In a worst-case scenario, one or more employees are seriously injured or killed. In addition to all of the financial consequences associated with an employee death, such as lost productivity, cost to find a replacement, workers compensation, and life insurance, this scenario may lead to a lawsuit by the victim's family. Bad publicity may result in an organization losing customers or stock value. Other employees may fear working for the company and leave.

Workplace violence may also cause disability losses. The most obvious form is when an employee is injured by another worker or a customer. The extent of the loss depends on the severity of the injuries. Less obvious are the losses caused by ongoing harassment or threats. Employees may become so fearful or ill that they cannot work. Employees may take frequent sick days, file a workers compensation disability claim, or even file lawsuits against the employer.

## Kidnap and Ransom

Data regarding kidnapping and ransom are difficult to access because most organizations consider such data confidential. Even a single loss will likely have severe financial and emotional consequences to both the employee and the organization, because kidnap and ransom often involve mid- and upper-level executives.

Kidnap and ransom can result in serious injury or death to the kidnapped employee. The employer suffers a loss, either temporary or permanent, of the employee's services, which results in a reduction of human resource potential of the organization. The severity of the loss depends on whether the kidnapped employee is a key person or someone whose services are more easily replaced. Kidnappers may believe that they will be able to demand a larger ransom for an executive or other important personnel. An organization's critical needs should determine whether to temporarily replace the kidnapped employee before the situation is resolved. Negative publicity and the costs of a replacement must both be considered.

An organization should consider paying the medical and rehabilitation (physical and mental) costs of the employee or death benefits to survivors if they are not already covered by some form of insurance. These costs may be covered by workers compensation. A voluntary payment of an employee's medical and rehabilitation costs may prevent or lessen the chance of the employees or their families asserting a legal claim against the organization.

Kidnapped employees may also require permanent relocation from the dangerous location where the kidnapping occurred. Even if an employee survives a kidnapping without physical injuries, the employee may suffer psychological harm that reduces his or her ability to perform. Other employees may also be negatively affected by the kidnapping, refusing to travel or to be assigned to a particular location. In some cases, the kidnap and ransom loss exposure in a particular location may be so great that an organization has to cease operating in that location entirely.

# ASSESSING PERSONNEL LOSS EXPOSURES

Risk management professionals need to assess the financial consequences of personnel losses.

A variety of methods may be used to identify and analyze personnel loss exposures. Some of these methods involve information that is unique and proprietary to an organization; others use information that is more standardized and publicly available. Each of the methods can be used to identify and analyze the human assets that are exposed to loss, the causes of loss, or the financial consequences of the loss to the organization.

These are the methods risk managers use to assess personnel loss exposures:

- Risk assessment questionnaires
- Loss histories
- Other records and documents
- Flowcharts and organizational charts
- Personal inspections
- Expertise within and beyond the organization

## Risk Assessment Questionnaires

Risk assessment questionnaires are useful for identifying personnel loss exposures because they usually include extensive lists of standardized questions that are designed to aid risk management professionals in developing a better understanding of the organization's loss exposures. Standardization is a strength because the questions are universally relevant. But standardization is also a weakness in that no standardized questionnaire can be expected to uncover all the loss exposures characteristic of a given industry, let alone those unique to a given organization. See the exhibit "Sample Question from IRMI's Exposure Survey Questionnaire."

## Loss Histories

Loss histories are a source of internal information about the causes of personnel losses. This information can be used to evaluate an organization's mortality or disability rates as well as retirement trends and voluntary and involuntary employee separation histories. However, although most organizations keep detailed records about death and disability that are work-related, they may not have records indicating death and disability that have occurred outside the workplace. An organization's Human Resources department is a good source of information about voluntary and involuntary employee separation and retirement trends, provided the data are maintained.

## Other Records and Documents

Many of the personnel losses an organization may experience may be projected by using reliable and widely available public data. Potential sources of these records include the United States Census Bureau, the National Center for Health Statistics, and the U.S. Bureau of Labor Statistics (BLS).

Two widely available sources of information are mortality and morbidity tables. An organization should expect its mortality experience to adhere fairly closely to the applicable mortality table. The larger the organization, the closer its mortality rates will be to the applicable mortality table. This is true as long as the organization's employees constitute a representative sample of the general population.

## Sample Question from IRMI's Exposure Survey Questionnaire

### PERSONNEL AND WORKERS COMPENSATION EXPOSURES

17.  a. Is there a potential for multiple injuries, illness, death, or disability of employees from:

| Event | Max. No. Employees Exposed | Estimate Likelihood | | | |
|---|---|---|---|---|---|
| | | Nil | Slight | Mod. | High |
| Corp. Owned Aircraft Disaster | | | | | |
| Commercial Aircraft Disaster | | | | | |
| Car or Van Pool Accidents | | | | | |
| Rail Travel Disaster | | | | | |
| Other Travel Disasters | | | | | |
| Epidemic | | | | | |
| Sabotage/Assassination | | | | | |
| Exposure to Asbestos, Silicon, Other Harmful Agents | | | | | |
| Industrial Accident (e.g., explosion, building collapse, pollution release, etc.) | | | | | |

Source: International Risk Management Institute, Inc., Exposure Survey Questionnaire (International Risk Management Institute, Inc., 1998), Chapter 15. [DA01925]

Morbidity tables provide data regarding health. Various injury statistics are also available. There are few publicly available data sources on retirement trends.

## Flowcharts and Organizational Charts

Flowcharts and organizational charts present risk management professionals with two methods that help identify key persons and key points in an organization's processes. The flowchart method identifies employees at critical junctions in an organization's activities. Each function or operating division should be charted, analyzed, and examined to determine how heavily it relies on key persons at various operational steps.

The organizational chart method of identifying personnel loss exposures involves studying job descriptions to identify the most important positions. This method highlights key persons who exercise unique talents, creativity, or special skills; make decisions vital to the organization; or manage and motivate the acts of others. This approach is comparable to identifying property loss exposures by starting with a list of properties. Such a list is most appropriate for identifying key owners, officers, and managers.

Identifying key personnel involves answering two questions:

1.  What would the organization do if this person suddenly were not available?

2.  If this person were unavailable, could the organization achieve its fundamental goals?

The first question helps determine whether, how, and when the person would be replaced. To manage the risk, a succession policy should be in place. The second question reveals the loss of efficiency or profits, if any, that would result from the loss of the person. A risk management professional should consider these additional questions:

*   Are all personnel located in the same facility?
*   Would it be safer to spread out employees over different locations, or will the organization suffer efficiency losses by doing so?
*   Are data backed up in an off-site facility?
*   If employees with specialized knowledge were lost, would replacement personnel be able to recreate their work?
*   What would be the effect on the organization if this employee were unavailable for any significant period of time?

## Personal Inspections

A personal inspection is a valuable method to help determine the extent of workplace hazards. Risk management professionals can use personal inspections to identify workplace hazards that may lead to the death, disability, or voluntary separation of employees who were not identified by the other methods of assessing personnel loss exposures. Personal inspections also provide the risk management professional with the opportunity to discuss with employees any other issues that may affect employee performance or morale.

## Expertise Within and Beyond the Organization

Expertise available within an organization may include human resources, system safety engineers, or senior managers. Interviews with these employees can help the risk management professional gather information about workplace hazards as well as information about employee productivity and morale. Former employees are an excellent source of information about an organization. Some organizations use exit interviews to aid in identifying problem areas. Employees who are leaving the organization often speak more freely than current employees because they do not fear reprisal for negative comments.

The risk management professional also may look beyond the organization for expertise regarding personnel loss exposures. There are organizations with expertise in personnel loss exposures that specialize in workplace safety and security to help minimize the workplace hazards. There are also outside experts who can aid an organization in building compensation packages that attract and retain quality employees.

# RISK TREATMENT FOR WORK-RELATED INJURY AND ILLNESS

Mitigating losses from work-related injury and illness help an organization protect its most important resource—its employees.

A risk management professional familiar with an organization's structure and procedures may select from a variety of risk control techniques to mitigate losses arising from work-related injury and illness:

- Avoidance
- Loss prevention
- Loss reduction
- Separation and duplication

## Avoidance

Avoidance reduces the probability of an activity's future loss to zero. For example, a tool manufacturer learns that the application of a rustproof coating on its tools will emit toxic vapors. The manufacturer could simply avoid using the product, thus protecting employees from potential related harm. Eliminating an existing loss exposure can be more difficult. If the tool manufacturer began to use the coating and then discontinued its use, it could eliminate its inventory of the coating material, avoiding future employee exposure to explosion and toxic vapors. However, the tool manufacturer cannot avoid exposures related to losses that could develop as a result of previous employee exposure to the coating.

## Loss Prevention

Loss prevention may be used when avoidance is impossible or undesirable. Safety engineering and workplace design can help prevent work-related injury and illness.

## Safety Engineering

Two basic causes of loss are associated with workplace injuries and illnesses: physical and procedural. Physical risk controls are sometimes called engineering controls, while procedural controls are sometimes called administrative controls.

Loss prevention physical controls include these:

- Materials substitution—This entails safer substitutions for hazardous materials.

- Isolation—Isolation is used to separate employees and others from hazardous materials or processes.

- Wet methods—Wet methods introduce moisture to a production process to keep harmful dusts out of the work environment.

- Guarding—Guarding is used to physically prevent someone from making contact with any potentially dangerous object or force.

- Ventilation—Ventilation removes hazardous vapors, dusts, mists, or heat from the work environment.

- Maintenance—Proper maintenance can prevent breakdowns and malfunctions.

- Housekeeping—Effective housekeeping helps prevent the slipping, tripping, and fire causes of loss.

- Personal protective equipment (PPE)—PPE includes devices or garments worn to protect workers from injury or illness.

Loss prevention procedural controls include these:

- Process change—Process change should be considered when a job or process poses a cause of loss.

- Education and training—Education focuses on a particular task's underlying efficiency and safety. Training explains what a task entails and how to perform it safely.

- Standard operating procedures (SOPs)—SOPs describe (ideally in written form), step-by-step, how to perform a task to avoid injury.

- Proper supervision—Proper supervision is required to ensure that employees do their jobs correctly and follow safety procedures.

- Medical controls—Medical controls in the form of medical examinations and testing can detect possible workplace-related health concerns.

- Job rotation—Job rotation attempts to reduce employee exposure to causes of loss by limiting the amount of time any single worker performs a particular task.

# Workplace Design

Workplace design coordinates a work environment's physical features, devices, and working conditions with the capabilities of the people in that environment. It is applied through methods that fall into these categories:

- Ergonomics
- Human factors engineering
- Biomechanics

Successful workplace design programs use **ergonomics** to enable employees to perform their jobs better, safely, and with less effort; to reduce injuries, accidents, workers compensation costs, and other accidental losses; and to increase profits or reduce operating costs.

Workplace design can reduce work injuries and maintain product quality and operating efficiency when it is applied in the context of six major areas of ergonomic concern:

- Manual materials handling—This refers to lifting, pulling, dragging, pushing, and transferring objects or materials by human power, with or without some mechanical assistance. Often this activity results in injuries to the back and is the leading cause of workers compensation claims. A full program for controlling injuries and other problems related to materials handling includes placing workers in appropriate jobs and training them in proper lifting procedures, as well as designing jobs to fit employees' capabilities.

- Cumulative trauma disorders (CTDs)—These are injuries caused by continuously performing a task over an extended period. CTDs can be caused by repetitive motions, overexertion, awkward postures, mechanical stresses (such as the pressure of a hand or foot on the sharp edges of tools or equipment), vibration, or exposure to cold. Most CTDs affect employees' upper extremities. One of the most common types of CTD is carpal tunnel syndrome. Various engineering, administrative, and medical measures can reduce employee exposure to CTDs. For employees who sit at desks, these measures include providing appropriate seating (chairs that are stable, are properly cushioned, have easily adjustable backrests and seats, and swivel to allow movement), sufficient leg space, arm supports, rounded or padded edges on work surfaces, and unoccupied space on the work surface nearest an employee to allow wrists and forearms to rest. For tasks best performed in a standing position, measures include structuring tasks to prevent prolonged, uninterrupted standing, eliminating foot controls, or if such controls are necessary, designing them for use by either foot, avoiding hard floors, and providing floor mats and footrests.

- Physical layout of workstations—The physical layout of workstations can cause vision difficulties, spinal strain, and poor posture. Often these stresses are the result of workstations that do not meet the physical requirements of a particular worker's body dimensions. The best way to

Ergonomics

The science of designing work space and equipment based on the needs of the people who use the work space and equipment.

control the causes of loss associated with office work is to make computer and other workstation elements as adjustable as possible.

- Displays and controls—Properly designed machine displays can reduce interpretation errors and errors caused by fatigue. Similarly, machine controls should be arranged to allow swift, efficient, and reliable interaction between the machine operator and the machine.

- Fatigue—Inadequate workplace design leads to fatigue whenever poor lighting, excess noise, work demands, or inadequate workspace interferes with employee performance. Unintentional errors resulting from fatigue cause many losses, including workplace accidents, defective output, and reduced productivity. Workplace design generally controls fatigue by keeping stresses on employees within manageable levels. Specific measures to control fatigue can be engineered (such as proper workspace design), administrative (such as providing employees with opportunities to appropriately modify their jobs or surroundings), or medical (such as identifying physiological or psychological evidence of chronic fatigue).

- Accommodating disabled employees—The Americans with Disabilities Act (ADA) requires most public employers to make reasonable accommodations for otherwise qualified employees. One of the basic strategies for reasonably accommodating a disabled person in a particular job is to modify the workplace so that the disabled employee can perform the essential tasks of that job.

**Human factors engineering**

A process that applies the knowledge of human behavior to design equipment people use on and off the job.

**Biomechanics**

A process that views people at work as special kinds of machines functioning within environments filled with other machines.

**Human factors engineering** combines the expertise of psychologists, engineers, and sociologists in the study of human behavior as it affects productivity. Human factors engineers attempt to design machine controls and gauges to reduce operator error and fatigue.

**Biomechanics** views people as a system of skeletal levers and muscular motors that exert force to achieve given results. Human machines function reliably only within the limits of their strength, agility, and endurance. Many biomechanical efforts have focused on properly designing hand tools that enable workers to apply maximum force to the objects without over-stressing their upper extremities.

To establish a workplace design program that combines all of these elements, an organization's senior management must be committed to the workplace design program, and supervisors and employees involved in the program must be trained appropriately. This often requires outside resources available from insurers, risk management consultants, or other specialized providers of risk management, ergonomic, and safety services.

Successful workplace design programs usually evolve through a reactive stage and a proactive stage. In the reactive stage, changes are made in response to ergonomic problems as they occur. These responses are relatively inefficient and fragmented because time and other resources are used to cope with actual difficulties rather than to prevent them. In the proactive stage, which typically occurs as a workplace design program matures, the organization's entire management works to recognize and manage ergonomic stresses before they produce significant losses.

## Loss Reduction

Loss reduction efforts associated with workplace-related injury and illness focus on rehabilitation, which is the process of restoring an injured and disabled person to his or her highest attainable level of functioning and independence in self-care, vocational, and recreational activities. Rehabilitation can be physical, psychological, or vocational. Rehabilitation management allows an organization to control the costs of bodily injury claims for employees and other injured claimants. It also reduces the severity of disability or employee income losses.

Rehabilitation management is an interdepartmental activity because losses and expenses associated with disabled claimants affect the entire organization. The risk management professional must coordinate the activities of the various departments involved with the treatment of the disabled person. Depending on the size of the organization, those departments may include personnel, claims, legal, and medical.

Rehabilitation management is cost-effective because it focuses on restoring the productivity of the employee as soon as possible. This reduces or eliminates the need for future surgery, hospital and treatment costs, legal fees, settlements, lost work time, and disability benefits. The variety of injuries a person can suffer provides numerous options for rehabilitation management. An organization's early involvement in a rehabilitation case helps to ensure that management will establish and maintain control of the administrative procedures, the persons involved, and the costs. Early involvement also encourages a good rapport among those involved and can prevent the injured or disabled persons from developing equally disabling psychological reactions associated with the injury or disability.

Effective rehabilitation management considers an individual's rehabilitation potential, which is the likelihood that the disabled individual will quickly return to maximum functional levels. The variables that influence an individual's potential for rehabilitation include these:

- Characteristics of the impairments, functional limitations, residual capacity (the capacity of the employee to work without further rehabilitation), and the prognosis of the disabled person
- Perception of the situation by the disabled person
- Environmental conditions, especially the perception of the situation by significant others, such as family members, healthcare professionals, and co-workers

Important relationships that influence an individual's rehabilitation potential include these:

- Employer and injured employee
- Physician and patient
- Claimant and insurer
- Injured employee and family
- Disabled person and rehabilitation specialist
- Injured employee and attorney

Rehabilitation management begins before an injury or an illness occurs. Procedures should be in place to address the needs of injured or disabled employees. By following those procedures, the risk management professional can better control the rehabilitation program, monitoring medical care and other services that might otherwise raise the costs of rehabilitation.

An appropriate first response to an injury or a disability includes providing the injured person with immediate medical attention and documenting the injury and the surrounding circumstances. This documentation (or initial disposition) should be done by a trained person as soon as possible after the injury. It is the employer's first line of defense in controlling the rehabilitation process. If the organization does not document its immediate actions and observations regarding the injured person, other physical problems not related to the injury might be associated with that injury, thus increasing the employer's liability for compensation.

After examining the injured person, a medically competent professional should assess the medical condition of the injured individual. The person should not be allowed to continue daily activities while in serious pain, because further injury can occur. He or she should be encouraged to see a physician and should not return to the job site until able to perform all of the motions necessary for the job without signs or complaints of pain.

When a referral to a physician is necessary, or when the employee has seen a physician on his or her own, the industrial nurse or designee should request this information:

- Results of any x-rays
- Diagnosis
- Medications prescribed
- Recommended rest and activity
- Anticipated return-to-work date
- Limitations on physical activities
- Physician's specialty

This information should be collected within the first two to five days after the injury, assuming the injured person has seen a physician. At this point, control of the information and the rehabilitation program must be established, either by the employer or the claim representative. For certain diagnoses, a rehabilitation consultant might also become involved.

Many factors may influence the success of rehabilitation management. For example, an injured person who is not making rapid progress in the rehabilitation program may become discouraged and give up. Other circumstances that may limit the effectiveness of the rehabilitation program and that must be managed include these:

- Extended hospitalization
- Uncoordinated medical treatment
- Extensive medication
- Lack of clear diagnosis
- Lack of clear prognosis
- Round-the-clock nursing care
- Non-goal-oriented physical therapy
- Lack of discharge planning
- Lack of specific date for returning to work

## Separation and Duplication

Separation of loss exposures involves arranging an organization's activities and resources so that no single event can cause simultaneous losses to all of them. For example, an organization might use separate buildings at different locations, maintain separate routes for its delivery trucks, or use several suppliers for key raw materials. Alternatively, an organization may prohibit key personnel from traveling together.

Duplication involves creating backup facilities or assets to be used only if the primary activity or asset suffers a loss. An example of duplication is cross-training employees so that each has a variety of skills. Duplication helps to offset the adverse financial effects of employee injuries and illnesses. If one employee is disabled by a work-related injury or illness, a cross-trained employee with acceptable skills can temporarily replace the disabled employee. Cross-training can also reduce an employee's exposure to financial loss from injury or illness. Assume that an employee suffers a work-related injury or illness that prevents him or her from performing a particular task. The diversity of skills developed through cross-training increases the employee's ability to perform other tasks that might not be affected by the disability.

## SUMMARY

The directors and officers of a corporation have various responsibilities and duties. Various liability loss exposures occur from the exercise of these duties and responsibilities.

Employers may be exposed to employment practices liability claims under state and federal laws. These claims may allege, for example, that the employer has wrongfully terminated the claimant's employment or illegally discriminated against the claimant, or that the claimant has been sexually harassed. A growing body of state and federal statutes, regulations, and court cases has more clearly defined unlawful employment practices and increased employers' exposure to such claims.

Benefit plans offered by nongovernmental entities are subject to ERISA, which, among other provisions, imposes fiduciary status on those involved in the management and administration of employee benefit plans.

An organization faces three major personnel causes of loss that must be controlled. They are work-related injury and illness, retirement and resignation, and work-related violence:

- Injuries are usually caused by an external physical force exerting stress on the human body, resulting in some externally manifested injury. An illness usually develops more slowly as the result of some organic or inorganic agent being absorbed, ingested, inhaled, or injected that impairs a function of a body.

- To control retirement and resignation, an organization first needs to identify the employees who will cause critical harm if they left.

- Workplace violence includes any violence or threat of violence that occurs in the work environment. Kidnap and ransom is an exposure that organizations in high-risk overseas locations are likely to face.

Risk management professionals have a variety of methods available to them to aid in identifying and analyzing personnel loss exposures. They include risk assessment questionnaires, loss histories, other records and documents, flow-charts and organizational charts, personal inspections, and expertise within and beyond the organization.

The risk control techniques of avoidance, loss prevention, loss reduction, separation, and duplication can be used to control loss exposures resulting in work-related injury or illness. Avoidance can be achieved by either never undertaking something that could cause injury or illness, or by ceasing to continue something that has caused injury or illness. Loss prevention measures that can be used include safety engineering, workplace design, and workplace design programs. Loss reduction measures focus on rehabilitating employees who have suffered injury or illness. Examples of separation measures include using separate buildings, using several different truck delivery routes, and preventing key employees from traveling together. Examples of duplication measures include cross-training of employees.

# ASSIGNMENT NOTES

1.  Equal Employment Opportunity Commission, "Shaping Employment Discrimination Law," www.eeoc.gov/EEOC/history/35th/1965-71/shaping.html (accessed November 12, 2010).

2.  Charles J. Muhl, "The Employment-at-Will Doctrine: Three Major Exceptions," Monthly Labor Review, January 2001, p. 7–8, http://findarticles.com/p/articles/mi_m1153/is_1_124/ai_71704724/pg_5/ (accessed November 12, 2010).

3.  Toussaint v. Blue Cross and Blue Shield of Michigan, 408 Mich. 579, 292 N.W.2d 880 (1980). Despite the date, this case continued to be frequently cited as a leading case relating to the implied-contract exception.

4.  Muhl, "The Employment-at-Will Doctrine: Three Major Exceptions," p. 10.

5.  Jeffrey O'Shaughnessy, "Small Firms Can Face Big EPL Exposures," P&C National Underwriter, March 29, 2010, www.property-casualty.com/Issues/2010 (accessed November 23, 2010).

6.  Len Strazewski, "Fiduciary Risk: A Sleeper Awakes," Risk & Insurance, August 2004, p. 38.

7.  Groom Law Group, "Employer Stock/Enron Litigation Update," May 28, 2004, www.americanbenefitscouncil.org/documents/employer_enronupdate061704.pdf (accessed January 16, 2008).

8.  "WorldCom Pension Settlement Reached," Business Insurance, July 12, 2004, p. 1.

# Segment C

**Assignment 8**
Environmental Risk

**Assignment 9**
Crime and Cyber Risk

**Assignment 10**
Fleet Risk

**Assignment 11**
Smart Products and Risk Management

# 8

# Environmental Risk

## Educational Objectives

After learning the content of this assignment, you should be able to:

▷ Explain how an organization can incur environmental liability under tort, contract, or statutory law.

▷ Describe the environmental loss exposures that might cause property, personnel, and net income losses.

▷ Summarize the basic purpose and distinguishing features of each of the environmental statutes described.

▷ Describe environmental risk control measures, the hierarchy in which they should be used, and the considerations involved in their selection.

▷ Explain how climate change can increase risk for organizations.

# Environmental Risk

**8**

## LEGAL FOUNDATIONS FOR ENVIRONMENTAL LIABILITY

Virtually every organization has environmental loss exposures, which can entail these consequences of pollutants (or, in some cases, substances that are not generally considered to be pollutants) being released into the environment:

- Liability for bodily injury to others or damage to their property
- The cost of cleaning up, or remediating, pollutants, either on the insured's own property or on the property of others

An organization can incur environmental liability under tort, contract, or statutory law. The source of liability for environmental losses is most frequently the actual or alleged release of pollutants, the violation of a law designed to protect human health and the environment from those pollutants, or the enforcement of environmental protection laws that require remediation expense payment.

### Tort Liability

Tort liability for pollution can be based on negligence, intentional torts, or strict liability. This discussion examines tort law concepts as they might apply in the context of environmental liability.

### Negligence

In many cases, pollution results from an organization's negligence or failure to exercise the legally required degree of care under the circumstances. If another party that has sustained injury makes a claim against the organization and proves that the organization breached its duty of care owed to the claimant, and that the breach of duty was the proximate cause of the claimant's injury, the organization can be held legally liable to pay the claimant's damages.

These are examples of negligent acts that have resulted in environmental liability claims:

- A contractor working at a manufacturing facility left a valve open on a process line overnight, causing the contents of a storage tank connected to the line to be released into an adjacent stream, which in turn caused property damage, bodily injury, and natural resource damage.

- A hazardous waste hauler transporting toxic waste to a disposal facility was at fault in causing an auto accident in the downtown section of a city, resulting in the release into the street of the hazardous liquid being transported. Passersby inhaled the fumes, and the business district of the city was evacuated for two days as cleanup contractors responded to the spill. Claims were filed against the transporter alleging bodily injury, property damage, and loss of business income.

Other possible sources of liability for the negligent release of pollutants include hazardous product manufacturing, testing, and transporting; hazardous waste disposal; product failures; inadequate emergency response procedures; and incompetent environmental consulting.

## Intentional Torts

The intentional torts most commonly alleged in environmental claims are nuisance and trespass. A property owner is entitled to the peaceful enjoyment of his or her property. If a neighbor or another third party engages in an activity that interferes with the owner's right of enjoyment of the property, the owner may bring an action alleging nuisance against the party causing the interference. Potential environmental liability exposures alleging nuisance can involve loud noises, noxious odors, bright lights, fog generation, electrical waves, and electromagnetic fields.

Trespass, unlike nuisance, involves the physical deposition of pollutants on the property of the claimant alleging injury. The material that is deposited may be a toxic substance, but it does not have to be.

Claims have resulted from releases or deposits of water, sand, and clean soil. As long as the deposits are objectionable to the property owner, a trespass claim can be brought against the party responsible for the release. Environmental claims for trespass could result from the release of dust or particulate matter into the air, the discharge of chemicals into a stream, the runoff of pesticides onto a neighbor's property, or thermal emissions into a river.

## Strict Liability

When manufacturing operations use inherently hazardous materials or processes, courts may impose strict liability, which eliminates the common-law defenses normally available to the defendant in a negligence suit. No degree of care is considered to be adequate for ultrahazardous activities or materials.

For example, a remediation contractor working on a job to incinerate nerve gas could face strict liability for ultrahazardous activities if a release of the nerve gas injures a third party, even though the contractor might exercise a very high degree of care in performing the work. Some examples of materials that could create strict liability for environmental injury include nuclear materials, explosives, pesticides, highly toxic chemicals, and hazardous waste.

## Contractual Liability

An organization can assume liability for environmental losses under a contract that contains a hold-harmless agreement. For example, a general contractor that agrees to indemnify a project owner for all claims made against the owner during the course of the project may incur an environmental loss under the contract if the proximate cause of the loss is a release of pollutants. A worker who is employed by a subcontractor at the project and is injured as a result of breathing ammonia might sue the project owner, thus activating the general contractor's contractual liability to the owner.

## Environmental Statutes

A new era of environmental legislation began with the passage of the National Environmental Policy Act (NEPA) of 1969. NEPA resulted from the efforts of conservationists to compel the federal government to consider the environmental ramifications of proposals for new highways, dams, and other public projects capable of affecting wildlife or scenic areas.

Since the passage of NEPA, environmental laws to protect human health and the environment have proliferated, beginning with laws to protect surface waters (such as the Clean Water Act) and the air (the Clean Air Act). As the environmental movement caught on, the more ambitious and complex Resource Conservation and Recovery Act (RCRA) of 1976 and the Comprehensive Environmental Response, Compensation, and Liability Act (CERCLA) of 1980 soon followed. Both CERCLA and RCRA have had a significant effect on the risk management programs of many organizations.

Many environmental laws do not require fault or negligence on the part of the party charged with responsibility, in effect creating strict liability by statute. One of the common threads that runs through most of these laws is the principle that the party that caused the pollution should be responsible for paying for the cleanup of that pollution in the case of a spill or release. This principle is commonly referred to as a "let the polluter pay" funding scheme.

Federal statutes provide the baseline standards for state and local environmental laws. Local governments are able to establish standards that are more restrictive than the federal standard. This legislative freedom and the public interest in laws protecting the environment lead to a profusion of environmental regulations that vary geographically.

The majority of environmental statutes regulate materials that are reactive, corrosive, toxic, or flammable. Environmental statutes contain provisions that can lead to injunctions, fines, and penalties for noncompliance. The statutes also contain provisions for the criminal prosecution of individuals, including corporate officers.

Although this latter point is not a subject of insurance, it is an important point to consider when developing environmental risk management programs. For insurance practitioners, the most common and significant risk management implications of these statutes are the cost recovery provisions for cleanup expenses and the proof of financial responsibility requirements.

The distinction of whether a material is a regulated hazardous material is important to the discussion of environmental insurance. Environmental insurance policies refer in their insuring agreements to cleanup cost obligations imposed on the insured by environmental laws. If the insured has loss exposures from unregulated materials, it is important to amend the environmental insurance policies to insure the loss exposure.

# Enforcement of Environmental Laws

For many years, the focus of environmental regulatory activities was compliance in a very technical sense. Under the Clean Air Act, the Clean Water Act, and several earlier environmental laws, compliance involved monitoring the outflow from pipes into streams and from smokestacks into the air. The Environmental Protection Agency (EPA) set standards, counted contaminants in parts per million, and enforced statutes with fines that could exceed hundreds of thousands of dollars per day.

The process was highly empirical. Technically trained inspectors met with the corporate mechanics who controlled the tools of compliance. Those subjected to enforcement actions were often the compliance personnel and technically trained employees who operated pollution control systems or the equipment that failed to meet the EPA standards. Risk managers were rarely involved in this process.

This enforcement model has changed dramatically in recent years. Now, an evaluation of compliance not only includes a review of the physical facilities, but it also considers management systems and control of the processes that pose a threat to the environment.

Such an evaluation reviews these items:

- The accountability of the board of directors for environmental matters
- The assignment of environmental responsibility within senior management ranks
- The effective dispersion of responsibility through all levels of the organization
- The day-to-day operation of the system in controlling activities that involve hazardous materials

Accordingly, not only the EPA but also the corporation's shareholders and employees now expect that a corporate environmental risk management program should have certain components. Such a program begins with a written corporate environmental policy, which is implemented by written procedures and carried out by the executives responsible for the management of day-to-day activities.

This formal plan should be adequately funded to ensure that it will be successful. A reporting system provides management personnel and the board of directors with enough information to ensure that everything is working as intended. When extraordinary events take place within a corporation, such as a major pollution incident or the corporation's merger with an organization having serious environmental loss exposures, additional expectations must be addressed.

Environmental insurance can be used as a tool to help manage environmental risks, not just insure them. Environmental underwriters are in a position to compare one applicant with another and are therefore able to provide useful advice on the adequacy of the environmental management systems relative to the applicant's peer group. Thus, the underwriting process may give early warnings to an organization that needs to improve its environmental management efforts. See the exhibit "Management's Responsibility for Environmental Compliance."

### Management's Responsibility for Environmental Compliance

One company's experience illustrates the current trend for regulators to focus on the responsibility of management in assessing environmental compliance. The company was involved in metal fabrication processes at thirteen plants geographically dispersed in seven states, with a total workforce of more than 8,000.

At one of the company's facilities, regulators were called in when neighbors discovered hydrocarbon solvents in their drinking water. An inspection of the facility found that the normal practice for cleaning up trichloroethylene spills from the shop floor was to hose the material out the door and let it run into storm water drains. Further inquiry revealed that the company had only one employee assigned to environmental compliance for all thirteen manufacturing facilities.

Fines were assessed against the corporate executives and the corporation for failure to adequately provide for environmental management within the company when the hazards associated with the materials in use were widely known. The chief executive officer of the firm was given a suspended sentence and three years' probation as a first offender, a result that would not occur today under the current mandatory minimum Federal Sentencing Guidelines for violations of environmental protection laws.

A shareholder suit against the officers and directors for failing to properly manage the firm's environmental matters quickly followed the environmental enforcement litigation. The shareholder suit alleged that because of the failure of senior management to develop an adequate environmental management protocol, the corporation incurred unnecessary expenses to resolve the ensuing enforcement actions.

The risk manager quickly learned how important an environmental risk management program is when she was asked to provide a detailed analysis of the incident and an explanation of what insurance protection the company had for this incident and future events of a similar nature. Of course, the insurance coverage available to help pay for this costly claim was of great interest to the directors and officers of the firm. It is easy to imagine the directors' and officers' disappointment when they were informed that the pollution exclusions in the firm's directors and officers liability policy, general liability policy, and umbrella liability policy effectively eliminated any possibility of an insurance recovery to help offset the expense of the legal actions.

[DA04894]

# OTHER ENVIRONMENTAL LOSS EXPOSURES

The magnitude, complexity, and dynamic nature of environmental regulations make liability loss exposures the predominant concern in environmental risk management. However, risk management professionals should also be aware of the primary property, personnel, and net income loss exposures that can arise from environmental pollution.

Although liability loss exposures are the predominant concern in environmental risk control, other loss exposures—particularly property, personnel, and net income loss exposures—may also arise from environmental pollution.

# Property Loss Exposures

Environmental pollution creates many loss exposures for an organization's real and personal property. For example, environmental pollution may prevent an organization from selling a piece of property. Potential real estate buyers often undertake detailed and exhaustive environmental studies to identify any potential environmental liability they might be assuming through the property transaction. In some states, this review is required before a sale can be made. Without prior cleanup and remediation of any pollution, the organization will not be able to sell the property.

Property, even if polluted, appears as an asset on an organization's balance sheet. However, the net value of the property may be a liability for the organization because of the combined legal and financial consequences of pollution cleanup.

Personal property is also at risk. Spills and leaks may result in substantial inventory losses for the organization. Exposure of processing equipment or other tangible assets to adverse substances may reduce their useful life and salvage value.

Moreover, after an environmental loss, costs are likely to increase to ensure that such loss exposures are not repeated. Following a major oil spill, one firm decided to retrofit its entire tanker fleet from single to double hulls.

# Personnel Loss Exposures

Worker health and safety issues are a social as well as a financial concern for organizations. Organizations have an obligation to provide a healthy and safe working environment for employees. The clear link between environmental protection and worker health and safety has caused many organizations to combine these two risk management areas into an environmental health and safety function.

Occupational exposure to hazardous materials can cause chemical burns or other on-the-job injuries. However, many work-environment contaminants have a cumulative effect on the human body that results in illness or disease.

Of considerable help are the Occupational Safety and Health Administration and the American College of Occupational and Environmental Medicine, which have standards for workplace safety and health. Use of these and other standards can help an organization assess the danger of the pollutants its personnel are exposed to.

# Net Income Loss Exposures

Any environmental pollution event is likely to result in some degree of business interruption and revenue reduction, which reduces the organization's net income. A spill or leak within a facility may shut down a manufacturing line or an area for repairs and cleanup.

Small events may disrupt business activity only slightly, and they are likely to produce little if any financial consequence. However, if raw materials or equipment needed for production are affected, the organization may miss production deadlines and lose business. In higher profile events, negative press may result in consumer boycotts.

Under extreme circumstances, the environmental liabilities may cause the enterprise to cease operation. Court-ordered injunctions on business operations (orders to cease certain activities) are common in certain industries, such as timber and oil development. For example, a court may order an organization to stop extracting timber or processing oil.

Significant expenses are also incurred in environmental cleanup. As well as the direct cleanup costs, legal and technical consulting services can consume significant funds that would otherwise be available to maintain or expand the business. The financial consequences of environmental liability losses are likely to be felt by customers, suppliers, and perhaps even local communities if the organization provides a primary source of employment for the area.

# ENVIRONMENTAL STATUTES

For insurance practitioners, the most common and significant implications of federal environmental laws and state statutes are the cost recovery provisions for cleanup expenses and the proof of financial responsibility requirements under some of the laws.

Some of the most influential federal environmental laws are summarized in the "Summary of Federal Environmental Laws" exhibit. Most states administer these laws under state statutes that have different names but virtually the same content as the federal laws. See the exhibit "Summary of Federal Environmental Laws."

## Clean Water Act

The Clean Water Act seeks to improve the quality of surface waters by prohibiting or regulating the discharge of pollutants into navigable waters and restoring them to fishable and swimmable quality. Many activities are regulated under the legislation, including pollutant discharge into waterways and storm water runoff. The Clean Water Act also mandates a Spill Prevention, Control, and Countermeasure Plan for certain regulated facilities, such as those for oil handling.

## Summary of Federal Environmental Laws

| Name of Law | Basic Purpose of Law |
| --- | --- |
| Clean Water Act | To improve the quality of surface waters by prohibiting or regulating the discharge of pollutants into navigable waters and restoring them to fishable or swimmable quality. |
| Clean Air Act | To improve the quality of ambient air by regulating emissions from both mobile and stationary sources of air pollution. |
| Motor Carrier Act of 1980 | To protect the environment from releases of harmful materials during transportation of such materials by motor carriers in interstate or intrastate commerce. |
| Toxic Substance Control Act | To regulate the chemical manufacturing industry and prevent the importation or manufacture of dangerous chemical substances without adequate safeguards. |
| Resource Conservation and Recovery Act (RCRA) | To provide "cradle-to-grave" regulation of hazardous waste. Imposes strict waste management requirements on generators and transporters of hazardous wastes and on hazardous waste treatment, storage, and disposal facilities. Also regulates underground storage tanks, medical wastes, and nonhazardous solid wastes. Includes proof of financial responsibility requirements for permit holders. |
| Comprehensive Environmental Response, Compensation, and Liability Act (CERCLA) | To facilitate the cleanup of any abandoned or uncontrolled sites containing hazardous substances. Imposes strict liability for cleanup costs on potentially responsible parties. |
| Oil Pollution Act of 1990 | To reduce the risk of spills of petroleum or hazardous materials into U.S. coastal or navigable waters by mandating technical standards and requiring proof of financial responsibility for facilities and vessels operating in or near such waters. |

[DA04895]

# Clean Air Act

The Clean Air Act seeks to improve the quality of ambient air by regulating emissions from both mobile and stationary sources of air pollution. Parties that intend to construct or operate sources of air emissions are required to obtain permits to do so. The terms of the permit vary from one emission source to another and from one pollutant to another.

Restrictions are stricter in areas of poor air quality (such as urban areas) than elsewhere. The zones around cities where ambient air quality fails to meet Clean Air Act requirements are classified as "Nonattainment Areas," wherein regulators can curtail new industrial or commercial development by denying the required air permits.

# Motor Carrier Act

The Motor Carrier Act of 1980 established minimum levels of financial responsibility for both private and for-hire carriers of hazardous materials. Its purpose is to protect the environment from releases of harmful materials during transportation of such materials by motor carriers in interstate or intrastate commerce.

One insurance mechanism that meets the act's requirements is the MCS 90 Endorsement. This endorsement, when attached to a commercial auto policy, promises that the insurer will pay any claims or judgments made against the transporter for public liability (bodily injury, property damage, or environmental restoration costs) resulting from operation of a covered auto.

The MCS 90 Endorsement is essentially a surety bond in that it requires the insured to reimburse the insurer for any payments made under the provisions of the MCS 90 that would not have been paid under the insurance policy in the absence of the endorsement. Because commercial auto insurance policies typically exclude most claims for loss caused by the release of pollutants from a covered auto, it is probable that the insured will have to reimburse the insurer for many losses that might be paid by the insurer under the MCS 90 for release of contaminants.

# Toxic Substance Control Act

The Toxic Substance Control Act, enacted in 1976, regulates the chemical manufacturing industry and prevents the importation or manufacture of dangerous chemical substances without adequate safeguards to ensure that their use does not harm human health or the environment. The act's statutory framework also facilitates extensive regulation of individual hazardous substances on a case-by-case basis.

Consequently, the act has been used to regulate polychlorinated biphenyls (PCBs) and, to a more limited extent, asbestos and radon. Under the Toxic Substance Control Act, manufacturers of chemical substances must provide extensive information to the Environmental Protection Agency (EPA) regarding the formulation, use, and risks of each substance they manufacture or import, including any information on known or suspected adverse health or environmental effects.

## Resource Conservation and Recovery Act

The Resource Conservation and Recovery Act (RCRA) provides "cradle-to-grave" regulation of hazardous waste. RCRA imposes strict waste management requirements on generators and transporters of hazardous wastes and on hazardous waste treatment, storage, and disposal facilities. RCRA also regulates underground storage tanks, medical wastes, and nonhazardous solid wastes, although the requirements for some of these waste categories are considerably less stringent than those for hazardous wastes.

RCRA was one of the first environmental statutes to adopt proof of financial responsibility requirements for permit holders. Under these provisions, the owners of hazardous waste treatment or storage facilities, landfills, and underground storage tanks are required to provide evidence that they have the financial resources to clean up any material from the facility that causes environmental damage and to compensate victims for bodily injury and property damage.

Permit holders have a number of options available to evidence this proof, including specially endorsed insurance policies, performance bonds, letters of credit, cash in escrow, self-insurer statuses, or, in some states, any financial arrangement acceptable to the regulators. The amounts of required proof vary by the type of facility and by state regulations. Insurance practitioners who need advice on compliance with these regulations should consult with the state environmental regulators for the current requirements and acceptable methods of providing the proof of financial responsibility.

## Comprehensive Environmental Response, Compensation, and Liability Act

Because RCRA regulations cover active but not abandoned waste disposal sites, the Comprehensive Environmental Response, Compensation, and Liability Act (CERCLA, or Superfund) was passed in 1980 to facilitate the cleanup of any abandoned or uncontrolled sites containing hazardous substances, including numerous old dump sites.

Potentially responsible parties (PRPs) are the persons or entities that are legally responsible for the costs of remediating a Superfund site. Parties involved with a Superfund site are referred to as PRPs until liability under the act is established. At that point, they become responsible parties (RPs). They are responsible for all costs associated with cleaning up the site, including the costs of identifying and evaluating contaminants and developing a plan for remediation. Following the "let the polluter pay" principle, the drafters of the original legislation included all parties who enjoyed an economic benefit from the waste disposal activities or from the ownership of the site.

PRPs can include any of these individuals:

- The current owners and operators of a site (even if they had no involvement with the original waste disposal activities)
- Prior owners and operators who may or may not have been involved with the site during the disposal of hazardous materials
- The generators of the waste materials disposed of at the site
- The transporters who hauled waste to the site
- Anyone who arranged for the disposal of materials at the site

Parent corporations may be liable for subsidiaries that are PRPs, depending on the extent of control over their subsidiaries and their involvement in waste disposal practices or decisions. Traditional notions of "piercing the corporate veil" (invalidating the legal protections of the corporate entity and suing the owners individually) will generally be applied during cost recovery efforts by the government.

Similarly, corporate successors may also be liable, depending on their involvement and the application of traditional principles of successor liability. Lessees may be liable as "operators" of the site, as may corporate officers or shareholders of closely held corporations. Even bankrupt parties may incur liability under CERCLA.

Superfund liability is strict (without regard to fault) and retroactive. This legislated liability is a significant deviation from traditional theories of recovery under the common law, which normally require negligence on the part of the defendant in order for the plaintiff to recover damages. In fact, many of the disposal sites that ultimately became Superfund sites were permitted legal operations at the time the sites were actively accepting waste.

Superfund liability is also joint and several, meaning any liable party may be responsible for the entire amount, regardless of its fair share, if, as is usually the case, the harm is indivisible. In allocating liability for the cleanup costs of a particular site, a PRP's assessment can be based on the volume of waste contributed to the site, not the toxicity of the waste. Therefore, the contributor of large volumes of nonhazardous materials to a Superfund site could be responsible for a large part of the cleanup cost even though it contributed only nonhazardous waste to the site.

Superfund is harsh and expensive for liable parties because it operates under a "let the polluter pay" funding scheme that features retroactive, strict liability. The passage of CERCLA and the resulting flood of claims by responsible parties under general liability policies were largely responsible for the proliferation of pollution exclusions in United States commercial insurance policies, beginning in 1986.

The far-reaching cost recovery provisions of CERCLA create a complex array of liability exposures for a broad spectrum of the U.S. economy. Most of the prospective loss exposures associated with Superfund can now be insured through a combination of various forms of environmental insurance.

## Oil Pollution Act

The Oil Pollution Act (OPA) of 1990 seeks to reduce the risk of spills of petroleum or hazardous materials into U.S. coastal or navigable waters by mandating technical standards for facilities and vessels operating in or near such waters. OPA also imposes requirements on owners of facilities and vessels to prevent releases and to pay for the costs of releases that are not prevented.

Similar in concept to the proof of financial responsibility requirements under RCRA, OPA mandates that each party responsible for a vessel or facility from which oil is discharged (or is threatening to be discharged) into or upon navigable waters, adjoining shorelines, or the exclusive economic zone of the U.S. is liable for removal costs and damages.

The amounts of required financial responsibility for a single vessel can be in the millions of dollars. Similar to RCRA, the methods that may be used to meet these requirements include specially endorsed insurance, a surety bond, a letter of credit, or qualification as a self-insurer.

# ENVIRONMENTAL RISK CONTROL

Risk management professionals must understand how risk control measures can be used to manage the environmental loss exposures of an organization.

An organization can apply these risk control measures—which have elements of avoidance, loss prevention, and loss reduction—to its environmental loss exposures:

- Source reduction
- Source treatment
- Disposal

## Source Reduction

**Source reduction** includes these basic risk control measures:

**Source reduction**

A procedure to reduce pollutants that emanate from an already existing source.

- Changing or modifying equipment—improving the efficiency of production equipment to produce less pollution
- Substituting materials—replacing a hazardous material with a safer one or substituting materials to improve process efficiency and to produce less pollution
- Redesigning process—improving the fundamental way an operation is accomplished to produce less pollution
- Redesigning the product—changing the fundamental product characteristics and features of the manufacturing process to produce less pollution
- Changing operations or human behavior—changing established procedures and practices (for example, maintenance and housekeeping procedures) to produce less pollution

# Source Treatment

**Source treatment**

A procedure to modify the pollutants that have already been produced.

To choose the appropriate **source treatment** risk control measure, risk management professionals should consider the pollutant's characteristics, the form it is in (solid, liquid, or gas), the media contaminated or threatened, government demands, and cost. The number of alternative technologies for risk control continues to grow as scientific understanding of the characteristics of pollutants increases.

Source treatment risk control measures include these:

- Recovery processes
- Physical and chemical processes
- Thermal processes
- Biological processes

## Recovery Processes

Certain wastes and emissions carry materials that can be reused. Recovery processes separate, remove, and concentrate reusable material from the waste. The reusable material is often sold or recycled back into the reusable process. When the reusable material is also the pollutant, the recovery process reduces the hazardous nature of the waste. However, in many cases, recovery processes are not an option for disposing of hazardous wastes, and additional treatment is required before the material can be safely and legally disposed of.

The equipment, chemicals, and chemical reactions in recovery processes often create a new set of wastes, residuals, and environmental loss exposures. Recovery processes are typically used to recover metals and solvents and are commonly used with liquid waste. Examples of recovery processes include these:

- Activated carbon absorption used in chemical spill response and industrial waste-water treatment exchange to recover metals from waste streams
- Distillation often used to recover solvents from waste streams

## Physical and Chemical Treatment Processes

Many physical and chemical processes are available to reduce the volume of waste, permit more economical and effective treatment, make waste less hazardous, and destroy the toxic components of waste. The processes are not significantly different from recovery processes but are used primarily for their treatment capabilities rather than for recovering and reusing materials. Both physical and chemical processes are used to separate and segregate waste components.

Chemical processes also alter the hazardous nature of the waste. However, as with recovery processes, the equipment and chemicals used and the residuals created from the treatment process create additional loss exposures. These processes may also require pretreatment to prepare the waste for treatment.

Examples of physical and chemical processes include filtration used to treat material such as oily waste water, chemical precipitation commonly used to treat corrosives, and dehalogenation used to treat PCBs and contaminated soil.

## Thermal Processes

Thermal processes dissolve wastes either through combustion or pyrolysis (chemical decomposition caused by heating in the absence of oxygen). Thermal processes can, in a matter of seconds, destroy materials that would take many years to deteriorate in a landfill. Many sophisticated thermal processes are available to treat materials such as solvents, PCBs, dioxins, contaminated soil, and infectious wastes. Depending on the thermal process used, treatment temperatures can range from several hundreds to several thousands of degrees.

Most thermal processes are managed by organizations specializing in waste management, although some wastes can be incinerated on site. Using waste as fuel, however, is carefully regulated. Many wastes, such as heavy metals, cyanides, insecticides, pesticides, PCBs, and radioactive materials, should not be incinerated because of safety considerations. Organizations using on-site incineration must also have a Resource Conservation and Recovery Act (RCRA) permit. Although typically very effective in destroying wastes, thermal processes are often expensive and have precise control requirements. Many thermal processes also create wastes that need management and disposal.

## Biological Processes

Biological processes, which use living organisms to treat waste, include aerobic digestion (needing oxygen), anaerobic digestion (not needing oxygen), and composting (or land application). Many chemicals are degradable through biological processes using formaldehyde, acetone, and isopropyl alcohol.

An ongoing challenge in using these processes is maintaining the right type of ecosystem for microbes. Temperature, moisture content, existence of other organisms, and oxygen supply are just some of the parameters that must be identified and controlled.

## Disposal

Disposal can be accomplished with **solidification, stabilization, and encapsulation processes**. These processes improve waste handling characteristics, decrease the surface area across which pollutants can transfer, or detoxify waste constituents.

Solidification, stabilization, and encapsulation processes

Processes that use additives to reduce the mobility of pollutants so that the waste meets land disposal requirements.

Solidification adds materials to the waste to produce a solid. Stabilization converts the waste to a more chemically stable form. This includes solidification but may also include chemical reactions. Encapsulation completely coats or encloses the waste with a new substance, either by individual particles or as an aggregate. These processes treat residuals from previous treatment processes so that they can be disposed of legally, and are becoming increasingly important because land disposal restrictions are becoming more stringent.

## Risk Control Measure Hierarchy

From a risk control perspective, there is a hierarchy of risk control measures. Source reduction is the preferred measure because loss exposures are avoided completely or reduced without creating new exposures in other areas.

If source reduction is not feasible, source treatment measures are the next in order of preference. There is also a hierarchy among the source treatment measures. First is the recovery process. In the recovery process, the pollutant is reused or recycled so that the organization is able to prevent or reduce pollutants. If the recovery process is not feasible, then the physical and chemical treatment process is the next preferred measure. Physical and chemical treatment processes decrease the potential environmental effect and are the most common measures used because they provide the highest degree of predictability and simplicity in dealing with environmental regulations. However, because those measures manage but do not prevent pollutants, some loss exposures might remain or new ones may be created.

Disposal, which includes the thermal, biological and solidification, stabilization and encapsulation processes, is the least desirable risk control measure for two reasons. First, introducing pollutants directly to environment implicitly entails the greatest risk. Second, environmental law dictates that liability for environmental harm remains with the organization—even if the organization contracts with another organization for this service.

## Risk Control Measure Selection Considerations

Several considerations influence which risk control measures should be selected. The first consideration is the technical feasibility of a risk control measure. The measure must be technically viable and appropriate given the specific context. Technical viability includes determining the commercial availability of the measure and performing an engineering study to determine whether the loss exposure would actually be controlled to the extent needed. The measure should also be appropriate in the broader context of business operations.

For example, a new piece of equipment might dramatically reduce waste volumes but substantially increase the time it takes to manufacture the product—a strategy unacceptable to management. Or a certain water treatment system might be technically ideal but unable to handle the amount of water wastes generated during peak production times.

The risk control team should ask questions such as these to determine the technical feasibility of a risk control measure:

- What are the space, operation, or management requirements of the measure?
- Is the measure commercially available?
- Is the measure compatible with current procedures, workflows, and production activities?
- Will the measure negatively affect product quality or other business concerns?
- Will the measure aggravate other environmental loss exposures or create new ones?
- Will the measure be sustainable for a long period?
- Will the measure withstand market, regulatory, and property use changes?
- Will new training, skills, or expertise be needed to manage the measure once it is in place?

A second consideration is the measure's economic feasibility. This includes capital costs (equipment, installation, and start-up), operating costs (supplies, parts, utilities, and labor), and intangible costs (potential loss of community goodwill and future liability costs). Economic benefits should also be calculated, including cost savings in environmental risk management and compliance, raw materials, maintenance and operation, and insurance.

The final and perhaps most important consideration is the feasibility of the measure regarding environmental regulatory demands. Environmental laws are often extremely prescriptive. Many environmental risk management activities, which on the surface appear to be effective and cost-efficient, may be illegal.

For example, an organization may want to improve the ambient air quality for its factory workers by venting solvent emissions to the outside. This practice is probably illegal under state clean-air statutes. Suppose an organization wants to establish an evaporation system to reduce the total volume of spent solvent sent to an off-site hazardous waste treatment facility. This seemingly effective strategy would be considered "on-site treatment" and illegal under RCRA without an appropriate permit.

In other situations, regulatory demands might mandate certain risk controls or technologies. In short, coordination with legal departments and regulatory specialists is essential to ensure that risk control measures under consideration do not exacerbate or create new environmental liability loss exposures.

# CLIMATE CHANGE RISK

Risk managers and insurers must address the potential effects of global warming and climate change on their organizations.

A growing body of scientific evidence has documented a gradual warming of the earth's atmosphere over the past century-and-a-half. Many scientists have attributed this phenomenon to human-caused emissions of greenhouse gases; however, global warming and its causes are subjects of continuing debate in both scientific and political circles. Controversy also surrounds the extent and nature of climate change; its implications for countries, businesses, and individuals; and appropriate responses.

As the debate continues, many governments, business organizations, and insurers are beginning to consider the potential for a wide variety of climate-change risks, including property, business, liability, environmental, regulatory, and reputational risk. Identifying, predicting, and treating these risks will become increasingly important to risk management professionals and others over coming decades.

## Climate Change Debate

Although some scientists contend that global warming is the result of natural climatic variations, a consensus of scientific bodies has attributed global warming to human emissions of the byproducts of fossil fuels and other substances, such as ozone, methane, and nitrous oxide, into the earth's atmosphere.

Various scientific scenarios of global warming's effect on the earth's climate, populations, countries, ecosystems, and economies have been presented. Shrinking sea ice, receding glaciers, and thawing of permafrost in and near polar areas have been cited as evidence of the effects of global warming. Among predicted results of continued warming are rising sea levels and sea temperatures, fundamental changes to ecosystems, and more frequent and severe weather events.

Indeed, the late twentieth and early twenty-first centuries have seen many severe weather events of record intensity. Hurricanes, river flooding, ice storms, hailstorms, windstorms, prairie and forest fires, heat waves, droughts, and tornadoes have caused record losses across the globe. Some experts suggest that these events and corresponding losses result from global warming; others attribute them to natural weather variations, which cause ever-increasing losses because of growing populations and development in vulnerable areas.

# Types of Climate Change Risks

Many organizations are considering the effects of climate change on future losses in these areas of risk:[1]

- Physical risks—Increasing frequency and severity of major storm events, such as hurricanes, in areas of significant population growth may dramatically increase losses by damaging property and interrupting transportation, power supplies, and distribution chains and by causing injury or death to employees. Coastal erosion and property damage from rising sea levels could increase property losses by billions of dollars. Water shortages resulting from decreased snowpack could significantly affect manufacturing operations. Medical facilities and organizations' employee health coverages could become inadequate to deal with increased health risks caused by heat and insect-borne diseases.

- Litigation risks—Organizations may face litigation for contributing to climate change. Such claims may arise from individual shareholder suits, class action suits, and regulatory agency actions. Stockholder lawsuits could focus on whether a company's officers and directors rendered a company unprofitable by failing to plan for climate change. Climate change mismanagement could become a more common type of litigation in class action lawsuits. Organizations may also face action by government agencies for failure to comply with environmental regulations.

- Stockholder risks—Stockholders and investors are demanding more "transparency" from corporate leaders relating to their fiduciary responsibility to take action in relation to climate change. Corporate investors may petition the Securities and Exchange Commission (SEC) to require companies to disclose climate change risks. An organization that ignores climate change risk can lose investors, who may prefer, instead, to invest in organizations perceived to be environmentally responsible.

- Regulatory risks—Many governmental agencies are strengthening disclosure requirements and performance standards for energy utilization and consumption and establishing greenhouse gas emission controls. For example, European Union (EU) countries have imposed mandatory emissions reduction targets with significant noncompliance penalties. The Kyoto Protocol of the United Nations Framework Convention on Climate Change, ratified by the EU and its member states in 2002, contains legally binding emissions targets for developed countries. As of 2012, the United States had not adopted the Kyoto Protocol. However, many U.S. states and regions are enacting regulations aimed at global warming and greenhouse emissions. Other regulatory risks can include carbon taxes; energy efficiency regulations; and mandated uses of greener technologies, building materials, and building design. Risk managers of companies with international operations or exposures should be aware of differences in regulations from country to country.

- Reputational risks—Publicity about poor environmental policies or high greenhouse gas emissions can damage an organization's reputation.

Repercussions of reputational damage can influence jurors in lawsuits involving the organization, local government bodies that grant zoning or construction permits, business news reporters, potential customers, environmental activists, and investors.

- Competition risks—An organization's ability to compete may be compromised by its failure to address climate change risks. Organizations that establish effective policies to deal with climate change exposures will have the competitive advantage among customers and interest groups who are concerned about environmental issues.

# Climate Change Risk Treatment

Climate change risk can be addressed through risk control, risk finance, and risk transfer techniques.

## Risk Control

Organizations can adopt a variety of risk control measures in relation to climate change, including these:

- Appointment of team or individual to be responsible for climate change risk management—A person or team with a working knowledge of climate change should be appointed to address the climate change exposure.

- Risk avoidance—An organization may choose to withdraw from business areas that present climate change risk. An analysis of environmental costs and risks for various products or processes could reveal new market and product opportunities that may reduce climate change risk.

- Disclosure of financial risks—A detailed disclosure of an organization's climate change risks indicates a company's good-faith effort to measure, mitigate, and control climate change loss exposures. Such a disclosure may help encourage and retain investors.

- Disaster planning—Organizations must develop disaster planning for catastrophic events such as hurricanes, which may increase in frequency and intensity. These plans may include evacuation procedures, arrangements for alternative facilities, stockpiling of emergency supplies, and more frequent computer data backup.

- Reduction of greenhouse gases—Companies that emit greenhouse gases should assess their internal emissions reduction opportunities in comparison with externally available approaches.

- Energy conservation and alternate energy usage—Energy conservation can include actions such as installing energy-efficient windows, using energy efficient lightbulbs, and adopting alternate energy approaches such as wind power and solar power.

- Adoption of "green" building measures and approaches—Structures can be built to promote energy conservation and use environmentally friendly construction products and processes such as geothermal heat pumps, rainwater collection, and radiant ceilings.

- Support for stricter building codes—Organizations should support and use stricter building codes that seek to prevent or reduce hurricane and other climate-related losses.

- Integration of climate change with overall business strategies—Climate change risk management decisions should be aligned with an organization's business strategies.

## Risk Finance

The key risk finance technique for climate change loss exposures is insurance, particularly coverages for property, general liability/environmental, and directors and officers (D&O) liability.

If climate change causes more frequent and severe events, such as floods, fires, and hurricanes, property losses will increase. Property insurance costs could rise, and some insurance coverages may be unavailable. Organizations should work closely with their insurance agents and brokers to determine the effects of climate change on their property loss exposures and take steps to mitigate and control the losses.

Whether climate change liability is covered under commercial general liability policies is uncertain; in some cases, coverage may depend on how the pollution exclusion is applied. Insurers could conceivably use the pollution exclusion to deny claims of loss resulting from greenhouse gas emissions. Even if a causal connection is established among an insured's emissions, specific climate change, and the loss, an insured could theoretically argue that the loss was proximately caused by an effect of climate change, such as flooding, and only secondarily caused by greenhouse gas emissions. For example, if an organization's emissions were proved to have contributed to warming the atmosphere sufficiently to cause sea levels to rise and flooding to occur, the proximate cause of loss would be flooding, thereby avoiding the pollution exclusion.

Because of this uncertainty, risk managers should consider special environmental liability coverage. However, these policies may apply only when a causal connection is established between the insured's action and measurable harm. Insurers could cite the continuing scientific debate about the cause of global warming and the difficulties of measuring effects in denying coverage under environmental liability policies.

Risk managers should also consider climate change risk as it relates to D&O liability insurance. Shareholders may sue directors and officers for failure to disclose liabilities, loss of revenues or market share, and reputational damage resulting from climate change exposures. However, some D&O policies specifically exclude coverage for liability relating to climate change or global warming. Risk managers should also review D&O policy provisions that exclude or limit coverage for bodily injury or property damage, personal injury torts, or intentional misconduct to determine how such provisions might apply to climate change risk. To mitigate risk under D&O policies, organizations should take measures to fully disclose their financial risks and should use alternate energy sources.

## Risk Transfer

Organizations may be able to transfer some climate change risk with techniques other than insurance. Two such techniques include weather derivatives and carbon trading.

Organizations can use weather derivatives to reduce financial risk associated with adverse weather conditions. A weather derivative is a financial contract whose value is based on the level of a weather-related index derived from variables such as average temperatures, snowfall, precipitation, or wind velocity during a designated period.

For example, a ski resort could purchase a weather derivative to mitigate the financial risk arising from insufficient snowfall or from higher-than-normal temperatures. Such a derivative could be designed to pay an agreed-upon amount for each inch the cumulative snowfall falls short of the base amount needed by the end of December to ensure the resort a profitable season.

Similarly, a power plant could use a derivative based on temperature to mitigate losses resulting from reduced energy use during a warmer-than-normal winter. Such a derivative could be designed to pay an agreed-upon amount per "heating degree days" (HDDs) within a designated period. The HDD measures the difference between average daily temperature and the base temperatures in a particular location. Financial organizations and experts continue to develop innovative indexes on which to base weather derivatives and innovative ways to gather data for such indexes. For example, derivatives based on indexes of soil moisture content could help farmers and agricultural businesses reduce the financial risk of drought; and soil moisture content can be derived from satellite images.

Carbon or emissions trading is used to control the overall amount of pollution in a given geographical area or country. Typically, a governing body establishes a cap on the amount of a pollutant that can be emitted. Companies are issued emission permits with credits or allowances that allow them to emit specific amounts of pollutants. The total amount of credits cannot exceed the cap. Organizations that need to exceed their emissions allowance limit can buy credits from organizations that pollute less. The transfer of these credits is called a trade.

In effect, the buyer of emissions credits pays for its emissions beyond its allowed allotment, and the seller is rewarded for reducing its emissions below its allotment. As a result, organizations that can easily reduce greenhouse emissions most inexpensively will do so, and the overall cost of reducing pollution is, in theory, reduced. Two of the largest carbon-emissions trading markets are the European Union Emissions Trading Scheme and the voluntary Chicago Climate Exchange program.

Critics of carbon trading suggest that the approach does not effectively reduce emissions. For example, caps that are set too high can result in surplus credits. Organizations are likely to purchase these readily available credits rather than reduce emissions. Furthermore, because credit allotments are based on past emission levels, an organization that successfully reduces its emissions may receive fewer credits in the future, reducing its incentive to reduce emissions even further. See the exhibit "Climate Change Litigation."

---

### Climate Change Litigation

In 2011, the United States Supreme Court ruled that federal regulation of emissions of carbon dioxide and other greenhouse gases preempts a plaintiff's right to sue under common law to stop a defendant's actions alleged to contribute to global warming.

Eight states and several conservation groups filed suit against the operators of five fossil-fuel fired power plants, demanding that they be required to reduce their emissions of carbon dioxide on the grounds that such emissions contribute to global warming. The district court dismissed the case, ruling that the environmental issues involved were within the purview of the legislative and executive branches rather than the courts.

The appeals court reversed the ruling on the basis that the executive branch's Environmental Protection Agency (EPA) did not at that time regulate carbon greenhouse gas emissions under the Clean Air Act; therefore, the plaintiffs could seek recourse in their common-law nuisance complaint. Although the EPA subsequently promulgated emission regulations, the Supreme Court ruled that even if the EPA were to decline to regulate emissions, the fact that Congress had delegated that authority to the EPA was sufficient to preempt common law actions.

---

State of Connecticut, et al., v. American Electric Power Company, Inc., et. al., 131 S.Ct. 2527 (2011). [DA08687]

## SUMMARY

Liability for pollution incidents can be based on negligence, intentional torts (such as nuisance or trespass), strict liability, or various environmental statutes. These environmental statutes have made environmental risk management and insurance much more important than in the past.

Although liability loss exposures are the predominant concern in environmental risk control, property, personnel, and net income loss exposures may also arise from environmental pollution. Environmental pollution can affect the value of real property, and spills and leaks can affect personal property. Personnel can be affected if they are not provided with a healthy and safe work environment, and environmental pollution events or environmental cleanup can result in significant net income losses.

One of the common threads that run through most environmental statutes is the principle that the party that caused the pollution should be responsible for paying for the cleanup of that pollution in the case of a spill or release.

The risk control measures that can be applied to environmental loss exposures—source reduction, source treatment, and disposal—contain elements of avoidance, loss prevention, and loss reduction. Source reduction is the preferred measure, followed by source treatment and then disposal. Three factors to consider in the selection of risk control measures are technical feasibility, economic feasibility, and regulatory demands.

Risk managers and insurers must address the potential effects of global warming and climate change on their organizations. Climate change risks include property, business, liability, environmental, regulatory, and reputational risk. Risk transfer, risk control, and risk finance techniques should be considered to address climate change risks.

## ASSIGNMENT NOTE

1. This section and the next are based on "Climate Change Risk Management Issues," an article written for the CPCU Society eJournal by Robin Olson (copyright 2008, International Risk Management Institute, Inc.), and a more general article of the same title in Practical Risk Management, Ed., Millie Workman, International Risk Management Institute (IRMI), Risk Management Notes #222, December 2007, www.irmi.come/online/pracrisk/ch0notes/prmn0222.aspx (accessed February 29, 2012). Used with permission.

# Direct Your Learning ▶▶

# 9

# Crime and Cyber Risk

## Educational Objectives

After learning the content of this assignment, you should be able to:

▷ Describe the distinctive features of crime risk and their implications for risk management.

▷ Describe the characteristics of common crimes.

▷ Explain how to use risk control measures against crime losses.

▷ Describe the cyber risk loss exposures in each of the following categories:

- Property
- Net income
- Liability

▷ Explain how organizations can control or finance their cyber risk exposures.

▷ Describe sources of social media risk and ways to control it.

# Crime and Cyber Risk

# 9

## DISTINCTIVE FEATURES OF CRIME RISK

Risk control strives to protect an organization, its employees, and its customers against the criminal intent or conduct of others, both outside and inside the organization.

A crime is an act (or sometimes a failure to act) that violates the rights of individuals or organizations. Crimes, whether committed against or by an organization, can result in property, personnel, liability, or net income losses. People, businesses, and other entities all face loss exposures from crime.

Hostile intent is one distinctive feature of criminal loss exposures. Organizations should continually evaluate their crime risk control efforts and adjust them when necessary.

### Hostile Intent

Human actions or faults contribute significantly to many types of loss. For example, ignorance or carelessness may cause property damage or bodily injury. A lack of reasonable care for others' safety may cause a negligence liability loss.

However, crime is not the result of an accident, negligence, or a natural event; it is an intentional act. Therefore, to reduce the frequency and severity or to improve the predictability of crime losses, risk control measures must focus on hostile intent. For example, both accidental fires and fires set by arsonists can seriously damage a building. However, some of the ordinary precautions against accidental fire damage, such as controls on ignition sources and on excessive accumulations of combustibles, are not as effective against fires set by arsonists. Arsonists supply their own rapidly burning fuels, fire accelerants, and ignition sources.

As another example, boards stored for use to protect exterior windows against windstorms may provide little protection against bricks hurled by vandals or rioters. Organizations may have some forewarning of windstorms, but they rarely have any advance warning of crimes. Similarly, a computerized quality control monitoring system, designed to ensure the uniformity of products from an automated assembly line, is not effective if the employees operating the system intentionally sabotage the company's products. Therefore, effective risk control measures against crime losses must recognize that criminals are driven by hostile intent.

Many people with criminal intentions constantly look for new opportunities for crime. Criminals search for high-value, easily transported items; unguarded property; vulnerable people; or unprotected key operations. A risk management professional needs to identify the organization's property, personnel, or operations that are particularly vulnerable to crime. The professional must also anticipate new opportunities for criminals to attack the organization and try to devise countermeasures in advance. New opportunities for crime are especially likely when an organization undergoes change (for example, acquires new facilities, develops new operating procedures, or hires new employees). Each of those changes creates potential gaps in the organization's security program.

## Continual Evaluation of Risk Control Efforts

Crime risk control efforts require continual evaluation because criminals may discover weaknesses in an organization's processes at any time. To illustrate, if the automatic fire detection/suppression system in a restaurant's kitchen is defective, several months or even years could pass before a fire accidentally starts in the kitchen and causes severe damage. However, if a disgruntled kitchen employee decides to intentionally set fire to the restaurant under circumstances that appear accidental, the employee could use the defect in the sprinkler system to facilitate and conceal the arson.

As another example, security procedures for depositing its daily cash receipts might require an organization's courier to randomly change the routes traveled to and from the bank. If the courier deviates from that procedure and follows more predictable routes, that predictability is a weakness in security procedures that criminals can exploit. The courier or the courier's supervisor may use detailed knowledge of the organization's operations to reveal potential opportunities to persons with whom he or she shares hostile intent that allow those persons to circumvent the organization's risk control measures.

Continual evaluation of risk control efforts is crucial in preventing any breakdowns or gaps in an organization's risk control measures. Most employees will report such breakdowns or gaps to management so that those problems can be corrected. However, some employees might be tempted to take advantage of those security weaknesses for reasons of personal gain. Therefore, it is important that the employees responsible for the daily functioning of an organization's risk control measures must be among its most trustworthy.

Risk control techniques should focus on taking precautions, such as these, to eliminate weaknesses that make the organization a relatively easy crime target:

- Shielding the organization's assets and activities by maintaining physical, procedural, and managerial barriers that reduce criminal opportunities
- Reducing criminals' perceptions that they can commit crimes against the organization without being detected and with legal impunity

# CHARACTERISTICS OF COMMON CRIMES

To develop effective crime risk control measures, an organization's risk manager must understand the characteristics of crimes to which the organization is vulnerable.

Crimes violate the peace and order of the general population. Crimes are defined either by common-law precedents (which are based on court decisions and recognized in most jurisdictions) or by statutes that apply only in the jurisdictions whose legislative bodies enacted those laws. Persons or organizations accused of criminal acts are prosecuted by local, state, or federal governments in criminal courts on behalf of the public. Courts impose punishments—for example, fines or imprisonment—on those found guilty of crimes.

Many crimes are also torts against the crime victims. The victims can sue wrongdoers in civil courts to collect monetary damages or to enforce other legal remedies. Therefore, anyone committing a crime could potentially be found liable in both a criminal and a civil court.

Common crimes include burglary, robbery, shoplifting, fraud, embezzlement, forgery and counterfeiting, vandalism, arson, terrorism, espionage, and computer crime. Each crime has specific characteristics.

## Burglary

**Burglary** may include breaking into or out of buildings; it may also involve entering a business when it is open to the public, hiding, and leaving the building after it is closed. A person can commit burglary even if property is not taken. For example, if criminals break through the wall of a bank to take money from the vault but flee before reaching the vault, they have still burglarized the bank. Even if they reach the vault only to find it empty, they have burglarized both the bank and the vault.

**Burglary**
The act of breaking into or out of any closed building or space not open for business to commit another felony.

## Robbery

**Robbery** is often used incorrectly to refer to theft; however, robbery involves the threat of force. In contrast to burglars, who normally steal property from buildings or unoccupied areas, robbers harm or threaten to harm people in order to steal from them. The safety of personnel and customers is usually a major concern during a robbery. Also important to consider is that the employees subjected to a robbery can sometimes help identify and prosecute the criminals.

**Robbery**
The act of taking tangible personal property from another person by force or by threat of force against that person or against another.

## Shoplifting

Merchants' annual losses from **shoplifting** can be several times their losses from robbery or burglary. Shoplifters typically conceal the stolen items on their person or in containers they are carrying. Shoplifters can work alone, in

**Shoplifting**
The removal of merchandise from a store by stealth without purchasing it.

teams, or in collusion with the store's employees or others, and they typically avoid confrontation and violence. They usually pose as customers or as others who have a legitimate purpose for being in the store, such as maintenance personnel or law enforcement officers.

Shoplifters want their thefts to pass unnoticed, so security procedures or surveillance systems aimed at detecting theft can be effective in both catching and discouraging shoplifters. Hidden safeguards such as security tags, cameras, and undercover security personnel are also useful to detect shoplifters.

Efforts to thwart shoplifters, as well as other thieves, can create other loss exposures. For example, a shoplifter confronted too aggressively may become violent, possibly injuring employees or customers or even creating a hostage situation. A person who is wrongfully accused of shoplifting or committing another theft can have a valid tort liability claim against the store for defamation, assault, wrongful imprisonment, or malicious prosecution. An organization's on-site procedures for handling suspected thieves must guard against both theft and these other possible types of losses.

# Fraud

**Fraud**

An intentional misrepresentation resulting in harm to a person or an organization.

Criminals may use **fraud** to induce another to act to his or her detriment. For example, deceiving someone into surrendering money or property is considered fraud. Victims may be persuaded to pay in advance for goods, services, rights to property ownership, or other benefits that they never receive or that are worth far less than they paid. Internet commerce enormously expands the global horizon for fraud.

Examples of fraud include these:

- A merchant collects payment in advance for goods that the merchant knows will not be delivered or will be greatly inferior to what the purchaser is entitled to receive.
- A customer accepts delivery of goods with the intention of not paying for them.
- An inventor sells all rights to an invention that has been developed and patented by another person.
- An unauthorized person acquires and uses the account number, personal identification number, or other identifying information of an organization's credit or debit card and charges personal items to the organization's account (in effect, impersonating an authorized card user).
- A person falsely claims to have been injured by a product and brings a large negligence suit against the manufacturer.

# Embezzlement

**Embezzlement**

The fraudulent taking of money or other personal property by one to whom that property has been entrusted.

**Embezzlement** may be committed by an employee or an agent acting in a fiduciary capacity. For example, an employee who makes personal use of money entrusted to him or her by an employer for business use or delivery commits embezzlement. Embezzlement can also involve a group of employees, perhaps in collusion with others, who interfere with the organization's selling or purchasing procedures to divert cash and merchandise for their own use.

Embezzlement is a crime of stealth or deception rather than a violent or forceful crime like robbery or burglary. It occurs because dishonest employees find and seize opportunities to secretly compromise the organization's procedures for their or others' benefit.

## Forgery and Counterfeiting

Both **forgery** and **counterfeiting** involve fraudulently creating or using false or unauthorized versions of currency, documents, artwork, or other property that only specified entities or persons have the right to make or use or unauthorized versions of documents such as stock certificates, birth records, lottery tickets, driver's or other licenses, passports, or other papers that only government agencies or other entities (such as corporations or banks) have the right to issue.

Counterfeiters and forgers can cause two broad types of crime losses:

- They can induce an organization to accept falsified currency, checks, credit cards, other negotiable instruments, documents, or artwork. When the organization exchanges something of value for the valueless items, the organization's immediate loss is the value of whatever it relinquished in the exchange. (The organization may incur additional costs to correct its original mistake of having accepted the counterfeit or forged items.)
- By creating or using unauthorized or stolen copies of the organization's own documents (for example, checks; identification cards; invoices; purchase orders; or even business cards, letterhead, and envelopes), they can impersonate the organization. Falsified documents can be used to manipulate funds, make seemingly valid promises, and issue "official" statements that harm the organization financially or damage its reputation.

**Forgery**
The act of creating or presenting false documents or artwork as genuine in order to commit fraud.

**Counterfeiting**
A form of forgery that involves privately duplicating a country's currency or presenting it as genuine with knowledge that it is not.

## Vandalism

**Vandalism** is often committed out of anger, revenge, envy, or simply boredom. It is done without the consent of the owner or the user of the property and without any just cause. Vandals usually damage property to attack those who own or use the property; they do not want the property itself.

**Vandalism**
Willful and malicious damage to or destruction of property.

## Arson

**Arson** may be either malicious or fraudulent and may involve the arsonist's property or property of another. An owner of property who conspires with others to burn it commits fraud by arson and, in some jurisdictions, can be convicted of arson as well.

**Arson**
The deliberate setting of fire to property for a fraudulent or malicious purpose.

# Terrorism

The September 11, 2001, terrorist attacks in the United States brought the crime of terrorism into persistent focus via the media, local and national governments, and risk management associations around the world.

Terrorists often have an underlying political agenda. Domestic terrorists may target an organization's property, persons, and activities with the intention of forcing the organization to change or close its business, for example, to stop research labs from using animals. Terrorism may also involve the deliberate contamination of property through chemical, biological, or radioactive materials, or the destruction of property by bombing or aerial impact.

Potentially high-risk targets are federal buildings, military operations, financial institutions, power plants, transportation hubs, communication networks, and biotechnology facilities. An attack could involve events such as a high-profile political, sporting, or monetary event, like a presidential inauguration, the Olympic Games, or an international trade conference.

# Espionage

**Espionage**

The act of obtaining confidential information through personal observation or mechanical, digital, or electronic techniques that circumvent efforts to protect the information's confidentiality.

Many organizations keep much of their operating information confidential to protect themselves from the results of **espionage**, which could include these:

- Interference with competitive advantage through the revelation of trade secrets
- Violation of employees' rights to keep their personal information from becoming public knowledge
- Revelation of national defense secrets

# Computer Crime

**Computer crime**

A criminal act using a computer to gain authorized or unauthorized access to steal, interrupt, or misuse computer system information.

**Computer sabotage**

The deliberate and hostile destruction of hardware or software or the disruption of productive processes.

**Computer crime** can involve damaging or using computer hardware or software to achieve an illegal purpose such as embezzlement, espionage, fraud, terrorism, or vandalism. Types of computer crimes can include these:

- **Computer sabotage**—Acts of computer sabotage include striking computer components with heavy objects, spilling caustic solutions on circuit boards and wires, introducing foreign matter into a computer's or printer's moving parts, or deliberately manipulating data to render a computer program unreliable.
- Fraud and embezzlement—By manipulating computer programs, embezzlers can drain an organization's financial resources for years without being detected. In collusion with other employees or outsiders, an employee can defraud an organization of sales revenue, inventories, and customer records resulting in large property and net income losses.
- Computer network breach—Vulnerable computer servers present loss exposures to computer operations because of their vital central

administrative role within computer networks. Password protections to reduce such exposures can fail if passwords are revealed.

- Theft through hacking—Computer hackers typically steal data to learn trade secrets or to determine a competitor's marketing or financial strategy. Hacking through the Internet can be an international activity, with criminals distributed around the world. Hackers may use computer viruses or "Trojan horses" that surreptitiously cull credit card data, passwords, or other sensitive information from an organization's systems.

- Theft of data storage systems—When no effective risk control measures exist, a thief with access to a server can quickly and easily remove or copy data. This type of crime is different from theft by hacking in that the theft can be committed by anyone with authorized access to the server. The data often include customer lists, product information, crucial operating procedures, general trade secrets, or other intellectual property. Prompt business recovery from such a theft may require off-site computer systems backup.

- Theft of computer time—Unauthorized use by employees of computer time for personal purposes can occur when computer use is not supervised or audited. This crime also increases the probability of loss from the surreptitious manipulation of data.

- Denial of service—A denial-of-service attack prevents proper network communications. During such an attack, the organization's server may be flooded with so much incoming data that it crashes. The attackers may follow-up with extortion e-mails. Alternatively, criminals may hack into customer databases and send out hundreds of thousands of e-mails illicitly, thereby wasting valuable computer time. Any denial of service can result in a business interruption loss.

- Espionage—Espionage can be committed indirectly by hacking or directly within the organization's own computer center. When information has been stolen but no evidence of its theft exists, the loss is doubly expensive because the victimized organization continues to operate on the assumption that the data are safe. If the breach in security had been known, additional losses and related expenses might have been prevented even if the data could not have been retrieved.

# CONTROLLING CRIME LOSSES

Crimes can result in property, personnel, liability, or net income losses. An organization can use risk control measures to protect itself, its employees, and its customers against the criminal intent or conduct of others, both outside and inside the organization.

An organization attempting to control crime risk must deter, detect, and deny. Deterrence seeks to prevent crime by reducing or eliminating the motivation and opportunity to commit a crime. If deterrence does not work or is not feasible, efforts should focus on detecting criminal behavior before it results in loss to the organization and, finally, denial of the facilities, tools, and other capabilities to those intent on causing loss.

Various crime risk control measures seek either to prevent losses or to reduce their frequency or severity. Loss prevention focuses deterrence and detection. Loss reduction focuses on reducing the severity of crimes that do occur by denying the criminal the chance to cause a large loss. Some loss reduction measures reduce the scale of crime; others assist an organization in recovering rapidly after a crime has been committed.

# Crime Risk Control Measures

Criminals tend to target vulnerable organizations. An organization's business cycle has peak periods during which the organization is more vulnerable than at other times, perhaps because of high inventory levels or seasonal production factors. Particular attention to risk control measures is needed during these peak periods.

Crime risk control measures that focus on deterrence and detection include these:

- Sound personnel policies
- Physical controls
- Procedural controls
- Managerial controls
- Investigation and prosecution of crimes

## Sound Personnel Policies

Sound personnel policies can help prevent employee crime. Effective personnel policy requirements and practices include background checks on potential employees, fair treatment of all employees, prompt and equitable resolution of grievances, and termination of or appropriate specified actions against employees who commit crimes against the organization. To implement these risk control measures, the risk management professional must work closely with the human resources department. This is particularly important because of legal limitations imposed on organizations doing employee background checks.

Some employees can become targets of violent crime. Violence in the workplace can cause work-related injuries, as well as property, personnel, liability, and net income losses for the organization. An organization should encourage employees and their supervisors to report situations that could lead to violence at work. However, because such situations can sometimes involve an employee's personal relationships, those who address such situations must protect employees' right to privacy. Wrongfully invading an employee's privacy or unduly interfering with an employee's personal relationships can expose an organization to tort liability.

Employees may become hostile toward an organization when faced with temptations or conflicts between obligations to their employer and obligations to others. For example, an employee facing financial problems might consider embezzling from the employer. Employees who perceive that they have been treated unfairly may also consider violence or other crimes against the employer. Sound personnel policies, accompanied by training, can help managers recognize potentially explosive situations and help employees resolve dilemmas constructively and peaceably.

Hostility toward an organization can also develop among customers, neighbors, and others, leading them to vandalize property; tamper with products; commit arson, computer-based fraud, or espionage; organize boycotts; or bring frivolous lawsuits against the organization. An organization's risk management professional should work cooperatively with its public relations department to recognize and defuse situations that could escalate into criminal activity.

## Physical Controls

Physical controls of crime losses are tangible barriers between would-be criminals and their targets. Physical controls include walls; fences; crash barriers; locked doors, vaults, and safes; guards and guard dogs; and automatic intruder-detection devices and alarms. Less apparent physical barriers include placing a particularly crucial or vulnerable facility in a remote location, conducting sensitive activities (such as chemical testing) near the center of an organization's facility, and surrounding property that criminals might be tempted to attack at night with intense lighting.

Although alarms can serve as deterrents, their primary function is to detect an intruder who has already entered the premises and thereby potentially reduce the loss. Various types of alarm systems are available, including these:

- A **perimeter system**—Electrical contacts or metal tapes on each door, window, or other building opening are wired so that an electrical current passes constantly through the system. Opening a door or a window interrupts the electrical current, which activates an alarm. A perimeter system provides no protection against entry through a roof or a wall.

- Foot pedal alarm—Alarms that are triggered by buttons or foot pedals can be situated so that a bank teller or store clerk, for example, can send a silent alarm to a central location or to the police while a crime is in progress.

- Interior alarm system—Systems that sound on the premises when unlawful entry is made can be effective in a store with security personnel on duty at all times but would be of little use in an industrial or a mercantile district where few people are present at night.

- Central station alarm—Some systems are connected to and constantly monitored at an alarm company central station. When the alarm sounds

**Perimeter system**

A type of burglar alarm system that is designed to signal an alarm whenever unauthorized entry is made into the building.

at the central station, a guard is sent to the alarm transmission site and police are notified.

- Automatic system—When central station service is not available, organizations can use an automatic system that dials the police telephone number and transmits a recorded message when the alarm is activated. However, such systems can be deactivated by placing telephone calls from nearby phones or by disconnecting the telephone lines.

One of the most significant issues relating to alarm systems is false alarms caused by accidental triggering. If false alarms occur frequently, police may assign a low priority to calls that originate from burglar alarm systems. Another deficiency is that alarm systems do not prevent burglaries but merely shorten a burglar's operating time. A delay of five to fifteen minutes or more from the time an alarm sounds until a guard or police officer arrives may give a burglar ample time to complete the theft and escape. Response time is a vital consideration in determining whether the expense of a sophisticated alarm system is worthwhile.

The quality and extent of protection provided by alarm systems vary. Insurance rate manuals generally give premium credits for approved alarm systems. Underwriters Laboratories, Inc., issues alarm certificates that indicate the grade, type, and protection extent of the certified system; insurers consider those certificates when granting insurance premium credits.

Organizations may use security guards to patrol the premises at periodic intervals. To ensure that inspections occur at the required times, a guard may carry a special clock that records visits to various stations when the guard inserts a key at each location. The weakness of this system is that no one is alerted if a guard is attacked by an intruder; therefore, some systems use a central station alarm that sends an alert if the guard fails to signal the station at an appointed time.

Many banks and other organizations with high robbery loss exposures install surveillance cameras that capture crimes in progress on film. These cameras can facilitate the identification, conviction, and incarceration of criminals; discourage robbery by increasing the probability of identification and conviction; and encourage criminals to look elsewhere for easier targets (termed "target displacement").

Physical controls also include passive restraints such as locks, bars, and safes or vaults. The type of lock used on a doorway can make a difference of several minutes in the entry time needed by a thief. Bars or grates can be installed across windows or doorways to block access. Passive restraints such as these may not prevent burglaries, but they may delay a burglar's entrance. See the exhibit "Physical Risk Control Measures Against Burglary and Robbery."

**Physical Risk Control Measures Against Burglary and Robbery**

**Burglary**

- Install and maintain perimeter protection of premises (such as fences, lighting, alarms, guards, and cleared space around premises)
- Use appropriate locks, vaults, safes, and exterior doors
- Install surveillance cameras attached to off-site videotape recorders
- Place marked cash and other property in vaults or safes to help trace and identify burglars
- Eliminate places of possible concealment for burglars

**Robbery**

- Install physical barriers inside premises to shield personnel from potential robbers
- Install safes and vaults with time locks that only a few employees know how to open
- Place surveillance cameras in vulnerable locations
- Employ guards and/or plainclothes security personnel
- Place marked cash or other valuables in registers or other locations to help trace robbers

[DA08674]

## Procedural Controls

Procedural controls define how particular tasks can be performed in ways that make it difficult for people to commit crimes, or they make crime detection more prompt or certain. For example, requiring identification or passwords before access is granted to an area can help combat robbery, burglary, shoplifting, vandalism, terrorism, computer crime, or violent attack.

Shoplifters and embezzlers often prefer to act alone or to go unobserved. Procedural controls are designed to make this difficult. For example, tasks such as cash handling, maintaining inventory or sales records, or conducting audits are often divided between two or more people. Regular audits can act as a procedural safeguard and a deterrent against embezzlement and fraud losses. Standard operating procedures that require at least two employees to be present when a store is open, or to work together when interviewing clients or providing medical care, provide some assurance that no single employee can attempt to defraud other persons. See the exhibit "Procedural Risk Control Measures Against Shoplifting and Embezzlement."

# Procedural Risk Control Measures Against Shoplifting and Embezzlement

## Shoplifting

- Train employees in how to spot and discourage potential shoplifters and in how to deal effectively with actual shoplifters without exposing themselves or the store to tort liability

- Screen present employees and job applicants for records of past shoplifting

- Establish procedures to prevent employees from sneaking merchandise out of the store at the end of their shifts

- Staff each cash register with at least two employees, with rotating assignments, to discourage employees from colluding among themselves or with others to shoplift

## Embezzlement

- Consecutively number all documents related to incoming or outgoing cash or credit transactions so that any misuse of these documents to embezzle funds can be readily recognized and traced

- Divide among several employees responsibility for performing and documenting all tasks related to incoming or outgoing cash and credit transactions so that no employee has complete control over both performing and recording any cash-related activity

- Require all employees to take vacations so that one employee's control over any task is not continuous for long periods

- Rotate employees among tasks for this same purpose

- Conduct regular, unannounced audits by both internal and external auditors

- Conduct independent checks of payroll and other payment records to ensure that they accurately reflect payments to actual persons or organizations that have provided the goods or services for which the payments were made

- Verify records of sales, deliveries, and purchases to confirm that they reflect real transactions

- Maintain strict controls of inventories of goods in process, merchandise, and supplies to counter embezzlement of property other than cash

- Inspect incoming and outgoing shipments of goods, supplies, and raw materials to detect shortages or defects through which employees, alone or through collusion with outsiders, may embezzle

- Implement procedural controls for computer crime losses, because embezzlement is often perpetrated through computers

- Screen job applicants or current employees seeking job transfers for records of past embezzlement convictions or attempts

[DA08675]

Crime and Cyber Risk 9.15
Crime and Cyber Risk 9.15

## Managerial Controls

Managerial controls that reduce criminal opportunity establish an atmosphere within an organization that deters or helps detect crime. Effective managerial controls can include education, applicant screening, and rotation of employees.

Employees can be educated about the organization's crime loss exposures, implemented crime risk control measures, and ways employees can help reduce crime losses. An educational program should include recognition or rewarding of employees who report criminal activities or suggest ways to deter or detect crimes. Classroom training on crime control should be supplemented with newsletters, bulletin boards, and participatory meetings.

All policies and procedures should be in writing and should include the corrective or disciplinary actions that will be taken if employees violate any crime control procedures. Employees should also be kept informed about the organization's work with law enforcement officials in prosecuting perpetrators of crimes against the organization. Projecting a tough attitude toward crime to employees (and through them to the public) can help an organization avoid becoming a target for criminals.

The primary goal of applicant screening is to hire and retain a suitable, trustworthy, and competent work force. Screening entails checking prospective employees' personal and professional references and verifying previous places of employment, education, and other personal data provided by the applicant. Because various state and federal laws that recognize employees' rights to continued employment can limit an organization's ability to discipline or dismiss an employee, applicant screening often provides the best opportunity to reduce the crime threats posed by employees.

Employee rotation can also deter crime. If employees are aware that their job assignments can be changed, they are less likely to commit crimes that might be discovered after they are transferred. Some managers may object to rotations on the grounds that they disrupt effective working relationships within departments, create unnecessary staffing and training needs, and complicate career planning. To reduce these complications, rotations should be included in job descriptions, occur in a reasonably predictable fashion, and be limited in frequency and duration. See the exhibit "Managerial Risk Control Measures Against Fraud and Counterfeiting/Forgery."

---

## Managerial Risk Control Measures Against Fraud and Counterfeiting/Forgery

**Fraud**

- Stay informed of new varieties of fraud, especially those new to the organization's industry or activities

- Alert managers and employees who deal with the public to the many possibilities for fraud

- Encourage supervisors and other managers to counsel with, or call to management's attention, any employee who is under such financial or other personal pressure that he or she may be tempted to commit fraud

- Bring criminal and civil charges against persons suspected of fraud

**Counterfeiting/Forgery**

- Educate personnel in the general methods and importance of controlling forgery and counterfeiting losses

- Recognize or award employees who make special efforts to control these losses

- Assist authorities in prosecuting forgers and counterfeiters and also initiate private tort suits for such wrongs as fraud

- Remain alert to new methods of making payments or other technological changes that may open new opportunities for forgery and counterfeiting

[DA08676]

## Investigation and Prosecution of Crimes

Organizations that investigate and actively pursue prosecution of suspected criminals by working with law enforcement officials reduce their crime losses in two ways:

- They can increase their opportunities to recover stolen property or to receive repayment or compensation from the criminals.

- They can establish a reputation for being tough on crime, discouraging criminals from targeting that organization.

An organization should establish specific procedures relating to investigation and prosecution of crime. Employee and management duties should include reporting suspected crimes and cooperating with law enforcement officials. Designated employees should receive training in interviewing witnesses and writing incident reports after a crime occurs.

## Reducing Scale of Crime and Recovery

Risk control measures for reduction of crime losses fall into two categories:

- Measures that reduce the scale of crime

- Measures that assist the organization in rapid recovery after a crime is committed.

The key to reducing the scale of crime lies in layers of defense against a criminal attack. The more layers of defense, the less severe the loss will likely be. These layers of defense include the types of risk control measures previously discussed, as well as computer-based security measures.

Post-crime recovery measures help restore an organization's operational functionality as rapidly as possible, further reducing losses. These risk control measures include having a full backup computer system with operational Web site, e-mail, and Internet links at an independent geographic location. Contingency plans are also needed to compensate for equipment, inventory, or other material theft or criminal damage. Vital legal and technical documents, as well as copies of computer storage disks, should be kept in a secure, fireproof, off-site repository, such as those operated by specialist commercial corporations.

# CYBER RISK LOSS EXPOSURES

Organizations that use the internet—for example, web-based sales and services—as part of their daily operations may have more value residing in their databases than in their warehouses. Therefore, they must consider the risks presented to their electronic systems and electronic data as well as to those of their customers and suppliers.

A typical organization may rely on a computer network, electronic data, digital devices (for example, cell phones), and a website to conduct its business operations. Such technology-based systems can be damaged and their security unintentionally or intentionally compromised by the organization's employees or by customers and suppliers. Therefore, the use of such systems increases an organization's exposure to property, net income, and liability loss.

## Property

All organizations, not just those that routinely conduct online business transactions, should consider whether they have cyber risk property loss exposures. For example, a plumbing contracting business that is not involved in online sales or that does not have a website may believe it has no cyber risk property loss exposures. However, this may not be the case if the plumbing contractor has a computer network that supports its accounting, finance, and customer database. The data in such a network is exposed to multiple cyber risks, including computer viruses and corruption, which could severely impair the contractor's operations.

Property exposed to loss because of cyber risk typically falls into one or both of the two categories of personal property: tangible property and intangible property. The distinction between tangible and intangible personal property is more relevant to commercial liability forms than to commercial property forms because many commercial liability forms define property damage to mean damage to tangible property only, and they also state that electronic data is not tangible property for coverage purposes. This provision was added in response to some courts holding that computer data is tangible personal property.

Although commercial property forms typically do not distinguish between tangible and intangible personal property, they usually limit coverage for loss of electronic data to an amount that is insufficient for most insureds. Consequently, a number of specific cyber risk loss exposures are not adequately covered, or not covered at all, by standard commercial property insurance policies. This limitation highlights the need that most organizations have for cyber risk coverage that covers loss of or damage to both tangible and intangible property as a result of cyber-related incidents.

Tangible property exposed to loss or damage because of computer network security breaches and other cyber-related incidents includes all types of computer equipment, such as laptop computers and mobile devices. Organizations should identify all possible threats against their computer networks originating externally and internally.

Although intangible personal property has no physical form, it is often of substantial value to an organization. In the context of cyber risk, electronic data is an especially valuable and vulnerable type of intangible property. For instance, consider a telemarketing organization that installs a software upgrade to its computer network. If the upgraded software contains a virus that corrupts the organization's data, the organization may be unable to perform its daily business operations because of the loss of its data.

A cyber criminal could obtain unauthorized access to an organization's computer network, damage or encrypt all the data in the network, and extort ransom from the organization to restore its data. In addition to damaging or encrypting data, criminals who hack into an organization's computer network can also steal confidential data, trade secrets, and other intellectual property. The possibility of these and similar losses occurring is a significant first-party property loss exposure.

## Net Income

An organization can assess the potential extent of its cyber risk net income loss exposures by considering how it might be affected by a reduction in or cessation of its normal business operations as a consequence of a computer network security breach. Such reductions in or cessations of normal business operations are commonly known as "business interruptions." Any possible business interruption that decreases revenues, increases expenses, or both should be considered by an organization when reviewing its cyber exposures. Cyber risk net income loss exposures can result not only from interruption of the organization's own computer network but also from interruption of its key customers' and suppliers' networks.

Net income exposed to cyber risk loss can be evaluated in terms of loss of business income (including contingent business income) and extra expenses. Both of these items can be affected should a cyber loss strike an organization.

Loss of business income occurs when an organization's net income is reduced because of an adverse event. In terms of cyber risk loss exposures, organizations typically consider events that can shut down or impair their computer networks. For example, a denial-of-service attack can slow or block users' access to a website, an email address, or a network by flooding an organization's network with requests for website pages or with numerous email messages. For an organization that generates business income on its website, a denial-of-service attack can be very costly, directly affecting sales revenue.

An additional example of a cyber risk business income loss exposure is one in which a virus infects an organization's network, corrupting data and destroying software. An organization should routinely create a duplicate copy (backup) of its data. Although software can be replaced, at a cost, the organization will sustain a business income loss if it cannot conduct its normal operations during the period of restoration.

Cyber risk contingent business income loss exposures relate to an organization's income that is contingent (or dependent) on a computer network that is not owned or operated by the primary organization. For example, a key customer of an electronics components manufacturer typically places its orders to the components manufacturer through the internet. If the key customer's computer network is attacked (for example, through a virus, a denial-of-service attack, or sabotage) and cannot be used to place orders, the resulting loss in revenue, if it cannot be replaced, is a contingent business income loss for the manufacturer. Additionally, an organization that uses a web-hosting company to manage its business website could suffer a contingent business income loss if the web-hosting company's server is rendered inoperable for an extended time.

Cyber risk contingent business income losses can also result from events affecting the computer networks of an organization's suppliers, utilities, or vendors, such as an extended shutdown of a cloud service's computer network because of a security breach.

In addition to normal operating expenses, including payroll, that an organization has during a time of suspended or impaired business operations, it may also need to incur extra expenses (in excess of its normal expenses) to minimize the effects of the business interruption or continue its operations. For example, an organization would incur extra expenses if, as a consequence of a network security breach, it needed to hire a contractor to recreate lost or stolen electronic data or pay its own employees overtime to restore its computer network and website to full service.

# Liability

Organizations that maintain a presence in cyber space face increased cyber risk liability loss exposures. These exposures arise from activities such as using email, maintaining websites, developing software, and conducting daily business operations (for example, sales and service) on the internet.

## Bodily Injury and Property Damage Liability

Organizations engaging in technology-related activities, such as transmitting electronic data, maintaining information on or conducting business through websites, or designing and supporting software, must be on guard against the bodily injury and property damage loss exposures generated by these activities.

Cyber risk bodily injury liability loss exposures can occur because of an organization's software development. For example, a software developer develops a program for physicians and pharmacists regarding the potential adverse interactions of different prescription medications. Because of a formulary error in the program, physicians and pharmacists conclude that a particular combination of prescription drugs is safe, while in reality the combination actually produces a serious or fatal reaction in a number of patients. The patients and their families sue because of the bodily injury that resulted from the software error.

Cyber risk property damage loss exposures can occur because of an organization's overall technology operations, including those related to software, hardware, and electronic data. For example, an insurance industry software provider issues an updated version of its software to an insurance brokerage. However, because of a security failure that occurred when the software upgrade was developed and transmitted to the brokerage, upon installation, the upgrade renders the brokerage's computer network inoperable, causing significant property damage to the system. The insurance brokerage then sues the software provider for the property damage to the network.

## Personal and Advertising Injury Liability

Many organizations assess their personal and advertising injury liability loss exposures as part of their general liability loss exposure analysis because Coverage B of the Commercial General Liability (CGL) Coverage Form covers the insured's liability to pay damages because of personal and advertising injury to which the insurance applies. Such loss exposures include the possibility of liability resulting from offenses such as false detention, malicious prosecution, slander, libel, disparagement, violation of a person's right of privacy, use of another's advertising idea in one's own advertisement, and infringing upon another's copyright or slogan. These and other offenses are listed in the CGL policy definition of personal and advertising injury.

However, CGL Coverage B is subject to several exclusions, and two of these exclusions apply specifically to cyber exposures. One of these cyber-related exclusions applies to personal and advertising injury committed by an insured whose business is any of these: advertising, broadcasting, publishing, or telecasting; designing or determining content of websites for others; or an internet search, access, content or service provider. Businesses of these types can obtain industry-specific professional liability policies to cover these and other types of cyber-related losses.

The other cyber-related exclusion in CGL Coverage B applies to personal and advertising injury arising out of an electronic chat room or bulletin board the insured owns, hosts, or controls. For an example of a cyber liability loss that could be excluded by this exclusion, consider an online stock market trading company that also offers discussion forums for its users. A forum user posing as an insider at Company A posts false information about the valuation of Company A and its stock, which eventually damages Company A's reputation as well as its market position. Company A sues the trading company for defamation.

Organizations that conduct business on websites should be concerned about any personal and advertising injury liability arising from the consequences of advertisements of products for which the insured has assumed liability under contract or agreement. The organization is responsible for any loss exposures and related liability that is assumed by contract. Consider an online tire retailer that contracts to advertise and sell a particular manufacturer's tires. The online retailer advertises "Tires last for 50,000 miles!" However, in reality, the manufacturer's tires wear out after only 15,000 miles. Customers sue the online tire retailer for false advertising relating to the representations made about the manufacturer's tires.

## Intellectual Property Liability

Cyber risk intellectual property liability loss exposures can affect an organization's copyrights, trademarks, patents, or trade secrets. For example, a copyright infringement loss exposure can occur when a major political blog site's owner posts on the blog copyrighted articles, in their entirety, from a well-known newspaper. If the site owner refuses to accede to the newspaper's demand that the blog stop posting the articles, the newspaper can sue the blog for copyright infringement.

Another example relates to trademark infringement. A new social media website could have as its trademark a design that is deceptively similar to a trademark that belongs to an established social media website. The established website's owner could sue the new website's owner for damages resulting from trademark infringement.

## Errors and Omissions Liability

As organizations continue to expand their business operations into cyber space, whether they are manufacturing traditional products for sale online, developing software for retail sale, or maintaining computer networks, they should be aware of cyber risk errors and omissions (E&O) liability. E&O liability presents the possibility of considerable damage to the organization, not only financially but also to its reputation, market standing, and goodwill.

Organizations should consider the scope of their daily business operations and how their actions or failure to act could result in E&O liability. For example, cyber risk E&O liability loss exposures can include design errors, manufacturing errors, or service errors.

Additional cyber risk E&O liability loss exposures can include loss resulting from errors relating to a company's product or the work it produces. For example, if a programmer creates a website for a retail client and neglects to include security safeguards to protect the site, the client could incur significant damages because of a business interruption if the website is hacked.

# CONTROLLING AND FINANCING CYBER RISK LOSS EXPOSURES

Internet-related technology has created new opportunities for growth for all types of organizations; however, these opportunities increase organizations' vulnerability to cyber risk loss exposures from many sources, both internal and external. Theft of information and electronic data has now surpassed physical theft at global companies.[1]

Because cyber risk loss exposures have the potential to damage an organization's assets, reputation, market standing, and customer and supplier relationships, risk control measures for these exposures are essential for any organization.

Many organizations will also need risk financing for their cyber risk loss exposures. Typical commercial insurance policies often exclude or restrict coverage for cyber risk loss exposures.

It is important for risk management and insurance professionals to be aware that cyber risk is rapidly evolving. As technology becomes more widely used and more complex, cyber risk loss exposures increase in both frequency and severity. In response, new companies and products enter the insurance market to provide coverage.

## Risk Control Measures for Cyber Risk

Specialized risk control measures are usually necessary for an organization to control cyber risk loss exposures involving property, net income, and liability. These risk control measures begin with an organization's determining the scope of its cyber risk loss exposures, often with assistance from a risk management or security specialist. A cyber risk security strategy should incorporate the organization's business objectives and available budget and should include an assessment of the appropriateness of the risk control measures for the loss exposures that are being addressed. Properly structured, a cyber risk security strategy can preserve an organization's resources, reduce the severity of losses that do occur, and hasten the organization's recovery from a cyber loss.

Specific risk control measures to prevent, deter, or mitigate cyber risk include these:

- Physical controls
- Procedural controls
- Personnel controls
- Managerial controls
- Investigation and prosecution of cyber crimes
- Post-cyber incident rapid recovery program

## Physical Controls

Physical controls place barriers between cyber criminals and their targets. Organizations should provide basic physical protection, such as guards, locked doors, central security alarms, and automatic devices to detect intruders. Additionally, organizations can physically limit access to computer equipment and programs and can implement other administrative and managerial safeguards that control physical access to systems or to the computer network environment.

Cyber criminals may use tactics to which computer hardware and software are particularly vulnerable, such as damaging them through the magnetic disruption and interruption of electrical power. Therefore, surveillance should be used for highly sensitive areas where data are stored. Access to such areas should be controlled by requiring personnel to identify themselves with badges or through **biometrics**.

**Biometrics**
Biological identification of an individual using anatomy or physiology.

## Procedural Controls

Procedural controls specify that tasks be performed in secure ways that prevent or reduce losses. In terms of cyber risk, procedural controls apply to how a computer system and all of its associated data are protected. Security policies should clearly state system authorization requirements for use of the system, levels of system access, and system response measures to unauthorized access.

Protection from hackers is a critical reason for organizations to create, implement, and regularly update procedural controls. Hackers have many motives for their attacks, including identity theft, extortion, destruction of competitive advantage, surveillance and reconnaissance, terrorism, political protest, and the satisfaction of defeating an organization's computer security system. If appropriate safeguards are not in place, organizations may never notice clandestine hacker intrusions that are designed to steal information. Other intrusions that use malicious software or codes (malware) are designed to deliberately and noticeably disrupt operations. Procedural controls that organizations use to thwart hackers include passwords, antivirus software, data encryption for stored data and data in transit, and firewalls.

Additionally, an organization can specify monitoring procedures in its procedural controls to prevent inappropriate access or use of its computers. For example, monitoring procedures may prohibit employees from using the organization's computers to access pornographic or other inappropriate websites, thereby eliminating activities that might expose the organization to a malware attack. Procedural controls may also be designed for network updates to ensure that new programs are tested before they are used to process actual data, possibly preventing an errors and omissions liability claim.

Other procedures can include establishment of a privacy policy and procedures for how, when, and under what terms an organization will allow material from other websites (such as hyperlinks or content) to appear on its own website. These policies and procedures could prevent claims for violation of privacy laws and for trademark or copyright infringement.

## Personnel Controls

The attitudes, performance, and behavior of employees can leave an organization exposed to a cyber attack, regardless of whether the resulting loss or damage was intended. Some employees are inadvertently the source of cyber losses—for example, employees who download software from the internet and unknowingly introduce a virus to the system. Others deliberately commit cyber crimes such as stealing intellectual property or committing identity theft. Disgruntled former employees with knowledge of or access to proprietary information are also potential sources of cyber losses.

Organizations can institute sound personnel controls to mitigate the cyber risk loss exposures presented by their employees. Personnel controls include such measures as preemployment screening, training, outlining unacceptable cyber behavior with associated consequences, and termination procedures that include revoking access and passwords.

Personnel controls can also extend to how the organization deals with its customers, suppliers, and neighbors. For example, a frustrated customer could become hostile and launch an electronic attack against the business by posting inflammatory information on public message boards and/or infecting the business's computer network with a virus or a **denial-of-service attack**. Consequently, the organization and its employees should try to maintain positive relationships with customers and other stakeholders and report any threat or suspicion of a cyber attack.

**Denial-of-service attack**

An attempt to overwhelm a computer system or network with excessive communications in order to deny users access.

## Managerial Controls

Managerial controls reduce cyber loss exposures by establishing an environment that prevents cyber losses or assists in their detection. Managerial controls include centralizing responsibility for cyber security. Many organizations have a chief information officer (CIO) or a chief risk officer (CRO) whose responsibilities include overseeing all technological aspects of the organization's operations. Managerial controls also involve ensuring that systems and procedures that have been adopted are monitored and followed to control cyber loss exposures. This effort can include monitoring the cyber risk security plan and ensuring compliance with risk control measures such as the creation and storage of backup files and the segregation of responsibilities to prevent any individual from having control of the entire system or inappropriate system access.

Additionally, an organization should continually evaluate and revise its risk control measures. As quickly as risk control measures are instituted to combat cyber risk, the technology that cyber criminals use to overcome them evolves. Therefore, organizations must be prepared to update their techniques accordingly.

## Investigation and Prosecution of Cyber Crimes

Often, organizations do not report cyber crimes to authorities because they fear negative publicity, worry that competitors could take advantage of an incident, or believe authorities cannot assist them in prosecuting cyber crimes. Although some initial negative publicity may result when an organization reveals that it has been attacked by a cyber criminal, the organization also may experience a public relations benefit by voluntarily releasing the news regarding a cyber crime, particularly if it is an innocent victim. The organization can describe the measures it is taking to prevent such an incident from recurring, thereby restoring consumer confidence and neutralizing any advantage competitors might gain from initial negative publicity. Additionally, many law enforcement agencies possess expertise in cyber crime and can help organizations control their loss exposures. Furthermore, organizations that vigilantly investigate and prosecute cyber criminals are less likely to be viewed as an "easy target" by cyber criminals.

Reporting certain types of cyber crimes may not be optional for some organizations. Most states now require organizations to disclose to authorities and affected individuals instances when data security breaches occur that expose personal information to identity theft or other types of cyber crime.

## Post-Cyber Incident Rapid Recovery Program

A post-cyber incident rapid recovery program aids in reducing the severity of an organization's cyber losses and in restoring operational functionality as soon as possible. Implementing a rapid recovery program focuses on the organization's ability to preserve and sustain its net income in the event of a cyber loss.

Risk control measures the organization can use as part of a post-cyber incident rapid recovery program include maintaining full backups of the computer system—complete with an operational website, email, and internet links—at an alternate location. Additionally, all vital legal and technical documents, as well as copies of computer storage media, should be secured in a fire-resistive, off-site repository, such as those operated by specialized data storage companies.

Contingency measures should be established to provide equipment, software, or any additional personnel that may be necessary to analyze, repair, cleanse, and restore lost or damaged data. Also, plans should be developed to address the effects on suppliers and customers.

A rapid recovery program should also include a public relations component so that, if necessary, the organization's public image, as well as customer and supplier relationships, can be preserved in the aftermath of a cyber loss.

# Risk Financing Measures for Cyber Risk

Organizations exposed to cyber risk must consider the financial consequences of a property, net income, or liability loss and whether they wish to transfer or retain those losses. Sources of risk financing can be arranged before (pre-loss financing) or after (post-loss financing) a loss occurs. Although an organization may have risk financing measures in place to address basic property, net income, and liability loss exposures, additional risk financing measures may be necessary to address cyber risk loss exposures. Risk financing measures include insurance, noninsurance risk transfer, and retention.

## Insurance

Because the field of cyber risk is a dynamic one, many organizations are uncertain of the value of cyber risk insurance or even of its availability as a technique for dealing with cyber risk. Cyber risk insurance coverage forms are still evolving. However, insurance is an important technique for organizations to use to manage their property, net income, or liability losses and the costs of compliance (for example, notification of customers after a theft of computer data) as a consequence of cyber risk loss exposures.

The cost of cyber risk can be significant. Hackers increasingly focus on attaining "back door" access to organizations and obtaining proprietary information that they can use for quick financial gain.

One serious cyber loss could threaten any organization's financial position. Therefore, it is important for organizations to carefully consider insurance coverage as part of their cyber risk management programs.

## Noninsurance Risk Transfer

**Hold-harmless agreement (or indemnity agreement)**
A contractual provision that obligates one of the parties to assume the legal liability of another party.

Organizations can use noninsurance risk transfer as one means of risk financing. When entering into contracts or online agreements, organizations must ensure that the contractual language properly protects them from cyber risk loss exposures. A **hold-harmless agreement, or indemnity agreement,** is a

## Reality Check

The cost of a data breach at an organization, whether or not the breach results in theft or damage, can be significant because of compliance with requirements to notify customers of the breach and other regulatory requirements. Even if no customer business is lost as a result of the notifications, the cost of the notifications and assistance to customers, such as monitoring their credit reports, can pose a risk to the bottom line of an organization.

"Attorney General Martha Coakley Announces Multi-State Settlement with the TJX Companies, Inc., Over Massive Data Breach," Office of the Attorney General, Commonwealth of Massachusetts, June 23, 2009, www.mass.gov/?pageID=cagopressrelease&L=1&L0=Home&sid=Cago&b=pressrelease&f=2009_06_23_tjx_settlement&csid=Cago (accessed November 15, 2010). [DA12640]

type of noninsurance measure that organizations can use to receive reimbursement for cyber risk losses or to transfer their cyber risk loss exposures. For example, a website-hosting company could sign a hold-harmless agreement promising to indemnify a customer, such as a retailer, for lost online sales if its server malfunctions. Another example is for an organization, through an indemnity agreement, to request to be named an additional insured under the indemnitor's insurance policy.

In addition to using hold-harmless agreements, many software firms also use liability disclaimers. While disclaimers do not transfer risk or act as risk financing, they can be used to limit the scope of liability. For example, organizations that collect their customers' personal information can post liability disclaimers and disclosure statements on their websites to fully inform customers of how their personal information may be used and the extent of the organization's liability should the information be illegally disclosed. They can also require electronic signatures from the customers to indicate consent.

## Retention

An organization may use **retention** to finance its cyber risk loss exposures. One advantage of retention is that it encourages risk control. For example, when an organization pays the cost of its own losses, it may have a greater incentive to prevent and reduce them. A disadvantage associated with retention is that when an organization decides to retain its cyber risk loss exposures, the associated uncertainty of loss outcomes can negatively affect its financial position.

Should an organization decide to finance its losses by retaining rather than transferring them, it faces the possibility that retained losses will be more frequent or severe than expected. Because of this uncertainty, an organization should limit its retention for each individual loss to a severity level at which it can tolerate the potential variability in the sum of its retained losses.

**Retention**

A risk financing technique by which losses are retained by generating funds within the organization to pay for the losses.

For example, a social networking website could purchase insurance for its third-party liability cyber risk loss exposures and decide to retain its first-party cyber risk loss exposures. Another organization could opt for both first-party and third-party coverage and strategically use deductibles when placing its coverage.

# SOCIAL MEDIA RISK

Organizations are increasingly using social media to communicate internally with employees and externally with customers, potential customers, and the public. However, use of social media exposes an organization to significant risks.

While the business advantages of engaging in two-way communication with people all over the world are significant, organizations using social media are exposed to reputational, legal, and operational risks and should develop programs to control these risks.

## The Nature of Social Media

Social media have allowed for an unprecedented level of two-way communication between business organizations and the public. Social media include social and business networking Web sites, personal and business blogs, interactive Web pages, online communities, various forms of group cell phone text messaging, and video-sharing Web sites.

Organizations that communicate with customers and potential customers through social media can develop ongoing relationships and create and convey a customer-friendly image that contributes to business success. Further, social media can be used to disseminate information and provide customer service and feedback.

Organizations can also use social media to monitor public perception of products and services and to respond quickly to significant changes in those perceptions—particularly negative ones. While negative comments can spread quickly, social media provide the opportunity to promptly mount an effective response and disseminate it widely.

An organization may consult business and social networks when gathering information about prospective employees; use interactive Web sites to provide customer service, feedback, and promotions; and monitor social networks and blogs for reference to its own and its competitors' products and services.

## Reputation Risk

Social media provide a vehicle for any message to be instantaneously multiplied, expanded upon, and communicated to millions of people. A single negative item of information—whether patently false, true, misinterpreted, or taken out of context—can reverse an organization's positive image and severely damage its reputation in a matter of hours, if not minutes.

For example, two airline passengers with time on their hands after their flight was canceled filmed themselves in an empty terminal racing wheelchairs, using a public address system, and exploring closed areas of the airport. They posted their film on a video-sharing Web site, and a national news network picked it up and broadcast it. Viewers complained of the apparent lack of airport security, and both the airline and the airport suffered reputational damage.[2]

Organizations are also exposed to reputational risk through the social networking activities of their employees. Employees may post negative comments about their employers, competitors, customers, or others associated with the organization or may inadvertently disclose confidential business information. Employees' online behavior may reflect poorly on the organization, particularly if it occurs in the organization's own social media location.[3]

# Legal Risk

Social media activities can lead to lawsuits or prosecution for violations of the law. Legal risks associated with social media can arise from an organization's employment or computer security practices or can relate to privacy or use of intellectual property. These risks exist in areas other than social media; however, the pervasiveness of social networking and the speed at which communication occurs can significantly increase the degree of exposure.

## Employment Risks

Personal information about employees and potential employees is readily available on social networking sites. Individuals post profiles, report on their social activities, and share their photographs. Some employers consider such information when making hiring or other employment-related decisions.

Employers may acquire information about prospective employees from social networking site profiles and postings or from Web searches. Hiring decisions based on any such information relating to race, age, disability, or religion may be discriminatory and in violation of federal statutes such as the Equal Employment Opportunity Act, the Civil Rights Act of 1964, the Age Discrimination Act, or the Americans with Disability Acts. In general, employers can base hiring decisions on personal information acquired from social media sources if the information relates to behavior that would directly affect an applicant's job responsibilities.

An organization that hires a company to screen job applicants may be subject to the Fair Credit Reporting Act. This law requires an applicant to receive advance notice of any adverse action taken on the basis of information acquired about him or her.

Organizations sometimes discipline or terminate employees because of comments made to other employees on social networks. Such actions may violate specific laws; for example, comments that relate to the employer-employee relationship—such as complaints about wages or working conditions—are protected under the National Labor Relations Act because they may relate to labor disputes or union organizing.

## Security Risks

Employees using social media may reveal confidential information that can threaten an organization's security. They may post comments on failed contract negotiations involving a client, safety problems with products under development, or a meeting with a well-known client. Posted photos of work activities may reveal information about an organization's culture, personnel, or products.

Security risks can also apply to personal safety. For example, revealing travel plans of executives on a social networking site could expose them to personal attack or, in some areas of the world, even kidnapping.

## Intellectual Property Risks

Copyright infringement and the disclosure of trade secrets are the primary intellectual property risks related to the use of social media. An organization may have legal permission to use another's copyrighted material; however, if the material or excerpts from it are copied and forwarded repeatedly, credit lines, copyright notices, or attribution may be lost, and the usage may extend far beyond the scope of original permission. As a result, the organization may be liable for copyright infringement. Copyright infringement also results from the unauthorized use and dissemination of copyrighted material from Web sites or articles posted electronically.

Social networkers may inadvertently disclose trade secrets belonging to their employer or its clients. Organizations may be liable for breach of contract if the intellectual property disclosed belongs to a client.[4]

## Defamation

**Defamation**

A false written or oral statement that harms another's reputation.

Disparaging remarks made on social media may lead to charges of **defamation**. An employee may disparage a competitor's product, for example, exposing the employer to liability. In some cases, an organization may be held liable for defamatory comments posted in public-commentary features of its Web page.

In some circumstances, even a positive statement about an organization can cause problems. For example, if an employee posts a positive review about the organization's product on a consumer Web site, truth in advertising laws may apply. The United States Federal Trade Commission's (FTC's) "Guides Concerning the Use of Endorsement and Testimonials in Advertising" state that an endorser of a product must disclose any connection the endorser has with the marketer of a product that would affect how people evaluate the endorsement.[5]

## Privacy Risks

Organizations must protect the privacy of those who visit their social media Web sites. The federal Electronic Communications Privacy Act prohibits the reading or disclosure of contents of electronic communications under some circumstances. Healthcare and financial organizations may be particularly vulnerable to privacy risks related to releasing personal health and financial information under the Health Insurance Portability and Accountability Act and the Gramm-Leach-Bliley Act, respectively. The Children's Online Privacy Protection Act applies to information that is posted or collected online and could be used to identify a child—such as full name, home address, e-mail address, or telephone number.

Privacy issues also arise from an organization's monitoring of employees' social media activities. An employer has no right to control what employees post on their private accounts.

An organization may also be liable for invasion of privacy if it uses an individual's photo or personal information for a commercial purpose, such as advertising, without the individual's consent.

## Operational Risk

Social network users can be vulnerable to risks posed by malicious software (malware), including computer viruses, worms, and "Trojan horses." Various malware applications can locate and copy confidential information, such as customers' credit card numbers or client lists, from internal systems; direct users to illegitimate Web sites designed to look legitimate ("spoofing"), such as banks and colleges, and request login information, passwords, and account numbers; track keystrokes to collect passwords and other confidential data ("keylogging"); corrupt systems; or destroy data on hard drives. Collected passwords, credit card numbers, and account numbers can be used to access victims' accounts.

Even applications ("apps") for cell phones, electronic tablets, and other handheld devices can contain malware. In such cases, not only may an organization's security be breached, but the organization could be held liable for failing to protect its clients' or customers' personal information.

## Controlling Social Media Risks

Organizations should develop sound and comprehensive risk control programs to address social media risks. Such programs should begin with an assessment of the risks. To manage social media legal risks, organizations should work with attorneys to identify the risks and any laws that might apply. An organization may want to designate specific individuals authorized to communicate online on behalf of the organization.

Some organizations prohibit all employees from using social media at work. Others limit access to designated individuals, sites that can be visited, or the amount of time an employee can spend using social media. Guidelines should be adopted for permitted uses.

A risk control program should include a written social media policy that describes the risks, lists the laws that apply, describes the types of behaviors that could lead to loss, and provides rules or guidelines on how to avoid loss. Periodic training of managers and employees should be provided to reinforce the policies. Organizations can also develop a social media agreement for employees to review and sign annually.

These are some examples of social risk management guidelines:

- Comments about the organization's products or services should not be posted anonymously.
- Unless authorized to do so, individuals should avoid any implication that they represent the organization.
- Anything posted in any social media form should be considered public information.
- Users should be cautious about sharing company information.
- Clients' and customers' privacy should be protected.
- Human rights and intellectual property rights violations should be avoided.
- Any material posted should be accurate—not defamatory, fraudulent, or misleading.
- Work-related posts should maintain a professional tone.

Another important aspect of social media risk control is monitoring of social networks and interactive Web sites. Monitoring can help organizations become aware of and control risky employee activity (with attention to potential employee privacy issues) and promptly detect negative posts about the organization, its products, or its services from customers or the public. Having a designated response team can help the organization mount a prompt and appropriate response to such postings.

### *Apply Your Knowledge*

Linda, a researcher at Westfork, Inc., belongs to a social networking interest group related to her line of research. She accesses this community in the evenings on her home computer. Her profile does not identify where she works.

One night, while participating in discussions in the online community, Linda responded angrily to several negative comments about the quality of Westfork's products: "Westfork's products are superior, and they have the data to prove it," she said. "And I happen to know that the company is introducing a new product late this year that has an innovative new design. It will blow the competitors out of the market. The combined IQ of you people must be about thirty. Come on, don't you know a good product when you see it?"

Linda's colleague Jon, also a member of the online community, saw Linda's remarks and reported them to Westfork's Social Media Response Team. Identify Westfork's potential social networking risks regarding Linda's online comments.

*Feedback*: Linda may be exposing Westfork to these risks:

- Violation of FTC truth-in-advertising rules—Linda's comments might be construed as an endorsement of Westfork's product. As an employee, she may expose Westfork to charges of violating FTC rules that require those who post product endorsements to reveal any connection with those who market the product.

- Disclosure of a trade secret—By discussing Westfork's new product and revealing a general timeline of when it will be introduced, Linda may be disclosing a trade secret.

- Damage to reputation—Even though Linda's profile does not identify her as a Westfork employee, other discussion participants are likely to conclude from her comments that she is associated with the company. Her rudeness may reflect on the company's image.

# SUMMARY

Criminal activity against an organization can cause it to incur property, personnel, liability, and net income losses. Unlike other loss exposures that strike by chance or out of human carelessness, a distinctive feature of criminal loss exposures is that they are guided by hostile intent. Because criminals constantly search for opportunities to commit crime, risk management professionals must continually evaluate risk control efforts.

To develop effective crime risk control measures, an organization's risk manager must understand the characteristics of crimes to which the organization is vulnerable. Such crimes can include burglary, robbery, shoplifting, fraud, embezzlement, forgery and counterfeiting, vandalism, arson, terrorism, espionage, and computer crime.

An organization can take specific risk control measures to deter, detect, or deny a criminal an opportunity to commit a crime. In general, these measures involve sound personnel policies; physical, procedural, and managerial controls; and investigation and prosecution of crimes. Adding layers of defense can reduce the severity of crimes, and backup of systems and facilities, as well as contingency plans, can reduce an organization's losses by ensuring rapid recovery after a crime.

Most organizations are exposed to cyber losses that can be broadly categorized as property, net income, and liability. Cyber risk property losses include damage to computer equipment and loss of data because of security breaches caused by cyber criminals. Cyber risk net income losses include loss of business income (including contingent business income) and the incurring of extra expenses as the result of a computer network shutdown caused by a security breach or other cyber incident. Cyber risk liability losses include liability for bodily injury and property damage, liability for personal and advertising injury, intellectual property liability, and errors and omissions liability resulting from cyber incidents.

Organizations control their cyber risk loss exposures through the use of a variety of risk control and risk financing techniques. Risk control measures include physical controls, procedural controls, personnel controls, managerial controls, investigation and prosecution of cyber crimes, and a post-cyber incident rapid recovery program. Risk financing measures include insurance, noninsurance risk transfers, and retention. By using these risk control and risk financing measures, organizations can control cyber risk loss exposures involving property, net income, and liability.

Organizations using social media are exposed to reputational risks, legal (including employment, security, intellectual, and property risks and risks related to defamation), and operational risks. Risk control programs to address social media risks should include assessment of the risks, identification of any laws that apply, development of a written social media policy, employee and manager training, monitoring of social media Web sites relevant to the organization, and appointment of a response team to address issues as they arise.

# ASSIGNMENT NOTES

1.   "Information Theft at Global Companies Surpasses All Other Forms of Fraud for First Time," Kroll Inc. news release, October 18, 2010, www.kroll.com/news/releases (accessed October 25, 2010).

2.   "Reputation Management: How's Your Brand Holding Up?" AON One, Q3 2011, September 2011, http://one.aon.com/reputation-management-hows-your-brand-holding (accessed March 8, 2012).

3.   Toby Merril, Kenneth Latham, Richard Santalesa, and David Navetta, "Social Media: The Business Benefits May Be Enormous, but Can the Risks—Reputational, Legal, Operational—Be Mitigated?" The John Liner Review, vol. 25, No. 2, Summer 2011, p. 73.

4.   Toby Merril, et. al., "Social Media: The Business Benefits May Be Enormous, but Can the Risks—Reputational, Legal, Operational—Be Mitigated?"

5.   "The FTC's Endorsement Guides: Being Up-Front With Consumers," Federal Trade Commission, www.ftc.gov/opa/reporter/advertising/endorsement.shtml (accessed March 8, 2012).

# Fleet Risk

## Educational Objectives

After learning the content of this assignment, you should be able to:

▷ Explain how fleets can be viewed as systems and the implications for fleet loss control.

▷ Explain how Federal Motor Carrier Safety Regulations apply to motor vehicle fleets.

▷ Explain how to control losses associated with the components of a motor vehicle fleet safety system.

▷ Describe the technological advances in motor vehicle fleet safety.

# Fleet Risk

## FLEETS AS SYSTEMS

Each vehicle in a fleet can be viewed as a component of a motor vehicle fleet system, which is a subsystem of an organization's larger transportation system. The organization uses such systems to assemble people, raw materials, supplies, and other inputs to produce and distribute goods and services. Fleet safety uses many system safety concepts, which are relevant to risk control and particularly useful for the transportation risk arising from motor vehicle fleets.

System safety rests on the premise that a system operates safely if its components enable it to fulfill its purpose within its environment without any system components failing throughout its life cycle. A motor vehicle fleet (fleet), like every system, has these four common features:

- Components
- Purpose
- Environment
- Life cycle

A system safety approach to reducing an organization's losses from its fleet begins by examining the four system features of a fleet.

## Components

A fleet system primarily includes these components, each of which poses risks that need to be controlled to maintain the fleet's safety:

- Vehicles
- Vehicle maintenance
- Operators
- Cargoes
- Routes
- Vehicle schedules

## Purpose

The essential purpose of any fleet system is to transport cargo or persons. To fulfill its purpose, an organization's fleet system should have these characteristics:

- Reliable—The fleet, with a high degree of certainty, completes all trips as scheduled without harm to the freight or passengers.
- Safe and well maintained—The fleet incurs few, if any, vehicle accident losses that might increase the transport time because of vehicle repair or maintenance.
- Efficient—The fleet operates at an acceptable cost.
- Environmentally neutral—The fleet's operation does not pollute or otherwise harm the environment in ways that could impose common law or statutory liability on the fleet operator or owner.
- Lawful—The fleet operates within the legal requirements of applicable local, state, and federal laws regarding issues such as size and weight restrictions.

Effective risk control generally enhances the attributes of a well-managed fleet. Increasing the safety of a fleet reduces the frequency and severity of losses that may harm it (or the fleets of others on which the organization relies), making it both more reliable and efficient. Moreover, focusing on liability risk control ensures that the fleet's operations are lawful.

Operating lawfully, in turn, enhances the efficiency of the fleet's operations by reducing the court judgments, fines, and delays that unlawful operations generate; as a result, deliveries are more reliable and rapid. In short, good fleet safety helps fulfill all purposes of motor vehicle fleet operations.

## Environment

The components of a fleet system, like any system, function within an environment. The most important environments in which a fleet system operates are physical, legal, economic, and competitive; all of these can affect a fleet's safety.

The physical environment encompasses the highways, weather conditions, terrain, communities, and other tangible objects and forces that the vehicles in the fleet encounter along their routes. Adverse weather conditions such as rain, fog, snow, wind, and ice can quickly affect the safe operation of any vehicle.

The legal environment consists of the laws under which a fleet operates. In general, most laws regarding fleet operations (statutes dealing with maximum speeds, maximum permissible weights, hours of service, mandated equipment, licensing of operators, and so on) tend to raise the level of fleet safety. However, differences among the laws of various jurisdictions, changes in those laws, and occasional conflicts among them can also make compliance difficult.

The managers of an organization's fleet operations may need to spend considerable time ensuring operation within the law.

Fleets also function within a changing economic environment that can affect fleet safety either positively or negatively. During prosperity, fleet safety is more likely to be supported by adequate budgets. However, in recessionary periods, budgets may be cut at the very time that economic forces intensify some major fleet risks. Operators anxious about keeping their jobs face greater temptation to speed, drive extra hours, and skip safety checks. Economic downturns can also lead to haphazard vehicle maintenance, labor union strikes, and civil disorders that may threaten the safe delivery of cargoes.

The competitive environment in which a fleet operates is closely related to its economic environment. When an organization is operating under normal competitive pressures from similar organizations, fleet safety is more likely to receive the emphasis and the financial and managerial support it deserves. However, when competition becomes intense, fleet safety efforts and expenditures may be lowered in efforts to save money in the short term. Such cost control measures can eventually jeopardize the long-term safety of vehicles, operators, and their cargoes.

## Life Cycle

An organization's fleet has a five-phase life cycle:

1.  Conceptual phase—determining what types of motor vehicles (as opposed to other modes of transportation) will meet an organization's needs

2.  Engineering phase—selecting the types of vehicles, operators, routes, roads, schedules, and maintenance that best meet the organization's fleet needs

3.  Production phase—purchasing the vehicles selected in the conceptual and engineering phases

4.  Operational phase—using the vehicles selected to transport freight or passengers over the selected routes on a predetermined schedule and maintaining the vehicles so that they can operate reliably, safely, efficiently, and lawfully, while being environmentally neutral

5.  Disposal phase—eliminating old vehicles unable to legally fulfill the purposes and attributes of the fleet because of age, technological obsolescence, or other reasons, and replacing those vehicles with vehicles that better fulfill the organization's transportation needs

Proper fleet safety management, as part of an overall organizational risk management effort, is important in all five of these phases. During the conceptual phase, an organization's risk management professionals and key executives should assess the exposures that could influence the organization's choices about when and where to use a fleet, which types of freight or passengers need to be transported, which routes to take, and which schedules to implement.

During the engineering phase, weighing alternatives for good control of the fleet's exposures is essential in specifying the characteristics of an appropriate fleet. Managers planning the fleet operations must be aware of the control aspects of each of the alternatives they are considering as they select the types and sizes of vehicles needed, select and train qualified vehicle operators, set detailed transportation schedules and routes, plan appropriate vehicle maintenance, and educate vehicle operators and other personnel about what to do after an accident.

During the production phase, the risk management professional uses selection criteria developed in the conceptual and engineering phases to purchase the appropriate vehicles.

During the operational phase, an organization's risk management professional must work with other personnel to implement and monitor measures that control the overall cost of risk (the sum of its sustained losses, insurance costs, safety measures, and administrative costs) attributable to the organization's fleet operations.

During the disposal phase, a crucial control concern is that the vehicles, their cargoes, and all other components that no longer function effectively are safely, legally, and ethically eliminated. Employees no longer qualified to operate their vehicles must legally be retired or reassigned in ways that recognize the value of their talents. Disposing of vehicles or dealing with their cargoes and operators in ways that are unsafe, illegal, or socially unacceptable can expose an organization to legal liability and raise the organization's operating cost, thereby jeopardizing its efficiency.

## Systems and Relationships

An organization's fleet system is part of several larger systems, such as its overall transportation system and the government's road systems. Similar to most systems, the fleet system tends to be nested within these other systems; it is composed of numerous vehicles, operators, cargoes, routes, schedules, and maintenance activities. Each of those components is, in turn, a system made up of several subsystems. For example, each vehicle is made up of a braking system, ignition system, fuel system, cargo-loading system, and other subsystems. Each vehicle operator, as a physical and psychological being, consists of a number of physiological subsystems (such as respiratory, circulatory, muscular, and nervous), as well as numerous psychological subsystems (knowledge, emotions, beliefs, and so on). Similarly, cargoes, routes, schedules, and maintenance activities consist of numerous subsystems.

That nesting of progressively smaller systems as subsystems within progressively larger systems has two implications for risk control and fleet safety management:

- When a smaller system fails, it becomes more likely that each of the larger systems of which the smaller system is a part will also fail. Because many of those failures cause accidents, they are a central risk control concern. For example, the failure of a pressure relief valve in the air-brake system of a large truck can cause the truck's brakes to fail. In turn, that brake failure is likely to precipitate a highway accident.

- The failure of a larger system degrades the environment in which its subsystems operate, increasing the strain on those subsystems and therefore the probability that those subsystems will fail. Again, accidents become more likely. As an illustration, if a truck is involved in an accident, smaller systems such as fuel, braking, and cooling could be compromised even though apparent signs of damage may not be obvious.

In short, the notion of systems and subsystems provides a basis for tracing the effects of one system component downward to smaller subsystems and upward to larger systems. It follows that the failure of any component of any system is likely to have wide-ranging effects. An effective fleet safety program takes account of, and works to prevent, the original failure and all its consequences throughout related systems.

# FEDERAL MOTOR CARRIER SAFETY REGULATIONS

The United States Federal Motor Carrier Safety Administration (FMCSA) works with law enforcement and the motor carrier industry to administer the Federal Motor Carrier Safety Regulations (FMCSR) and to monitor, promote, and ensure safety related to motor carriers.

Motor carriers and their drivers are required by federal law to follow the FMCSR. These rules identify parties that are subject to the rules and specify qualifications for motor carrier drivers, and they provide significant rules governing other aspects of the motor carrier industry. Additionally, the FMCSA conducts a compliance, safety, and accountability (CSA) initiative to fulfill its goals. A risk management professional should be familiar with the FMCSR as part of the legal environment within which a fleet operates and recognize its role in ensuring fleet safety.

## Application to Fleet Operations

Fleet operations must comply with FMCSR, provided the vehicles in and the operations of the fleet meet the definitions provided by FMCSR. A commercial motor vehicle (CMV) or a combination of motor vehicles that is used to transport property or people must match one of these descriptions:

- Have a gross vehicle weight rating (GVWR) of 26,001 or more pounds.
- Have a GCWR of 26,001 or more pounds, including any towed vehicle with a GVWR exceeding 10,000 pounds.

- Transport sixteen or more people, including the driver.
- Transport hazardous materials as identified by the Hazardous Materials Transportation Act and subject to the Hazardous Materials Regulations. (This can apply to any size of vehicle.)

Fleets that are subject to the FMCSR are generally those that include any truck exceeding 10,001 pounds; a bus driven for-hire (for compensation) that can transport sixteen or more people, including the driver, and that is operated over state lines; or a truck or bus for-hire that is operated within a state, but for which operation either begins or ends in another state. Additionally, fleets with vehicles that haul hazardous cargo, regardless of whether they operate in multiple states, are usually subject to the Hazardous Materials Regulations. Fleets with vehicles meeting any of these descriptions are most likely subject to the Minimum Financial Responsibility Requirements. Notably, taxis, school buses, and van pools are exempt from the FMCSR.

## Significant Rules

The FMCSR regulates most aspects of motor carriers that use CMVs to transport property and people on U.S. roadways. Some significant rules involve driver qualification, drug testing for specified employees, hours of service, accident reporting, record keeping, and electronic device usage.

## Driver Qualification Rules

The FMCSR requires all drivers of CMVs to have a single valid commercial driver's license (CDL). These regulations establish testing procedures and methods; knowledge and skills to be tested; minimum passing scores; and other licensing requirements for state motor vehicle licensing departments to use in issuing CDLs to qualified CMV operators. The regulations also set forth penalties and disqualification terms for CMV operators convicted of certain criminal and other offenses and serious traffic violations. A CMV operator whose license or driving privileges have been suspended, revoked, or canceled must inform their employer and the motor vehicle department of his or her state or jurisdiction of domicile. The regulations further require CMV drivers to provide previous employment information to prospective employers, and they prohibit employers from allowing any individual whose CDL has been suspended to operate a commercial vehicle.

Every CMV driver must prepare a list of motor vehicle law violations (other than parking) of which he or she has been convicted or forfeited bond or collateral during the previous twelve months. The driver must furnish this list of violations or certification of no violations annually to his or her employer, the motor carrier.

## Drug Testing for Employees Who Perform "Safety-Sensitive" Functions

The FMCSR requires compliance with the Department of Transportation (DOT) regulations on drug and alcohol testing for employees who drive CMVs and who are required to hold a CDL. These employees are said to perform "safety-sensitive" functions. The FMCSR specifies that safety-sensitive functions include all functions performed during the time from which a driver begins to work, or is required to be ready to work, until the time he or she is relieved from work and work responsibilities. These functions include driving a CMV, waiting to be dispatched, inspecting equipment, loading or unloading a CMV or overseeing these activities, performing maintenance, or otherwise attending to a CMV.

A motor carrier/employer, anyone who owns or leases CMVs, and any CMV driver must comply with the DOT alcohol and drug testing regulations and may not perform any safety-sensitive functions while using alcohol, within four hours after using alcohol, or while having a positive breath alcohol concentration. Refusing to submit to an alcohol test is prohibited, as is using alcohol within eight hours after an accident or before post-accident testing.

Alcohol testing can be completed through a breath or saliva analysis, and drug testing is completed through urine analysis. Testing may be performed for these reasons:

- Preemployment
- Random
- Reasonable suspicion/reasonable cause
- Post-accident
- Return-to-duty
- Follow-up

If the alcohol test result is positive—a blood alcohol concentration of 0.02 percent or higher—the driver must be removed from safety-sensitive duties for at least twenty-four hours.

Any unauthorized use of specified, controlled substances is prohibited for drivers at any time. The FMCSR also prohibits the use of certain legally prescribed controlled substances. If an employer receives a positive drug test result—a drug urine test result between 0.02 and 0.039—or testing cannot be validated (a specimen was tampered with or substituted, or a testing error occurred), the employer must temporarily remove the employee from performing safety-sensitive functions—a procedure called "standing-down" an employee. A licensed physician must verify the findings before any subsequent action may be taken against a stood-down employee. When an employee has violated any DOT drug regulations and has been removed from safety-sensitive duties for any employer, he or she must complete an appropriate education and/or treatment program, administered by a substance abuse professional, before returning to safety-sensitive duty.

In the first twelve months after a driver returns to duty following a positive alcohol or drug test result, the FMCSR requires at least six unannounced follow-up tests to be conducted. If the employee fails, the employer may take personnel action in compliance with its policies or labor agreements.

The DOT regulation provides full details on the testing and evaluation procedures; chain of custody of urine specimens; materials, supplies, equipment, and facilities to be used; documentation and forms to be completed; and training and education of parties involved in the testing. Regulations also ensure strict confidentiality of all drug-testing information and records, which may only be released with the written consent of the driver, except as required in the testing and for certain legal proceedings.[1]

## Hours of Service Rules

The FMCSR specifies the maximum number of hours that an operator may drive a CMV and be on duty. On-duty time includes driving time; time that a driver is waiting to be dispatched from any motor carrier facility; time inspecting, servicing, or conditioning a CMV; time loading or unloading a CMV and handling associated paperwork or supervising such activities; time spent in service to or attendance of a disabled CMV; time associated with providing a carrier's alcohol or drug testing; time performing any other work for the carrier or for another person if compensated; and all time spent in or on a CMV, except for time resting in a parked CMV or in a sleeper berth or passenger seat.

FMCSR driving time limits vary depending on whether property or passengers are being carried; however, the rules clearly describe maximum driving time limits, minimum break times, maximum on-duty time limits, and maximum weekly hours of duty with a thirty-four-hour off-duty break that includes specified early morning hours. Maximum weekly hours vary depending on whether the carrier operates six or seven days per week. Risk managers should be alert for potential hours-of-service rule violations.

Hours of service rules for a driver that is carrying property (no passengers and no hazardous materials) and works for a carrier that operates six days per week, include these:

- Following a minimum ten-hour off-duty break, the driver may only drive for an eleven-hour period.
- After every eight hours of on-duty time, the driver must take a minimum thirty-minute rest break.
- The driver must not drive a CMV during these breaks.
- The driver may not drive beyond the fourteenth consecutive hour after starting an on-duty period that follows a minimum ten-hour off-duty break.

The intent is that the driver should sleep during a portion of the ten-hour off-duty period, and certain rules explain that provision. The rules are based on research of the minimum rest periods needed to reduce driver-fatigue and exhaustion that may lead to accidents.

Drivers transporting certain explosive materials are considered on duty at any time they are "in attendance" of the CMV or are performing other work duties; therefore, special rules apply for their rest periods. Special provisions for all drivers apply in emergencies, during adverse driving conditions, and for driver-salespersons and oil field operation drivers. Less-restrictive provisions apply for most short-haul driving (within 100 air-mile radius from the driver's normal reporting site) and for retail store deliveries, but only when a CDL is required.

FMCSR rules specify that, if a motor carrier requires a driver to use a FMCSR-compliant automatic on-board recording device in the CMV to track hours of service, the driver must comply. Any such device must be fully accessible to authorities from within the CMV and from a related support system within the motor carrier's terminal. Any manual entries made by the driver must be legible and signed.

### Apply Your Knowledge

Troy works for a motor carrier and has been assigned to carry a load of lumber across three states to another terminal. Troy began his on-duty period after a ten-hour, off-duty break. He started his work (on-duty) at 8:00 a.m. and spent one hour loading the CMV. The trip is expected to take fifteen hours, and he began driving immediately after loading. By what time must Troy take a minimum, thirty-minute, off-duty rest break (based on his starting terminal's time zone)?

a. 5:00 p.m.
b. 8:00 p.m.
c. 4:00 p.m.
d. 7:00 p.m.

*Feedback: c.* Troy must take a minimum, thirty-minute, off-duty rest break after eight consecutive on-duty hours, regardless of whether he is driving while on duty. Therefore, he must take a rest break eight hours after starting work, which would be 4:00 p.m.

## Accident Reporting Rules

CMV accident reports are used in investigations and special studies. Accident reports must be available to the FMCSA and state and local agencies or authorities. The FMCSR requires motor carriers to record accidents in a

10.12   Risk Assessment and Treatment

compliant register that must be retained for at least one year after the accident occurs.

The FMCSR defines an accident as an occurrence involving a CMV that has any of these results:

- A fatality
- Bodily injury to a person who immediately receives medical treatment for the injury away from the scene of the accident
- One or more motor vehicles that incur disabling damage as a result and which requires the disabled vehicle(s) to be transported from the scene by a tow truck or other motor vehicle

An accident does not include an occurrence involving an individual boarding or exiting a stationary motor vehicle or involving loading or unloading cargo.

The FMCSR specifies that the accident register must list all accidents. The list must include the accident date, city or town nearest the accident location and state, driver's name, number of injuries, number of fatalities, and whether hazardous materials were released. The accident register must include copies of accident reports required by any government entities and insurers.

## Record Keeping Rules

The FMCSR specifies minimum record retention requirements for motor carriers and obligates them to maintain DOT-required records supporting their financial and operational data. Beyond those requirements, company management may destroy records at its discretion if other governmental body retention laws are met.

The specific records for retentions are described and categorized in an appendix to the FMCSR with minimum retention dates. Except for records that are commonly maintained according to another authority, most general business records must be retained for three years or for three years beyond their settlement or disposition date. Items having expiration dates may be retained based on their expiration or cancelation date. Generally, shipping records must be retained for one year, while transportation records' retention varies from one to three years.

The FMCSR describes hazards from which records must be protected and requires reporting to the DOT secretary if records are damaged or destroyed or other hardships occur. Additionally, the FMCSR explains organizations' record retention responsibilities when they are dissolved or merged with other organizations.

## Electronic Device Usage Rules

To minimize driver distractions and resultant accidents, and to increase situational awareness, decision making, and performance, the FMCSR prohibits drivers from using electronic devices while driving a CMV for interstate commerce. The FMCSR defines an "electronic device" to include a cellular telephone; personal digital assistant; pager; computer; or any other device used to input, write, send, receive, or read text. Similar FMCSR regulations ban text messaging by CMV drivers carrying hazardous materials for intrastate commerce.

Violations for using an electronic device while driving are punishable by fines against the driver and, for repeated offenses, disqualification from operating a CMV for up to four months. Employers that allow their employees/drivers to use hand-held cellular phones or to engage in texting while driving (except emergency use with officials) are subject to significant penalties. Before the FMCSA began applying such penalties, many large carriers had established policies against hand-held telephone use by employees while driving CMVs. Many carriers are expected to establish similar policies.[2]

## Compliance, Safety, and Accountability (CSA) Program

In 2010, the FMCSA developed the CSA initiative to improve safety of CMVs and reduce accidents, injuries, and fatalities. Under this initiative, the FMCSA works with state partners through a nationwide system to improve highway safety.

The CSA uses Safety Measurement System (SMS) technology to track and update safety performance data. Tools are used to evaluate the reasons for safety problems. Officials use this information to recommend remedies, to encourage corrective action, and, if inadequate, to access penalties. The CSA has led to more efficient and effective intervention and the ability to reach more carriers than was possible with compliance reviews; carriers are also better able to identify and correct their own safety issues.

The SMS collects motor carrier data through roadside inspections, safety-based violations, state-reported accidents, and the federal motor carrier census to quantify carriers' performance and assign a safety score. The score is developed based on unsafe driving, hours-of-service issues, driver fitness, controlled substance or alcohol driver impairments, vehicle maintenance, cargo-related issues, and accident frequency and severity.

A policy process determines appropriate carrier intervention, which can range from warning letters to on-site comprehensive investigations. Letters provide the safety score, suggested remedies, and consequences for not correcting problems. Less intensive off-site and on-site investigations are used when appropriate for the problems identified. In all cases, the carrier can access all data used to develop the score and many roadside inspectors can access the data to conduct targeted inspections.

Carriers may voluntarily develop comprehensive safety plans (CSPs) using a template provided by the FMCSA. When safety concerns merit a response from the carrier, the CSA issues a notice of violation (NOV). If the regulatory violations are severe enough to warrant civil penalties, a notice of claim (NOC) is issued, and, in the most extreme cases, an operations out-of-service (OOS) order is issued to require the carrier to cease all motor vehicle operations.[3]

# CONTROLLING LOSSES ASSOCIATED WITH MOTOR VEHICLE SAFETY SYSTEMS

From a frequency and severity perspective, an organization's transportation loss exposures arising from its motor vehicle fleet can be one of the most likely areas to sustain substantial loss. Because an organization can depend heavily on motor vehicles in its day-to-day operations, motor vehicle fleets pose many risk management challenges and opportunities for loss control.

Each of the components of a fleet system generates loss exposures that can lead to vehicle accidents. In addition, the environment within which those components function as a system can jeopardize one or more of them and, therefore, threaten system failure. Consequently, a thorough fleet safety program encompasses each of those components and the elements of the environment in which they operate. This section discusses how to control the risks associated with these components:

- Vehicles
- Vehicle maintenance
- Drivers
- Cargoes
- Routes
- Vehicle schedules

## Vehicles

An organization's fleet safety is influenced by the selection of task-appropriate vehicles for purchase, the establishment of safe operating practices, and vehicle maintenance and replacement. Through these measures, a company can reduce the number of accidents and contain unnecessary expenses resulting from accidents and breakdowns.

### Vehicle Selection

Selecting vehicles suitable for particular tasks requires a full understanding of the intended use. Factors to consider when selecting appropriate vehicles are the anticipated cargo (size and weight), characteristics of cargo (potential for load shifts, high center of gravity, and other physical characteristics), number of passengers, and the geographic area in which the vehicle will be operated. The underlying goal is to choose vehicles that can safely and efficiently transport the anticipated cargoes and passengers. Achieving that goal requires careful monitoring of the vehicles' actual use.

Vehicles selected must have a sufficient gross vehicle weight rating (GVWR) for the maximum load or number of passengers they will be used to carry. The GVWR is a predetermined specification assigned by the manufacturer. It is the maximum allowable weight at which a fully loaded vehicle can operate safely, including the weight of the vehicle, its options and accessories, all liquids—such as gas and oil—when their receptacles are filled to capacity, any passengers and cargo placed inside the vehicle or secured on top, and any other factors that might increase the total weight of the vehicle. The GVWR determines the class of license that drivers are required to have, how much they may be paid (higher classes command higher salaries), and the safety regulations and training required of them.

Vehicles selected must have good safety records. Statistics are available from the National Association of Automobile Manufacturers and the Insurance Institute for Highway Safety indicating the relative safety of the various makes and models of vehicles and the types of accidents to which each is most subject. Products liability claims brought against manufacturers for specific types of vehicles and any recalls indicate vehicle models to avoid.

When selecting fleet vehicles, ease of maintenance requires consideration. A vehicle that can readily be repaired in an organization's own garage or at roadside by its own drivers will generally be more productive in the long run than a vehicle that can be maintained or repaired only by highly trained mechanics using specialized tools. Buying vehicles from the same manufacturer can simplify maintenance. Vehicles whose performance records indicate they can operate reliably for extended periods tend to be safer and more productive than those that require frequent care.

Uniformity among the vehicles selected for a fleet increases fleet safety. If vehicles are fundamentally alike, most drivers will be able to operate any fleet vehicle safely, with knowledge and confidence. Similarity among vehicles also facilitates roadside repairs because an organization's emergency repair vehicles can carry and use parts compatible with all vehicles.

## Safety Equipment

Most makes and models of vehicles come equipped with several important safety features. Solid body construction, high maneuverability, and an exterior color that is easily visible in low lighting conditions are three such features.

Specialized vehicles need additional safety equipment. For example, dump trucks need lights, or other indicators to show when the truck body is raised, and a cab protector or canopy. Other large trucks require equipment such as a low air-pressure warning system (for air brakes), audible backup signal, appropriate tie downs to prevent loads from shifting or falling, and rock guards over driving (powered) tires. Rescue vehicles need sirens and warning lights, extensive first-aid medical supplies, and appropriate radio communication equipment.

## Vehicle Replacement

Unless its fleet needs are declining, an organization must replace fleet vehicles whenever they wear out or become obsolete, or when they are damaged to the point that it is not cost-effective to repair them. Replacing some of the vehicles in a fleet gives the organization the opportunity to reconsider its original purchase decisions or to gradually alter the composition of the fleet to reflect changing environmental or business conditions.

## Vehicle Maintenance

Vehicle maintenance on an organization's fleet affects its losses from fleet operations in two ways. First, proper maintenance tends to improve the fleet's safety record and, therefore, to reduce vehicle losses. Second, because motor vehicle maintenance is a potentially hazardous activity, it must be performed safely. Controlling maintenance loss exposures is essential to overall fleet safety.

Regular preventive maintenance—done on a scheduled basis, irrespective of mechanical problems—is crucial to safe, reliable vehicle performance. Scheduling a vehicle's trips must allow time for monthly or more frequent inspections at one of the organization's garages or at another facility properly equipped and staffed to check and replace brakes, lights, tires, engine belts, and other vehicle components before they fail. Preventive maintenance can keep accidents from happening and enable vehicles to complete trips on time without breaking down.

## Drivers

Drivers are a crucial component of a fleet system. The majority of vehicle accidents on or off public roadways result from driver error, inattention, lack of training, or another human fault. Because accidents involving driver error tend to be preventable, fleet safety management often focuses on how drivers are selected; trained; supervised; licensed; and, when necessary, dismissed.

### Driver Selection

The essential steps in selecting new drivers for any motor vehicle include these:

- Analyzing job functions—determining what specific tasks drivers will perform
- Recruiting applicants—advertising, prescreening, and reviewing applications

- Screening applicants—interviewing and administering written and road tests
- Hiring employees—making the initial job offer (subject to checks and a physical exam), conducting background checks, conducting a physical examination, and confirming the job offer
- Orienting employees—conducting new-employee orientations and establishing and maintaining qualification files

Screening applicants involves several steps that can best be tracked through a decision flowchart. See the exhibit "New-Driver Hiring Decision Flowchart."

A criteria matrix based on motor vehicle records (MVRs) showing the number of at-fault accidents and the number of moving violations can help determine acceptable MVRs for hiring drivers and for employment continuation. The employer should establish the number of years within which at-fault accidents and moving violations should be considered or may use the years reported on MVRs for the employer's jurisdiction. See the exhibit "Motor Vehicle Record Criteria Matrix."

## Driver Training

Driver training is an extensive, specialized field that encompasses several forms of training in various areas. An organization with a large fleet might provide its own driver training, especially if it has very specific needs. Other organizations tend to rely more heavily on independent driver-training firms to provide the training their drivers require.

Driver training might involve classroom instruction; behind-the-wheel training; simulations; or independent study using textbooks, films, or interactive computer programs. Classroom and independent study are best suited for learning traffic laws, the hazards associated with particular cargoes, procedures in case of accidents, and similar subjects. Behind-the-wheel training is essential for learning the skills needed to operate a vehicle safely and for the remedial training of drivers who have been involved in accidents. The classroom and behind-the-wheel coaching are also appropriate for practicing the procedures a driver should follow immediately after an accident.

Each driver's qualification file should document the type and content of the training the driver has received. The file should indicate that the driver has passed performance or written tests that document completion of fleet training.

## Driver Supervision

Supervisors of vehicle drivers must focus on reinforcing safe, efficient driver behavior and on discouraging or disciplining unsafe, inefficient behavior. Supervising vehicle drivers is especially challenging because drivers, unlike most employees, spend virtually all of their work time away from direct

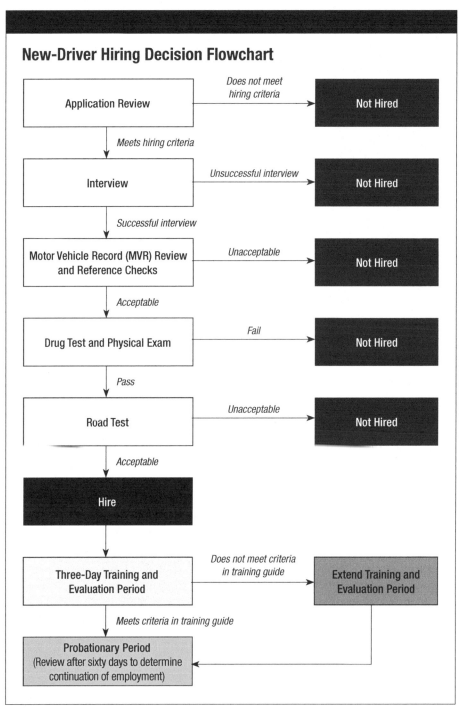

[DA08688]

## Motor Vehicle Record Criteria Matrix

At-Fault Accidents

| | | 0 | 1 | 2 | 3 |
|---|---|---|---|---|---|
| Moving Violations | 0 | OK | OK | OK* | NO |
| | 1 | OK | OK | OK* | NO |
| | 2 | OK | OK* | NO | NO |
| | 3 | OK* | NO | NO | NO |
| | 4 | NO | NO | NO | NO |

*Borderline drivers—Current drivers who are borderline can remain employed. Applicants who are borderline cannot be hired.

[DA08689]

managerial observation and beyond their supervisors' personal control and feedback.

Some organizations, especially common carriers (companies that sell transport services to the public for people or property) with large fleets, try to compensate for this lack of direct personal contact by using procedural and physical controls. For example, many drivers are asked to keep a written log of times when they leave or reach particular stops along their routes and stop for fuel, food, or rest. Other drivers might be given an extremely precise route and schedule and be asked to call the fleet manager's office at predetermined times to report their locations.

Many vehicles carry two-way radios or cell phones so that the fleet dispatcher or supervisor can randomly contact each driver to monitor the driver's location and activity. Some fleets are equipped with automatic devices that make continuous-time recordings of the speed and direction of the vehicles' movements and the times when the vehicles are not moving. Those records are either turned in to the fleet dispatcher or supervisor at the end of each day or trip or submitted through real-time, electronic reporting.

Organizations that are not common carriers or that have relatively small fleets often adopt less formal methods for supervising drivers (such as meetings or even occasionally riding with the driver).

Some fleet managers emphasize rewards for outstanding performance or discipline for substandard performance. Those managers focus on bonuses, safe-driving contests, on-schedule awards, or other forms of positive recognition that give drivers incentives to achieve the organization's fleet safety, efficiency, and other performance goals.

Highly positive, reward-centered fleet supervision programs can be especially effective when they fit the organization's general management style and the expectations of the vehicle drivers. In other organizations, emphasizing rewards for outstanding safety records can lead drivers to falsify reports of safety checks, disguise potentially damaging incidents, and fail to report genuine accidents. Such behavior can impair the communication and cooperation on which any effective fleet supervision effort should be based.

## Driver Licensing

Vehicle drivers should be licensed to drive every vehicle used at work (including the driver's personal vehicle, if applicable). Requiring a valid driver's license is a crucial aspect of fleet safety for these reasons:

- Failure to confirm that drivers have current, valid licenses exposes organizations to liability for any accidents their unlicensed or improperly licensed drivers cause.

- Some states have relatively liberal standards for licensing drivers; therefore, not all states' licenses document the level of competence that some organizations seek in their vehicle drivers (especially for those residing in other states).

- Each state has different, frequently changing requirements for the types of licenses drivers must have to operate certain kinds of commercial vehicles, particularly large trucks, buses, ambulances, and other specialty vehicles.

- Federal laws can add to or supersede these state requirements, especially for vehicles that transport hazardous materials—such as fuels, chemicals, and wastes—in interstate commerce.

To fully understand the licensing requirements and classifications of commercial vehicle drivers, fleet managers should research both state and federal requirements, particularly for drivers involved in interstate commerce.

## Driver Dismissal

An employer may want to replace a driver for a variety of positive or negative reasons. Positively, an employer may promote a driver to other work within the organization. Negatively, an employer may need to dismiss or transfer a driver because some aspect of that driver's performance—such as efficiency, reliability, safety, or timeliness—is below standard and is not improving after intervention measures.

Some vehicle drivers may also need to be dismissed or laid off because their employer's volume of business markedly declines. Dismissing or replacing a vehicle driver can have significant implications from a fleet safety perspective and from a risk management perspective.

From a fleet safety perspective, each dismissal or replacement of a vehicle driver should raise, or at least maintain, the overall level of safety in the fleet. These factors can be a significant safety concern:

- Before a driver is dismissed because of a poor safety record, the employer should confirm that the driver's deficiencies have been the predominant cause of the poor record and that those deficiencies cannot be corrected.
- If a dismissed driver is replaced, the replacement driver should be able to safely operate the vehicle(s) to which he or she is assigned.
- The dismissal or replacement should not have an overly adverse effect on the safety performance or conduct of the remaining drivers.

Risk management concerns can arise from poor management of the replacement process. All legal rights of the dismissed driver must be respected so that the employer is not exposed to potential liability for replacing the driver. In addition, the dismissal and replacement process should be structured to minimize emotional stress and thereby reduce the possibility of careless, angry, or distraught work performance that might lead to workers compensation or automobile negligence liability claims against the employer.

# Cargoes

A primary component of a fleet system is the cargo being transported. In this section, cargo is used as a broad term that encompasses both freight and passengers. Cargo can be transported in any kind of passenger car, truck, bus, or other motor vehicle on or off public roads.

## Suitability to Vehicle

In general, a specific cargo is suitable for a particular vehicle only if the vehicle poses no unreasonable risks to the cargo and the cargo poses no unreasonable risks to the vehicle.

Vehicles can easily damage cargoes. Consequently, various kinds of cargoes require specialized vehicles for their safe transport. Consider, for example, such cargoes as passengers, bulk petroleum products, livestock, packaged frozen foods, newly forested logs, bulldozers or other large earth-moving equipment, and the major components of modular housing units. Each requires its own type of vehicle for safe transport. Trying to transport many of these cargoes in an all-purpose vehicle, such as a utility van or flatbed truck, is likely to cause accidental losses such as these:

- The bulk petroleum catches fire or explodes because the vehicle was not properly grounded and bonded to neutralize static electricity.
- Livestock suffer because of inadequate space or ventilation.
- The frozen food thaws and spoils because of improper refrigeration.
- The logs or the bulldozer shifts and rolls off the truck.
- The modular housing units slam together, are knocked out of alignment, and no longer fit together as designed.

Conversely, a cargo can damage a vehicle or driver because the cargo is too heavy for the vehicle, too corrosive to its interior, too toxic to the vehicle driver, or otherwise so hazardous that only a highly specialized vehicle can safely transport it. Moreover, as a vehicle ages with use, a cargo it once could carry properly can exceed the vehicle's capabilities. An organization must regularly check that its cargoes and vehicles are matched safely.

## Proper Loading

Because transporting cargo is expensive, a common fleet operation goal is to maximize payload and minimize downtime. However, if loading is not closely monitored, the potential to overload or not properly secure cargo can become a serious issue. Drivers need specific training on loading procedures and on securing cargo for the vehicles they operate. Fleet management and drivers should be familiar with the cargo securement requirements in the Federal Motor Carrier Safety Regulations (FMCSR). Improper loading does not save time in the long run because it is likely to cause cargo damage, vehicle damage, and missed delivery schedules and, in the event of an accident, to create additional liability for the organization.

## Suitability of Routes

When an organization has a choice of routes, it should select a motor vehicle route only if it presents no unreasonable risks to the cargo and if the cargo presents no unreasonable risk to the properties or persons along the route or in the surrounding environment.

Specific routes can unduly threaten particular cargoes when those routes create hazardous environments. For example, it would be unwise to use a refrigerated truck to transport frozen foods through a desert during the summer if another route offers cooler weather during that season without substantial added cost. If a cargo is vulnerable to salty ocean air, an inland route is preferable to a coastal one.

In addition, hazardous cargoes can cause particularly severe losses if they escape into the communities or environment along densely populated or otherwise vulnerable routes. For example, it is dangerous to transport hazardous waste through urban areas, especially during high-traffic periods. Roadway accidents may result in the release of hazardous material into crowded surroundings, causing great property damage, widespread bodily injuries, and potentially large liability losses for all parties responsible for the shipment. Transporting hazardous material along a mountain road that follows the course of a large river is risky because, should an accident occur, the truck or cargo could fall into the river and carry contamination to all populations and properties along the river.

## Safeguards Against Inherent Vice

"Inherent vice" refers to a condition that can cause property to deteriorate or destroy itself. Frozen food spoiling in an unrefrigerated vehicle is an example of inherent vice, as is decorative porcelains breaking when jostled together during shipping or packages of soap powder transported in a nonwatertight vehicle getting wet and being ruined during a rainstorm.

The vehicle must provide an appropriate environment for the cargo. Specially designed environmental controls on the vehicle must be working, and nothing must happen during the trip to jeopardize that environment. For example, the heating or refrigeration in a truck should operate whether or not the truck's engine is running. Similarly, the truck carrying the soap powder should be equipped with moisture sensors that enable the driver to confirm, without opening the cargo to the rainstorm, that the cargo is dry.

# Routes

Suitably safe, cost-effective, reliable routes are those that present no unacceptable risks to vehicles, drivers, and cargoes; are reasonable in distance; and offer some flexibility of alternatives if the main route is blocked or closed.

Some routes are naturally safer than others for almost any vehicle or cargo. One route could be significantly less hazardous than others because the roads are better designed or have less traffic, because it is less subject to natural causes of loss such as avalanches or flooding, or because it offers better two-way radio or cell phone transmission and reception to summon help. Steeply graded roads, the absence of restaurants or other facilities where drivers can make scheduled rest stops, poor roadway lighting, and any number of other adverse conditions can make one route inherently riskier than another. Unless other factors strongly indicate to the contrary, good fleet safety management requires selecting the least hazardous route whenever a reasonable choice exists.

Distance is another important factor in selecting safe, economical routes. The less distance a vehicle travels, the less likely it is to experience an accident.

Also, the shorter the route, the more likely the trip can be completed on or close to schedule without any unforeseen events causing delays.

## Vehicle Schedules

A sound safety-oriented vehicle schedule provides enough time for vehicle drivers to complete their trips on schedule without rushing and without scheduling conflicts. A driver's schedule should allow flexibility to deal with unforeseen events.

A suitable schedule allows (and requires) vehicle drivers to work at a reasonable pace. A schedule that is too demanding requires drivers to rush or to overextend themselves and could result in driving errors. A schedule that is too lax is inefficient and likely to tempt some drivers to extend their overnight stops or rest breaks because they know they will have plenty of time to catch up on their schedule later. To make schedules more acceptable to their vehicle drivers, many fleet managers seek input from drivers to develop reasonable schedule standards.

Schedules that pay vehicle drivers on an incentive scale reward drivers for driving the greatest distance in the least possible time. Such incentive systems tend to jeopardize safety because drivers may be tempted to exceed speed limits, drive too many hours each day, rush or skip daily vehicle safety and maintenance checks, take hazardous shortcuts, or try other dangerous activities to increase their incentive-pay rewards. Organizations committed to incentive-pay systems for their vehicle drivers should also include incentives for safety-related conduct (or deduct money if drivers fail to document their safety-related actions).

Setting reasonable driver schedules also entails avoiding schedule conflicts. Those setting drivers' schedules must be sure that no driver is scheduled to be driving and sleeping at the same time or asked to make a preventive maintenance check during a required rest period. Computerized fleet scheduling/dispatch software can help to prevent those conflicts and to test the reasonability of each driver's schedule.

Reasonable scheduling also allows some flexibility for unforeseen difficulties such as a stalled engine, a truck being delayed at a mandatory weigh station stop, or a drawbridge being stuck open. The driver facing such situations should have enough leeway in the route schedule to complete the trip within a reasonably acceptable time.

# TECHNOLOGICAL ADVANCES IN MOTOR VEHICLE FLEET SAFETY

Organizations depend heavily on motor vehicle fleets in their day-to-day operations. Safeguarding motor vehicles and their cargo using advanced technology can contribute greatly to helping an organization achieve its risk management goals.

Many organizations generate most of their revenue by providing customers with temporary use of vehicles such as taxis, ambulances, trucks, hearses, and luxury automobiles. For those companies, keeping a sufficient fleet of vehicles ready for customers' immediate, safe, and reliable use is essential to their business success. Organizations can use technological advances in fleet safety to minimize accident potential and liability.

In practice, an organization's fleet safety program must focus almost entirely on its own vehicles and vehicle drivers to achieve the most benefit from its limited risk management resources. Exceptions exist when an organization advises its major suppliers or customers on how to improve their fleet safety (or refuses to deal with them until their dangerous fleet practices improve) and when an organization supports various industry, legislative, and law enforcement efforts to improve fleet safety.

## Need for Technology

Driver error is the most frequent cause of motor vehicle accidents. Driver supervision is often minimal because of driver mobility, so it can be difficult for management to know if drivers are engaging in risky behaviors such as speeding or tailgating while driving, or if they are exceeding the federal hours of service requirements for commercial motor vehicles. These behaviors may be discovered only after an accident occurs—when it is too late. Technological advances in fleet safety can help an organization significantly reduce accidents.

## Technological Advances

With technological advances in fleet safety, onboard computers can capture information about risky driving behavior and enable risk management professionals to evaluate operator performance before an accident, thereby reducing accident potential and liability for the organization. Effectively using the captured information is crucial. For example, if an organization acquires data indicating that a particular driver is a habitual speeder and does nothing to change this behavior, the organization could be exposed to additional liability if the driver is involved in an accident, especially if the primary cause of the accident is excessive speed.

In addition to onboard computers, the following safety technologies also exist for fleet operations:

- Stability control systems sense when a vehicle is traveling too fast in a curve and automatically apply the vehicle's brakes.
- Rear-mounted video cameras provide the operator with a better vision of what is happening behind the vehicle.

- Antilock braking systems prevent a vehicle's brakes from locking up and perpetuating a loss of traction during a skid.

- Real-time tire pressure monitors alert drivers to improperly inflated tire conditions that can cause excessive tire wear, loss of fuel efficiency, and unsafe driving conditions. For eight-wheeled vehicles and "run flat" tires, these monitors can alert the driver to a flat tire and the need to decrease speed and seek an appropriate repair location.

- Onboard tire inflation systems keep proper air pressure in select tires to reduce the chance that the driver will lose control of the vehicle.

- Satellite communication with global positioning system (GPS) capabilities allows an employer to monitor a vehicle's position and progress en route and enables a driver to stay on course and reduce the likelihood of unexpected risks encountered on an unplanned route.

- Onboard scales measure temperature and pressure to determine gross vehicle weight, net weight, and axle group weights. These features enable a vehicle to carry the maximum legal weight and to assist with efficient and proper load distribution for effective and safe vehicle loading and operation.

- Dash-mounted video cameras provide video surveillance in front of a vehicle, which serves as evidence for the cause of an accident or other road incident, helps avoid paying fraudulent claims for staged accidents, provides information for driver evaluations, and can serve in a collision warning system.

- Lane departure warning systems (LDWS) are collision warning systems that alert drivers when they have crossed into another lane to avoid side swipe collisions or head-on collisions and when they have crossed onto a shoulder or off the roadway to avoid collisions with fixed objects and rollover accidents.

- Forward Collision Warning Systems (FCWS) are collision warning systems that alert drivers when they approach a dangerous situation, such as a stopped or slow-moving vehicle on the roadway, and help drivers maintain an adequate following distance.

The Federal Motor Carrier Safety Administration (FMCSA) recommends that fleet operators use a combination of these safety systems to prevent accidents. See the exhibit "Estimated Collisions Preventable by Using Specified Safety Systems."

## Estimated Collisions Preventable by Using Specified Safety Systems

### Integrated Vehicle-Based Systems

**Lane Departure Warning Systems (LDWS):**

| | |
|---|---|
| • Same or opposite direction sideswipes | 88% |
| • Opposite direction head-ons | 38% |
| • Single vehicle rollovers | 44% |
| • Single vehicle collisions with a fixed object | 78% |

**Forward Collision Warning Systems (FCWS):**

| | |
|---|---|
| • Rear-end collisions with a slow or stopped vehicle | 67% |

### Collision Mitigation Systems

**Roll Stability Control (RSC) Systems:**

| | |
|---|---|
| • Rollovers from excess speed in a curve | 42% |

**Electronic Stability Control (ESC) Systems:**

| | |
|---|---|
| • Jackknifes from loss of control | 66% |

Adapted from Federal Motor Carrier Safety Administration, Office of Analysis, Research, and Technology presentation, "Onboard Safety System Deployment Program," 2008, estimated using commercial motor carrier crash data from multiple sources spanning 2001 through 2005. [DA08690]

# SUMMARY

An organization's fleet is a system. A fleet has components, the purpose of which is to safely and efficiently transport cargo or persons and to achieve the organization's goals within its physical, legal, economic, and competitive environments. The five phases of a fleet's life cycle are conceptual, engineering, production, operational, and disposal. Each of a fleet's components is a system made up of several subsystems. The nesting of progressively smaller systems as subsystems within progressively larger systems provides a basis for tracing the effects of a failure downward to smaller systems and upward to larger systems. A risk management professional works to prevent a system failure and is aware of its consequences throughout related systems.

Motor carriers and their drivers are required to follow the rules in the FMCSR if their CMVs and fleets meet the specified qualifications. The FMCSR provides rules governing many aspects of the motor carrier industry, including significant rules involving driver qualifications, drug testing, hours of service, accident reporting, record keeping, and electronic device usage. Additionally, the FMCSA conducts a CSA initiative to fulfill its goals for motor carriers and improve highway safety. A risk management professional should be familiar with the FMCSR as part of the legal environment within which a fleet operates and recognize its role in ensuring fleet safety.

A vehicle fleet owner can reduce the number of accidents and contain unnecessary expenses resulting from accidents and breakdowns by purchasing task-appropriate vehicles, establishing safe operating practices, properly maintaining vehicles, and replacing vehicles as appropriate. Selecting drivers for their skills, knowledge, and driving record is crucial. All vehicle drivers should be, and should remain, properly licensed to operate each of the types of vehicles they use on the job. Cargo should be suited to the vehicle transporting it, properly loaded and secured, appropriate for the route the vehicle is to travel, and free from uncontrolled inherent vice. Vehicle routes should be as safe as scheduling and cost constraints allow. Unreasonable schedules place excessive demands on drivers and can undermine fleet safety.

Organizations can use advanced technology in fleet safety to minimize accident potential and liability. Because operator error is a significant cause of motor vehicle accidents, being able to monitor and control inappropriate behaviors is a crucial risk control measure. Many advanced safety technologies are available to help reduce the frequency and severity of accidents.

## ASSIGNMENT NOTES

1.  Office of Drug and Alcohol Policy and Compliance, Selected portions of Department of Transportation Rule 49 CFR Part 40: 49 U.S.C.A. § 40 (2010).

2.  U.S. Department of Transportation, Office of Public Affairs, "News Release: U.S. Transportation Secretary LaHood Announces Final Rule That Bans Hand-Held Cell Phone Use by Drivers of Buses and Large Trucks," November 23, 2011, www.fmcsa.dot.gov/about/news/news-releases/2011/Secretary-LaHood-Announces-Step-towards-Safer-Highways.aspx (accessed March 1, 2012).

3.  U.S. Department of Transportation, Federal Motor Carrier Safety Administration, selected passages of the Federal Motor Carrier Safety Regulations Rule 49 CFR all parts: 49 U.S.C.A. § 300-399 (2012).

# Smart Products and Risk Management

## Educational Objectives

After learning the content of this assignment, you should be able to:

▷ Demonstrate how smart products can be applied to risk management.

▷ Illustrate how data produced by smart products enables risk assessment and control.

▷ Describe the exposures associated with using smart products to manage risks.

# Smart Products and Risk Management

11

## HOW SMART PRODUCTS APPLY TO RISK MANAGEMENT

Historically, risk managers' assessments of the probability of adverse events were limited by the boundaries of human perception. Today, however, previously imperceptible risk factors, such as a worker's hydration level, the presence of a hazardous chemical in the air, or the catastrophic intersection of seemingly disconnected financial transactions, can be factored into risk management decision making.

This new world of risk assessment data has been revealed by **smart products** that sense their environment, process data, and communicate with other smart products and smart operations. These interactions generate **big data**—to which advanced analytics can be applied, ultimately reducing the uncertainty associated with predicting future events.

As technology evolves, the availability and sophistication of smart products that can help refine risk management techniques continue to grow. Here are just a few examples:

- Wearables such as helmets that monitor fatigue or wristwatches that measure vital signs can sense, monitor, report, and analyze workers' health or well-being and their surrounding environments. Data generated by wearables may be specific to one employee or aggregated for a project, team, or organization.

- Drones can be used in surveillance and aerial photography; being unmanned and highly versatile makes them ideal for assessing conditions or risks in dangerous or unknown areas. The data generated by drones relies heavily on other technologies, such as computer vision, image recognition, and artificial intelligence, to mine the data collected and form conclusions about detected objects.

- In addition to performing activities and capturing information from sensors in a workplace, robots can measure, respond to, and produce data for monitored hazards or changing environmental conditions. For example, sensors in conjunction with high-definition cameras can scan and inspect bridges for erosion or other unsafe conditions.

**Smart product**

An innovative item that uses sensors; wireless sensor networks; and data collection, transmission, and analysis to further enable the item to be faster, more useful, or otherwise improved.

**Big data**

Sets of data that are too large to be gathered and analyzed by traditional methods.

Smart products have introduced a new dimension of depth and precision to risk assessment and control in a variety of contexts, including these:

- Property management
- Supply chain management
- Transportation management
- Catastrophe management
- Workplace safety management
- Construction and engineering management

## Property Management

**Wireless sensor network (WSN)**

A wireless network consisting of individual sensors placed at various locations to exchange data.

Property managers can use **wireless sensor networks (WSNs)** to detect and respond to leaks and malfunctions or prevent on-site falls and injuries. For example, temperature and water sensors can monitor heat irregularities and detect the first signs of leakage before tenants (especially lower-level ones in multistory buildings) sustain water damage to drywall, carpets, furniture, or other belongings. Temperature sensors provide alerts before a pipe freezes and are particularly useful in vacant or temporarily unoccupied buildings. Light sensors monitor illumination and provide lighting when needed around the perimeter of buildings, in parking lots, on stairs, and in underground parking garages, eliminating hazards that could lead to liability claims and lawsuits. Motion sensors and surveillance cameras can deter crime before it occurs and document suspicious activities. Thermal sensors, current sensors, and smoke detectors assess impending fire conditions so that first responders can be notified before a fire begins or actions can be taken to lessen the extent and cost of damage if one does occur.

Because the sensors in a WSN work together, multiple buildings can be remotely managed, producing data that shows real-time and historical maintenance reports and service records, as well as comparisons among properties or units, floors, or departments within a property. Some sensors only need to be placed in the desired locations and activated. Many applications allow further monitoring or interaction opportunities. And surveillance cameras, enabled with computer vision, capture images that can be analyzed for additional insights, allowing for loss prevention and reduction and ensuring continuous climate control, controlled power consumption, and compliance with building codes.

## Supply Chain Management

Supply chain management involves the risk of not only product, service, or shipment disruptions caused by unforeseen events but also the downstream effects that interruptions cause to other products, services, or shipments. Risk assessment, which involves identifying potential or actual disruptions, and risk control, which involves preventing or reducing disruptions, use many emerging technologies to manage supply chain risks.

For example, radio frequency identification (RFID), which uses radio frequency to identify objects, wireless protocols, and the Global Positioning System (GPS), is particularly important to managing supply chain risks. Supply chain assets were previously tracked using standard bar codes, which must be in close proximity to a reader. In contrast, RFID tags identify assets and compile their characteristics without human intervention.

RFID technology is wireless, supports an automated process, does not require the reader to be in close proximity to the asset, and provides specific information on each asset to facilitate logistics and transport. This technology, especially when used with GPS for additional location tracking, enables a mixed shipment of freight to be identified and tracked without the need to remove any external wrapping. Furthermore, each item of freight can be easily cataloged by the reader according to description and condition, manufacture and expiration dates, arrival location and time, and relationship to current inventory. When a shipment is incomplete or damaged, RFID technology can be used to assess the risk, automatically call for replacements, and manage the replacement process.

Additionally, RFID tags provide unique identifiers, which offer real-time, accurate record storage and retrieval in a closed-loop system. With this readily available, detailed data on supply chain assets, companies can immediately identify discrepancies and interruptions and quickly prevent and reduce supply chain risk. Furthermore, RFID's process-automation capability can generate real-time alerts for those who need to receive the information and oversee remediation.

Other kinds of sensors can empower more precise supply chain management. For example, sensor data can inform a supply chain manager that weather conditions have interrupted the production of parts or that cargo has been stolen.

## Transportation Management

Transportation management that facilitates risk assessment and control involves incorporating technologies from the **Internet of Things (IoT)** to connect vehicles and their drivers with solutions for awareness, safety, efficiency, and reliability. These same technologies also help organizations manage their vehicle fleets.

Internet of Things (IoT)
A network of objects that transmit data to and from each other without human interaction.

Some of these technologies even provide driver assistance. Examples include crash avoidance; self-parking; cameras on the back of trucks to facilitate lane changing; and, in some cases, full autonomous driving capabilities enabled by cameras that use computer vision to discern people from other objects or vehicles, as well as to recognize changes in pavement types or abrupt lane changes in construction zones.

**Smart transportation**

The integration of strategic vehicle management solutions with innovative technologies.

**Smart transportation** is also key to transportation management. As with many smart operations in a variety of contexts, it can be described as a series of layers:

- A sensing layer, which uses a variety of sensors, cameras, and data-collection capabilities to make (or help the driver to make) necessary corrections and provide information to others
- A communications layer that provides data transmission to and from drivers and managers using wireless protocols that ensure necessary capabilities, such as recording, data uploading, navigating, video recording, and centralized monitoring for both the sensing layer and the service layer
- A service layer, which employs applications using data processing, cloud computing, and storage and analysis of large amounts of the data captured by vehicle sensors and provided by drivers

The results of this interaction among layers are improved remote diagnostics, prompt driver response from real-time analysis of his or her driving habits or physical condition, fuel and/or vehicle repair savings because of implemented corrections, preventive maintenance alerts before a costly mechanical breakdown, and customizable products and services (such as comparisons of nearby hotels and restaurants) to make rides easier for drivers and more enjoyable for passengers.

These advancements are also attributable to the photos, images, diagnostics, trip logs, and other vast amounts of data and statistics created by the sensing layer, analyzed by the service layer, and supported by the communications layer. The resulting data is, in turn, used to monitor performance and further refine the processes.

**Telematics**

The use of technological devices to transmit data via wireless communication and GPS tracking.

For example, accelerometers, devices that measure acceleration, motion, and tilt, are combined with special software to detect and measure linear motion. Through **telematics**, accelerometer technology can generate information about vehicle fleets, such as operator acceleration and braking. It can also be used for many other applications, such as to detect excessive vibration in an industrial machine that is about to explode and may injure workers and/or damage property.

Additionally, augmented reality technology can integrate a digital experience into a user's physical environment. One such example, head-up displays in or near aircraft and car windshields, reduces distractions for pilots and drivers by displaying information, such as speed and warning signals, within their lines of sight.

# Catastrophe Management

Sensors and WSNs are also used in catastrophe management. As long as a sensor can withstand a harsh environment, it can continuously monitor an area for light, temperature, specific gases, and more. Alternatively, a sensor or WSN can measure local changes when a catastrophe is predicted or has occurred.

By continuously sensing the environment, sensors and WSNs can detect and analyze changes over time and help predict a catastrophe and allow for adequate preparation. For example, an accelerometer can continuously monitor earth movements to determine where an earthquake will occur, and underwater pressure sensors can measure water weight on sensors to help determine how fast and in which direction a tsunami will travel. In fire-prone areas, gas sensors, thermal sensors, and anemometers can be strategically placed on the outer proximity of an area to warn of approaching forest fires.

**Lidar** is a technology used to, among other things, improve the performance and accuracy of autonomous vehicles. It can work with optical sensors, such as high-definition cameras, to detect images, even through shadows or blinding sunshine. Lidar has applications to catastrophe management, both before and after a natural disaster:

**Lidar**
A sensor similar to radar that uses infrared light to detect nearby objects.

- It provides images even under lighting conditions that are inadequate because of cloudiness, intense sunshine, or shadows. Furthermore, its high-definition three-dimensional mapping technology provides more realistic and usable data than two-dimensional mapping.

- It can capture and produce accurate elevation data, enhancing the mapping of flood-prone areas before a flood and helping to determine the flood levels that will be reached based on current water levels in surrounding rivers. It can also help identify regions, neighborhoods, or even individual structures that may need to be evacuated before a flood.

- Furthermore, lidar images after a flood, and the additional data it collects on air pressure, temperature, wind turbulence, and location, provide information that assists in prioritizing rescue and remediation efforts. This information can also be used to analyze and compare various flood events.

- Lidar can help determine the optimal location for emergency communications equipment after a disaster disrupts cell or internet service. Models produced using lidar images identify the optimal locations for placing mobile Wi-Fi terminals (linked to satellites) to provide a signal for up to a thirty-mile radius. After a catastrophe such as a tsunami or an earthquake, lidar can provide street-by-street or even structure-by-structure analysis of locations with the highest risk, thus helping rescue and remediation resources be deployed efficiently.

## Workplace Safety Management

Many smart products ultimately may be used to improve workplace safety and productivity:

- Wearables allow workers to wear sensors in comfortable and familiar ways (such as in safety vests or work boots) and still have their hands free to do their jobs.

- Drones provide information and help assess and control risks by going into unknown and potentially dangerous areas without putting humans at risk; they can accomplish this on the ground, in the air, or underwater.

- Robots—no longer clunky, human-like machines—operate in close proximity to workers but do more of the repetitive and heavy-lifting jobs. This allows workers to better use their skills and for humans and machines to be better integrated in the workplace.

## Construction and Engineering Management

Mechanical sensors detect and measure a physical quantity and produce a signal that is readable by the user or another device. They are generally used with machinery and have many applications in construction and engineering:

- Motion sensors have many applications, including surveillance and security.

- Pressure sensors are similar to strain sensors, which convert pressure or tension into a measurement of electrical resistance.

- Current sensors are useful in protecting electronic systems and batteries from heat buildup.

- Position sensors are used when components are to be activated only when they are in the optimal places for a particular process to continue. They are used, for example, in car-wash machinery that senses the size of vehicles and adapts the cleaning process accordingly.

- Proximity sensors, slightly different from position sensors, respond when an object reaches a threshold area within range of the sensor. For example, proximity sensors in smartphones can sense the presence of an ear and turn off the backlight and touch-screen functions to save power.

- An inertial measurement unit (IMU) tracks an object's position using accelerometers and gyroscopes. IMUs are used in navigation systems, as orientation (location) sensors in personal devices, and to measure motion in fitness trackers and gaming systems. They are also key sensors for autonomous vehicles.

# HOW DATA ANALYTICS EMPOWERS SMART PRODUCTS

Smart products and operations gather vast amounts of data that ultimately can help improve risk assessment and control through preventive analytics. Preventive analytics leverages modern technology, big data, and advanced analytics to identify root causes and their interactions. It is particularly effective because it can continuously monitor activity—whether arising from humans or machines.

Traditionally, to take corrective actions to prevent future losses, risk professionals have applied **root cause analysis (RCA)**, which identifies the predominant cause of an accident. However, RCA looks backward and is only undertaken periodically—perhaps once per year—limiting its effectiveness. Furthermore, it may not identify all root causes and the related events that contribute to a loss.

**Root cause analysis (RCA)**

A step-by-step evaluation method to identify the root cause of an undesirable outcome and the actions that can be taken to prevent its recurrence.

In recent years, risk professionals have used predictive analytics by constructing analytical models to predict losses based on various predictive attributes. Preventive analytics are able to take advantage of the sheer volume of data available through smart products. For example, in the case of fraud prevention, every financial transaction provides data, which a machine can analyze and ultimately use to identify both legitimate and potentially fraudulent transactions.

This type of approach has become more useful through the incorporation of big data and more sophisticated through the advancement of analytical techniques such as these:

- Classification analysis
- Text mining
- Pattern matching
- Neural network analysis

## Classification Analysis

Emerging technologies, such as sensors, radio frequency identification (RFID) tags, and computer vision, produce an abundance of data. One of the basic techniques used to analyze this data to make predictions is **classification analysis**.

**Classification analysis**

A supervised learning technique to segment data according to the values of known attributes to determine the value of a categorical target variable.

Sensor technology is particularly useful in the field of worker safety. For example, helmets can detect toxic fumes, shirts and wristbands can monitor workers' stress levels, and vests can detect unsafe motions.

While information harvested from workplace sensors and wearables is potentially useful in isolation—if, for example, an employee's wearable indicates an unsafe fatigue level, or a machine sensor signals an impending malfunction—

it is only fully useful if relationships among accumulated data points illustrate the extent to which environmental conditions, worker attributes, and other relevant factors affect the probability of an accident and lead to preventive actions. This can be accomplished through classification analysis, either alone or in combination with other advanced analytical techniques.

Consider a simple example of how, after sufficient data is collected from sensors, a construction contractor's risk manager can employ a classification tree model to determine the probability of a workplace accident. Data from each sensor is used in tandem with other data to develop combinations of attributes that help predict workplace accidents. These attributes are combined with traditional workplace-accident attributes not collected through sensors, such as equipment status and hours worked in a given shift.

The ovals in a classification tree diagram represent the attributes under analysis, while the rectangles show the classification as "Accident" or "No Accident." Classification results derive from the combination of attributes connected to the rectangles through a sequence of arrows, each of which depicts the value of the attribute to which it is connected. The classification probabilities shown in the rectangles indicate the ratio of the number of times the model predicted the classified result (Accident or No Accident) to the total number of predictions made by the model. See the exhibit "Worker Data Classification Tree."

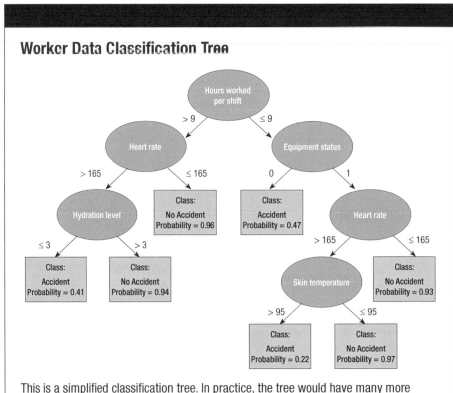

**Worker Data Classification Tree**

This is a simplified classification tree. In practice, the tree would have many more branches and attributes that are constructed by using a computer algorithm.

# Text Mining

Artificial intelligence has greatly expanded the ability to derive useful data from text. While a person can read one document at a time, a computer can read many. Computers' efficiency is one reason more and more businesses are investing in artificial intelligence. But after a computer reads text, how does it interpret and process it? It does so through **text mining**.

Developing models to analyze text is more difficult than developing models to analyze other types of data because text is unstructured and typically contains neither organized fields nor numerical values. Because the text in claims files, social media posts, news stories, and consumer reviews is generally not meaningful to a machine or an **algorithm**, it must be preprocessed to account for capitalization discrepancies, misspellings, abbreviations, spaces, punctuation, words that convey little meaning (such as "and" and "the"), and synonyms.

To apply a modeling algorithm to text, the text must be put into a form the algorithm can recognize. This is accomplished by turning a body of text into numerical values representing the number of times each word appears—a process that turns unstructured data (text) into structured data (numbers). These numbers are then analyzed using advanced statistical techniques.

**Natural language processing**, a component of text mining, can be used to derive the inferred meaning of certain words. It can be used to help a computer learn context, which is often very important for certain text mining applications, such as **sentiment analysis**. It is also used along with robots to automate certain claims processes, read documents in different languages, and mine public information. The latter is particularly helpful in obtaining public information on tiers of suppliers in order to assess supply chain risk.

Text mining has a large number of additional risk management applications. These range from mining workers compensation data for potentially fraudulent claims to mining social media to determine sentiment level for or against an organization to assess its reputation risk.

# Pattern Matching

**Pattern matching** can also be used in risk assessment and control. For example, by using computer vision, drones can take images of crops to analyze their health or the moisture level in soil. They can also take images of buildings to analyze damage after a loss. While these tasks could be performed by humans, drones perform them more efficiently by incorporating artificial intelligence, which can match the images collected with patterns from other images to determine the potential for severe loss.

As computer vision science evolves, it is becoming increasingly better at accounting for nuances. For example, cameras can distinguish between products and people by using large amounts of data to train a neural network using deep learning. A computer that is fed massive numbers of images, such as

**Text mining**
Obtaining information through language recognition.

**Algorithm**
An operational sequence used to solve mathematical problems and to create computer programs.

**Natural language processing**
A component of text mining that uses linguistics to understand human speech or read documents.

**Sentiment analysis**
The process of determining the opinion or emotion behind a selection of text.

**Pattern matching**
The science of finding matching patterns in data.

those of human limbs and robots, teaches itself to distinguish between humans and robots in general, rather than just between an individual person's limb and a specific robot. A computer vision algorithm, then, can learn to distinguish between humans and robots on a factory floor and trigger an automatic loss prevention process if the two come in close proximity to each other.

Pattern matching can also be used to find fraud in financial transactions and network security issues and breaches. This is done by analyzing transaction data to find fraudulent patterns. As transactions take place in real time, potentially fraudulent ones are flagged for review based on data the machine has previously analyzed.

# Neural Network Analysis

**Neural network**

A data analysis technique composed of three layers, including an input layer, a hidden layer with nonlinear functions, and an output layer, that is used for complex problems.

**Neural networks** are designed to replicate the functions of the human brain. Although neural networks cannot actually behave like a human brain, they can operate in similar ways when sorting through input data. They can also complete activities that the human brain cannot, such as rapidly performing thousands of mathematical calculations with large amounts of data.

Neural networks consist of three layers. The input layer provides data for the network to analyze, the output layer provides results of the analysis, and the hidden layer resides between these two layers. The hidden layer is so named because the processes used by the computer are not transparent or easily understood. This layer performs various mathematical functions to match inputs to outputs. Typically, a neural network uses thousands of neurons and links to perform calculations, enabling it to process a very large volume of data.

When applied to the big data generated by smart products and operations, neural networks enable deep learning of the relationships among the data. In addition to their ability to analyze very large quantities of data, another characteristic of neural networks is their ability to work with incomplete data. Their conclusions can be based on observations, detected correlations, and new concepts.

For example, neural network analysis can be applied to supply chain networks to predict second-tier suppliers (suppliers of suppliers) and third-tier suppliers based on publicly available data. When this extended supply chain data is layered on top of hazard information (such as natural-disaster potential) by geography, a risk profile of an organization's supply chain can be developed.

Neural networks are often considered a type of machine learning. Machine learning begins with a model that has been developed and tested by data scientists to perform a predictive analysis. As the computer applies the model, it learns from the results and new data.

Neural networks are less dependent on rules than other forms of machine learning are. They are able to make independent observations about the data they receive and then provide intuitive results.

When provided data from sensors, high-definition cameras, wearables, drones, robots, smart buildings, and other smart products and operations, neural networks have many applications in risk assessment and control. They enable complex analyses for predicting machine failure, catastrophes, financial improprieties, and defective products, among many other uses.

# THE RISKS OF USING SMART PRODUCTS

Smart products, smart operations, and preventive analytics present significant risk assessment and control opportunities. However, these technologies are so new that some of the risks associated with their use cannot yet be measured. For example, as artificial intelligence (AI) automates processes, will employees lose their jobs? And because human drivers may not control autonomous vehicles, who will be liable for accidents that occur?

Businesses must weigh the benefits of emerging technologies against the risks they present. To do so, they should first understand the risks that emerging technology creates. They can then determine the best ways to protect themselves from the consequences.

## Property Risks

Smart operations are increasingly used to manage property, supply chains, and transportation, among other business processes. But what risks do these operations pose to the property involved?

Smart operations typically run on Wi-Fi or another common communication protocol, which various smart objects use to communicate with one another. This creates an opportunity for a cyber attack that could shut down operations and damage equipment and products.

AI increases the risk of industrial espionage—essentially, corporate spying—and the more smart devices there are, the more opportunities hackers have to monitor a business's activities and disrupt its operations. And halting one business's operations can have a ripple effect if that business is involved in a supply chain. For example, if the wearable of a manufacturing company's employee is hacked, the operations of the manufacturer's customers may be affected.

Typically, smart technology is also more complicated and expensive to repair and replace than other types of property. Risk professionals should help organizations ensure that they have access to professionals with the specialized skills needed to fix smart products and operations.

# Liability Risks

Emerging technologies present many new liability exposures, such as these:

- Liability for property damage and bodily injury may be difficult to determine when autonomous vehicles are involved. It makes sense to assume that liability will shift from the driver to the product manufacturer. But what if human drivers have the option to take control of the vehicles? Are they then liable for accidents? Most legal experts assume that if autonomous vehicles become more common, liability for car accidents will become a products liability issue; however, insurance and risk professionals will need to adjust as this industry evolves.

- Sensors in automobiles that monitor driving habits, sensors on employees that monitor work habits and activities, and sensors on smartphones that monitor users' daily habits all present privacy issues. For example, if a commercial driver is being monitored through his smartphone as part of a fleet safety initiative, his personal contacts and information may be exposed along with his driving habits.

- The interconnectivity of the Internet of Things (IoT) means that the personal, financial, and proprietary data of both people and businesses is frequently transferred and is therefore increasingly susceptible to attack. One unsecured device or server can compromise huge amounts of data, making companies liable for these breaches. Interconnectivity also makes smart devices susceptible to attack, which may lead to products liability claims. For example, the heating controls of a seasonal business that closes during the winter could be tampered with, leading to frozen pipes and extensive water damage.

- Wearables create several liability concerns for the companies that develop and manufacture them, for vendors, and for businesses that use them as part of their risk management programs. Wearables can lead to bodily injury claims ranging from minor skin irritation from wearing a device to severe injury caused by the failure of a wearable to monitor its user's medical condition. For example, if an employee has a heart condition and uses a wearable to monitor his heart rate, he or his family may pursue a claim against his organization or the wearable manufacturer if he suffers a heart attack.

- Radio frequency identification (RFID) is increasingly used to help manage supply chain risks. However, RFID's use also creates risks, many of which are related to privacy and security. Because RFID transmits information via wireless technology, data can be intercepted by an unauthorized party. If a business transmits data to a customer or supplier, that business could be liable if the data falls into the wrong hands.

- Drones have the potential to cause property damage and bodily injury. For example, if a drone loses its connection and global positioning signal, it could fall from the sky and land on whoever or whatever is under it.

- A company could face errors and omissions liability for a poorly designed algorithm that results in faulty decisions and bodily injury or property damage to others.

# Personnel Risks

When companies require their employees to use emerging technologies, such as wearables, they may be liable if private or medical information is accessed or used inappropriately. For example, what if health information about professional athletes, gathered from wearable devices, was used to negotiate contracts and was considered more important than a player's performance history? And what if athletic teams, or any type of employer, began instructing employees how to behave during their personal time? See the exhibit "Implementing Smart Products."

---

### Implementing Smart Products

Making sure that the appropriate smart products are chosen for a project or an organization is key to successfully integrating them with employees and stakeholders. However, even when carefully chosen and backed by science, smart products can prove risky because of the large investment required in both money and time.

Acceptance of smart products at work, especially wearables that affect employees, may be easier for factory, construction, unionized, or field personnel, who may immediately see their safety benefits, than for office or service employees. Younger employees, who likely grew up around smart products, and those with previous positive experiences with such products may also be more likely to understand the value of the products and embrace them.

For some, embracing wearables for safety may lead to concerns of other risks: Is this headwear harming my brain? How will my sensitive skin react to this vest? Have these smart glasses been tested to ensure that I will not lose my vision in ten years? What happens if I misplace these very expensive smart boots?

For all smart products, employees are particularly concerned about privacy regarding the use and dissemination of collected personal data, and employers are concerned about the appropriate safeguarding of this data and the cyber liability exposure created by collecting, using, and storing it. Capturing medical data through sensors may be subject to healthcare privacy regulations.

In addition, without proper training, smart products may be more of a hindrance than a help. Employees may come to overtrust them and, as a result, become less attentive. In cases of drones and robots, workers may fear that they will be replaced by these machines and thus resist their implementation.

---

[DA12660]

# Net Income Risks

Emerging technologies can affect a business's net income. Because the IoT exposes businesses to cyber attacks (for example, ransomware), a company that uses such technology may have its operations shut down by a malicious party. Businesses must also be aware of potential data breaches that would affect their customers. The cost to an organization of repairing its reputation and notifying and assisting customers after a data breach can be significant.

An organization's response to a breach can determine the extent of its overall loss. If an organization fails to take prompt action to halt a breach and to report it to regulators and its customers, damages mount, and the organization can face penalties for failing to report the breach and for violating privacy statutes.

Additionally, any manager or officer of the organization who knew about the breach and failed to act appropriately may also be terminated. Loss of the organization's chief information officer and chief executive officer, for example, could be expensive for the organization in terms of recruiting a suitable replacement and of allocating funds for an updated employment package.

Even when prompt action is taken after a breach, the organization incurs legal fees for counsel in handling the breach, managing employee terminations and hiring, and resolving any customer losses. The organization may also incur costs for providing credit monitoring for customers affected by the breach or for all customers.

Ultimately, the organization that experienced the breach suffers reputational loss. Swift measures to halt the breach and repair any security lapses, to avoid a breach before one occurs, and to have a plan in place for a breach can help limit reputational costs and financial losses. For a small to midsize organization, the costs of a breach can result in business failure.

# Controlling Risks Arising From Emerging Technologies

In particular, organizations seek to control **cyber risk**. While building a secure system is always simpler than retrofitting an existing one, an organization can use either approach to control its emerging technology risks.

## Physical Controls

**Cyber risk**

The possibility that data will end up in the possession of a party who is not authorized to have that data and who can use it in a manner that is harmful to the individual or organization that is the subject of the data and/or the party that collected and stored the data.

A botnet is created when a group of computers and other IoT objects becomes infected with malicious software. One way to prevent botnets is through network and device security—for example, firewalls and user authentication. It is critical for organizations to understand that one unsecure system component can compromise an entire network and lead to a data breach. Additionally, controlling the risk of bodily injury and property damage from smart devices is often tied to protecting them from attack. When their controls are not tampered with, devices are more likely to run as they should.

## Procedural Controls

Improving the interoperability among various IoT-connected devices, with an emphasis on security standards, is a key way for an organization to control risk from emerging technologies. However, data from different devices is generated in different ways, so there is often no standard communication protocol for a network. This can make it more difficult to establish effective security, so organizations are encouraged to standardize their approach to data collection as much as possible.

Standards about the data itself can also help mitigate risks. For example, data governance can dictate what type of data will be collected (avoiding collection of any that is unnecessary) and how long it is kept. Risk professionals should remember that if an organization stores data, it may be liable for breaches of that data.

## Managerial Controls

Management sets an organization's standards for how smart products and operations will be implemented and their risks managed. However, managers can follow best practices for security. The Federal Trade Commission (FTC) provides guidelines for organizations trying to secure their devices and networks. The FTC's report, *Internet of Things: Privacy & Security in a Connected World*, provides fair information practice principles on entities' collection and use of personal information in the context of the IoT[1]:

- Security—The FTC recommends building security into devices, training all employees about good security, retaining capable service providers, defending against identified risks, limiting unauthorized access to devices and the network, and continuously monitoring smart products.

- Data minimization—Organizations should limit the data they collect and retain. Large stores of data attract those wishing to steal it.

- Notice and choice—An organization's customers should be given notice when their data is collected and used in an unexpected way and a choice as to whether they consent to this use.

# SUMMARY

Smart products can be used to enhance risk assessment and control in a variety of contexts, including these:

- Property management
- Supply chain management
- Transportation management

- Catastrophe management
- Workplace safety management
- Construction and engineering management

Techniques that can be used to convert the data gathered by smart products into actionable risk management data include these:

- Classification analysis
- Text mining
- Pattern matching
- Neural network analysis

Businesses should understand the property, liability, personnel, and net income risk exposures that emerging technology creates. They can then determine the best ways to protect themselves from the associated risks.

# ASSIGNMENT NOTE

1. Federal Trade Commission, "Internet of Things: Privacy & Security in a Connected World," January 2015, www.ftc.gov/system/files/documents/reports/federal-trade-commission-staff-report-november-2013-workshop-entitled-internet-things-privacy/150127iotrpt.pdf (accessed July 31, 2017).

# Index

Page numbers in boldface refer to pages where the word or phrase is defined.